THE EFFECTIVENESS

OF EARLY INTERVENTION

FOR AT-RISK AND

HANDICAPPED CHILDREN

THE EFFECTIVENESS OF EARLY INTERVENTION FOR AT-RISK AND HANDICAPPED CHILDREN

Edited by

MICHAEL J. GURALNICK
FORREST C. BENNETT

Child Development and Mental Retardation Center
University of Washington
Seattle, Washington

1987

ACADEMIC PRESS, INC.
Harcourt Brace Jovanovich, Publishers
Orlando   San Diego   New York   Austin
Boston   London   Sydney   Tokyo   Toronto

ACADEMIC PRESS, INC.
Orlando, Florida 32887

United Kingdom Edition published by
ACADEMIC PRESS INC. (LONDON) LTD.
24–28 Oval Road, London NW1 7DX

Library of Congress Cataloging in Publication Data

The Effectiveness of early intervention for at-risk and
    handicapped children.

    Includes index.
    1. Developmental disabilities—Treatment.   2. Handi-
capped children—Rehabilitation.   I. Guralnick,
Michael J.   II. Bennett, Forrest C.   [DNLM: 1. Educa-
tion, Special.   2. Handicapped.   LC 4015 E27]
RJ135.E34   1987   618.92   86-10875
ISBN 0—12—307910—1 (alk. paper)

PRINTED IN THE UNITED STATES OF AMERICA

87 88 89 90   9 8 7 6 5 4 3 2 1

Contents

Part I Introduction and Overview

Chapter 1 A Framework for Early Intervention
Michael J. Guralnick and Forrest C. Bennett

Part II Children at Risk

Chapter 2 An Analysis of the Effectiveness of Early Intervention Programs for Environmentally At-Risk Children
Donna M. Bryant and Craig T. Ramey

Part III   Children with Documented Handicaps

Part IV   Current and Future Perspectives

Preface

Early intervention programs for children at risk for developmental problems and for those with documented handicaps are now prominent features of our service system. In many respects, our ability to provide effective intervention programs for young children reflects our understanding of developmental processes and how events in the life of the child and family affect those processes. It also reflects our ability to generate comprehensive service programs based upon this knowledge while remaining responsive to the special needs of children and families.

Those seeking to examine how effective these programs are must confront immediately issues related to the heterogeneity of the population of at-risk and handicapped children, the complex array of programs that have been established, the diversity of outcome measures that have been employed, and the variability in the quality of the experimental approaches that have been taken. Accordingly, gaining even a modest understanding of the outcomes of early intervention as well as the factors that have contributed to those outcomes is a very difficult and demanding task, and some organizing framework is essential.

The approach taken in this volume has been to organize the literature on the effectiveness of early intervention by the traditional grouping of children by disability area and at-risk category. These groupings not only constitute a major source of variability in our outcome measures but also provide a means of organizing any patterns that may exist for a specified group of children within the network of interacting variables that includes child, family, and program characteristics. Despite many limitations in the available data, we have emphasized throughout this volume that any current or future analysis of the effectiveness of early intervention can best be achieved by examining these separate and definable populations of children in conjunction with other variables that influence the outcomes of early intervention programs.

Within this structure, chapter authors have sought to provide a readily accessible account of the important research that has been carried out to date, to identify patterns and trends, and to recommend directions for future work. To help accomplish this, we have deviated from the usual approach of presenting study-by-study summaries and critiques. Instead, each chapter contains summaries *in tabular format* of relevant information including subject characteristics, intervention models and parameters, experimental designs, assessment approaches, and outcomes. With this reference guide to existing research as a framework, chapter authors were able to devote considerably more of their efforts toward commenting on salient features of the literature and to discussing patterns of outcomes.

At the same time, however, we felt that extensive background material would be essential to place the outcomes of early intervention programs in perspective. Accordingly, descriptions of the populations being reviewed, their developmental characteristics, and the specific forms early interventions have taken have been provided and occupy substantial segments of each of the chapters.

As discussed in the first chapter, we realize the limitations of any single approach to evaluating the effectiveness of early intervention as well as the limitations imposed by the nature of the data in this field. In many ways, we saw our task from the beginning as one designed to bring the complexities of the field into focus, to identify patterns, relationships, and trends, and to raise and examine issues of significance. To the extent that this has occurred, we will have accomplished the major goals of this volume.

Developing chapters within the overall framework of this volume was a very challenging task, and we are extremely grateful to each of the contributors. We also wish to offer special thanks to Kathleen Bethel for her outstanding editing of the manuscripts.

Michael J. Guralnick
Forrest C. Bennett

Part I

Introduction and Overview

Chapter 1

A Framework for Early Intervention

MICHAEL J. GURALNICK
FORREST C. BENNETT

Child Development and Mental Retardation Center
University of Washington
Seattle, Washington 98195

INTRODUCTION

Early intervention services for children at risk for developmental problems and for those with documented handicaps can now be found in virtually every community in the United States and in numerous other countries. Commitments to early intervention by health, educational, and social agencies are now well established. Encouraged by national priorities and legislation, concerted efforts by parents, professionals, and special interest groups are meeting with considerable success at almost every level in mandating permanent, coordinated, comprehensive, and adequately funded systems for providing early intervention services.

The achievements of this early intervention movement are truly remarkable when it is recognized that only 2 decades ago most parents concerned about the problems of their young children were faced with the almost insurmountable task of independently seeking out professional help and services. The more fortunate ones were able to find a professional sensitive to their concerns and knowledgeable about developmental and behavioral issues affecting young children. Unfortunately, a further search for organized health, educational, and social services was frequently frustrating and disappointing.

It almost seems inevitable that rapidly developing movements such as early intervention will experience various periods of disillusionment, criticism, and

3

THE EFFECTIVENESS OF EARLY INTERVENTION
FOR AT-RISK AND HANDICAPPED CHILDREN

self-doubt regarding their effectiveness. This was certainly true for those initial preschool intervention programs designed for disadvantaged children—programs that now appear to have reached a rapprochement with their critics and are in the process of developing a realistic set of strategies for the future (Caldwell, 1974; Zigler & Berman, 1983). Nevertheless, existing early intervention programs for many groups of at-risk and handicapped children now appear to be undergoing a similar experience, perhaps not one of disillusionment at this stage but certainly one of concern and even skepticism regarding the overall benefits that can result from these programs.

Commitments to early intervention notwithstanding, the issue of what can be accomplished for these children and their families within existing knowledge and resources is a critical one and of great interest and importance to professionals, program planners, policymakers, and consumers. More specifically, it is important to determine for those at risk if adverse biological or psychosocial factors can be prevented from having an impact on development or, failing this, whether their effects can be minimized. For those whose disabilities have been clearly established, the question is whether strategies can be developed that ensure optimal development. A corresponding issue here concerns the possibility of accelerating substantially the development of children with documented handicaps through the provision of intensive early intervention services.

These and related questions will be addressed for different groups of at-risk and handicapped children in separate chapters in this book. However, in order to provide a perspective and context for these analyses, this chapter first will present a brief overview of the nature of the children considered in this review and appraisal of the effectiveness of early intervention, including discussions of the characteristics of certain groups of children, etiological issues, and expectations from primary prevention efforts. This will be followed by a discussion of the lines of evidence that provide a rationale for early intervention. Topics to be considered include environmental influences during the early years, issues of developmental continuity, the possibly unique effects of early experiences for children with documented handicaps, and the role of secondary complications. Finally, a framework for understanding different approaches to early intervention, the nature of the available evidence, and details regarding the organization and plan of this book will be presented.

NATURE OF THE POPULATIONS
FOR EARLY INTERVENTION

In considering the effectiveness of different early intervention approaches, it is important to distinguish clearly and to differentiate three broad target populations of children who might be the recipients of early intervention services (see

Tjossem, 1976). The specific groups are: (1) infants and children at increased environmental risk (e.g., poverty, low socioeconomic status, single parent, adolescent mother), (2) infants and children at increased biological risk (e.g., premature/low birthweight graduates of neonatal intensive care, asphyxiated fullterm infants), and (3) infants and children with established developmental delays, deviations, or disabilities. Early intervention for infants and children at risk for developmental problems have primarily a prevention orientation with a particular recent focus on "doubly vulnerable" infants (those at additive risk both environmentally and biologically).

As noted in a subsequent section of this chapter, for children in the third group—those with documented handicaps—this book is organized according to primary functional areas of developmental disability: cognitive (general developmental) delays, motor impairment, language/communication delays and disorders, the clinical syndrome of autism, and major sensory impairments of hearing and/or vision. Although it is important to discuss and differentiate these general categories of developmental dysfunction individually, it is equally important to appreciate their frequent overlaps, common specific etiologies and associated problems, and mutual occurrence in the same child. For example, a child born very prematurely with a complicated neonatal course may survive and develop without any adverse developmental sequelae or may suffer a motor impairment such as cerebral palsy, generalized developmental delays, a relatively specific central communication disorder, one or more major sensory impairments, or any combination of these disabilities. In this context of overlapping and associated handicaps, the motor disability of cerebral palsy is frequently complicated by significant cognitive impairment (50%), communication disorders (25%), and/or hearing/vision impairments (20%); primary cognitive (general developmental) delays may be accompanied by motor impairments (40%), communication disorders (30%), and/or hearing/vision impairments (20%) (Thompson & O'Quinn, 1979). Thus, the various developmental disabilities should appropriately be regarded as different points on the continuum of brain and/or sensory dysfunction, rather than as unique, unrelated disorders.

Specific Etiological Considerations

Effective developmental intervention should always be preceded by a thorough developmental diagnosis. Most parents expend a considerable amount of energy directly or indirectly in attempting to find the specific cause of their child's developmental problem. The diagnostic process can clarify etiological misconceptions and often alleviate parental guilt. It can also provide meaningful medical, developmental, and behavioral prognostic information, guide certain aspects of early intervention, and establish recurrence risk estimates for future family planning. In the search for contributing factors to an individual child's

TABLE 1

Etiologies of developmental disorders

Timing	Common etiologies
Prenatal	Chromosomal syndromes Idiopathic syndromes CNS malformations Intrauterine infections Drugs, medications Maternal diseases X-Irradiation X-Linked mental retardation
Perinatal	Low birthweight/premature infant a. Hypoxia, hypercarbia, acidosis b. Intracranial hemorrhage c. Hypoglycemia, hyperbilirubinemia d. Sepsis, meningitis Perinatal asphyxia a. Obstetric complications b. Abnormal presentations c. Large infants d. Low Apgar scores
Postnatal	Metabolic, progressive disorders Congenital hypothyroidism Neurocutaneous syndromes CNS infections CNS trauma Anoxic insults Heavy metal intoxication Child abuse Environmental deprivation

atypical development, the following must be considered: (1) the nature of the disorder (genetic, hypoxic, infectious, traumatic, toxic, nutritional, psychosocial), (2) the timing of the disorder (prenatal, perinatal, postnatal), and (3) the specific developmental areas affected. Common etiologies of developmental disorders are enumerated by their timing in Table 1. Even though it is not currently possible to offer an exact diagnosis in many cases of atypical child development, "approximate" diagnoses that describe the most likely nature and timing of the problem can be extremely helpful, and their importance should not be underestimated.

A detailed classification of the nature of the developmentally disabled population included in this book is presented in Table 2. Generally accepted incidence

TABLE 2

Nature of the population: A developmental disabilities classification[a]

Developmental disability (primary area of functional impairment)	Incidence	Types and timing	Severity
1. Cognitive delay (mental retardation)	2–3%	Types: Specific etiologies by timing Timing for severe impairment: Prenatal: 80–85% Perinatal: 5–10% Postnatal: 5–10%	Mild: 70–85% Moderate: 8–12% Severe: 5–6% Profound: 2–3%
2. Motor impairments (cerebral palsy)	General: 1/400 <2500 g: 1/100 <1500 g: 1/12	Types: Spastic: 60–70% Hemiplegic: 30% Diplegic: 20% Quadriplegic: 15% Extrapyramidal: 15–20% Mixed: 20% Timing: Prenatal: 50–60% Perinatal: 20–40% Postnatal: 10%	Minimal (subtle neuromotor abnormalities) to severe (nonambulatory, wheelchair-dependent)
Others a. Meningomyelocele (spina bifida)	1/1000–1500		
b. Floppy infant syndrome (e.g., spinal muscular atrophy)			
c. Duchenne's muscular dystrophy	1/3000 males		
d. Spinal cord injuries			

(continued)

TABLE 2 (*Continued*)

Developmental disability (primary area of functional impairment)	Incidence	Types and timing	Severity

3. Communication disorders	5–7% as broadly defined; male predilection	Types
		a. Receptive and/or expressive language disorders (developmental dysphasia/aphasia)
		b. Speech disorders
		  1. Articulation (dyslalia, dyspraxia, dysarthria)
		  2. Rhythm (dysfluency, stutter)
		  3. Voice (dysphonia)
			Mild misarticulation to severe receptive and expressive language disability

4. Autism	1/2000; males 3:1		
5. Major sensory impairments a. Hearing impairment	Congenital deafness: 1/1000	Types: Sensorineural, conductive, mixed Timing: Prenatal: >50% Perinatal: 10–20% Postnatal: 20–30%	Mild (25–40 dB) to profound (>90 dB)
b. Visual impairment	Congenital blindness: 1/2500–3000	Types: Central, peripheral Timing: Prenatal: >50% Perinatal: 25–30% Postnatal: 10%	Totally blind to legally blind (20/200 or less) to partially sighted for educational purposes (20/80 or less)
c. Deaf/blind multiple handicap	5% of hearing impaired and 5% of visually impaired; 4000 children in United States	Timing: Prenatal: >50% Perinatal: 25% Postnatal: <10%	

[a]Based on Drillien and Drummond (1977), Northern and Downs (1978), Smith and Keen (1979), Stanley and Alberman (1984), and Thompson and O'Quinn (1979).

and prevalence estimates, specific types, and the severity spectrum are outlined for each primary area of functional impairment. It should be emphasized that this table results from a comprehensive literature review and is by no means identical to the classification system used by any single investigator. Definitions and subgroups of the different developmental disorders will be discussed in the individual chapters. Similarly, the listed ratios and percentages are approximations and represent our own attempt to synthesize and reflect accurately often divergent epidemiological data. Despite some uncertainties, one can only be impressed by the current magnitude, scope, and dimensions of childhood developmental dysfunction and the corresponding necessity to evaluate critically the large number of approaches to early intervention.

Prevention Capabilities

A major goal of medical and social science during the past 2 decades has been the prevention of conditions known to result always or frequently in developmental disability. Certainly all professionals involved in the care of children with central nervous system handicaps would agree that preventing such disorders and their associated medical, psychological, and financial costs should always be a high individual and societal priority. The most important primary preventive activities consist of rubella immunization, genetic counseling, improved prenatal care, avoidance of adverse agents during pregnancy, perinatal/neonatal intensive care, kernicterus (bilirubin encephalopathy) prevention, reduction of heavy metal (e.g., lead) exposure, antimicrobials, accident prevention, and public efforts in child health, education, and welfare and in reducing malparenting. Indeed, early intervention programs for children at biological or psychosocial risk constitute important preventive efforts. Secondary prevention activities, those intended to provide early identification of a potentially handicapping condition and thus permit prompt medical intervention to avert an outcome with a disability, focus primarily on prenatal diagnosis and newborn screening. These strategies considered together have dramatically altered the epidemiology of developmental disability in the United States and represent significant public health achievements. For example, routine newborn blood screening has made possible the prevention of mental retardation in phenylketonuria, the incidence of kernicterus has been markedly reduced by the prevention of maternal Rh sensitization, widespread immunization has resulted in the reduction of the congenital rubella syndrome to such a degree that it no longer is the most prevalent type of intrauterine infection nor the leading cause of combined hearing and visual impairment, and increased awareness of the importance of "mothering from conception" is steadily changing maternal prenatal behavior.

Nevertheless, despite these advances in recent years, it is estimated that we can currently affect the incidence of only 20–30% of the various causes of developmental disability (Crocker, 1982). Even though the number of specific disorders amenable to prenatal diagnostic methodologies continues to increase, most infants with serious developmental impairments will not be detected in this manner, and, of course, the absence of prenatal diagnostic abnormalities is certainly no guarantee of normal neurodevelopmental outcome. For example, in at least 40% of children with severe cognitive impairment, the specific cause, and therefore also the prevention, of the disability remains unknown even following extensive medical investigation (Smith & Simons, 1975). Changing lifestyles have increased the prevalence and etiologic importance of such infectious agents as herpes simplex virus and cytomegalovirus for which no safe, effective vaccines are presently available; the automobile is increasingly the leading single cause of childhood mortality and acquired neurological disorders; and the combined effects of poverty and malparenting, including all forms of child abuse and neglect, continue to exact a staggering toll in terms of impaired child heath, development, and behavior. Thus, the majority of cases of mental retardation, cerebral palsy, communication disorders, and related handicaps remain incompletely understood and currently unpreventable. Accordingly, it is even more essential that continuing efforts be made to improve our knowledge and understanding of early intervention programs with regard to their role in maximizing the development and general well-being of handicapped children and their families.

RATIONALE FOR EARLY INTERVENTION

Before discussing the different approaches to early intervention and evaluation issues, it is important to consider some of the reasons why such intensive efforts have been devoted to intervention during the first few years of life. Although it is difficult to trace certain antecedents with such a limited historical perspective, forces that were especially influential in the last 30 years or so can be readily identified. In many respects, the rationale for early intervention was closely connected to conceptualizations that stressed the importance of the early years for normally developing children and the role environmental factors play in that development. As might be expected, support for the notion that the early years are in fact special ones and that environmental events can substantially alter the course of development during that period was established as a result of findings from diverse areas of inquiry. For example, working in laboratory-like settings in the 1950s and 1960s developmental psychologists discovered that, contrary to prevailing thinking, infants were extraordinarily sophisticated and competent beings, processing information and actively participating in their own development (see Appleton, Clifton, & Goldberg, 1975). Clearly, the potential for influencing even very early development was there. Theoretical speculations at the neuropsychological level (e.g., Hebb, 1949) and the interpretation of then-existing data that a significant proportion of our intellectual competence is determined by 4 years of age (B. S. Bloom, 1964) further stimulated interest in the early period. Similarly, extrapolations from ethological and psychoanalytic thought, emphasizing both the primacy of early experience and the long-term and pervasive consequences for later social and personality development from adverse early life events (see Bowlby, 1951; Hunt, 1961), focused attention on those early childhood relationships that could support adequate growth and development. Indeed, when reports of research suggesting that the long-term prognosis of retarded children, for example, or those raised in radically depriving environments such as institutions, could be significantly altered through early intervention, it was considered by many as confirmatory evidence for both the importance and malleability of early childhood development (see Horowitz, 1980; Hunt, 1976).

Of course, many initial claims in relation to early experience and early intervention must now be tempered in light of methodological concerns and new information. In fact, intense debate continues today as to whether early experience in general exerts an unusual and disproportionate influence upon development as a whole (Clarke & Clarke, 1976). The corollary proposition that intervention that is provided early is likely to have the most profound impact has provoked an equally intense debate (Rutter, 1980). Moreover, a renewed respect for the power of genetic–maturational factors governing even complex psychological processes has emerged (e.g., Kagan, 1982), and our understanding of the limits of environmental events in overcoming biological insult has increased substantially.

At the same time, however, more recent research and developmental theories have served to clarify and extend these original views and can now be invoked to provide a contemporary rationale suggesting the importance of the early years. Specifically, the relation between early environmental factors and developmental outcome has now been demonstrated not only for children raised in highly depriving settings but also for children from more typical environments. Parental characteristics such as responsivity contingent on child initiations, the quality and quantity of verbal interactions, the provision of a wide array of toys and materials, the existence of social support networks, the expression of warmth and affection, and maternal sensitivity have all been found to be associated with a child's concurrent or later developmental functioning (Bee et al., 1982; Bradley & Caldwell, 1976; Clarke-Stewart, 1973; Wachs & Gruen, 1982).

The nature of the language environment as provided by caregivers has received special attention and serves as an excellent model for examining environmental influences. Numerous studies have now demonstrated that parents of normally developing children carefully adjust their language and related communicative interactions in accordance with the changing cognitive and linguistic levels of their children in a manner that is particularly suited to fostering language development. Supported by general parental characteristics related to responsivity, sensitivity, and of course the desire to understand and communicate, a rather remarkable array of parent–child language strategies have been identified that appear to have instructional value. Adjustments in pitch, in semantic and syntactic complexity, care in pacing and in reducing disfluencies, the proper timing of modeling and imitation, and the creation of dialogues and conversational sequences that expand and add clarity to child language forms and functions all seem to contribute to this incredible achievement of language learning during the first few years of life (L. Bloom & Lahey, 1978; Hoff-Ginsberg & Shatz, 1982; McLean & Snyder-McLean, 1978; Moerk, 1977). However, should parents' input fail to adjust or match the language learning strategies of their children, the process of language acquisition is likely to be slowed (Nelson, 1973). In fact, the importance of establishing a reasonable match between the interaction patterns of children and parental styles has also been demonstrated for those characteristics referred to as temperament; a parent–child mismatch in this domain is associated with adverse developmental consequences (Thomas & Chess, 1977).

In fairness, although evidence continues to mount regarding the importance of physical and social environmental factors in relation to developmental outcome, the evidence itself is not only correlational but relationships tend to be complex and sometimes inconsistent. We have not yet reached a sufficient level of understanding to suggest the exact nature and timing of specific environmental events that yield optimal developmental outcomes, and additional research would do well to help disentangle the web of interrelationships. Nevertheless, the impact of these variables is difficult to deny.

Developmental Continuity and Early Experience

Assuming that these early caregiver–child interactions are in fact causally related to later outcomes, what developmental processes might account for these effects and how are they related to long-term continuities of development? Of course, care must be taken to avoid simplifying a complicated process, as the impact of many events and combinations of events are surely age- and developmental-domain-specific and are moderated by a host of individual difference factors. It is also recognized that discontinuities are as much a part of human development as are continuities and that certain aspects of behavior are susceptible to change, sometimes radical change, at virtually any point in the life cycle. However, it is worthwhile examining, at least at a more global level, developmental processes that might account for the continuities that do exist as well as the significance of these processes in relation to early experience and early intervention.

One influential model suggests that continuity originates from early contingent parental responsiveness, which creates a generalized expectancy in infants that they can have an effect on their environment (Lewis & Goldberg, 1969). As a consequence, very young children who experience a higher level of responsiveness are more likely to explore and be interactive, to probe continually and extract information from the social and physical environment, and to create a generally highly favorable and developmentally stimulating environment for themselves. Accordingly, contingent responsiveness is related to a motivational construct—one that is likely to promote continuities in development given the continued availability of a varied and responsive environment.

From a more comprehensive perspective, the construct of attachments formed between caregivers and children during the first 2 years can be seen as an important process mediating early relationships and later developmental outcome. In fact, attachments that are considered secure are, as might be expected, closely correlated with maternal characteristics such as responsivity, mutuality, stimulation, warmth and expressing affection (see Wachs & Gruen, 1982). Moreover, and of considerable importance, Sroufe and his colleagues (Sroufe, 1979; Waters, Wippman, & Sroufe, 1979) have not only documented that individual differences in attachment are relatively stable but also that they predict later and highly important developmental characteristics such as play behavior, problem-solving skills, and peer relationships.

The suggestion from these and other studies as well as from corresponding theoretical constructs is that, discontinuities in developing cognitive structures notwithstanding, the quality of a child's affective, social, and motivational processes emerges from the quality of early caregiver–child interactions. In turn, these processes serve to mediate and modulate subsequent interactions of both a cognitive and noncognitive nature, further strengthening behavioral dispositions and establishing firm directions for development. The integrity and coherence of a child's interactions with the world even during this period suggest that substantial modifications at a later time may be extremely difficult to achieve. With regard to difficulties anticipated as a result of problematic early relationships, the robustness of continuities in human development and the interrelationships among adaptive processes have been so impressive that Sroufe (1979) felt confident enough to state: ''We cannot assume that early experiences will somehow be canceled out by later experience. Lasting consequences of early inadequate experience may be subtle and complex, taking the form of increased vulnerability to certain kinds of stress, for example, or becoming manifest only when the individual attempts to establish intimate adult relationships or engage in parenting. But there will be consequences'' (p. 840).

Early Experience and Children
with Documented Handicaps

The controversy over the resiliency of children in overcoming adverse events in infancy and early childhood will be with us for a long time to come. There is no doubt that such resiliency is impressive (Clarke & Clarke, 1976; Rutter, 1980). But, as we have seen, it also has been possible to develop a rationale suggesting that, under some circumstances, the events occurring during the early years exert if not irreversible effects, at least ones that may well have disproportionate influences on later development.

In fact, as we will argue, it is quite possible that the early years are even more crucial for children with documented handicaps. The disabilities these children manifest and the conditions surrounding the existence of their handicaps may serve to intensify the significance of early experiences. Although not denying that even seriously handicapped children can be highly resilient and capable of overcoming a difficult period in early childhood, their abilities to cope, adapt, and reorient may be much more limited and fragile. Moreover, as will be described, many of these children appear to become partners in uncertain relationships, establishing interaction patterns that are known to be counterproductive with regard to development. In doing so, these youngsters become prone to numerous complications secondary to their primary handicap during the early years—complications that often affect their social and emotional development or create unnecessary imbalances across different developmental domains.

The processes that are responsible for these patterns are not entirely clear at this time. However, as described next, it does appear that certain characteristics of handicapped children themselves make it extremely difficult for parents to create a social and physical environment that is likely to maximize development. The bidirectional nature of caregiver–child interactions (Bell, 1968) is most apparent when handicapped children are involved. When compounded by the stress experienced by family members, it is understandable why disruptions to developmentally supportive relationships can occur. Of perhaps most importance for this discussion is the fact that these patterns are not likely to correct themselves spontaneously. Accordingly, in order to provide an environment that ensures proper growth and development, some form of early intervention will be necessary for many handicapped children and their families. Described below are some examples of the types of problems that may arise in this regard and their probable consequences.

Disruptions in Caregiver–Child Interactions

Recent research indicates that establishing secure attachments during neonatal and early infancy periods between handicapped children and their caregivers is a very difficult process to accomplish (Blacher & Meyers, 1983; Stone Chesney,

1978). That such difficulties in attachment should exist is not surprising for two reasons. The first relates to certain characteristics of handicapped children, especially their inability to signal and display affective responses that engage the caregiver. For example, eye contact has long been recognized as an important mediator of this process. However, it is not only visually impaired infants who experience difficulties (Fraiberg, 1974), but also children with other handicaps, particularly those with Down syndrome (Berger & Cunningham, 1981). Moreover, Down syndrome children's poorly developed capacity for smiling and higher threshold for affective responses (both laughter and crying) pose further and special problems for caregivers seeking to "read" their child's signals and to establish warm, responsive, and affectionate relationships (Cicchetti & Sroufe, 1978; Emde, Katz, & Thorpe, 1978). These children, and probably other developmentally delayed children as well (Kogan, 1980), exhibit special deficits in physiological arousal that do not seem to be directly tied to or explainable by their cognitive delays (Cicchetti & Sroufe, 1978).

Although the emphasis in this section is on children with documented handicaps, it should be noted that infants born at risk due to biological factors, many being graduates of neonatal intensive care units or having experienced extended hospitalization, show a similar pattern. Deficits in responsivity, positive affect, and the modulation of arousal have been well documented for these youngsters (Field, Sostek, Goldberg, & Shuman, 1979). Moreover, mothers appear to be extremely controlling and overly active, tend to perceive their child's temperament as difficult, and often end interactions with their child crying or averting their gaze.

Second, it is of course understandable that parents' awareness of their child's handicap or even potential handicap, and the often disruptive and stress-producing processes that accompany this awareness, may well interfere at least initially with processes related to the formation of secure attachments (Battle, 1974; Waisbren, 1980). Of course, problems in early caregiver–child relations vary with the type of disability, family characteristics, resources, and the like (Murphy, 1982). It appears that excessive caregiving demands, lack of child responsiveness, and any unusual behavior patterns are closely associated with stress levels in parents (Beckman-Bell, 1981). However, just the existence of a handicap seems certain to place that child and family at a considerably greater risk for developing patterns that are not likely to be optimal for development.

Various forms of nonoptimal patterns of interaction can be observed beyond infancy also. For example, in comparison to mothers of normally developing children, mothers of hearing-impaired youngsters seem to become less involved over time with their children (Wedell-Monnig & Lumley, 1980). Although they still dominate interactions, the frequency with which these mothers interact with their children declines during the first to second year. Moreover, hearing-impaired children become less interactive and more passive over this period.

These authors speculate that the declining interactions of hearing-impaired children may well have been a result of difficulties mothers experience in responding accurately to the intent of their children. From the children's perspective, the absence of appropriate feedback can easily lead to a cognitive orientation in which expectations for failure or helplessness predominate. Similar social interaction and attachment difficulties are apparent for preschool-age hearing-impaired children also (Greenberg & Marvin, 1979; Schlesinger & Meadow, 1972).

Patterns similar to those for hearing-impaired children have been observed for children with general developmental delays and cerebral palsy. Comparisons with developmentally matched groups of nonhandicapped children indicate that mothers of young developmentally delayed children are not only more dominant, using many commands and initiating most of the interactions with their children, but are also not as likely to provide positive feedback when their children comply (Cunningham, Reuler, Blackwell, & Deck, 1981; Terdal, Jackson, & Garner, 1976). A pattern of lowered responsivity of delayed children has also been observed in these studies. For children with cerebral palsy, observations of tutorial and related sessions suggest that parents become less accepting, less positive, and less warm to their children over time (Kogan, Tyler, & Turner, 1974).

Earlier, the importance and role of parental input to language development in normally developing children was emphasized. Unfortunately, disruptions in relationships between parents and their handicapped children can also create a pattern that tends to depress the child's development of communicative competence. Whereas parents of normally developing children are generally able to adjust their communicative and linguistic interactions to foster the language competence of their child, the lack of responsiveness of many handicapped children often produces mismatches between a child's abilities and language input. These discrepancies, in conjunction with increased parental dominance, reduced social interactions, and an overall lowered responsivity combine to create conditions that often fail to establish a press for developing communicative competence (Cunningham et al., 1981; Lasky & Klopp, 1982; Mahoney & Seely, 1976). In fact, even the prelinguistic communications between parents and their Down syndrome infants are often not optimal, with considerable difficulties in vocal turn taking being observed (Berger & Cunningham, 1983). Although due in part to the vocalization patterns of the children themselves, less of a "dialogue" is evident and fewer expansions and extensions of the child's activity occur. This is the case despite the fact that parents of Down syndrome infants tend to be highly interactive, at least initially. Moreover, in comparison to developmentally matched normally developing children, Down syndrome children do not use eye contact very effectively as a basis for initiating interactions, for confirming expectations, or for questioning their caretakers (Jones,

1980). Failure to use this very powerful signal as a source of information and as a means of establishing a prelinguistic dialogue (e.g., turn taking) is a serious problem given the importance of these patterns in forming the groundwork for future communicative development (Bruner, 1977).

Related Complications and Factors

Any problems young handicapped children experience during this period unfortunately tend to be neither transient nor circumscribed. Interrelations among different developmental domains and organizational components of behavior are cardinal features of developmental processes (ses Hayden & McGinness, 1977). Problems in one area are likely to affect others. As a consequence, failure to obtain a comprehensive understanding of the issues early on sets the stage for subsequent and unnecessary problems that may pose more difficulties in the long run than the so-called primary handicap.

Although many secondary complications do not become manifest until children enter different phases of their lives, often the roots of these problems can be detected during the first few years. Difficulties in establishing relationships with one's peers, an important predictor of later adjustment problems (Hartup, 1976), is perhaps the best example. Research has now documented the unusual difficulties young children with handicaps have in establishing these peer relationships and in engaging in productive social play (e.g., Guralnick & Weinhouse, 1984; Higgenbotham & Baker, 1981; Markovits & Strayer, 1982). In a real sense, these difficulties are partly reflections of other problems such as communicative disorders, lack of responsiveness of peers, an inability to appropriately initiate social interactions, and even emotional/behavioral problems that seem to be evident in the early years.

This latter problem is particularly perplexing and potentially most damaging. Relatively little is known about the adjustment problems of most disability groups during the first few years or the extent to which adjustment problems are secondary complications or another direct manifestation of the primary disability. Nevertheless, the longer term problems of children with developmental disabilities have been well documented. Specifically, children with virtually any type of handicap appear to be at considerably greater risk for developing later social and emotional difficulties (Baker & Cantwell, 1982; Eaton & Menolascino, 1982; Meadow & Trybus, 1979; Reiss, Levitan, & McNally, 1982). Moreover, recent evidence indicates that an unusually high percentage of children at biological risk show clear signs of emotional and behavioral problems at as young as 2 years of age (Escalona, 1982).

Complications can also be found at levels beyond the individual child, as the birth and presence of a handicapped child is likely to alter substantially relationships within families, affecting virtually every member. Although certainly not a uniform response, the added stress created by the handicapped child can lead to emotional problems of parents and siblings, and in some extreme instances can contribute to the dissolution of that family unit (see Friedrich, Greenberg, & Crnic, in press). Early intervention in the form of counseling, the provision of support groups, and even psychotherapeutic interventions may be able to prevent these difficulties from reaching critical stages. If these problems are allowed to follow their normal course during the early years, severe disruptions to the family may result that are certain to have significant effects for all concerned (Bronfenbrenner, 1977).

Finally, failure to intervene during the first 5 years of life to press development to its limits and to minimize any secondary problems is likely to place a child at a disadvantage with regard to future opportunities to develop. Following the preschool years, a decision about subsequent schooling must be made. Depending on the community, alternatives may be extensive, ranging from primary placement in a regular classroom with supportive services to placement in a completely separate program consisting only of children with similar disabilities. Administrative decisions regarding placement are highly dependent on the developmental and behavioral characteristics of the child at the time. Although movement from setting to setting can occur at any point in the child's life, experience suggests that the expectations of teachers and parents are likely to be highly correlated with the initial placement decision. Because even a constant rate of development on the part of a handicapped child results each year in greater and greater discrepancies between the developmental domains affected and those of their normally developing peers, such expectations may be further reduced. Failure to intervene early to ensure the least restrictive nature of this initial placement will surely have lifelong consequences.

Summary

A considerable theoretical and empirical literature is now available indicating that developmental outcomes can be substantially altered by the nature of the social and physical environment during the first few years of life (Sameroff & Chandler, 1975; Wachs & Gruen, 1982). Developmental continuity and the significance of early experiences are seen as important themes in human development. At the same time, ample evidence exists to suggest that interactions between caregivers and their handicapped children, or with children at risk for a handicapping condition, can be easily disrupted. Effective parenting is not an easy task, even with healthy, normally developing children under ideal conditions. When children's signaling, feedback, and affective systems are not intact, as is common for many children with handicaps or those at risk, it is not difficult to realize how readily patterns that are not optimal for development can arise. We have seen how caregiver responsiveness can decline over the years, reflecting in part parents' own personal conflicts and stress as well as actual difficulties in adjusting their interactions to the reduced responsiveness and more limited signaling capacities of their child. As a result of a host of factors, the ability to establish secure parent–child attachments is jeopardized. The consequences of this are far-reaching because these relationships lie at the very heart of those processes that affect the integrity and continuity of development.

Moreover, discrepancies between a child's communicative skills and parental communicative input are common, perhaps contributing inadvertently to a child's communicative disabilities. In conjunction with these difficulties in communication, a problem that affects all areas of development, it is not surprising that young handicapped children manifest marked deficiencies in their peer relations, exhibit problems in related aspects of social and emotional development, and are more vulnerable to a host of social, emotional, and behavioral disorders in later life. Disruptions to family life, the intrinsic interrelationships existing across different developmental domains, and the developmental consequences of the initial placement decision for subsequent schooling all converge to suggest that the early years are not only precarious ones but may well carry a crucial and disproportionate burden for a handicapped child's later development and overall well-being.

Finally, it is important to reiterate that many of these difficulties are not at all inevitable. Families differ dramatically in terms of their abilities to cope with major problems and to establish warm, supportive relationships. The success of parents through sometimes heroic efforts to build and provide a well-matched yet stimulating environment and to establish affectionate, responsive, and synchronous relationships is not at all uncommon. Yet the difficulties of this task can be found at every milestone. Although no precise statistical data can be cited at this time, unless some form of intervention is provided much too large a proportion of children are likely to be trapped in a cycle of events during their early years that appear to be counterproductive to their development. Even if the effects of these early events are reversible, they appear to be affecting processes that may require extraordinary and costly efforts in order to restore development to its optimal course at a later time.

GENERAL APPROACHES TO EARLY INTERVENTION

Early intervention services constitute a systematic and planned effort to promote development through a series of manipulations of environmental or experiential factors initiated during the first 5 years of life. As Simeonsson, Cooper, and Scheiner (1982) pointed out, these interventions may consist of some form of traditional speech, physical, or occupational therapy, or they may be part of more comprehensive programs. This volume will also consider some of the more nontraditional approaches to early intervention.

For children with documented handicaps in particular, the developmental perspective and potential problems facing these children and their families, aspects of which have been outlined earlier, provide the field with a valuable framework to help guide the development of specific early intervention strategies and programs. Ideally, within this framework a comprehensive developmental profile is obtained at the outset. Included in this profile are efforts to identify the strengths and adaptive styles of children, aspects of the physical and social environment that do not appear to be optimal with regard to a child's development, and an evaluation of child characteristics that might contribute to any possible difficulties. This rather extensive series of assessments—which includes a careful analysis of the child and family, related health and medical issues, and a sense for the community of which the child is a member—is accomplished in a highly systematic way, usually drawing upon evaluations from numerous disciplines. This information is then gathered together to generate one coherent, individualized, positive plan for intervention.

For the most part, the focus of the intervention that is planned within this model is designed to ensure that developmental processes and relationships closely approximate those compatible with the principles of normal child development and sound family and community functioning. It is not that the interventions that are planned are not special or extraordinary. On the contrary, early intervention specialists from virtually every discipline have been extremely creative in developing instructional techniques, curricula, adaptive equipment, highly specialized materials, counseling procedures, and electromechanical devices that help foster the development of young handicapped children and strengthen family–child relationships. Anyone observing a good comprehensive early intervention program, for example, is likely to find a highly stimulating, responsive, but organized environment that contains an array of curricula and materials, all sensitively tuned to each child's needs. Highly directive, demanding, and intense activities may be evident from time to time and special devices to encourage exploration or to supplement or even replace normal modes of communication would likely be available also. Moreover, such a program might include a series of strategies to help parents recognize some of the unique aspects of their child or to provide assistance in recognizing communicative signals to help establish a well-matched linguistic environment (see Tjossem, 1976).

Even though some of the intervention techniques may appear to violate normal developmental patterns, such as when substitute methods for communication are used, these efforts are nevertheless designed so that the child either remains on or is restored to a path compatible with general developmental principles and processes. Most traditional therapeutic approaches, irrespective of discipline, are consistent with this framework. Although models of development may differ widely from program to program, they remain developmental models of one form or another. In addition, this approach contains a strong preventive component, one primarily designed to maintain conditions when they are developmentally appropriate and to minimize the occurrence of any secondary complications. For example, by providing anticipatory guidance to help avoid serious social or emotional problems from emerging or by instruction in techniques that help prevent self-stimulatory behaviors from establishing a foothold, potentially serious complications can either be avoided entirely or their impact significantly reduced. Accordingly, it is through processes attempting to establish the most developmentally appropriate environment as well as those reducing the impact of or even avoiding secondary complications that interventions are expected to be effective on both immediate and long-term bases.

But of course there are many variations in the approach to early intervention. One alternative, for example, seeks to accelerate development to a level beyond that which would be expected by a straightforward application of the developmental principles and preventive strategies described earlier. In essence, it is anticipated that by gathering together and implementing a series of highly intensive clinical techniques or educational strategies, by placing an unusually high level of demands upon children, and by committing extensive personnel and related resources successful programs will have a major impact. Although a similar body of knowledge is drawn upon by most approaches to early intervention, this particular type of approach can be distinguished by its technical and empirical orientation as well as by its intensive and demanding nature. These latter aspects are especially important in forming the expectations of the model. After all, there is no reason to expect any easy experiential routes to major developmental changes, but those more comprehensive, intensive, and technologically oriented efforts carry with them the understandable expectations that such unusual efforts will yield substantial gains.[1]

This discussion was intended only to provide the reader with an orientation to early intervention strategies and inevitably oversimplifies the nature of existing programs. In particular, it fails to reflect fairly the blending of approaches common to many intervention efforts and the variations in scope that are evident. It is hoped, however, that this discussion has served to introduce a point that will be stressed repeatedly throughout this volume: that early intervention is not a singular construct but rather is a term that refers to a collection of different "early interventions,"[2] each varying widely in its goals, nature, and scope. For any group of handicapped children the different forms these early interventions can take can range considerably. Variations in focus (comprehensive to limited, e.g., full range of services in a preschool intervention program in contrast to vestibular stimulation to foster motor development), rationale (type of develop-

[1]As noted, this discussion does not refer to biomedical treatments but only to experiential ones. However, in the final chapter some of the major, highly visible biomedical approaches will be considered.

[2]We thank Rune Simeonsson for suggesting this terminology.

mental or educational model), timing (onset of intervention), duration (length of intervention over time), intensity (daily proportion of time devoted to treatment, location (home or center based), and the object of the intervention (child and/or family) are only some of the important dimensions across which early interventions can differ. Any statements relating to the effectiveness of early intervention must consider these variations.

Finally, it is important to note that these general approaches to early intervention for children with documented handicaps can also characterize the preventive intervention efforts for children at risk due to biological or psychosocial factors. A developmental model is particularly apparent for the latter group, with special attention placed on certain developmental processes and family interaction patterns identified for that subgroup of children (see Chapter 2). Programs for children at biological risk, although generally being cast within a developmental framework, often include specialized forms of contrived stimulation (see Chapter 3). Clearly, it is essential to maintain a perspective with regard to the nature of the specific interventions, their assumptions, and expectations.

THE NATURE OF THE EVIDENCE
FOR EARLY INTERVENTION

Because early interventions have so many components that vary in so many different ways, it is likely to be extraordinarily difficult to extract unequivocal and totally scientifically defensible statements about effectiveness from existing data (see Dunst & Rheingrover, 1981; Simeonsson et al., 1982). To these difficulties, others must be added. The definition of handicapped populations and even at-risk groups and their samples for research purposes have often been ambiguous. The dimensions of severity of handicap and corresponding associated disabilities are two parameters that have powerful moderating influences on interventions, but often fail to be adequately described. In fact, the remarkable heterogeneity of handicapped children and the very low incidence of many disability groups add to these evaluation problems. Because ethical and legal considerations often require that some form of intervention be provided to all handicapped children, it is easy to see why many fundamental procedures for establishing proper comparisons cannot be followed. When instrumentation problems are added to this mix, it is apparent why it might be possible to reject much of the intervention research that exists outright, to select data to fit one's own biases, or to fall prey to many false generalizations through an uncritical acceptance of the findings.

As might be expected, the primary experimental design problem plaguing researchers in this field is the establishment of proper comparison groups. Although some studies have been able to randomly assign subjects to various conditions (including alternative intervention contrast groups or control groups receiving routine care), a substantial proportion have been forced to rely on other approaches. One strategy has been to create comparison groups by selecting children, either singly or in intact groups, who for a variety of reasons have not received services. In an effort to avoid selection bias, child and other relevant characteristics are matched to those of the early intervention subjects as closely as possible. Sometimes these comparison groups are identified or formed during a preintervention period and tested at that time along with the intervention group as one measure of initial group equivalence. Both groups are then tested again following the intervention period to yield comparative data (pre–post comparisons). More typically, the comparison group is tested (and often formed) following the early intervention period (a post-only comparison). The major problem with this general approach is that one can never be sure whether equivalence has been achieved; when intact groups in particular are selected, matching problems are inevitable. The believability of this approach clearly rests with the researcher's ability to ensure a sound and credible match.

The second major strategy for evaluating effectiveness in the absence of random assignment is to appeal to historical or normative data. The weaker approach is to evaluate gains in terms of previous rates of development for individual children (pre–post with no controls). If more rapid gains correlate with the intervention period, a degree of effectiveness is suggested. If this approach is carried out systematically by including a group that delays entry to the program for a specified period of time or by using certain single-subject designs (typically some form of a multiple baseline approach), then it may be possible to rule out maturational and related factors, thereby enhancing the researcher's ability to attribute change to the intervention itself.

Alternatively, certain groups of children at risk or even those with documented handicaps can also appeal to extensive normative data to present their case for effectiveness. Normative data are not only available for the general population of children for a given chronological age but for certain at-risk or disability subgroups also. For example, longitudinal studies of children with Down syndrome or disadvantaged children who have not received early intervention allow some useful normative comparisons. For this to be a fair and valid comparison, assurance must be obtained that the intervention group is a representative sample of the larger normative comparison group, differing only in regard to their receiving early intervention services.

It cannot be overemphasized that the threats to internal validity (Campbell & Stanley, 1966) associated with the absence of random assignment are considerable. Moreover, retrospective studies, in which subjects are tracked down at a point subsequent to intervention, or other similar approaches add additional hazards to meaningful interpretations of outcomes. Although many studies have been especially creative in combining various experimental designs and finding ways of testing and ruling out competing hypotheses, issues of potential bias are of great concern.

Yet this is too important an area to dismiss because of difficulties in experimental design and evaluation. Scientific and clinical judgments must always adapt to the special circumstances of the problem under study, but such an adaptation does not at all imply that the principles of scientific inquiry or clinical practice must be compromised. After all, when faced with families of handicapped children seeking advice, conclusions, however tentative, must be drawn and actions taken even in the absence of elegantly constructed designs and a firm data base.

Although the attitude of a scientific purist probably lurks deep within us all, a balanced and reasonable approach is one that exhibits a willingness to broaden one's concept of the nature of the data that can be useful in evaluating the effectiveness of early intervention programs while maintaining a critical perspective. As will be seen, in some instances quite sophisticated investigations have been conducted. However, whether or not such studies are available, it is important to attempt to identify program elements that appear robust across studies, to consider carefully patterns that may appear and internal consistencies that may emerge, and to weigh outcomes in terms of their logical and developmental credibility. Isolated bits of evidence may seem tangential and circumstantial at first glance, but in their totality may help establish important directions regarding the effectiveness of early interventions.

THE ROLE OF PRIMARY CARE PROFESSIONALS

Perhaps the most vocal critics of early intervention programs in recent years have been physicians (e.g., Ferry, 1981). The questions posed by the medical community regarding the effectiveness of intervention programs and the potential hazards to the family resulting from false expectations and the significant expenditures of time and energy needed to comply with program requirements are important ones and should receive the proper attention of researchers in the field. Because the primary care physician or associated practitioner occupies a pivotal position regarding the early identification of developmental problems and then the referral of these children and families to appropriate early intervention services, it is increasingly imperative that these professionals become acquainted with the critical issues and research in the field. Primary care physicians are often the first professionals to encounter initial parental concerns about their child's development and/or behavior. Depending upon the physicians' knowledge, clinical skills, and attitudes, they can either ignore these early signs and symptoms or effectively investigate the concerns, consult with other professionals, make appropriate referrals (which may include early intervention programs), and participate in the child's developmental management.

Accordingly, a number of issues in this book regarding early intervention will be directed toward physicians. It is hoped that primary care physicians' improved

understanding of the different types of early intervention efforts and their underlying rationales and documentation of their specific effectiveness and utility will
be helpful in developing realistic attitudes toward what can be accomplished for
at-risk and handicapped children during infancy and early childhood. In addition,
this understanding may also serve to alter attitudes about the quality of life for
developmentally disabled children, provide alternative perspectives with regard
to related medical/ethical decisions, and change the nature of the counseling and
recommendations given to parents.

PURPOSE AND ORGANIZATION OF THIS BOOK

This book is concerned with the outcomes of efforts occurring during the first
few years of life designed to achieve some influence on the development of
children at risk for developmental problems as well as those with established
disabilities. It should be noted that we labor under no illusions about the strength
of the data base, the quality of the work in this area, or our ability to arrive at
specific answers to even a fraction of the important questions in this field. In
fact, we do not see our task here as an effort to generate firm conclusions
regarding the effectiveness of early intervention. Rather, we see it as one that
takes inventory, notes trends, patterns, and problems, and raises and examines
issues of significance. In some cases patterns, trends, and the quality of the
research may be strong enough to generate conclusions that carry some degree of
confidence. We do feel, however, that it is appropriate in all instances to make
recommendations at this time based on existing knowledge about the value of
various forms of early intervention. Educational, clinical, and public policy
decisions continue to be made in the area of early intervention, and we hope that
this volume will enhance the quality of those decisions.

The approach taken here organizes the early intervention field in the more
traditional manner. For children with documented handicaps, separate chapters
focus on children with motor, cognitive, hearing, visual, and language and
communicative delays or dysfunctions. In addition, a chapter examining the
effects of early intervention for children classified as autistic will be presented.
Two other chapters consider children who are at risk from either predominantly
biological or environmental sources. The final chapter attempts to provide a
broad perspective on the major findings and issues facing the field.[3]

---

[3]Please note that we have deliberately excluded children who are considered to have behavioral or
emotional disturbances as their primary disability. Although this was not an easy decision, it was felt
that the definitional problems and other complexities could not be adequately addressed in this
volume. However, the chapter on autism does focus on a subset of the more severely disturbed of this
group. In addition, both definitional and conceptual problems led us to exclude children considered
learning disabled or disordered or children diagnosed as hyperactive. A subset of those children
included in the communicative disorder chapter are likely to be diagnosed as learning disabled
sometime during their elementary school years.

This organization is not intended to imply that we see intervention approaches as isolated within each disability area or that children with handicaps can be placed easily in one or another disability category. On the contrary, we subscribe to the notions not only of the overlap of developmental disorders (as discussed earlier and stressed in each of the individual chapters) but also that multidisciplinary involvement in early intervention is almost always the strategy of choice. Moreover, the interaction and co-occurrence of biological and environmental risk factors has been well recognized. The organization by disability or risk status does, however, reflect the existence of a certain integrity within each area and serves as a useful means of gathering and communicating information.

Finally, we have also attempted to achieve communicative clarity by asking contributors to organize their chapters in a consistent manner. Included in each chapter will be a description of the population of children being considered, general developmental characteristics, and classification systems. Following this, descriptions of the forms early interventions have taken, including specific approaches and their theoretical underpinnings will be presented. In addition to sections dealing with typical approaches to assessment and evaluation, an important component of each chapter will be a tabular summary of articles selected primarily from the peer-reviewed literature within a recent period. With these tables we hope to provide the reader with a useful perspective of the scope and nature of the research for each disability or risk area. It is from analyses of these studies and related information that recommendations will be developed.

REFERENCES

Appleton, T., Clifton, R., & Goldberg, S. (1975). The development of behavioral competence in infancy. In F. D. Horowitz (Ed.), *Review of child development research* (Vol. 4, pp. 101–186). Chicago: University of Chicago Press.

Baker, L., & Cantwell, D. P. (1982). Developmental, social and behavioral characteristics of speech and language disordered children. *Child Psychiatry and Human Development, 12,* 195–206.

Battle, C. U. (1974). Disruptions in the socialization of a young, severely handicapped child. *Rehabilitation Literature, 35,* 130–140.

Beckman-Bell, P. (1981). Child-related stress in families of handicapped children. *Topics in Early Childhood Special Education, 1*(3), 45–53.

Bee, H. L., Barnard, K. E., Eyres, S. J., Gray, C. A., Hammond, M. A., Spietz, A. L., Snyder, C., & Clark, B. (1982). Prediction of IQ and language skill from perinatal status, child performance, family characteristics, and mother–infant interaction. *Child Development, 53,* 1134–1156.

Bell, R. Q. (1968). A reinterpretation of the direction of effects in studies of socialization. *Psychological Review, 75,* 81–95.

Berger, J., & Cunningham, C. C. (1981). The development of eye contact between mothers and normal versus Down's syndrome infants. *Developmental Psychology, 17,* 678–689.

Berger, J., & Cunningham, C. C. (1983). Development of early vocal behaviors and interactions in

Down syndrome and nonhandicapped infant–mother pairs. *Developmental Psychology, 19,* 322–331.

Blacher, J., & Meyers, C. E. (1983). A review of attachment formation and disorder of handicapped children. *American Journal of Mental Deficiency, 87,* 359–371.

Bloom, B. S. (1964). *Stability and change in human characteristics.* New York: John Wiley & Sons.

Bloom, L., & Lahey, M. (1978). *Language development and language disorders.* New York: Wiley.

Bowlby, J. (1951). *Maternal care and mental health* (Monograph Series No. 2). Geneva: World Health Organization.

Bradley, R., & Caldwell, B. (1976). Early home environment and changes in mental test performance in children from 6–36 months. *Developmental Psychology, 12,* 93–97.

Bronfenbrenner, U. (1977). Toward an experimental ecology of human development. *American Psychologist, 32,* 513–531.

Bruner, J. S. (1977). Early social interaction and language acquisition. In H. R. Schaffer (Ed.), *Studies in mother–infant interaction* (pp. 271–289). London: Academic Press.

Caldwell, B. M. (1974). A decade of early intervention programs: What we have learned. *American Journal of Orthopsychiatry, 44,* 491–496.

Campbell, D. T., & Stanley, J. C. (1966). *Experimental and quasi-experimental designs for research.* Chicago: Rand McNally.

Cicchetti, D., & Sroufe, L. A. (1978). An organizational view of affect: Illustration from the study of Down's syndrome infants. In M. Lewis & L. A. Rosenblum (Eds.), *The development of affect* (pp. 309–350). New York: Plenum Press.

Clarke, A. M., & Clarke, A. D. B. (1976). *Early experience: Myth and evidence.* New York: The Free Press.

Clarke-Stewart, K. A. (1973). Interactions between mothers and their young children: Characteristics and consequences. *Monographs of the Society for Research in Child Development, 38*(6–7, Serial No. 153).

Crocker, A. C. (1982). Current strategies in prevention of mental retardation. *Pediatric Annals, 11*(5), 450–457.

Cunningham, C. E., Reuler, E. Blackwell, J., & Deck, J. (1981). Behavioral and linguistic developments in the interactions of normal and retarded children with their mothers. *Child Development, 52,* 62–70.

Drillien, C. M., & Drummond, M. B. (Eds.). (1977). *Neurodevelopmental problems in early childhood.* Oxford, England: Blackwell Scientific Publications.

Dunst, C. J., & Rheingrover, R. M. (1981). An analysis of the efficacy of infant intervention programs with organically handicapped children. *Evaluation and Program Planning, 4,* 287–323.

Eaton, L. F., & Menolascino, F. J. (1982). Psychiatric disorders in the mentally retarded: Types, problems, and challenges. *American Journal of Psychiatry, 139,* 1297–1303.

Emde, R. N., Katz, E. L., & Thorpe, J. K. (1978). Emotional expression in infancy: II. Early deviations in Down's syndrome. In M. Lewis & L. A. Rosenblum (Ed.), *The development of affect* (pp. 351–360). New York: Plenum Press.

Escalona, S. K. (1982). Babies at double hazard: Early development of infants at biologic and social risk. *Pediatrics, 70,* 670–676.

Ferry, P. C. (1981). On growing new neurons: Are early intervention programs effective? *Pediatrics, 67,* 38–41.

Field, T. M., Sostek, A. M., Goldberg, S., & Shuman, H. H. (1979). *Infants born at risk: Behavior and development.* New York: SP Medical & Scientific Books.

Fraiberg, S. (1974). Blind infants and their mothers: An examination of the sign system. In M. Lewis & L. A. Rosenblum (Eds.), *The origins of behavior: Vol. 1. The effect of the infant on its caregiver* (pp. 215–232). New York: Wiley.

Friedrich, W. N., Greenberg, M. T., & Crnic, K. A. (in press). Empirical studies of handicapped children and their families: Measurement issues in conceptual framework. In S. Landesman-Dwyer & P. Vietze (Eds.), *Research on the impact of residential settings on mentally retarded persons.* Baltimore: University Park Press.

Greenberg, M. T., & Marvin, R. S. (1979). Attachment patterns in profoundly deaf preschool children. *Merrill-Palmer Quarterly, 25,* 265–279.

Guralnick, M. J., & Weinhouse, E. M. (1984). Peer-related social interactions of developmentally delayed young children: Development and characteristics. *Developmental Psychology, 20,* 815–827.

Hartup, W. W. (1976). Peer interaction and the behavioral development of the individual child. In E. Schopler & R. J. Reichler (Eds.), *Psychopathology and child development: Research and treatment* (pp. 203–218). New York: Plenum Press.

Hayden, A. H., & McGinness, G. D. (1977). Bases for early intervention. In E. Sontag (Ed.), *Educational programming for the severely and profoundly handicapped* (pp. 153–165). Reston, VA: Council for Exceptional Children.

Hebb, D. O. (1949). *The organization of behavior.* New York: Wiley.

Higgenbotham, J., & Baker, B. M. (1981). Social participation and cognitive play differences in hearing-impaired and normally hearing preschoolers. *The Volta Review, 83,* 135–149.

Hoff-Ginsberg, E., & Shatz, M. (1982). Linguistic input and the child's acquisition of language. *Psychological Bulletin, 92,* 3–26.

Horowitz, F. D. (1980). Intervention and its effects on early development: What model of development is appropriate? In R. R. Turner & H. W. Reese (Eds.), *Life-span developmental psychology: Intervention* (pp. 235–248). New York: Academic Press.

Hunt, J. M. (1961). *Intelligence and experience.* New York: Ronald Press.

Hunt, J. M. (1976). Environmental programming to foster competence and prevent mental retardation in infancy. In R. N. Walsh & W. T. Greenough (Eds.), *Environments as therapy for brain dysfunction* (pp. 201–255). New York: Plenum Press.

Jones, O. H. M. (1980). Prelinguistic communication skills in Down's syndrome and normal infants. In T. M. Field, S. Goldberg, D. Stern, & A. M. Sostek (Eds.), *High-risk infants and children: Adult and peer interactions* (pp. 205–225). New York: Academic Press.

Kagan, J. (1982). Canalization of early psychological development. *Pediatrics, 70,* 474–483.

Kogan, K. L. (1980). Interaction systems between preschool handicapped or developmentally delayed children and their parents. In T. M. Field, S. Goldberg, D. Stern, & A. M. Sostek (Eds.), *High-risk infants and children: Adult and peer interactions* (pp. 227–247). New York: Academic Press.

Kogan, K. L., Tyler, N., & Turner, P. (1974). The process of interpersonal adaptation between mothers and their cerebral palsied children. *Developmental Medicine and Child Neurology, 16,* 518–527.

Lasky, W. Z., & Klopp, K. (1982). Parent–child interactions in normal and language-disordered children. *Journal of Speech and Hearing Disorders, 47,* 7–18.

Lewis, M., & Goldberg, S. (1969). Perceptual-cognitive development in infancy: A generalized expectancy model as a function of mother–infant interaction. *Merrill-Palmer Quarterly, 15,* 81–100.

Mahoney, G. J., & Seely, P. B. (1976). The role of the social agent in language acquisition: Implications for language intervention. In N. R. Ellis (Ed.), *International review of research in mental retardation* (Vol. 8, pp. 57–103). New York: Academic Press.

Markovits, H., & Strayer, F. F. (1982). Toward an applied social ethology: A case study of social skills among blind children. In K. H. Rubin & H. S. Ross (Eds.), *Peer relationships and social skills in childhood* (pp. 301–322). New York: Springer-Verlag.

McLean, J. E., & Snyder-McLean, L. K. (1978). *A transactional approach to early language training.* Columbus, OH: Merrill.

Meadow, K. P., & Trybus, R. J. (1979). Behavioral and emotional problems of deaf children: An overview. In L. J. Bradford & W. G. Hardy (Eds.), *Hearing and hearing impairment* (pp. 395–403). New York: Grune & Stratton.

Moerk, E. L. (1977). *Pragmatic and semantic aspects of early language development.* Baltimore: University Park Press.

Murphy, M. A. (1982). The family with a handicapped child: A review of the literature. *Journal of Developmental and Behavioral Pediatrics, 3,* 73–82.

Nelson, K. (1973). Structure and strategy in learning to talk. *Monographs of the Society for Research in Child Development, 38*(1 and 2, Serial No. 149).

Northern, J. L., & Downs, M. P. (1978). *Hearing in children* (2nd ed.). Baltimore: Williams & Wilkins.

Reiss, S., Levitan, G. W., & McNally, R. J. (1982). Emotionally disturbed mentally retarded people: An underserved population. *American Psychologist, 37,* 361–367.

Rutter, M. (1980). The long-term effects of early experience. *Developmental Medicine and Child Neurology, 22,* 800–815.

Sameroff, A. J., & Chandler, M. J. (1975). Reproductive risk and the continuum of caretaking casualty. In F. D. Horowitz, M. Hetherington, S. Scarr-Salapatek, and G. Siegel (Eds.), *Review of child development research* (Vol. 4, pp. 187–244). Chicago: University of Chicago Press.

Schlesinger, H. S., & Meadow, K. P. (1972). *Sound and sign: Childhood deafness and mental health.* Berkeley, CA: University of California Press.

Simeonsson, R. J., Cooper, D. H., & Scheiner, A. P. (1982). A review and analysis of the effectiveness of early intervention programs. *Pediatrics, 69,* 635–641.

Smith, V., & Keen, J. (Eds.). (1979). *Visual handicap in children* (Clinics in Developmental Medicine No. 73) London: Spastics International Medical Publications.

Smith, D. W., & Simons, F. E. R. (1975). Rational diagnostic evaluation of the child with mental deficiency. *American Journal of Diseases of Children, 129,* 1285–1290.

Sroufe, L. A. (1979). The coherence of individual development: Early care, attachment, and subsequent developmental issues. *American Psychologist, 34,* 834–841.

Stanley, F., & Alberman, E. (Eds.). (1984). *The epidemiology of the cerebral palsies* (Clinics in Developmental Medicine No. 87). Oxford: Spastics International Medical Publications.

Stone, N. W., & Chesney, B. H. (1978). Attachment behaviors in handicapped infants. *Mental Retardation, 16,* 8–12.

Terdal, L., Jackson, R. H., & Garner, A. M. (1976). Mother–child interactions: A comparison between normal and developmentally delayed groups. In E. J. Mash, L. A. Hamerlynck, & L. C. Handy (Eds.), *Behavior modification and families* (pp. 249–264). New York: Brunner/Mazel.

Thomas, A., & Chess, S. (1977). *Temperament and development.* New York: Brunner/Mazel.

Thompson, R. J., Jr., & O'Quinn, A. N. (1979). *Developmental disabilities.* New York: Oxford University Press.

Tjossem, T. D. (Ed.). (1976). *Intervention strategies for high risk infants and young children.* Baltimore: University Park Press.

Wachs, T. D., & Gruen, G. E. (1982). *Early experience and human development.* New York: Plenum Press.

Waisbren, S. E. (1980). Parents' reactions after the birth of a developmentally disabled child. *American Journal of Mental Deficiency, 84,* 345–351.

Waters, E., Wippman, J., & Sroufe, L. A. (1979). Attachment, positive affect, and competence in the peer group: Two studies in construct validation. *Child Development, 50,* 821–829.

Wedell-Monnig, J., & Lumley, J. M. (1980). Child deafness and mother–child interaction. *Child Development, 51,* 766–774.

Zigler, E., & Berman, W. (1983). Discerning the future of early childhood intervention. *American Psychologist, 38,* 894–906.

Part II

Children at Risk

Chapter 2

An Analysis of the Effectiveness of Early Intervention Programs for Environmentally At-Risk Children

DONNA M. BRYANT
CRAIG T. RAMEY

Frank Porter Graham Child Development Center
University of North Carolina
Chapel Hill, North Carolina 27514

INTRODUCTION

The question of the effectiveness of early intervention or compensatory education for infants and children from socially disadvantaged families has been investigated in many ways by many social scientists over the past 25 years. This chapter will summarize what is known about the efficacy of early education by carefully analyzing several exemplary intervention studies. Frequently developed for preschool-aged children and/or their families, early education programs have attempted to modify the course of early development to better prepare socially disadvantaged, at-risk children for public school.

This approach to breaking the cycle of poverty has been taken because it has been established repeatedly that the children who perform most poorly scholas-

33

tically and intellectually tend to come disproportionately from lower socioeconomic families (e.g., Heber, Dever & Conry, 1968; Knobloch & Pasamanick, 1953; Kushlick & Blunden, 1974; Ramey, Stedman, Borders-Patterson, & Mengel, 1978). This is often attributed to impoverished environments, but it is also true that many other potential causes of developmental retardation are associated with low socioeconomic status. Medical complications of pregnancy are more prevalent among the poor. Also associated with poverty is the lack of financial resources to provide for basic necessities such as healthy food and safe shelter. Mothers' education, a powerful predictor of first-grade intelligence and achievement (Ramey et al., 1978), is also lower among the poor. These different environmental risk factors contribute to the later developmental delays but with less predictability or specificity than an organically caused deficit. The lack of a physical syndrome at birth also makes it difficult to identify at an early stage which children are likely to be most at risk and which are likely to benefit most from preventive efforts.

Some of the very early reports of early education (Klaus & Gray, 1968; Weikart, 1967) showed that preschool programs were indeed raising children's IQs. These results were followed by a negative evaluation of the early Head Start programs (Westinghouse Learning Corporation, 1969), which led to a widely held belief that compensatory education caused gains in IQ that "washed out" once the child left the special program and entered public school. A reliance on IQ measures has indeed been one of the problems of early education research programs. Compensatory education programs have been controversial because these efforts have frequently been evaluated with IQ tests; IQ tests are controversial primarily because of the continuing debate concerning the roles that genetic influences and environmental factors play in determining performance on tests of intelligence (see, for example, Herrnstein, 1982; Jensen, 1969). Whatever their inadequacies, intellectual tests are the only developmental measure common to all of the compensatory education studies; such tests are therefore the one measure that allows direct comparison of outcome across studies.

Different paradigms and theories have guided early intervention research over the years. but two have had a pervasive influence on this area of research. The early experience paradigm was used in the works of Hunt (1961) and Bloom (1964) that provided a major impetus for preschool intervention programs. Both emphasized that early experiences in life are important for successful intellectual development, although Bloom believed more specifically in certain critical periods for learning. Both moved the field toward greater acceptance of early preschool education as an important experience for children, particularly disadvantaged children.

Another theory that has been especially influential in the design of early intervention programs and assessment of their outcomes has been the transactional model of development (Sameroff & Chandler, 1975). This theory emphasizes the dynamic interplay between the biology (including genotype) of the child and the environment that the child encounters. As the child grows, he or she is influenced by his own biology in interaction with social values, family attitudes and values, and financial resources. The general systems theory that has guided the two early intervention studies conducted at our site is an expanded transactional model, emphasizing the family and broader cultural milieu (Ramey, Mac-Phee, & Yeates, 1982). Models such as these are important because they provide the theoretical rationale for aspects of the curriculum or intervention delivered to children and/or families.

In this chapter we will summarize the programmatic features and intellectual results (outcome in terms of IQ) from exemplary educational experiments, and then discuss what we have learned and the implications of those results.

THE RESEARCH STUDIES

Criteria for Review

Although a very large number of service and demonstration projects have been conducted since the mid-1960s, relatively few studies have met the basic criteria required to be considered true experiments. The most frequent research design flaw has been the failure to ensure adequately the initial equivalence of educationally treated and untreated (control) groups. In social and behavioral science, the most traditional and simplest experimental method to ensure initial equivalence is to assign individuals at random to groups that are then treated differently. Given a sufficient number of cases in each group, sampling theory allows one to interpret subsequent mean differences between groups as plausibly due to the educational procedures used. In the absence of initial equivalence of groups, subsequent group differences are not scientifically interpretable in any straightforward manner.

In this chapter we have restricted our attention to studies that the various authors described as true experiments. In doing this, we omit some well-known studies of early intervention that used quasi-experimental designs (Madden, Levenstein, & Levenstein, 1976; Schaefer & Aaronson, 1972; Slaughter, 1983). By so restricting our choice of projects to those using randomization, we hope to arrive at generalizations of effects that are, at most, conservative estimates of the current knowledge base concerning early intervention. We had also hoped that some of the Head Start programs (Zigler & Anderson, 1979) had been conducted using an adequate experimental design, but to our knowledge this is not the case.

The seventeen studies that met our criteria to be reviewed in this chapter are presented in Table 1, along with the references we used in researching their subject characteristics, intervention description, research design, and IQ results.

TABLE 1

Seventeen compensatory education research studies: Years of
intervention and follow-up and references used

Infancy programs

Center-based, child- and parent-focused
1. Milwaukee Project
   Intervention, 1966–1972; follow-up, through 1983
   (Garber, 1982; Garber & Heber, 1981; Heber & Garber, 1971)
2. Project CARE
   Intervention, 1978–present; follow-up continuing
   (Ramey, Bryant, Sparling, & Wasik, 1985; Ramey, Sparling, & Wasik, 1981)
3. Carolina Abecedarian Project
   Intervention, 1972–1985; follow-up, continuing
   (Ramey & Bryant, 1983; Ramey, MacPhee, & Yeates, 1982; Ramey, Yeates, & Short,
   1984)
4. Field's Center–Home Visit Comparison
   Intervention, 1979–1980; follow-up, 1981
   (Field, 1982)

Center-based, parent-focused
5. Birmingham PCDC[a]
   Intervention, 1970–1973; follow-up, 1974
   (Andrews, Blumenthal, Johnson, Kahn, Ferguson, Lasater, Malone, & Wallace, 1982)
6. Houston PCDC
   Intervention 1970–1973; follow-up 1974
   (Andrews et al., 1982)
7. New Orleans PCDC
   Intervention, 1970–1973; follow-up, 1974
   (Andrews et al., 1982)

Home visit, parent-focused
8. Mobile Unit for Child Health
   Intervention, 1965–69; follow up, 1970–1972
   (Gutelius, Kirsch, MacDonald, Brooks, McErlean, & Newcomb, 1972; Gutelius, Kirsch,
   MacDonald, Brooks, & McErlean, 1977)
9. Florida Parent Education Project
   Intervention, 1966–1972; follow-up, 1974, 1976, 1978, 1980
   (Gordon & Guinagh, 1974, 1978; Guinagh & Gordon, 1976; Olmsted, Rubin, True, and
   Revicki, 1980)
10. Ypsilanti–Carnegie Infant Education Project
    Intervention, 1968–1970; follow-up 1974–1975
    (Epstein & Weikart, 1979; Lambie, Bond, & Weikart, 1974)
11. Family-Oriented Home Visiting Program
    Intervention, 1972–1975; follow-up, 1976
    (Gray & Ruttle, 1980)

TABLE 1 (*Continued*)

Infancy programs

12. Field's Home Visit Study
    Intervention, 1977–1979; follow-up, 1980
    (Field, 1982; Field, Widmayer, Stringer, & Ignatoff, 1980)

Early childhood (preschool) programs

Center-based, child- and/or parent-focused
13. Perry Preschool Project
    Intervention, 1962–1966; follow-up, 1967–1970, 1975
    (Schweinhart & Weikart, 1980)
14. Early Training Project
    Intervention, 1962–1965; follow-up, 1968, 1975, 1979
    (Gray & Klaus, 1970; Gray, Ramsey, & Klaus, 1982; Klaus & Gray, 1968)
15. Academic Preschool Project
    Intervention, 1965–1968
    (Bereiter & Engelmann, 1966)
16. Curriculum Comparison Study
    Intervention, 1968–1969; follow-up, 1971, 1975–1977
    (Miller & Dyer, 1975; Miller & Bizzell, 1983)
17. Five Preschool Comparisons
    Intervention, 1965–1967; follow-up, 1969
    (Karnes, Hodgins, Teska, & Kirk, 1969)

[a]PCDC, Parent–Child Development Center.

In many cases, more than one primary source was used to obtain this information, and in some cases, the different sources reported slightly different information—for example, in numbers of subjects or the process of group assignment. In these cases we used our best judgment as to which numbers to report here and cited the specific source of the information in the tables that follow.

Organization of the Review of the Studies

The programs have been grouped in Table 1 under two developmental periods corresponding to the time at which the child entered the program: (1) infancy and (2) early childhood. The projects that began in infancy have been further classified as to whether they were (a) center-based with a child and parent focus, (b) center-based but primarily parent-focused, or (c) home-based and primarily parent-focused. Within each of these headings, programs are arranged in order of their apparent intensity of education, as judged by the number of hours per month that projects sought to have contact with parents and/or children. The early childhood programs have also been ordered in intensity of contact from those that had the most hours or years of contact to those that had the least. Throughout this chapter the studies will be grouped in the same order.

Table 1 also indicates the years during which each of the 17 projects conducted their intervention program(s) and years in which systematic follow-up data have been reported. The projects varied in the years of their inception from the early 1960s to the late 1970s. Thus, these projects were conducted during a historical period of rapid development of many social action programs aimed at reducing the impact of poverty. One might easily question whether the natural ecologies of the environments in which these projects were conducted were comparable. Programs that began later may have operated in social climates that were richer in resources than earlier projects. If this is so, then the performance of control group children might be expected, on average, to be somewhat higher in the later projects than in the earlier ones—all other factors being equal. That is, to the extent that President Johnson's Great Society programs were successfully developed and implemented, the effect on poor families would be expected to be positive and the contrast between treated and control groups lessened.

Most of the individual projects lasted for a relatively brief historical period, about 3–5 years. There has been some systematic follow-up by investigators, but less than might have been anticipated. The monograph by Lazar, Darlington, Murray, Royce, and Snipper (1982), which reported follow-up on some of the projects to be discussed here, made a major contribution to the area. Gray, Ramsey, and Klaus (1982) followed the life course of the children from the Early Training Project through age 20. Berrueta-Clement, Schweinhart, Barnett, Epstein, and Weikart (1984) have written follow-up results on the Perry Preschool Project children through age 19. The Carolina Abecedarian Project (Ramey & Campbell, 1984) is currently collecting follow-up data on 12-year olds and their families. These follow-up studies are important because they tell us about real-world outcomes: school success, employment potential, and social adjustment.

Most of the projects discussed in this chapter are no longer actively involved in compensatory education. The exception to this is Project CARE, a study being conducted at the Frank Porter Graham Child Development Center at the University of North Carolina at Chapel Hill. Intervention will continue for these children through the third year in public school. Children are currently 6–8 years of age. Intervention has ended in all other studies reported.

Our review of the 17 intervention studies and their findings will look at four major areas: (1) characteristics of the subjects, (2) research design, (3) characteristics of the intervention, and (4) IQ results.

Characteristics of the Subjects

Table 2 contains a brief description of each project including children's age at entry, race of participants, type of community in which the project was con-

TABLE 2

Characteristics of the subjects

Name of study	Child's age at entry	Race	Type of community	Family characteristics
Infancy programs				
1. Center-based, child- and parent-focused				
Milwaukee Project	3–6 months	Black	Urban (Milwaukee, WI)	From economically depressed census tract in inner city; mother's IQ <75
Project CARE	3 months	95% black, 5% white	Small town (Chapel Hill, NC)	Family's average income = $6,500; mother's and father's education = 11; average IQ of mothers = 87; about 25% 2-parent families
Carolina Abecedarian Project	3 months	Black	Small town (Chapel Hill, NC)	Average earned income = $1,455; mother's education = 10 years; average IQ of mothers = 85; 25% 2-parent families
Field's Center–Home Visit Comparison	Birth	Black	Urban (Miami, FL)	Teen mothers ≦19 years old; full-term babies
2. Center-based parent-focused				
Birmingham PCDC	3–5 months	Black	Urban (Birmingham, AL)	Approximately $4,000 yearly income; mother's education = 11 years; average number people in home = 5; about 50% fathers head of household; most lived in public housing; less than 50% received welfare
Houston PCDC	1 year	Mexican American	Urban (Houston, TX)	Average income = $6,000; most owned or rented their house; mother's education = 7.5 years; 90% fathers present; more than 5 people in home; $\frac{1}{3}$ of mothers spoke only Spanish

(continued)

TABLE 2 (*Continued*)

Name of study	Child's age at entry	Race	Type of community	Family characteristics
New Orleans PCDC	2 months	Black	Urban (New Orleans, LA)	Average income = $4,000; about $\frac{1}{3}$ lived in public housing; mother's education = 10–11 years; approximately 5 people in home; approximately 50% fathers head of household
3. Home visit, parent-focused				
Mobile Unit for Child Health	At 7 months of pregnancy	Black	Urban (Washington, DC)	Teenage unmarried mothers living in low-income area; most income from unskilled labor; only 3 families receiving public assistance at entry; mother's score >20 on Peabody; for most, grandmother was head of household
Florida Parent Education Project	3 months	80% black, 20% white	Urban, small town, and rural (Gainesville, FL, and surrounding 12 counties)	Families below poverty level as defined by hospital criteria
Ypsilanti–Carnegie Infant Education Project	3, 7, or 11 months	Black and white	Urban (Ypsilanti, MI)	Few parents employed; mother's and father's education = 10 years, approximately 6 people in home
Family-oriented Home Visiting Program	17–24 months with sibling aged 2–5	50% black, 50% white	Urban (Nashville, TN)	Average income <$4,137; mother's education = 10 years; 72% 2-parent families; mother had to be nonworking or working at night (so visits could be made)

Study	Age at entry	Race	Location	Family characteristics
Field's Home Visit Study	Birth (preterm babies)	Black	Urban (Miami, FL)	Lowest SES; teenage, unmarried mothers; mother's education = 10 years; most lived with their mother who was often the primary caregiver

Early childhood programs
1. Center-based, child- and/or parent-focused

Study	Age at entry	Race	Location	Family characteristics
Perry Preschool Project	1st cohort = 4 years; 2nd–5th cohorts = 3 years	Black	Urban (Ypsilanti, MI)	70% had at least 1 parent employed; mother's education = 9.7, father's education = 8.8; 53% 2-parent families; approximately 7 people in home
Early Training Project	3 or 4 years	Black	Small towns (Tennessee)	Average income <$3,000; unskilled or semi-skilled occupations; mother's education $\leq$8 years; 67% 2-parent families; approximately 6–7 people in home
Academic Preschool Project	4 years	Mostly black	Urban (Champaign, IL)	30–40% were receiving some form of welfare; parents usually unskilled or semi-skilled laborers
Curriculum Comparison	4 years	Mostly black	Urban (Louisville, KY)	Average income = $3,440; 30–50% received welfare; mother's and father's education = 11 years; 39% 2-parent families; approximately 5–7 people in home
Five Preschool Comparisons	4 years	67% black 33% white	Urban (Champaign, IL)	Families from economically depressed neighborhoods of the city

ducted, and salient family characteristics as reported by the investigators. With
the exception of the Mobile Unit for Child Health Project, in which subjects were
selected before birth, all of the studies were begun when the children were
between birth and 5 years of age; two thirds of the studies began when the
children were infants.

These experiments in compensatory education have been conducted with children from socially, educationally, and economically disadvantaged families.
This has been the case because such children are at elevated risk for lower scores
on standardized tests of intelligence and academic achievement (see, for example, Broman, Nichols, & Kennedy, 1975; Knobloch & Pasamanick, 1953;
Ramey, et al., 1978). Therefore, it has been hypothesized that systematic educational programs might be especially advantageous to this vulnerable segment of
the population—especially as our society becomes increasingly more tech-
nological. As a result of this special targeting, most of the children who participated in early intervention studies were black and lived in urban settings in the
Eastern half of the United States. Urban black families were particularly targeted
for assistance in the 1960s and 1970s because of social and economic injustices;
it should be noted that, as a result, what we know about the effects of early
compensatory education comes from studies that concentrated heavily on a subgroup of the socially disadvantaged population. The notable exception to this is
the Houston Parent Child Development Center (PCDC), which targeted intervention to low-socioeconomic status (SES) Mexican American children and their
families.

The children came from families of low economic and educational status and
lived in homes having, on average, 5–7 people in the household. Within this
general description, however, there were dramatic differences in the families.
For example, in some studies, children lived with single parents (e.g., Field's
Center–Home Visit Comparison), while in others (e.g., Houston PCDC) almost
all lived with both parents. Some were children of teenage mothers, but most
were not. In most of the studies, some of the families lived in public housing or
received some form of public assistance. The percentage of these families varied
considerably among the studies, however. Although these 17 studies are comparable in the low-SES, mostly black composition of their samples, other family
characteristics that might be related to outcome have not been varied systematically and are not directly comparable across projects.

Research Design

Table 3 contains a brief description of each of the 17 projects' sampling plan,
intervention research design, the IQ assessment instruments and standardization
norms, the number of child participants, and data on sample attrition.

From Table 3 it will be noticed that most of the projects recruited a pool of

TABLE 3

Research design

Name of study	Sampling plan	Intervention design[a]	IQ assessments	Numbers Entry	Numbers End	Attrition
Infancy programs						
1. Center-based child- and parent-focused						
Milwaukee Project	Families assigned by alternate monthly cohorts to E or C group	E = parent training and daycare C = testing only	Gesell, 10– 22 months; Stanford–Binet (1960 norms), 2–6 years; WISCs, 7–10 years	E = 20 C = 20	17 18	E = 15% C = 10%
Project CARE	Families ranked by mother's IQ and High-Risk Index, then randomly assigned to 1 of 3 groups	E1 = daycare plus home visits and infant formula E2 = home visits and infant formula C = infant formula	Bayleys through 2 years; Stanford–Binets (1972 norms) at 2 and 3 years; McCarthy at $2\frac{1}{2}$	E1 = 16 E2 = 27 C = 23	14 25 22	E1 = 12% E2 = 7% C = 4%
Carolina Abecedarian Project	Families ranked by mother's IQ and High-Risk Index, then randomly assigned to E or C group	E = daycare, social work services and infant formula C = social work services and infant formula	Bayleys, 3–18 months; Stanford-Binet (1972 norms), 2, 3, 4, and 5 years; McCarthy, $2\frac{1}{2}$, $3\frac{1}{2}$, $4\frac{1}{2}$; WPPSI at 5 years	E = 57 C = 54	49 47	E = 14% C = 13% through age 5
Field's Center–Home Visit Comparison	Mothers randomly assigned to E1, E2, or C group	E1 = daycare and parent training E2 = home visits C = testing only	Denver at 4 months; Bayleys at 8 and 12 months	E1 = 20 E2 = 20 C = 20	NR[b] NR NR	NR

(continued)

TABLE 3 (*Continued*)

Name of study	Sampling plan	Intervention design[a]	IQ assessments	Numbers Entry	End	Attrition
2. Center-based, parent-focused						
Birmingham PCDC	Randomly assigned to E or C after agreeing to participate in either group	E = daycare, parent training, and work experience in daycare C = small stipend for testing	Bayleys at 4, 10, and 20 months; Stanford–Binet (1960 norms) at 36 and 48 months	E = 162 C = 89	71 65	E = 56% C = 27%
Houston PCDC	Eligible families randomly assigned to E or C, then invited to participate in the assigned group	E = home visits, daycare and family services C = testing only	Bayleys at 12 and 24 months; Stanford–Binet (1960 norms) at 36 months	E = 97 C = 119	44 58	E = 55% C = 51%
New Orleans PCDC	Recruited mothers randomly assigned to E or C groups	E = daycare, parent training and family services C = offered health services and stipend for testing	Bayleys at 7, 13, 19, and 25 months; Stanford–Binet (1960 norms) at 36 and 48 months	E = 67 C = 59	NR NR	E = 50% C = 25%
3. Home visit, parent-focused						
Mobile Unit for Child Health	Mothers were recruited during pregnancy and randomly assigned to E or C before child's birth	E = medical services and infant stimulation services at home C = referred to other available health services	Bayleys through 2 years; Stanford–Binet (1960 norms) at 3 years	E = 47 C = 48	44 45	E = 6% C = 6%

Program	Sample/Assignment	Treatment	Measures	Initial N	Final N	Attrition
Florida Parent Education Project	Families randomly assigned to various E groups or C group; later, more were randomly assigned to the E = Home Learning Center or C group; assignment was made by area of town or county	E = 1 of 6 home visit and/or playgroup combinations of 1, 2 or 3 years' duration C = testing only	Griffiths at 1 year; Bayley at 2 years; Stanford–Binet (1960 norms) at 3–6 years; WISC-R at 10 years	3 years = NR 2 years = NR 1 years = NR C = NR Total 309	24 35 83 50 192	37% overall
Ypsilanti–Carnegie Infant Education Project	Stratified random sample by age of entry	E = home visits C = testing only	Bayleys at 3–37 months; Stanford–Binet (1960 norms) at 6 and 7 years	E = NR C = NR	22 22	Total = 26%; significantly more whites than blacks dropped out
Family-Oriented Home Visiting Program	3 waves recruited and randomly assigned to E or C groups	E = home visits C = 4 social visits, photographs of children, and noneducational presents	Bayley at pretest (17–24 months) and Stanford–Binets (1972 norms) at posttests (26–52 months)	E = 27 C = 20	20 17	E = 26% C = 15%
Field's Home Visit Study	Mothers agreed to participate, then randomly assigned to E or C group	E = home visits C = testing only	Denver at 4 months; Bayley at 8 and 12 months	E = 30 C = 30	27 25	E = 10% C = 17%
Early childhood programs 1. Center-based, child- and/or parent-focused						
Perry Preschool Project	Recruited children with IQs 70–85; stratified random sample by	E = 2 years preschool C = testing only	Stanford–Binet (1960 norms) yearly at 3–10; WISC at 14	E = 61 C = 67	58 65	E = 5% C = 3%

(continued)

TABLE 3 (*Continued*)

Name of study	Sampling plan	Intervention design[a]	IQ assessments	Numbers Entry	Numbers End	Numbers Attrition
	IQ with adjustments made for SES, sex, siblings, and mother's ability to participate in the E group					
Early Training Project	Children were randomly assigned to E1, E2, or C conditions	E1 = 3 years of summer school and home visits E2 = 2 years of summer school and home visits C = occasional gifts, picnics, and twice-weekly play periods in the last summer.	Stanford–Binet (1960 norms) administered to all children before and after each summer program, at 1st- and 2nd-grade entry, and at 2nd- and 4th-grade exit; WISC at 17	E1 = 22 E2 = 21 C1 = 18	19 19 18	E = 12% C = 0%
Academic Preschool Project	Stratified sample (by IQ) with adjustments for race and sex	E = 2 years of Academic Preschool C = 1 year of traditional preschool and 1 year of public school kindergarten	Stanford–Binet (1960 norms) 1st year fall and spring; 2nd year spring only	E = 15 C = 28	12 NR	E = 20% C = NR

Study	Assignment	Treatment	Measure			
Curriculum Comparison[c]	Stratified random assignment (by sex) to E or non-E classes within each of 4 schools	E = 1 of 4 types of prekindergarten programs: Bereiter–Engelmann, Traditional, DARCEE, and Montessori	Stanford–Binet (1960 norms) before and after preschool, at end of kindergarten, 1st and 2nd grades	E = 214	213	E <1%
Five Preschool Comparisons[d]	Stratified sample (by IQ); children assigned to class units; adjustments made for race and sex, each class then randomly assigned to a treatment	E = 1 of 5 types of preschool: Traditional, Ameliorative, Direct Verbal, Community-Integrated, and Montessori	Stanford–Binet (1960 norms) before and after preschool	Traditional (Tr) = 30	25	Tr = 17%
				Ameliorative (Am) = 30	24	Am = 20%
				Direct Verbal (DV) = NR	23	DV = NR
				Community-Integrated (CI) = NR	16	CI = NR
				Montessori (Mo) = NR	13	Mo = NR

[a]E and C are used to refer to the experimental and control groups.

[b]NR = not reported.

[c]Non-E children were not tested. This study included a nonrandom comparison group of children from Head Start waiting lists who received no preschool. Results from this group are not discussed here.

[d]At school entry, all Ss were placed nonrandomly into a public kindergarten or Bereiter–Englemann class. These results are not discussed here.

potential subjects and then randomly assigned children and/or families to a single treatment condition or to an educationally nontreated control condition. However, several noteworthy exceptions to this relatively simple assignment procedure occurred. Specifically, the Milwaukee Project assigned children to experimental or control groups by monthly cohorts instead of randomly assigning each individual. The Florida Parent Education Project used a combination of random assignment of individuals and assignment of geographic areas to various treatment conditions or to a control group. Five studies—the Ypsilanti–Carnegie Infant Education Project, the Perry Preschool, the Academic Preschool, the Curriculum Comparison, and the Five Preschool Comparisons—used stratified random sample assignment to groups. This procedure is standard; however, some of the studies also made nonrandom "adjustments" in the groups to balance for race or sex. When assignment procedures vary from truly random, our interpretation of results should be cautious.

Several projects had more than one experimental condition. Project CARE compared daycare plus home visits to home visits only to controls; Field also compared center plus home visit to home visits only to controls; the Florida Parent Education Project compared the timing and duration of six home visit and/or playgroup combinations to a control group; the Early Training Project compared 3 years of summer school and home visits to a 2-year program to controls; the Curriculum Comparison Project compared four types of prekindergarten programs including Bereiter–Engelmann, Montessori, Ameliorative, and traditional, but had no randomly assigned control group; and the Five Preschool Comparisons also compared prekindergarten programs, but had no randomly assigned control group.

With respect to intellectual assessment instruments, the most commonly used measure during early childhood was the Stanford–Binet (Terman & Merrill, 1973). During the infancy period, various projects, as noted, used the Gesell (Gesell & Amatruda, 1947), the Griffiths Mental Development Scales (Griffiths, 1954) and/or the Denver Developmental Screening Test (Frankenberg & Dodds, 1968), although the Bayley Scales of Infant Development (Bayley, 1969) was the most widely used test. The extent to which the scores from these various infant tests are similar—especially for these samples of socially disadvantaged, primarily black samples—is, at present, not known.

Another difference among the intellectual results of the projects is the norms used in the scoring of the Stanford–Binet—that is, 1960 or 1972. Although many of the projects were completed after 1972, many researchers continued to use 1960 norms, apparently for continuity in testing procedures. This difference should be noted, however, particularly when interpreting the results of the Milwaukee Project, the Birmingham, Houston, and New Orleans PCDCs, the Mobile Unit for Child Health, the Florida Parent Education Project, the Ypsilanti–Carnegie Infant Education Project, the Perry Preschool Project, the Early

Training Project, the Academic Preschool Project, the Curriculum Comparison, and the Five Preschool Comparisons, all of which used the 1960 Stanford–Binet norms. Using the 1972 norms were Project CARE, the Carolina Abecedarian Project, and the Family-Oriented Home Visiting Project. Although the difference in norms will not affect the magnitude of group differences within projects, it will affect comparability across projects of mean performances in both experimental and control groups. In general, the use of 1972 norms results in about a 10-point lower IQ than that of identically performing children who are scored using 1960 norms (Bryant, Burchinal, & Ramey, 1985).

It should also be noted that most of the projects have a relatively small number of children per experimental or control condition (typically 20–30) and that there was a wide range of attrition across projects, ranging from 0% for control subjects in the Early Training Project to 55% of the experimental group children in the Houston PCDC. Because initial sample sizes were small, the potential for systematic bias in the results of projects due to selective attrition cannot be dismissed lightly, even though statistical comparisons of families who dropped and those who stayed may not be significant. Given the low statistical power for such small samples, fairly large differences between those participants who dropped out and those who continued participation could be apparent but not statistically significant. However, even if attrition can be presumed to be random (i.e., not selective across or within groups), it may be particularly important to examine the overall differential attrition rates to determine the probable future appeal of programs with varying formats or programmatic characteristics.

Characteristics of the Intervention

Although it is very difficult, and undoubtedly an injustice to the complexity of the educational programs, we have attempted a capsule description of the characteristics of the intervention process for each of the 17 programs. Table 4 summarizes (1) the site of the educational intervention (usually either the family's home or a child development center), (2) the targets of the intervention (usually either the child, the mother, or both), (3) the duration of the educational treatment, (4) the intensity of the treatment or treatments within projects, and (5) a brief description of typical activities as reported by the projects. In Table 4 we have followed the convention established in Table 2 of ordering projects by intensity within developmental periods.

Typically, a center or school was the intervention site for the studies ranked most intense within their age of intervention category. This is probably so because it is easier and perhaps more cost-effective for a child or parent to spend several hours in a daycare center than it is for a home visitor or teacher to spend several hours in one child's home. Most home visit programs consisted of 90 minutes of intervention conducted once a week or less often. The most intense

TABLE 4

Characteristics of the intervention

Name of study	Intervention site	Primary target(s)	Duration	Intensity	Activities
Infancy programs					
1. Center-based, child- and parent-focused					
Milwaukee Project	Home and Center	Child and mother	Home = 4 months Center = 6 years for child; 2 years for mother	Many hours of HVs[a] in 1st 4 months, then full-day daycare year-round	Children in educational program having a cognitive–language orientation in a structured environment using prescriptive teaching techniques. Vocational and social education program for mothers including job training and remedial education
Project CARE	Center and Home	Child and mother in Center/HV group; mother in home group	5 years; project continues to age 8	Full-day daycare, year-round plus weekly HVs to Center/HV group; weekly HVs to home group	Children in educational daycare program with focus on language and cognitive development and adaptive social behavior. All medical care provided. HVs to both E groups with focus on responsive parenting, learning activities, behavior management, and problem solving

Carolina Abecedarian Project	Center	Child	8 years	Full-day daycare, year-round	Children in educational daycare program with focus on language and cognitive development and adaptive social behavior. All medical care provided
Field's Center–Home Visit Comparison	Center or home	Mother and child for Center group; mother for home group	12 months	Center = 20 hours/week; home = $\frac{1}{2}$ hour HV biweekly	Curriculum items modeled by HV; activities designed from the Denver and Bayley test items. Parent training in child development and in job skills via CETA employment
2. Center-based parent-focused					
Birmingham PCDC	Center	Mother and child	31–33 months	To 11 months = 12 hours/week; 12–17 months = 20 hours/week; 18–36 months = 40 hours/week	To 11 months = Training in parenting and child development; mothers cared for own child with assistance from center staff. 12–17 months = 4 half-days as understudies to teaching mothers; 1 half-day training in child development and family topics. 18–30 months = 4 mornings as teaching mothers,

(continued)

TABLE 4 (*Continued*)

Name of study	Intervention site	Primary target(s)	Duration	Intensity	Activities
					remaining time in training, taking care of own child, class preparation, and social groups
Houston PCDC	Year 1, home; year 2, center	Mother, child, and family	24 months	Year 1 = $1\frac{1}{2}$ hour HVs for 30 weeks plus 4 family workshops; Year 2 = 3-hour sessions for 4 days/week for 8 months plus nightly meetings	Year 1 = HV topics in child development, parenting, home as learning environment, parent–child activities. Family workshops for problem solving and communication skills. Year 2 = Training in home management, child development, and parenting; videotape and discussions of parent–child interactions. English classes offered weekly
New Orleans PCDC	Center	Mother and child	34 months	3 hours, 2 times/week	One weekly session to counsel on child development with 1-hour discussion group and 2-hour parent–child laboratory experience. One weekly session focused on adult and family life

Mobile Unit for Child Health	Home and mobile health unit	Mother and child	3 years	At least 20 health-related and 24 infant education 1-hour HVs over 3 years	Prenatal counseling; well-baby care; infant stimulation activities with emphasis on language; educational toy given to family often. 1st cohort received training on child development and family problems
Florida Parent Education Project	Home	Mother for 1st 2 years, mother and child in last year	3 years for 1 group, 2 years for 3 groups, and 1 year for 3 groups	Weekly 1-hour HVs for 3 years plus playgroup for 2 hours twice a week in 3rd year	HVs used infant stimulation activities with child and mother to help mother become more effective teacher of her child. Home Learning Center in 3rd year, supervised by experienced parents, was a backyard playgroup for socialization skills
Ypsilanti–Carnegie Infant Education Project	Home	Mother and child	16 months	Weekly 60–90 minute HVs	Focus on mothers as teachers of their children. Piagetian-based formal set of infant activities to support objectives for mothers; emphasis on fine and gross motor skills

(continued)

TABLE 4 (*Continued*)

Name of study	Intervention site	Primary target(s)	Duration	Intensity	Activities
Family-Oriented Home Visiting Program	Home	Mother	9 months	30 weekly 60–90 minute HVs	Activities were based on DARCEE principles and materials for mothers of toddlers (Giesy, 1970). Intervention tailored to each family, but emphasized teaching style, competence, language, and behavior management. Used inexpensive homemade materials
Field's Home Visit Study	Home	Mother	12 months	Biweekly $\frac{1}{2}$-hour HVs	Curriculum items modelled by HV; activities designed from the Denver and Bayley test items. Goals to educate mothers on developmental milestones and to facilitate mother–child interaction
Early childhood programs 1. Center-based child- and/or parent-focused Perry Preschool Project	School and home	Center = child; home = child and mother	1st cohort = 30 weeks; cohorts 2–5 = 60 weeks	Center = $12\frac{1}{2}$ hours/week; Home = weekly $1\frac{1}{2}$ hour HV	High/Scope Cognitively Oriented Curriculum used; Piagetian-based; emphasis on concrete

Early Training Project	School and home	Summer = child; winter = child and mother	E1 = 3 summers and 3 winters; E2 = 2 summers and 2 winters	Summer program = 4 hours daily for 10 weeks; winter program = weekly 1-hour HVs for 9 months	experience and expression in language Curriculum focused on perceptual and language development and acquisition of basic concepts. Tried to improve achievement motivation, persistence, and delay of gratification. Used common preschool toys and materials; the HV program tried to involve the parent in the child's education
Academic Preschool Project	School	Child	2 school terms	2 hours/day	Direct instruction (Bereiter–Engelmann curriculum) was provided in relation to 15 learning objectives; focus was on rapid attainment of basic academic concepts
Curriculum Comparison Study	School	Child	9-month school term	6½ hours/day	Adopted the curriculum and activities of 4 previously developed programs: 1. Bereiter–Engelmann (4 classes)

(*continued*)

TABLE 4 (*Continued*)

Name of study	Intervention site	Primary target(s)	Duration	Intensity	Activities
					2. DARCEE (4 classes)
					3. Montessori (2 classes)
					4. traditional preschool (4 classes)
Five Preschool Comparisons	School	Child	7–8 months	2 hours and 15 minutes/day	Used the curriculum and activities of 4 previously developed programs:
					1. Traditional (2 classes)
					2. Ameliorative (2 classes)
					3. Bereiter–Engelmann (2 classes)
					4. Community-integrated (1 class)
					5. Montessori (1 class)

[a]HV = home visit.

infancy and early childhood programs included center training as well as home visiting, thus attempting to alter the child's developmental course by changing the child directly and by changing parents' behavior and/or attitudes. Some of the most intense programs (e.g., the Milwaukee Project) also taught job skills to the mothers; if successful, this would affect an even broader range of the child's environment.

The duration of the most intense studies lasted from birth until public school entry. Other studies intervened for a year or 2 during infancy, during early childhood, or for the 1 year preceding public school entry. A comparison of some of these studies based on age at intervention might pinpoint more definitively just how early the early experiences have to occur in order to have an effect, either short-term or long-term, on intellectual development.

All studies included as part of their treatment specific educational activities designed to teach the infant or child certain concepts or skills. Depending on the mechanism targeted, these activities were either taught directly to the child (e.g., Abecedarian Project) or were taught to the mother so that she could teach her child (e.g., Florida Parent Education Program). These activities were many and varied: gross motor, perceptual, language, adaptive social behavior, and Piagetian-based activities. Three of the preschool programs used the Bereiter–Engelmann curriculum (Direct Verbal or DISTAR, as it is now called) in comparison to control groups or to groups who received other forms of preschool education.

Many projects included curricula for parents in order to encourage greater parent involvement in the child's intellectual, emotional, and social development. The Milwaukee Project, Project CARE, the PCDCs, and the Mobile Unit Project included parent training in areas such as problem solving, family life, and communication. Field's Center–Home Visit Comparison and the Milwaukee Project also included job training as part of the experimental treatment.

It is difficult to make a general summary statement about treatments, given the diversity of activities conducted as part of the interventions. Some treatments were described in a few pages or less, and some treatments used curricula that have been published and widely circulated. Most treatments were reported to be based on clearly defined theoretical models, yet the intervention was not specified in enough detail to determine that. It is clear that even if we determine that some compensatory education programs have significant effects on IQ, little research to date has addressed the question of which components of the programs are most effective.

IQ Results

The data base for the discussion to follow is composed of the mean IQ measures of experimental (E) and control (C) groups, where appropriate, in each of the 17 intervention studies. These scores are presented in Table 5. Standard

TABLE 5

Summary of group mean IQ results from eighteen compensatory education studies reporting random assignment to groups[a]

	N at entry	4–7	10–13	18–19	22–25	27–33	35–37	38–43
				Age in months				
INFANCY PROGRAMS								
1. Center-based, child- and parent-focused								
Milwaukee Project								
Experimental (E)	20		117[G]	118*[,G]	125*[,S]	124*	126*	125*
Control (C)	20		113	101	96	94	94	95
Project CARE								
E1 (DC + HV)	16	109	119*	119*	114*	108*[,M]	105*	
E2 (HV only)	27	107	108	94	89	90	89	
C	23	105	108	103	97	100	93	
Carolina Abecedarian Project								
E	57	107	111*	107*	96*[,S]	102*[,M]	101*	
C	54	101	105	90	85	93	84	
Field's Center–Home Visit Comparison								
E1 (DC)	20	35[D]	119*					
E2 (HV)	20	NR	108					
C	20	36	106					
2. Center-based, parent focused								
Birmingham PCDC								
E	162	113*	111		97*		98*	
C	89	106	107		89		91	
Houston PCDC								
E	97		103		99*		108	
C	119		102		91		104	
New Orleans PCDC								
E	67	121	111	97	101		105*	
C	59	123	107	99	100		99	
3. Home visit, parent-focused								
Mobile Unit for Child Health								
E	47	106	108*		100*		99*	
C	48	103	102		91		91	
Florida Parent Education Program								
E1 (3 years	NR				85		99*	
E2 (2 years)	NR				83		95	
E3 (1 year)	NR				90		94	
All E groups[b]	NR		111*[,R]		85		95	
C	NR		107		91		91	
	Total N = 309							

	Age in years (grade in parentheses)								
4	5 (K)	6 (1st)	7 (2nd)	8 (3rd)	9 (4th)	10 (5th)	Later follow-up	Percent attrition	Stanford–Binet norms
126*	118*	119*	103*,W	103*,W	103*,W	104*,W		15	1960
96	93	87	81	83	84	86		10	
								12	1972
								7	
								4	
102*	101*,P							14	1972
89	94							13	
								NR	NA
100*								56	1960
95								27	
								55	1960
								51	
109*								50	1960
97								25	
								6	1960
								6	
98*	98*	97*				89W		37[d]	1960
96*	94	95				87			
95*	94	95				81			
94*	94*	94*				88*			
88	89	88				78			

(*continued*)

TABLE 5 (*Continued*)

	N at entry	Age in months						
		4–7	10–13	18–19	22–25	27–33	35–37	38–43
Ypsilanti–Carnegie Infant Education Program								
E	NR	96	104	110	106		104	
C	NR	92	98	106	102		101	
Family-Oriented Home Visit Program[c]								
E	27			99		89		93*
C	20			94		83		85
Field's Home Visit Study[c]								
E	30	35*,D	115*					
C	30	31	105					

EARLY CHILDHOOD PROGRAMS

1. Center-based, child- and/or parent-focused

	N at entry	4–7	10–13	18–19	22–25	27–33	35–37	38–43
Perry Preschool Project								
E	61						79	
C	67						78	
Early Training Project								
E	43						90	97*
C	18						85	88
Academic Preschool Project								
E	15							
C	28							
Curriculum Comparison Study								
Bereiter–Engelmann	NR						93	
DARCEE	NR						96	
Montessori	NR						92	
Traditional	NR						90	
All E groups	214						93	
Five Preschool Comparisons								
Traditional	30							
Ameliorative	30							
Bereiter–Engelmann	NR							
Community-Integrated	NR							
Montessori	NR							

[a]Results at the various ages are from the following tests, unless indicated otherwise: 4–25 months, Bayley Mental Development Index; 27 months–10 years, Stanford–Binet Intelligence Test; 13–17 years, Wechsler Intelligence Scale for Children (WISC). *, Significant at the .05 level or better. ___ Underlined E group scores indicate pre- or postintervention results; nonunderlined scores are tests given during intervention; _ _ _ dotted lines indicate that the pretest was given 8 weeks after intervention began. Percent attrition figures are given for endpoint of educational intervention except as noted. Abbreviations: DC, an educational daycare program delivered daily; HV, home visits made to families by professional or paraprofessional educators; NR, not reported; NA, not applicable; PCDC, Parent Child Development Center; D, Denver Developmental Screening Test; G, Gesell Developmental Schedules; M, McCarthy Scales of Children's Abilities; P, Wechsler Preschool and

Age in years (grade in parentheses)							Later follow-up	Percent attrition	Stanford–Binet norms
4	5 (K)	6 (1st)	7 (2nd)	8 (3rd)	9 (4th)	10 (5th)			
		111	106					26^d	1960
		111	106						
93								26	1972
87								15	
								10	NA
								17	
96*	95*	91*	92*	88	88	85	81^{W,e}	5	1960
83	84	86	87	87	87	84	81	3	
95	97*	96*	99*	94*		88	79^{W,f}	12	1960
90	88	83	91	88		85	76	0	
95	112*	121*						20	1960
95	102	100						NR	
98	94	90	87				83^g		1960
97	94	94	91				85		
97	95	95	93				88		
96	94	93	90				86		
97*	94	92	90				85	<1	
94	102							17	1960
96	110							20	
95	108							NR	
93	98							NR	
93	99							NR	

Primary Scale of Intelligence; ^{R}, Griffiths Mental Development Scales; ^{S}, Stanford–Binet; ^{W}, WISC or WISC-R.

^{b}Figures used after age 2 are from Lazar and Darlington, 1982.

^{c}Scores at entry (16–24 months), at end of intervention (27–33 months), and at follow-ups (37–43 months and 53 months).

^{d}Overall attrition

^{e}At age 14.

^{f}At age 17.

^{g}At age 13.

deviations are not presented because they were not reported in some of the studies. Unless indicated otherwise, the early scores (4–25 months) are from the Bayley Mental Development Index (MDI) and the later scores are from the Stanford–Binet. Pre- and postintervention means are indicated with underlined E scores. Scores from tests given during the intervention are not underlined. Statistically significant E–C group differences are indicated by asterisks (*).

The Ypsilanti–Carnegie Infant Education Program, the Family-Oriented Home Visit Program, and Field's Center–Home Visit Comparison originally included other experimental groups, which, due to attrition or other problems, were not included in the data analyses of the original studies. We have also eliminated those groups from our discussion. The Florida Parent Education Program and the Miller and Dyer Curriculum Comparison Study of four preschool programs each included several treatment groups. For these two studies, we have elected to include in Table 5 a row of scores that describe the mean IQ scores of all E groups combined. These scores are from the monograph by the Consortium for Longitudinal Studies (Lazar et al., 1982).

Our discussion of results will be divided into three sections: results from infant intervention studies through age 2, results from a subset of the infant interventions that lasted through age 3, and early childhood IQ results from the preschool interventions for 3–5 year olds.

Infancy Results

Eleven of the 17 studies intervened during infancy. Table 6 presents a summary of their results. A comparison of the 9 studies that gave Bayley tests at 12 months indicates that the mean MDI scores of both experimental and control groups were unusually high for low-SES populations presumed to be at elevated risk for lower development (E mean = 111; C mean = 104). The scores of the experimental groups were always greater than the scores of the control groups. In 5 of the 9 studies the differences were statistically significant; however, in 2 of those 5 studies (both of Field's studies) the curriculum was based on the test items, so those differences are to be expected. Of the remaining 3 studies, Project CARE showed an 11-point E–C difference at 12 months, and the Carolina Abecedarian and Mobile Unit for Child Health projects each showed a 6-point difference. The Florida Project also showed a 4-point difference on the Griffiths test, a small difference that was significant presumably because of the large number of subjects participating. With the exception of Project CARE, and Field's studies, then, few of the 11 infancy intervention projects showed a striking advantage for the treated groups by 12 months, perhaps because the scores of the control groups were still at or above average. Biological or maturational factors may play primary roles in the development of intelligence during infancy and thus individual differences may not be highly correlated with en-

TABLE 6

Early infancy studies ranked by E–C difference at 2 years[a]

	E–C differences		Experimental scores			Control scores		
	12 months	24 months	12 months	24 months	Change	12 months	24 months	Change
Milwaukee Project	4	29	117g	125*,s	+8	113	96	−17
Project CARE	11	17	119*	114*	−5	108	97	−11
Carolina Abecedarian Project	6	9	111*	96*,s	−15	105	85	−20
Mobile Unit for Child Health	6	9	108*	100*	−8	102	91	−11
Birmingham PCDC	4	8	111	97	−14	107	89	−18
Houston PCDC	1	8	103	99*	−4	102	91	−11
Ypsilanti–Carnegie Infant Education Project	6	4	104	106	+2	98	102	+4
New Orleans PCDC	4	1	111	101	−10	107	100	−7
Field's Center–Home Visit	13		119*			106		
Field's Home Visit Study	10		115*			105		
Florida Parent Education Project	4	−6	111*,r	85	−26	107	91	−16
Mean Bayley MDI			111.2 (N = 9)	100.3 (N = 7)		104.4 (N = 9)	94.4 (N = 7)	

[a] All tests are Bayley MDIs except where indicated otherwise: g, Gesell at 10 months; s, Stanford–Binet at 2 years; r, Griffiths at 12 months; *, difference between E and C group significant at the .05 level or better.

vironmental differences (McCall, 1981). During infancy perhaps the developmental process will occur if the infant is given at least minimal levels of sustenance and stimulation.

Of the 11 studies that intervened during infancy, 9 reported 2-year scores. Seven projects used Bayley tests and the Milwaukee and Carolina Abecedarian projects used the Stanford–Binet. A comparison of the 2-year Bayley MDI scores indicated that E scores were greater than C scores for all studies (E mean = 100; C mean = 94) except for the Florida Parent Education Project. The Carolina Abecedarian Project and Milwaukee E-group Stanford–Binets were also significantly greater than the C-group scores (E mean = 111; C mean = 91). In all, 6 of the 9 studies reported that the E–C differences were statistically significant, indicating that the effects of the interventions on IQ did seem to be measurable by 2 years of age.

Why were these differences significant? Were the E scores improving or were the C scores decreasing? In 5 of the 6 studies that tested with the Bayley at both 12 and 24 months, the E *and* C scores dropped over that time. The average C drop was 12 points and the average E drop was 8 points. Thus, the early intervention did not improve Bayley scores for the E groups, but it prevented the large decline that occurred in the untreated control groups.

The Ypsilanti–Cargenie Infant Education Project was the only study that showed Bayley gains for both groups, 2 points for the Es and 4 points for the Cs. The Milwaukee Project, which reported the largest E–C difference at 2 years (29 IQ points), was the only study to show an E group increase (8 points) and a C group decrease (17 points). However, subjects received the Gesell at 10 months and the Stanford–Binet at 24 months, making it difficult to evaluate these change scores.

It is interesting to note that the range of 24-month C scores was 85–102, and that in only two of the studies were the scores below 90–85 in the Carolina Abecedarian Project (which used the Stanford–Binet at age 2) and 89 in the Birmingham PCDC study. In general, the C scores were within the normal range, although most were somewhat lower than the standardization mean of 100. It should be noted, however, that they were not in the range that would have been labeled mild mental retardation, regardless of the criteria used.

The two projects that showed the largest E–C differences at 2 years—the Milwaukee Project (29 points) and Project CARE (17 points)—also had the highest absolute E scores at 2 years (125 and 114, respectively). Both projects provided full-day, year-round day care for E children as well as support services for the family, such as family education via center training and home visits. The Milwaukee Project also provided job training and placements for the E mothers. These most intense studies yielded the most dramatic results at 2 years. It should be noted, however, that the Milwaukee Project used the 1960 standardization norms of the Stanford–Binet, resulting in scores that are about 10 points higher than if the 1972 norms had been used; Project CARE used the later norms. The scores at age 2 would thus appear to be virtually identical for these two most intense studies.

Four other projects showed statistically significant intervention effects at 2 years, although the effects were less dramatic than those of the Milwaukee or CARE projects. The Carolina Abecedarian Project, the Mobile Unit for Child Health, and the Birmingham and Houston PCDC studies all showed significant 8- or 9-point E–C differences and absolute 2-year E scores ranging from 96 to 100. The Carolina Abecedarian Project was a full-day, year-round day care intervention with fewer family support services than the Milwaukee or CARE projects. In type of treatment, though, it was most closely related to the most intense studies, yet in 2-year outcome it was more similar to the parent-focused studies. Perhaps this was because the 1972 version of the Stanford–Binet was the test used at 2 years, whereas all other studies used the Bayley or the 1960 version of the Stanford–Binet. A 10-point increase in Carolina Abecedarian Project E and C scores would have put it in the results range (for both E and C groups) of the most intense intervention studies. Instead, its results appear to fall in the moderate range.

The other three projects that showed moderate but statistically significant intervention effects at 2 years were parent-focused studies. Two of these studies were PCDC interventions at Birmingham and Houston, which included extensive center training for parents. The third project, the Mobile Unit for Child Health, was also a parent home visit program that included the provision of medical care, nutritional supplements, and educational activities for the infants. These moderately intense programs showed significant intervention effects with E group IQ scores averaging about 100. The PCDC studies, however, had over 50% attrition from the treatment groups, so results should be looked at with caution.

The remaining infancy interventions were all home visit programs, the least intense treatments reviewed in this chapter. None resulted in statistically significant 2-year outcomes. The E-group Bayley scores of the Ypsilanti–Carnegie Infant Education Program and the New Orleans PCDC averaged around 100, but the C-group scores averaged around 100 as well. If these samples of children were at risk for developmental delay, it was not evidenced in the 2-year C scores, nor were the E scores significantly higher as a result of treatment. Gordon's Florida Parent Education Program also showed no treatment effect by age 2, and all E groups combined actually scored lower than the C group. The conclusion from these studies seems to be that weekly parent-focused home visits alone are not enough intervention to significantly alter the child's intellectual status by age 2.

Taken all together, the 2-year results from the 11 infancy interventions support an intensity hypothesis. Home visits alone have not been shown to alter scores of intellectual development by age 2. Home visits plus medical and educational intervention or parent-focused center training have moderate effects on IQ.

TABLE 7

Early childhood results at age 3

	E–C difference	Stanford–Binet scores		Norms used
		E	C	
Milwaukee Project	32	126[a]	94	1960
Carolina Abecedarian Project	17	101[a]	84	1972
Project CARE	12	105[a]	93	1972
Mobile Unit for Child Health	8	99[a]	91	1960
Family Oriented Home Visiting Program	8	93[a]	85	1972
Birmingham PCDC	7	98[a]	91	1960
New Orleans PCDC	6	105[a]	99	1960
Houston PCDC	4	108	104	1960
Florida Parent Education Project	4	95	91	1960
Ypsilanti–Carnegie Infant Education Project	3	104	101	1960

[a]Difference between the E and C group significant at the .05 level or better.

Providing daycare plus other family services causes the most improvement in intellectual development. Based on outcome, it is unclear whether providing daycare alone is a most intense or moderately intense level of intervention.

Results from Interventions through Age 3

With the exception of Field's 2 studies, all of the infant intervention studies discussed in the previous section continued intervention and data collection through age 3. In addition, Gray's Family-Oriented Home Visit Program, which started when the children were 16–24 months old, also collected follow-up scores around age 3 (actually 38–43 months). Table 7 presents a comparison of the 3-year results of these 10 studies with a rank-ordering based on magnitude of E–C differences in Stanford–Binet scores.

When the 10 studies are ranked on the basis of the magnitude of treatment effect, the order is very similar to age 2 results and they seem to cluster into four groups. The Milwaukee Project, one of the 3 most intense treatments, showed the largest E–C difference (32 points) and forms a category of its own. The other 2 full-day daycare projects, Carolina Abecedarian and Project CARE, showed E–C differences of about one standard deviation, 17 and 12 points respectively, and form a second cluster. These 3 most intense studies, taken together, produced the strongest treatment effects.

The third cluster of studies includes four programs that had significant group differences, but the magnitude of the differences were 6, 7, or 8 IQ points, approximately one-half standard deviation. Two of these were PCDC center-based, parent-focused interventions. The other two were home visit, parent-focused studies. In our presumed hierarchy of intensity, the Mobile Unit for Child Health seemed more intense and lasted for twice as long as the Family-Oriented Home Visiting Program, yet both had effects of 8 points. These latter two studies used different Stanford–Binet norms, but that should not have affected difference scores, although it may have affected absolute scores. The Family-Oriented Home Visiting Program was the least intense of the seven studies that showed significant treatment effects. It was also the project with the lowest mean E group IQ, 93 points.

The fourth cluster of studies with results through age 3 includes the three projects with no significant E–C group differences. These are the Houston PCDC program, the Florida Parent Education Program, and the Ypsilanti–Carnegie Infant Education Program. In two of these three studies (Houston and Ypsilanti) both the E and C groups had mean Stanford–Binet scores greater than 100. In the Florida Parent Education Project experimental subjects who had participated in all 3 years of intervention were performing significantly higher than controls; however, when all E groups were combined (including 1- and 2-year treatment groups) the difference was not significant.

On the basis of the mean IQ of the experimental group children, the 10 studies form two groups—the Milwaukee Project (E mean = 126) and all the other studies (E mean = 101, range 93–108). Given the range of intensities represented by the other 9 studies, none of the E groups approach the high level of performance of the Milwaukee subjects. It is important to bear in mind that the Milwaukee Project used 1960 Stanford–Binet norms, but even taking this into account their performance still surpassed all the others, including the two full-day, year-round daycare projects—Carolina Abecedarian and CARE. The job training skills and experiences provided for the mothers by the Milwaukee Project in the first 2 years may have been a significant intervention above and beyond daycare and parenting skills, or some other aspect of their program perhaps undocumented, may have been responsible for the large group difference and high E scores.

Among the other studies, the intensity hypothesis, which was supported by the rankings of E–C differences, is less clearly supported by the absolute scores of the experimental children. For example, one of the least intense studies, the Houston PCDC (E mean = 108), had higher E scores than one of the most intense studies, Project CARE (E mean = 105), although the differences between the 1960 Binet scores in the Houston Program and the 1972 norms in Project CARE may account for this apparent anomoly. A 3-year program of home visits and play groups, the Florida Parent Education Program (E mean =

95), had only slightly higher scores than a 9-month home visit program, Family-Oriented Home Visiting Program (E mean = 93).

All but one study that had significant treatment effects at age 2 continued to show significant E–C differences at age 3 (all but Houston PCDC). In addition, the New Orleans PCDC and the Family-Oriented Home Visiting Program showed significant effects for the first time at age 3. Patterns that were established earlier still seem to be present at age 3, although there were more changes in the E scores from 2 to 3 years of age than there were in the C scores. These changes are difficult to evaluate because most studies changed tests from the 2-year assessment to the 3-year assessment.

Preschool Results

The data base for discussion of IQ changes in the preschool years (ages 3–5) is composed of fewer studies than were available for the infancy period or the period through age 3. Three studies used random assignment to E or C groups and intervened for 1–3 years beginning at age 3 or 4 (Perry Preschool, Early Training Project, and Academic Preschool). Two studies intervened during the last preschool year (beginning at about age 4), but had no randomly assigned control group (Miller and Dyer's Curriculum Comparison Study of four preschool programs and Karnes's Five Preschool Comparisons). Both studies, however, used random assignment to the various experimental groups. Two studies that began intervention in infancy continued continued treatment through the preschool years (Milwaukee Project and Carolina Abecedarian Project) and another is still in progress (Project CARE). Two studies ceased intervention at age 3, but continued to test children during the preschool years (Florida Parent Program and Ypsilanti–Carnegie Infant Education Program). Results from these studies are presented in Table 8. The first five studies in Table 8 are the programs that intervened only during the early childhood years. They are ordered based on intensity of contact. The last four studies in Table 8 are the programs that intervened during infancy and continued intervention and/or follow-up assessments through the early childhood period. In some studies, the IQ tests were given before and after preschool attendance rather than on the child's birthday, so the ages are approximately 3, 4, or 5 years.

Two studies showed a remarkable improvement in IQ scores of the E group after intervention. Experimental children in the Academic Preschool Project improved 17 points and experimental children in the Perry Preschool Project improved 16 points. Perry Preschool children were initially selected based on IQ scores less than 85, whereas Academic Preschool children were selected from a disadvantaged population but had an average IQ of 95 upon entry. Scores of the control group children in both of these studies also improved about 6 or 7 points. Both of these studies involved at least one full school term of intervention and succeeded in producing significant E–C differences.

The Early Training Project intervened most intensely during 10-week summer

TABLE 8

Preschool IQ results

	Experimental scores				Control scores			
	3 years	4 years	5 years	Change	3 years	4 years	5 years	Change
Perry Preschool Project	79		95[a]	+16	78		84	+6
Early Training Project	90		97[a]	+7	95		88	−7
Academic Preschool Project		95	112[a]	+17		95	102	+7
Curriculum Comparison Study	93	97		+4	No randomly assigned control			
Five Preschool Comparisons		94	103	+9	No controls			
Milwaukee Project	126*		118[a]	−8	94		93	−1
Carolina Abecedarian Project	101*		101[a,b]	0	84		94	+10
Florida Parent Education Project	95	94[a]	−1		91		89	−2
Ypsilanti–Carnegie Infant Education Project	104		111	+7	101		111	+10

[a]Difference between the E and C group significant at the .05 level or better.
[b]The Wechsler Preschool and Primary Scale of Intelligence was given at age 5.

sessions, with home visits during the year. This study also produced significant E–C differences by 5 years, differences of about the same magnitude as the Perry Preschool Project. In absolute gains, the Es in the Early Training Project gained only 7 IQ points over 2 years of intervention, but because the Cs decreased 7 points over the same time period, the outcome scores at age 5 are very similar to the Perry Preschool Project.

The Miller and Dyer and the Karnes preschool comparison studies have no randomly assigned control groups, so the only comparisons that can be made are among various types of interventions. None of the Miller and Dyer treatments seemed to affect IQ to a significant degree, and the range of scores, both for pretests and posttests, was very small: None of the treatment groups had pretest scores less than 90 nor did any have posttest scores greater than 100. Presumably, these disadvantaged children had not had any other intervention before age 3, yet their IQ scores, although below average, were not very far below average.

The same was true for the children in the Karnes preschool comparison. None of the E groups' average entry IQs was less than 93 at age 4. The ameliorative and the Bereiter–Engelmann interventions seemed to produce the most IQ change at the end of the school term, but the group differences were not statistically significant.

Results from the two studies that continued intervention up to school entry, the

Milwaukee and Carolina Abecedarian Projects, showed significant E–C differences at age 5. The Milwaukee E children still averaged far above the mean (Stanford–Binet IQ = 118) and the Abecedarian E children scored right at the mean (Wechsler Preschool and Primary Scale of Intelligence [WPPSI] IQ = 101). The intensity differences between these two studies have been discussed previously and may be the reason for the difference in the absolute E scores. The tests used by the two studies were also different.

The Florida Parent Education Project continued testing, although it did not continue intervention past age 3. The IQs of the E children were significantly higher than those of the C children at ages 4 and 5. Since age 3, the scores of the control children had fallen a few points to 88 or 89. The controls in the Florida Education Project illustrate that the 3–5-year-old range is the age at which the C children in some of the projects, but not all, begin falling to the levels that might be considered mild mental retardation and that might target them for special education classes in elementary school. However, the Ypsilanti–Carnegie study, which also continued testing beyond the end of intervention, was one that showed no IQ differences in preschool and showed no relative disadvantage for the children in the untreated control group. As a matter of fact, both E and C groups averaged 111 on the Stanford–Binet, well above average. These subjects were perhaps less disadvantaged than the Florida sample, yet for a disadvantaged sample they scored quite high.

Overall, the preschool results seem to show that continuing interventions continued to have effects on intelligence, and that programs that began at age 3 or 4 also were able to raise IQ levels significantly. No studies in the preschool period experimentally addressed the issue of timing of the intervention, but the Perry Preschool and the Early Training projects, which began at age 3, and the Academic Preschool, which began at age 4, were all able to produce significant IQ gains by age 5 in the children who received the experimental treatment.

Long-Term Results

Although most of the projects reviewed here lasted for brief periods, about 3–5 years, some longer-term follow-ups have been conducted. The Consortium for Longitudinal Studies (Lazar et al., 1982) conducted a follow-up in 1976 and 1980 of several early intervention projects begun in the late 1950s and early 1960s. Many of the subjects were already young adults, themselves parents of young children. The Consortium found results in three main areas: (1) Children who received early education programs were less likely to repeat a grade or be referred to special education classes; (2) these children were more achievement-oriented; and (3) their parents had higher educational and occupational aspirations for them than control children's parents. These children also completed high school more often and were more likely to find employment.

The Perry Preschool Project has also followed children for many years, through age 19. The young adults who were in the education program were more often employed, had fewer experiences of unemployment, had higher incomes, were more satisfied with their work, and made less use of public welfare benefits than the control group (Schweinhart & Weikart, 1980). There was also a lower frequency of teenage pregnancy among girls in the treatment group (Berrueta-Clement et al., 1984). Although few in number, these projects reporting long-term follow-up findings add support to the claims that preschool can be an "inoculation against failure" (Woodhead, 1985).

CONCLUSIONS FROM EMPIRICAL STUDIES

Our review of 17 compensatory education programs summarized the subjects, design, and intervention of the studies themselves, and concluded with a close look at the IQ results of each of the studies. What have we learned from this exercise?

First, we have learned that experimentally adequate research designs can be implemented in a longitudinal fashion with socially disadvantaged families. Most parents do want to provide good educational experiences for their children and are willing to and are often enthusiastic about participating in educational research studies. Although this is primarily a logistical point, it is a basic and necessary step to test strong hypotheses concerning intellectual malleability in young children. Therefore, for evaluation research purposes, quasi-experimental designs, with many of the variables likely to be confounded, should not be considered as adequate.

The preponderance of evidence seems to suggest that the intensity of programs (defined by amount and breadth of contact with children and/or families) is likely to have a direct and positive relationship to the degree of intellectual benefit derived by children participating in such programs. The results from the intervention studies reviewed show that educational home visits alone are not very effective. Home visits plus medical and educational intervention or parent-focused center training are moderately effective. The most improvement in intellectual development is seen when children attend daycare and families receive parent training or other services.

We have also learned that intellectual benefits can be derived by children when compensatory education is begun at various points during the preschool years. Although the data are not perfectly clear on this issue, it appears that significant benefits can be obtained whether programs are begun in infancy, early childhood, or during the preschool years. In addition, the results from programs that began at birth or within the first few months cause one to question whether sufficient risk exists during the first year of life (for most disadvantaged infants) to warrant *intensive* educational efforts during the first 12 months. In the only studies that varied the timing of intervention, the Florida Parent Education Program and the Ypsilanti–Carnegie Infant Education Program, children who began in very early infancy were not significantly more advanced than those who began as toddlers.

From these studies, we have learned that the function of systematic early education is not primarily to enhance early intellectual development to above average or levels of performance, but rather to prevent or slow the declines from average performance. The results from the Milwaukee Project and possibly from the Academic Preschool Project are exceptions to this generalization. Without intervention, the normative pattern of disadvantaged infants is one of relative decline on intellectual test scores after the first 12–18 months. Possible reasons for the decline are (1) differences in what infant tests and tests for older children actually assess, (2) cultural language differences being measured on tests that become more language-based, and (3) emergence of different abilities stressed in the culture but not on the tests. Regardless of the reasons for the decline, the evidence shows that intervention prevents or slows it.

Some of the studies reviewed directly compared different curricula; others compared one curriculum to a control group. We have learned that it is not likely that variations across currently well-developed educational methods and practices are strongly implicated in differential intellectual enhancement and development. This is not to imply that variations in systematic curricula cannot be important but only that within the range of alternatives explored thus far— traditional nursery school, concentrated didactic teaching, Montessori's methods, and so on—that these variations on a theme seem not to be particularly potent.

In contrast to a previous point about parents' willingness to participate in educational research, we suspect that the high attrition rates in projects requiring *extraordinary* participation by disadvantaged mothers on a frequent and sustained basis may indicate that this change mechanism is not perceived by families as particularly desirable. Requiring more than one or two hours of parent participation, whether during a home visit or in a larger group, may lead to higher attrition or noncompliance. To the extent that a given curriculum requires this of parents, it may be less effective. However, to the extent that the curriculum can be tailored to the life-styles and experiences of the participants, it can be more effective (Slaughter, 1983). Parents may be more willing or able to meet the needs of their children if the program is meeting some of their needs as adults and as parents. That is why Project CARE has included a problem-solving curriculum for parents (Wasik, 1984).

Honig (1984) discussed the many possible reasons why parent involvement programs are not overwhelmingly effective, beginning with the main reason that a parent's beliefs and interactions are quite complex and not changeable in a few visits per month. Many parents have too many personal problems of their own and too few resources to draw upon to be able to provide sustained attention and love to a child. Parents may have difficulty seeing themselves as the primary educator in their child's life. Parent educators in the home may spend too much time teaching specific activities and procedures and not integrate ideas or help parents emotionally. Some visitors may not respect a parent's alternative life-style, which impedes building a relationship of trust with the parent. All of these obstacles to effective program delivery have been faced by most of the intervention studies reviewed in this chapter. Yet parent involvement is still seen as the key to sustaining program gains once intervention has ended.

Last, we have learned through an examination of control group intellectual performance that during the preschool years relatively few children score below the level that would officially earn them the diagnostic label of mentally retarded. However, it is unclear why this is the case. There are three major plausible explanations for this fact. First, the use of 1960 Stanford–Binet norms by even fairly recent projects may overestimate the relative performance of these groups. Second, the location of most of these projects near universities, perhaps with an accompanying increased availability of social, medical, and other services, may not have allowed the recruitment of those individuals most at risk for retarded development. Alternatively, social action programs such as Aid to Families of Dependent Children and the Women, Infants, and Children (WIC) food program are now more widely available and the debilitating social conditions present in the first half of this century may have been, to some degree, ameliorated, thus buffering the impact of what would otherwise have been the natural ecology. Third, the developmental course of nonorganically caused mental retardation may not be fully expressed during the preschool years, so a longer developmental perspective may be needed to show the full detrimental impact of poverty on intellectual achievement.

IMPLICATIONS OF EARLY INTERVENTION IQ RESULTS

As we discussed earlier in this chapter, the early experience paradigm and the transactional model of development have been among the most important theoretical issues raised in early education research. The results of the studies reviewed in this chapter lead to implications about those paradigms.

In the broadest sense, the IQ results provide support for the idea that early experience is important for optimal development during the preschool years for children from socially disadvantaged families. This support takes the form of data that strongly imply that without some sort of systematic educational experience, a significant portion of children from socially disadvantaged families are not likely to approach their full intellectual potential. On the other hand, if systematic education is provided, intellectual levels can be boosted by modest to quite dramatic amounts, depending primarily upon the intensity of the educational treatments. Unfortunately for policymakers, however, we are unlikely to find that inexpensive programs have the magnitude of effects that were once anticipated. However, if mild interventions are not likely to produce strong positive effects on intellectual modifiability. then relatively brief and mildly deleterious environments are also not likely to leave permanent intellectual scars. In short, the young child appears to be responsive to *sustained* alternations in the quality of the environment, whether the approach is one of prevention or of remediation—at least during the preschool period. However, the demonstrated malleability during various phases of the preschool years does call into question strict interpretations of the critical period hypothesis, at least for variations in timing within this relatively brief developmental period.

Although the importance (if not the criticalness) of early experience has been supported by the IQ results, we are still unclear about which specific aspects of early experience are causally linked to specific aspects of intellectual development. Did children learn more from their many experiences with educational materials and toys, or from the expressive descriptive language used by their caregivers as they played with the toys, or from the emotional support they felt, allowing a more confident exploration of the environment? Did language learning improve more than perceptual–motor? Was social growth facilitated by the language development? Changes have been measured at specific times in some studies, but the interactive nature of changes is not well known.

Given the results of the curriculum comparison studies, it appears that systematic variations within what Scarr and Weinberg (1978) have called "humane environments" may be functionally equivalent for intellectual development—at least when it is measured somewhat summatively and, therefore, globally, as has been done with IQ tests. There might well be a direct parallel between cumulative risk as described by Rutter (1981) and cumulative competence or intellectual adaptability. More specifically, Rutter has shown that individual risk factors are not as highly related to deleterious outcomes as are the number of risk factors present for a given child or family. Similarly, there may be many paths to intellectual competence depending on the number of strengths or supportive or protective factors in the child's environment. Multiple measures of intellectual competence need to be used (not just IQ) to enable programs to try to enhance the specific cognitive processes that are most vulnerable in high-risk children.

With respect to the transactional hypothesis, the compensatory education experiments afford some indirect, if not direct, support. The notion that the infant's intellectual development can be altered by modifying the behaviors or tendencies of caregivers through systematic education has plausibility, even though the magnitude of the impact is modest and below that which has been shown by working directly with the child. Some interventions have resulted in parent attitude changes or improvements in the home environment, although these measures are not taken by as many studies as is IQ and they are measured with diverse instruments. However, the theoretically important point seems to be that intellectual development can potentially be influenced by systematic efforts aimed at a variety of nodes in the social–interactional system of infants and their caregivers.

ACKNOWLEDGMENTS

Preparation of this paper was partially supported by grants from NIH (5R01HD19757), the Department of Education (G008300011), and the Robert Wood Johnson Foundation (9367).

REFERENCES

Andrews, S. R., Blumenthal, J. B., Johnson, D. L., Kahn, A. J., Ferguson, C. J., Lasater, T. M., Malone, P. E., & Wallace, D. B. (1982). The skills of mothering: A study of Parent Child Development Centers. *Monographs of the Society for Research in Child Development, 47*(6, Serial No. 198).

Bayley, N. (1969). *Manual for the Bayley Scales of Infant Development.* New York: The Psychological Corporation.

Bereiter, C., & Engelmann, S. (1966). *The effectiveness of direct verbal instruction performance and achievement in reading and arithmetic.* Champaign, IL: Academic Preschool. (ERIC Document Reproduction Service No. ED 030 496)

Berrueta-Clement, J. R. B.,Schweinhart, L. J., Barnett, W. S., Epstein, A. S., & Weikart, D. P. (1984). Changed lives: The effects of the Perry Preschool Program on youths through age 19. *Monographs of the High/Scope Educational Research Foundation* (No. 8.) Ypsilanti, MI: The High/Scope Press.

Bloom, B. S. (1964). *Stability and change in human characteristics.* New York: Wiley.

Broman, S. H., Nichols., P. L., & Kennedy, A. (1975). *Preschool IQ: Prenatal and early developmental correlates.* Hillsdale, NJ: Erlbaum.

Bryant, D. M., Burchinal, M. B., & Ramey, C. T. (1985). *A comparison of treatment effects on Bayley MDI and Stanford–Binet IQ scores of disadvantaged two-year-olds.* Manuscript submitted for publication.

Epstein, A. S., & Weikart, D. B. (1979). *The Ypsilanti–Carnegie Infant Education Project: Longitudinal follow-up.* Ypsilanti, MI: High/Scope Educational Research Foundation.

Field, T. M. (1982). Infants born at risk: Early compensatory experiences. In L. Bond & J. Joffe (Eds.), *Facilitating infant and early childhood development.* Burlington, VT: University of Vermont Press.

Field, T., Widmayer, S., Stringer, S., & Ignatoff, E. (1980). Teenage, lower class black mothers and their preterm infants: An intervention and developmental follow-up. *Child Development, 51,* 426–436.

Frankenberg, W., & Dodds, J. (1968). *Denver Developmental Screening Test.* Denver: University of Colorado Medical Center.

Garber, H. (1982, August). *Preventing mild mental retardation: Decimating a complex.* Paper presented at the International Association of the Scientific Study of Mental Deficiency. (IASSMD) symposium, Toronto.

Garber, H., & Heber, R. (1981). The efficacy of early intervention with family rehabilitation. In M. Begab, H. C. Haywood, & H. L. Garber (Eds.), *Psychosocial influences in retarded performance*. Baltimore: University Park Press.

Gesell, A., & Amatruda, C. S. (1947). *Developmental diagnosis* (2nd ed.). New York: Hoeber.

Giesy, R. (1970). *A guide for home visitors*. Demonstration and Research Center for Early Education, Peabody College, Nashville, TN.

Gordon, I. J., & Guinagh, B. J. (1974). *A home learning center approach to early stimulation* (Final report to the National Institute of Mental Health). Gainesville, FL: Institute for Development of Human Resources, University of Florida. Published in *JSAS Catalog of Selected Documents in Psychology, 8*(6) (Ms. No. 1634).

Gordon, I. J., & Guinagh, B. J. (1978, March). *Middle school performance as a function of early stimulation*. (Final report to the Administration of Children, Youth, and Families, Project No. NIH-HEW-OCD-90-C-908). Gainesville, FL: University of Florida, Institute for Development of Human Resources; and Chapel Hill, NC: University of North Carolina, School of Education.

Gray, S. W., & Klaus, R. A. (1970). The early training project: A seventh year report. *Child Development, 41*, 909–924.

Gray, S. W., Ramsey, B. K., & Klaus, R.A. (1982). *From 3 to 20: The Early Training Project*. Baltimore: University Park Press.

Gray, S., & Ruttle, K. (1980). The Family-Oriented Home Visiting Program: A longitudinal study. *Genetic Psychology Monographs, 102*, 299–316.

Griffiths, R. (1954). *The abilities of babies*. London: University of London Press.

Guinagh, B. J., & Gordon, I.J. (1976). *School performance as a function of early stimulation* (Final report to OCD, Grant No. NIH-HEW-09-C-638). Gainesville: University of Florida.

Gutelius, M. F., Kirsch, A. D., MacDonald, S., Brooks, M. R., & McErlean, T. (1977). Controlled study of child health supervision: Behavioral results. *Pediatrics, 60*, 294–304.

Gutelius, M. F., Kirsch, A. D., MacDonald, S., Brooks, M. R., McErlean, T., & Newcomb, C. (1972). Promising results from a cognitive stimulation program in infancy. *Clinical Pediatrics, 11*, 585–593.

Heber, R. F., Dever, R. B., & Conry, J. (1968). The influence of environmental and genetic variables on intellectual development. In H. Prehm, L. A. Hamerlynck, & J. E. Crosson (Eds.), *Behavioral research in mental retardation*. Eugene: University of Oregon Press.

Heber, R., & Garber, H. (1971, October). *Rehabilitation of families at risk for mental retardation. A progress report*. Madison, WI: Rehabilitation Research and Training Center in Mental Retardation.

Herrnstein, R. J. (1982). IQ testing and the media. *The Atlantic, 250*(2), 68–74.

Honig, A. S. (1984). Reflections on infant intervention programs: What have we learned: *Journal of Children in Contemporary Society, 17*(1), 81–92.

Hunt, J. McV. (1961). *Intelligence and experience*. New York: Ronald Press.

Jensen, A. R. (1969). How much can we boost IQ and scholastic achievement? *Harvard Educational Review, 39*, 1–123.

Karnes, M. B., Hodgins, A. S., Teska, J. A., & Kirk, S. A. (1969). *Investigations of classroom and at-home interventions: Research and development program on preschool disadvantaged children* (Final Report). Urbana: University of Illinois. (ERIC Document Reproduction Service No. Ed 036 663)

Klaus, R. A., & Gray, S. W. (1968). The early training project for disadvantaged children: A report after five years. *Monographs of the Society for Research in Child Development, 33*(4, Serial No. 120).

Knobloch, H., & Pasamanick, B. (1953). Further observation on the behavioral development of Negro children. *Journal of Genetic Psychology, 83*, 137–157.

Kushlick, A., & Blunden, R. (1974). The epidemiology of mental subnormality. In A. M. Clarke & A. D. B. Clarke (Eds.), *Mental deficiency: The changing outlook*. New York: The Free Press.

Lambie, D. Z., Bond, J. T., & Weikart, D. P. (1974). *Home teaching with mothers and infants: The Ypsilanti–Carnegie Infant Education Project—An experiment.* Ypsilanti, MI: High/Scope Educational Research Foundation.

Lazar, I., Darlington, R., Murray, H., Royce, J., & Snipper, A. (1982). Lasting effects of early education: A report from the Consortium for Longitudinal Studies. *Monographs of the Society for Research in Child Development, 47*(2–3, Serial No. 195).

Madden, J., Levenstein, P., & Levenstein, S. (1976). Longitudinal IQ outcomes of the Mother–Child Home Program. *Child Development, 46,* 1015–1025.

McCall, R. B. (1981). Nature–nurture and the two realms of development: A proposed integration with respect to mental development. *Child Development, 52,* 1–12.

Miller, L. B., & Dyer, J. L. (1975). Four preschool programs: Their dimensions and effects. *Monographs of the Society for Research in Child Development, 40*(5–6, Serial No. 162).

Olmsted, P. P., Rubin, R. I., True, J. H., & Revicki, D. A. (1980). *Parent education, the contributions of Ira J. Gordon.* Washington, DC: Association for Childhood Education International.

Ramey, C. T., & Bryant, D. M. (August, 1983). *Enhancing the development of the socially disadvantaged child with programs of varying intensity.* Paper presented at the American Psychological Association meeting, Los Angeles, California.

Ramey, C. T., Bryant, D. M., Sparling, J. J., & Wasik, B. H. (1985). Educational interventions to enhance intellectual development: Comprehensive day care versus family education. In S. Harel & N. Anastasiow (Eds.), *The at-risk infant: Psycho/socio/medical aspects.* Baltimore, MD: Paul H. Brookes.

Ramey, C. T., & Campbell, F. A. (1984). Preventive education for high-risk children: Cognitive consequences of the Carolina Abecedarian Project. *Special Issue: American Journal of Mental Deficiency, 88*(5), 515–523.

Ramey, C. T., MacPhee, D., & Yeates, K. O. (1982). Preventing developmental retardation: A general systems model. In L. A. Bond & J. M. Joffe (Eds.), *Facilitating infant and early childhood development.* Hanover, NH: University Press of New England.

Ramey, C. T., Sparling, J. J., & Wasik, B. H. (1981). Creating social environments to facilitate language development. In R. Scheifelbush & D. Bricker (Eds.), *Early language intervention.* Baltimore: University Park Press.

Ramey, C. T., Stedman, D. J., Borders-Patterson, A., & Mengel, W. (1978). Predicting school failure from information available at birth. *American Journal of Mental Deficiency, 82,* 525–534.

Ramey,C. T., Yeates, K. O., & Short, E. J. (1984). The plasticity of intellectual development: Insights from preventive intervention. *Child Development, 55,* 1913–1925.

Rutter, M. (1981). Stress, coping, and development: Some issues and questions. *Journal of Child Psychology and Psychiatry, 22,* 323–356.

Sameroff, A. J., & Chandler, M. J. (1975). Reproductive risk and the continuum of caretaking casualty. In F. D. Horowitz (Ed.), *Review of child development research* (Vol. 4). Chicago: University of Chicago Press.

Scarr, S., & Weinberg, R. A. (1978). The influence of "family background" on intellectual attainment. *American Sociological Review, 43,* 674–692.

Schaefer, E. S., & Aaronson, M. (1972). Infant education research project: Implementation and implications of a home tutoring program. In R. K. Parker (Ed.), *The preschool in action* (pp. 410–430). Boston: Allyn & Bacon.

Schweinhart, L. J., & Weikart, D. B. (1980). *Young children grow up: The effects of the Perry Preschool Program on youths through age 15.* Ypsilanti, MI: High/Scope Educational Research Foundation.

Slaughter, D. T. (1983). Early intervention and its effects on maternal and child development. *Monographs of the Society for Research in Child Development, 48*(4, Serial No. 202).

Terman, L. M., & Merrill, M. A. (1973). *The Stanford-Binet Intelligence Scale.* New York: Houghton Mifflin.

Wasik, B. H. (1984). *A manual for teaching parents problem solving skills.* Chapel Hill, NC: Frank Porter Graham Child Development Center.

Weikart, D. P. (Ed.). (1967). *Preschool intervention: Preliminary results of the Perry Preschool Project.* Ann Arbor, MI: Campus Publishers.

Westinghouse Learning Corporation. (1969). *The impact of Head Start: An evaluation of Head Start on children's cognitive and affective development.* Executive Summary, Ohio University report to the Office of Economic Opportunity. Washington, D.C.: Clearinghouse for Federal Scientific and Technical Information. (ED036321)

Woodhead, M. (1985). Pre-school education has long-term effects: But can they be generalised? *Oxford Review of Education, 11*(2), 133–155.

Zigler, E., & Anderson, K. (1979). An idea whose time had come. In E. Zigler & J. Valentine (Eds.), *Project Head Start: A legacy of the war on poverty.* New York: Free Press.

Chapter 3

The Effectiveness of Early Intervention for Infants at Increased Biologic Risk

FORREST C. BENNETT

Child Development and Mental Retardation Center
University of Washington
Seattle, Washington 98195

INTRODUCTION

The concept of increased biologic risk is generally used to identify and include any newborn, infant, or child who has experienced a potentially brain-injurious event or sequence of events that have been associated with adverse, long-term, neurodevelopmental and/or neurobehavioral sequelae. This risk concept closely parallels the similar concept of increased environmental risk discussed in the chapter by Bryant and Ramey (Chapter 2, this volume). It clearly is not meant to encompass infants and children with established, diagnosed developmental dysfunctions and disabilities as discussed in the various chapters in the book, but rather to highlight an earlier stage of vulnerability prior to the actual emergence of any permanent developmental disorder. Thus, the "high-risk" label must always be applied cautiously with the understanding that, for the majority of biologic insults, most survivors will *not* develop the developmental complications for which they have an increased epidemiological risk (Scott & Masi, 1979). As a corollary to this important distinction, severe developmental disabilities are commonly and idiopathically encountered in infants with no apparent biologic risks. These facts emphasize the need to differentiate precisely risk and disability, both clinically and for research purposes, to avoid carelessly inferring one from the other or using the terms interchangeably. Accordingly, the

79

early interventions discussed in this chapter all share the primary goal of prevention rather than amelioration, of preventing the development of central nervous system handicapping conditions in an identified risk population.

NATURE OF THE POPULATION

Who is the biologically at-risk infant or child? The prototype is certainly the premature/low birthweight neonatal intensive care unit (NICU) graduate. However, other common at-risk conditions include perinatal asphyxia, central nervous system infection (e.g., meningitis, encephalitis), central nervous system trauma (e.g., accidents, abuse), ingestion of central nervous system toxins (e.g., lead, arsenic), and sustained hypoxia, such as might occur during a prolonged asthma attack or uncontrolled seizure episode. Because of the increasing prevalence of surviving low birthweight infants and the corresponding increase of both intense early developmental intervention efforts and long-term follow-up investigations, this chapter will focus exclusively on the premature/low birthweight infant as the contemporary model for a critical examination of the early intervention proposals for infants at increased biologic risk (Bennett, 1984).

Although most premature (preterm) infants can also be classified as low birthweight, these two categories are not identical and should be clearly defined. *Prematurity* refers specifically to a shortened gestational time and is generally applied to pregnancies of less than a 37-week duration. *Low birthweight,* by definition, includes infants weighing 2,500 g (about $5\frac{1}{2}$ lb) or less at birth, with *very low birthweight* reserved for those infants weighing 1,500 g (about $3\frac{1}{2}$ lb) or less at birth. Thus, the concept of prematurity rests solely on gestational age regardless of birthweight. For example, a 40-week gestational age (full-term) infant suffering from intrauterine growth retardation and weighing only 1,800 g (4 lb) at birth is certainly low birthweight but not premature, whereas an infant with the identical birthweight but of a 32-week gestational age is both low birthweight and premature.

Approximately 180,000 premature infants are born annually in the United States. Considering birthweight alone, about 6% of all live births in the white population are 2,500 g or less (low birthweight) and about 1% are 1,500 g or less (very low birthweight); these birthweight statistics are at least doubled (i.e., 12% and 2–3% respectively) in nonwhite populations (McCormick, 1985). Because these prematurity and low birthweight incidence estimates have remained surprisingly stable since the 1960s, reductions in neonatal mortality are steadily increasing the prevalence of biologically vulnerable infants in the overall population. Much debate and large differences of opinion persist when considering the effects of neonatal intensive care on the long-term neurodevelopmental morbidity encountered in low birthweight infants; most investigators, however, are

TABLE 1

Neonatal mortality for very low birthweight infants

	Birthweight (g)		
Years	500–1000	1,001–1,500	≤1,500
1960s	614/677 (91%)	456/1,039 (44%)	1,070/1,716 (62%)
Early 1970s	248/291 (85%)	176/583 (30%)	424/874 (49%)
Late 1970s	502/866 (58%)	325/1,845 (18%)	827/2,711 (31%)

in current agreement that the single clearest result of this technically enhanced care has been a dramatic and continuing reduction in neonatal mortality since the early 1960s, particularly for very low birthweight infants since the mid-1970s (Paneth et al., 1982; Philip, Little, Polivy, & Lucey, 1981). Simply stated, with the present standards of practice in neonatal intensive care units, many more very premature, very low birthweight infants are surviving to be discharged home than even in the 1970s. Table 1, using combined data from several centers, summarizes neonatal mortality for very low birthweight infants since the 1960s. Table 2 illustrates expected 1980 survival, as averaged from reporting NICUs, for individual birthweight groups of low birthweight infants. As can be seen, survival approaches 50% even at 801 grams and does not become more infrequent until below this birthweight. A 1983 report (Hirata et al., 1983) from a large San Francisco, California, NICU extends this striking trend by describing a 40% survival rate between 500 and 750g birthweight. Figure 1 graphically por-

TABLE 2

1980s NICU survival rate by birthweight

Birthweight (g)	Survival (%)
500–600	10
601–800	30
801–1,000	48
1,001–1,200	70
1,201–1,400	82
1,401–1,600	87
1,601–1,800	90
1,801–2,000	92
2,001–2,500	94
Total ≤ 2,500 gm	81

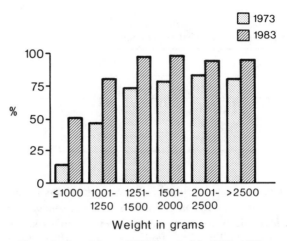

Figure 1. Comparison of NICU survival for 1973–1983.

trays that whereas survival continues to increase in all low birthweight categories, the greatest impact of neonatal intensive care technology in recent years has
clearly been on the smallest (and sickest) infants.

  With continued reductions in the neonatal mortality of premature/low birthweight infants, serious concerns persist that this improved survival may be
accompanied by increased neurodevelopmental morbidity, specifically in an increased number of permanently handicapped and brain-damaged children. The
major central nervous system/sensory handicapping conditions associated with
prematurity are: cerebral palsy (particularly the spastic diplegia type), mental or
developmental retardation (IQ or DQ < 70), sensorineural hearing loss, and
visual impairment (primarily the consequences of retrolental fibroplasia). These
handicaps frequently occur together in the same child, are usually apparent by 2
years of age, and vary in severity from mild to profound. Their incidence increases with decreasing birthweight and gestational age; the handicap rate in
males consistently exceeds that in females (Fitzhardinge, 1975; Hack, Fanaroff,
& Merkatz, 1979). Table 3 provides current combined incidence figures by
birthweight group for these major handicapping conditions. Such major morbidity statistics may be viewed both optimistically and pessimistically. On the
one hand, the occurrence of these major sequelae is far less than initially predicted at the beginning of the NICU era, and many more nonhandicapped than
handicapped (15 : 1) survivors are being added to the population. Conversely, the
major handicap rate has changed little since 1970 in spite of ongoing mortality
decreases, and data from Sweden (Hagberg, Hagberg, & Olow, 1984), Australia
(Stanley, 1979), and the United States (Paneth, Kiely, Stein, & Susser, 1981)

strongly suggest an actual current increase in major handicaps among the smallest and sickest survivors.

Further, while major handicapping sequelae are the easiest for NICUs to quantify and report, numerous long-term follow-up studies are clearly indicating that so-called minor neurodevelopmental and neurobehavioral sequelae are at least, if not more, prevalent in surviving premature/low birthweight infants and become increasingly apparent in a variety of clinical manifestations with increasing age during the first 6 years of life (Ehrlich, Shapiro, Kimball, & Huttner, 1973; Klein, Hack, Gallagher, & Fanaroff, 1985). These early, often subtle, developmental and behavioral delays and differences are not necessarily outgrown, but frequently portend future school dysfunction and, thus, often become *major* impediments to normal academic and social progress. Specific types of minor developmental handicap include borderline intelligence (IQ 70–84), minor persistent neuromotor abnormalities on the same continuum but of less severity than cerebral palsy (gross and fine motor milestone delays, mild muscle hypertonia or hypotonia, mild asymmetries, immature balance and coordination), and communication disorders (receptive and/or expressive language milestone delays, speech dysfunctions such as malarticulation and dysfluency). Specific areas of observed preterm–term behavioral difference include neonatal behavior (poorer and more variable performance in most assessed areas, particularly visual and auditory orienting, habituation, and behavioral organization), infant and child temperament (more "difficult" with less adaptability to change, less attentive, less mastery motivation, less smiling, more negative mood, and more irritability), and social competence (less social perception and more emotional immaturity) (Field, 1983; Kurtzberg et al., 1979). As with major handicaps, the overall incidence of these "minor" handicapping conditions increases with decreasing birthweight and gestational age and is also greater in male survivors. Current estimates in very low birthweight infants vary between 15%

TABLE 3

Surviving low birthweight infants with one or more major handicaps

Birthweight (g)	Major handicapping conditions (%)
1,500–2,500	10%
	(5–20%)
1,000–1,500	20%
	(5–30%)
≤1,000	30%
	(8–40%)

and 25%. Accordingly, when the 20% major handicap rate is also considered, between 35% and 45% of very low birthweight survivors demonstrate a residual, neurodevelopmental problem that compromises their age-expected function (Saigal, Rosenbaum, Stoskopf, & Milner, 1982).

The occurrence of most of the major and minor neurodevelopmental sequelae associated with prematurity and low birthweight is also related to the severity of perinatal/neonatal illness. That is, low birthweight infants experiencing a prolonged course with many medical complications have an increased likelihood of developing some type of developmental dysfunction. Specific events highly associated with suboptimal outcomes include intrauterine growth retardation, severe perinatal asphyxia, neonatal meningitis/encephalitis, symptomatic intracranial hemorrhage (particularly extensive intraventricular and/or intraparenchymal hemorrhage), and neonatal seizures. Typical neonatal complications that are not so strongly linked to adverse outcomes include respiratory distress syndrome and milder forms of chronic bronchopulmonary dysplasia, apnea of prematurity, and transient metabolic abnormalities (e.g., hypoglycemia, hypocalcemia). However, it must be emphasized and constantly considered that despite the large number of positive group associations, individual neurodevelopmental outcome remains very difficult to predict accurately and prospectively in the NICU, and infants with apparently similar neonatal courses may develop remarkably differently. This repeated observation should be a source of caution and humility to those making critical neonatal care decisions and also to those providing follow-up evaluations.

Finally, as increasing numbers of studies are able to follow premature/low birthweight infants longitudinally into the school years, the full spectrum of these children's learning and behavioral performance is emerging and becoming clearer. Although incidence estimates of school problems vary between reports, almost all investigators currently agree that low birthweight survivors have a distinctly increased risk of school dysfunction in some form (Drillien, Thomson, & Burgoyne, 1980; Dunn et al., 1980). Very low birthweight estimates approximate 50%; Nickel, Bennett, and Lamson (1982) reported that 65% of extremely low birthweight (≤1,000 g) survivors were experiencing school problems, with particular difficulties in reading comprehension, mathematics, perceptual skills, and fine motor balance and coordination. There is also general agreement that although this significant risk certainly exists independent of the single most powerfully predictive variable, socioeconomic status, the combination and interaction of *both* biologic and environmental risks constitutes an especially worrisome "doubly vulnerable" milieu and a highly appropriate target population for early intervention efforts. Expectedly, as with antecedent major and minor handicapping conditions, school learning and/or behavioral problems also occur with greatest frequency in the smallest and sickest NICU graduates. This enlarging phenomenon has been termed by some the *new morbidity* of prematurity.

Even though most low birthweight children are not functionally impaired, compared on a group basis with normal birthweight, full-term children they perform and score lower on most measures of mental development, language proficiency, and scholastic achievement throughout childhood and thus, particularly in the case of very low birthweight children, should be considered at long-term higher risk developmentally and behaviorally.

It can be concluded from this brief overview of a tremendously diverse and complex literature that because the severity of neonatal illness by itself is an unreliable predictor of neurodevelopmental outcome and because many of these infants demonstrate early, transient neuromotor abnormalities (Drillien, 1972), all premature/low birthweight infants merit sensitive, continuous developmental screening and developmental assessment and management, if indicated, throughout infancy, childhood, and adolescence. But whereas regular developmental surveillance in this "high-risk" population is important, an attitude of supportive, cautious optimism, rather than presumption of handicap, is usually appropriate and reinforced by current follow-up information. Counseling and interventions directed at those infants who are also at increased environmental and parenting risk demand high priority because of the documented importance of environmental variables in the ultimate prognosis of premature/low birthweight infants (Kopp, 1983).

ENVIRONMENT OF THE PREMATURE/LOW BIRTHWEIGHT INFANT

Before the rationale and specific forms of early developmental neonatal intervention are described, it is worthwhile to picture briefly the NICU environment in which the sick premature infant first experiences extrauterine life. It is hoped that such a portrayal will explain the great interest and concern surrounding developmental interventions for premature/low birthweight newborns and will also provide the appropriate background setting for the remainder of this chapter.

The contemporary NICU is a highly unique, life-saving, intensive medical care world experienced by the premature newborn for an average duration of 1–3 months and occasionally longer, depending on the degree of prematurity and the extent of complications. Common neonatal complications of being born too soon and/or too small that prolong the duration of hospitalization include several types of respiratory distress syndrome often requiring assisted mechanical ventilation and often resulting in chronic lung disease, patent ductus arteriosus often requiring surgical closure, apnea often requiring assisted ventilation, varying grades of intracranial hemorrhage, overwhelming infection (neonatal sepsis) often including meningitis and encephalitis, necrotizing enterocolitis occasionally requiring surgical bowel resection, hypoglycemia, hypocalcemia, hyperbilirubinemia usually necessitating phototherapy, and anemia often requiring multiple blood trans-fusions. Rarer complications such as major vascular obstructions with resultant tissue infarction are particularly devastating and potentially disfiguring.

Proper care of all of these neonatal complications requires marked invas-iveness and disruption of diurnal sleep/wake patterns, such as isolettes with continuous bright light and loud noise, mechanical respirators with oral or nasal intubation, indwelling catheters for fluid and caloric administration and blood sampling, gastric and intestinal tubes for feeding, prolonged phototherapy with eye patching, multiple needle punctures for blood, urine, and spinal fluid collec-tion, multiple radiological and ultrasound procedures, countless different exam-iners and nurses with repetitive, disruptive handling, and, at best, significantly restricted opportunities for normal parent–infant interaction (Gottfried, Hodgman, & Brown, 1984). Dr. Jerold Lucey (1977), a prominent neo-natologist, questioned: "Is intensive care becoming too intensive?" He vividly contrasted the world of the sleeping, quiescent intrauterine fetus with the vastly different extrauterine world of the sick premature newborn. He painted a stark, but quite realistic, picture of the NICU resident:

Picture yourself in a brightly lit room, nude, defenseless, and your eyes hurting from silver nitrate. You are blindfolded, chilly, and surrounded by a tepid fog. You are gasping for air, fighting to breathe, and choking and gagging every so often on mucous. You are unable to clear your throat or cough. A mask is placed over your face, and blasts of air are forced into your lungs. Somebody sticks a catheter into your mouth, occasionally too far, causing you to retch or vomit. You are startled and frightened by loud, strange noises (beepers, voices, roaring respirators, telephones, radios, incubator noise). Some giant is pouring food into a tube which has been forced through your nose or throat into your stomach. It is uncomfortable and obstructs your nasal airway. You are probably nauseated; you are certainly not hungry, but you are expected to eat—and soon.

You have a headache, probably the worst one of your life. You are sleep deprived. Every-time you doze off, somebody gets worried about you. They think you are in a coma. You have to be very careful to breathe very regularly. You are not allowed the multiple long pauses (15 seconds or more) of a sleeping, dreaming adult. If you do pause, a bell goes off, waking you up, and somebody slaps your feet or pulls your hair to see if you will or can cry. If you are exhausted or unresponsive, you are in trouble. If you have any jerky movements, you are suspected of having a convulsion.

Every few hours somebody cuts your foot or sticks a needle into your scalp or one of your arteries. Your arms and legs are taped down to boards. Electrodes are attached to your chest. You are immobilized. You may even have an itch, but you can't scratch. Cool, rude hands probe your abdomen every so often, feeling for your liver, kidneys, or bladder. After a few days of this intensive care you are exhausted and you may need assistance to continue breathing just because you are too tired to do it on your own. (pp. 1064–1065)

Considering all of this, the increasingly prevalent suggestion that contemporary management of newborns receiving intensive care may be responsible for newly recognized iatrogenic complications and may contribute to the developmental deficits associated with prematurity is certainly not surprising.

NEONATAL INTERVENTION RATIONALE

Two major, incompletely resolved debates have markedly influenced the rationale and direction of neonatal developmental intervention (Meisels, Jones, & Stiefel, 1983). The first issue deals with the appropriate developmental perspective and theoretical construct of a premature newborn. Specifically, one school of thought argues that the premature infant should be viewed essentially as an extrauterine fetus, with neonatal intervention efforts therefore aimed primarily at simulating the intrauterine environment. Proponents of this interpretation emphasize the importance of peaceful, restful, womblike experiences and attempt to recreate artifically this lost natural milieu. Conversely, others vigorously assert that because most body systems undergo profound physiological changes at birth, it is quite reasonable to presume that the central nervous and sensory systems also change and thus that the premature infant differs significantly from the fetus and requires neonatal interventions simulating the extrauterine environment experienced by full-term infants. Advocates of this position tend to encourage more active, awake supplemental sensory stimulations similar to the normal newborn nursery and the home. Als, Lester, Tronick, and Brazelton (1982), in attempting to provide a more phenomenological view of life for the premature infant immediately following birth, state the following:

> The 32-week old organism is adapted to an intrauterine environment of a regulated temperature, contained movement pattern, suspension of gravity, muted and regular sensory inputs, and physiological supports which have evolved to ensure normal intrauterine development for a large percentage of fetuses. Should a premature delivery ensue, one could predict that most fetuses would die, since their organismic adaptations do not fit the environment they find themselves in. Modern technology and medicine have changed this but are still searching for how best to provide for such organisms after birth, given the incongruence of the situation. Artificial recreation of the intrauterine environment for the preterm infant is inappropriate since the transitions at birth automatically trigger independent functioning of organ systems necessary for survival, such as the respiratory, cardiac, and digestive systems. (pp. 14–15)

These writers go on to caution that "when one realizes the current organizational issues for the preterm infant, one becomes aware of the flaws and possible dangers of intervention programs which consider preterm infants to be deficient full-term infants and which, therefore, are intended to 'train' infants in behavior appropriate for full-term babies.'' (p. 17).

The second, and closely related, key issue concerns the appropriate developmental interpretation of the NICU environment. Does this unusual medical setting constitute a source of (1) sensory deprivation, requiring a variety of added stimulations, (2) constant overstimulation, requiring *less* handling and *less* intervention of all types and more time for uninterrupted sleep, or (3) an inappropriate *pattern* of interactions rather than simply too much or too little stimulation and including aspects of both deprivation and overstimulation? Most recent ecological investigations of the NICU support this third orientation. Pertaining strictly to physical stimulation, these careful observational studies (Gottfried & Gaiter, 1984; Gottfried, Wallace-Lande, & Sherman-Brown, 1981) indicate that premature newborns are not sensorially deprived, but, in fact, receive large amounts of ongoing stimulation. Newborns monitored in these studies were continuously exposed to cool-white fluorescent lighting with illumination not varying across day and night. Likewise, recording of the acoustic environment revealed continuously high sounds levels, higher than in a home or even a busy office. Mean characteristic sound levels were in the range of 70–80 dB; conversational speech predominates between 30–60 dB. For extended periods, sound levels were potentially hazardous with upper levels reaching 120 dB. These noise levels are comparable to automobile traffic, and at times the noise reached levels of large machinery. Isolettes provided no sheltering from this visual and auditory insult; recordings of light and sound were virtually identical both outside and inside the incubator. The data also indicated that premature newborns have extensive contact with caregivers. However, almost all contacts were with staff members. In spite of open visiting policies, a minimal percentage of contacts involved family members. This is of particular concern because mothers provide a more important source of stimulation to their newborns than nursing personnel. The average frequency of daily contacts ranged from 40–70 with some newborns receiving as many as 100 contacts. Virtually all contacts involved medical/nursing care with some form of handling. Contacts were brief (2–5 min. in duration) and occurred on the average of every 18–30 min. In a given day, sick newborns received a total of 2.5–3.5 hr of contact with caregivers.

In contrast to the high magnitude of visual, auditory, and tactile stimulation, these time–motion studies found that premature newborns received infrequent social experiences. Despite the fact that newborns were in contact with persons, they seldom received social types of stimulation. The preponderance of contacts between caregivers and newborns could be appropriately described as nonsocial. Contacts almost exclusively were oriented toward medical/nursing activities and were seldom oriented toward social events. If social stimulation occurred, it was embedded within routine care. Approaching an infant for the sole aim of providing social stimulation was a rare event. In more than half the instances when newborns cried during contacts, caregivers did not attempt to soothe them. Additionally, the integration of social sensory experiences was not impressively high. It was not uncommon for newborns to be handled and not talked to or positioned in such a way that they could not see caregivers. Quite often social stimulation was given independent of the newborns' behavioral states. For example, in no more than approximately half the situations when social events occurred did the newborns have their eyes opened. Surprisingly, even in the intermediate care nurseries (i.e., growing and gaining weight, less acute needs) assessed, the large majority of contacts with newborns were devoid of social events. Social touching, rocking, or talking to newborns, all of which are felt to be developmentally advantageous, occurred during less than one third of the contacts.

In summary, with respect to social stimulation, many premature newborns may indeed be sensorially deprived throughout their course of hospitalization. Despite the constant bombardment of visual, auditory, and tactile physical stimulations, the NICU appears to be a startling, nonsocial environment for newborns. Unfortunately, there is also frequently little or no organization, rhythmicity, or developmentally appropriate pattern of either physical or social stimulation incorporated into the treatment plan of newborn intensive care.

In light of the foregoing controversial issues, it is no surprise that the specific rationales—i.e. the philosophical goals and objectives—guiding neonatal developmental intervention programs also lack widespread agreement and, in fact, continue to evolve over time. This ongoing theoretical evolution of purpose has dramatically altered the focus and form of current neonatal intervention strategies. Through the end of the 1970s, three prominent rationales variously influenced the types and emphases of initial neonatal intervention efforts (Meisels et al., 1983). Determination as to which of these three original rationales was functionally dominant at the individual NICU was, of course, predicated on personal, local interpretations of the previously discussed developmental debates. Succinctly, the three neonatal intervention rationales predominating during the 1970–1979 decade may be stated as follows: (1) to attempt to normalize and humanize the disruptive effects of the NICU environment so that it more closely resembles the environment of full-term newborns, (2) to correct for presumed sensory deprivation endured by the premature newborn treated in the NICU and thereby to optimize subsequent development and decrease the likelihood of long-term neurodevelopmental complications, and (3) to compensate for intrauterine experiences lost as a result of premature birth.

However, because of continued dispute and complete absence of consensus regarding the necessity, nature, and effectiveness of neonatal developmental interventions based solely on these initial principles, there has been a clear shift in focus and orientation since approximately 1980 away from exclusively newborn and infant-directed measures and toward more family-centered interventions emphasizing and facilitating parent–premature infant interactions. As we shall see, this recent redirection and alteration of a guiding rationale should not be viewed as a total departure from past approaches nor as a scientific repudiation of earlier efforts, but rather as a very reasonable, practical, and necessary outgrowth of our expanded awareness of the developmental importance of early parent–infant interaction and communication (Bee et al., 1982).

TYPES OF INTERVENTION

Although there is great interstudy variability in terms of the specific neonatal interventions (independent variables) utilized, practically all reporting centers in the 1970s employed early supplemental stimulation and/or environmental modification in basically one or more of four major sensory areas (Field, 1980). In fact, the majority of published investigations are multimodal—they have combined sensory manipulations in more than one circumscribed area. Despite their broad variations, these traditional interventions, taken as a whole, relate in part to all three of the initial rationales or experimental hypotheses described earlier.

The four major sensory modalities recommended for neonatal developmental intervention include: (1) visual stimulation (decoration of surroundings, mobiles with brightly colored objects), (2) auditory stimulation (talking, singing, music boxes, recorded mother's voice, recorded heartbeat), (3) tactile stimulation (non nutritive sucking, stroking, flexing, massaging, rubbing, handling, positioning), and (4) vestibular–kinesthetic stimulation (rocking, oscillating beds—e.g., waterbeds). Many different combinations of these infant-focused interventions have been described and analyzed, including stroking, handling, and rocking; specific cephalocaudal massage treatment and rocking administered by mothers; rocking bed and heartbeat recording; visual decoration and body rubbing; rocking waterbed, simulated heartbeat, and tape of mother's voice played during rocking; bright mobiles, rubbing, rocking, talking, singing, and music boxes (thus, all four modalities represented in this case). As can immediately be appreciated, the number of individual protocols is almost limitless, and intervention programs further vary in terms of their specificity or lack thereof within a given sensory area. For example, one program may utilize a variety of vestibular stimulations in differing amounts and sequences, while another may have chosen to assess the effects of vestibular stimulation as specifically provided by a motorized hammock or, alternatively, by an oscillating waterbed. Such marked variability between individual intervention programs seriously impairs both the interpretation and generalizability of outcome results.

A relatively unique type of physical stimulation recently advocated by some is neonatal hydrotherapy (Sweeney, 1983). This approach is generally used as an adjunct to the more traditional intervention modalities, particularly in conjunction with tactile stimulations such as rubbing, handling, and positioning. Required equipment for this intervention technique includes a standard infant bassinet or other suitable tub, warm water in which the premature newborn is immersed, and an overhead radiant heater placed above the tub.

As previously suggested, there has been an entirely new dimension and direction added to the field of early developmental intervention for biologically vulnerable infants in the 1980s (Meisels et al., 1983; Ramey, Bryant, Sparling, & Wasik, 1984). This more recent type of intervention focuses primarily on the enhancement of the parent–premature infant relationship by means of both the facilitation of optimal social functioning on the part of the premature infant and also, correspondingly, direct parent-training strategies. In this current parent-focused redirection, this type of neonatal intervention now closely resembles and parallels the goals and objectives of early developmental intervention for infants at increased environmental risk (see chapter by Bryant and Ramey, this volume). In fact, intervention recommendations and protocols for the two risk populations will frequently appear quite similar with numerous overlaps and shared rationale; it is not unusual at individual sites for the premature/low birthweight intervention plans to have been adapted directly from existing intervention programs for poverty/low socioeconomic status infants and families. An example of this phenomenon exists at the Frank Porter Graham Child Development Center in Chapel Hill, North Carolina, where a comprehensive parent-focused intervention curriculum (*Partners for Learning Curriculum,* Sparling & Lewis, 1985) for neonatal intensive care unit graduates has recently been adapted and expanded from a similar parent-focused curriculum (*Learning Games for the First Three Years,* Sparling & Lewis, 1981) originally designed and intended for environmentally vulnerable infants.

Interventions aimed at improving parent–premature infant interaction have taken various forms, usually including both a component of infant preparation and readiness for such intimate contact and also a component of parent instruction in initiating dialogue and responding to the fragile infant's communicative overtures. The premature newborn and infant, when medically appropriate, should be assisted through environmental structuring, support, and facilitation in interacting with his or her immediate environment in such a way that he or she confirms expectations for positive parent–infant social elicitation and feedback. For example, when the premature infant becomes overloaded with stimuli, he or she may withdraw, become rigid, or may even demonstrate signs of autonomic nervous system stress and dysfunction including gagging, vomiting, apnea, bradycardia, and cyanosis. In each of these cases the infant becomes unavailable to the environment for obtaining information or for giving positive feedback and, in turn, may cause parents and other caregivers to feel less competent and less effective. Thus, to the extent that reciprocal social transactions are contingent on the readability and predictability of the infant's signals and on the caregiver's ability to respond appropriately to these signals, it becomes critical for infants at risk to engage in interactions without experiencing great expense to physiologic, motor, and state regulation.

Likewise and concurrently, contemporary neonatal intervention programs emphasize the necessity for parents to understand premature newborn and infant behavior. Parmelee (1981) has stressed the importance of carefully interpreting the individual infant's different behaviors to the parent as a key first step. He states that is is also helpful to model techniques of dealing with the baby very specifically for the parent and to reinforce positively the parent's successful spontaneous interactions with the infant. Ideally, parents should be assisted in correctly modifying their perceptions of their infant's medical status, should become more successful in implementing programs of brief behavioral intervention, and should be aided in constructing a positive and enhancing psychological environment for themselves and their vulnerable infants. Additionally, because the coexistence of both biologic and environmental risks constitutes a particularly common background for developmental failure, efforts at comprehensive, broad-based intervention must often include both an intensive home visitation component and an understanding of the parents' (especially the mother's) coping abilities, support services for their physical and mental health, and economic support for the family, including adequate, stable daycare for the infant and siblings when required. Neonatal intervention programs that are based on a framework such as that described in this last section will have the potential for enhancing parent–premature infant interactions and thereby for reducing the probability of subsequent caretaking and developmental casualties.

INTERVENTION PARAMETERS AND SETTINGS

As with the specific combinations of sensory stimulations, great variability among reports also exists in terms of the onset, frequency, and duration of interventions. Timing of initial developmental intervention varies from immediately after birth to some relatively arbitrary starting point such as 14 days of age to the time when the premature newborn is deemed clinically and physiologically stable. Likewise, even though most studies provided an intervention program that took place at least several times daily, marked interstudy variability in intervention frequency is again the norm. Some stimulations were only administered during feedings, some were prescribed every 15 min regardless of the infant's readiness or state of alertness, and some were continuous, discontinuous, or contingent upon the infant's own activity and responsiveness. Examining the duration of intervention programs reveals the greatest variation of all. For example, typical intervention end points include term gestational age, regain of birthweight, or nursery discharge. Thus, overall length of sensory stimulation might be 1 week or 8 weeks. Further, although most interventions with premature infants have focused exclusively on manipulating the environment during the infant's initial hospitalization, in recent years an increasing number additionally provide interventions for parents and/or infants that continue after hospital discharge into the home. These home follow-through programs also vary in duration from several months to the entire first year of life.

Neonatal intensive care unit nurses have been the principal neonatal intervention agents in most reports of the more traditional forms of stimulation described earlier. Other types of provider are physical therapists, occupational therapists, and early childhood special educators, including the recently created subgroup of early neonatal interventionists. With the previously discussed evolution from solely infant-focused programs to more parent-focused strategies, parents and other family members are, naturally, increasingly involved in the active intervention plans.

INTERVENTION SUBJECT SELECTION

The study of comparability of experiments involving neonatal developmental interventions is further hampered by inconsistent reporting of and limited information provided on sample characteristics. This too, then, constitutes a source of great interstudy and intrastudy variability. Many studies have involved families of low socioeconomic status with predominantly black, young, unmarried mothers. Unfortunately, most have also involved relatively healthy premature infants without early signs and symptoms of neurological dysfunction; infants who may theoretically benefit from intervention the most, such as extremely low birthweight infants weighing less than 1,000 g at birth and experiencing numerous neonatal complications, are quite underrepresented in most published investigations. Thus, the bulk of experimental evidence has been accumulated on those infants who biologically and medically are at relatively lower risk and environmentally are at higher risk. Nevertheless, study differences abound in such basic infant characteristics as birthweight mean and range (700–2,400 g), gestational age mean and range (24–37 weeks), inborn/outborn status, severity of neonatal illness, types of medical intervention, and duration of hospitalization. These are important sources of variability in interpreting intervention results because all have been associated to some degree with neurodevelopmental outcome in premature infants. Other sources of variation that prevent direct comparison of results include socioeconomic status, race, and maternal age and parity.

INTERVENTION OUTCOME MEASURES

Adding to the variability of the study populations and methodologies is the extensive variability of types of dependent outcome measures. Assessed outcome parameters of neonatal intervention can most conveniently and coherently be grouped into three broad categories: developmental, medical, and parental. The various developmental outcome measures employed include performance on standardized neurodevelopmental and neurobehavioral evaluations (e.g., Brazelton Neonatal Behavioral Assessment Scale [Brazelton, 1973] Bayley Scales of Infant Development [Bayley, 1969], Cattell Infant Intelligence Scale [Cattell, 1940]), performance on specific cognitive–sensory tasks (e.g., visual orienting, auditory responsivity, recognition memory), sleep/wake state organization and stabilization, temperament characteristics such as activity level and irritability, and neuromotor criteria such as muscle tone and volitional movement. Typically assessed medical dependent variables are weight gain, head growth, change in vital signs such as heart and/or respiratory rate, frequency of apnea, frequency of emesis, and length of hospitalization. Parental outcome measures have included the frequency of parental visitation and attempted evaluation of the quality of the parent–infant interaction.

Studies vary considerably in both the number and types of intervention outcome measures utilized. For example, one study may only examine a single medical outcome (such as the frequency of apnea) with different sensory stimulations and another may evaluate a combination of developmental, medical, and parental results of very similar interventions. In summary, as should be readily apparent at this point, critical, scientific appraisal of neonatal intervention involves a difficult, confusing search for effects amid a most complex mixture of structural, methodological, sampling, and outcome variability.

RESULTS OF NEONATAL DEVELOPMENTAL INTERVENTION

As might certainly be anticipated, reported results are as various as the methodologies employed, and patterns of outcome reveal great variability in terms of their exact nature, extent, significance, and duration. Positive developmental outcomes most frequently reported include improved neonatal neurobehavioral performance (particularly on visual and auditory orienting and general maturation items), increased state stabilization, higher performance on infant developmental (both mental and motor) assessment scales, normalized muscle tone, and more manageable temperament with decreased irritability and increased positive affect. Encouraging medical outcomes typically cited include improved weight gain with better feeding, decreased incidence of apnea, and more mature heart rate responses. Optimistic parental outcomes reported involve primarily increased frequency of parental visitation and enhanced parent–infant interaction. However, although most studies report at least some measured benefit attributable to the specific intervention employed, many of these positive trends are not replicated by other investigations that in contrast, report essentially negative findings. Because of these frequently contradictory results, generalizability from most of the individual, isolated outcomes is limited.

Table 4 provides a comprehensive review of 17 neonatal developmental intervention studies published since 1970. Criteria for selection included clear specification of intervention type and mode, adequate description of subject characteristics, and use of an appropriate research design including assignment to experimental or control groups. Additionally, all studies repeatedly cited in other reviews of this topic were included. Descriptive reports of nursery intervention programs without an experimental design were excluded.

Studies were able to be categorized fairly readily into three groups according to the basic intervention philosophy employed: (1) 12 investigations of infant-focused, sensory stimulation interventions, (2) 3 investigations of parent-focused, training interventions, and (3) 2 investigations of a combination of both infant-focused and parent-focused interventions. The 12 traditional infant-focused studies were further subdivided on the basis of the specific sensory modalities utilized: two reports (Katz, 1971; Segall, 1972) of auditory stimulation alone, one report (Powell, 1974) of tactile stimulation alone, one report (Korner, Kraemer, Haffner, & Cosper, 1975) of vestibular–kinesthetic stimulation alone, three reports (Barnard, 1973; Burns, Deddish, Burns, & Hatcher, 1983; Kramer & Pierpont, 1976) of combined auditory and vestibular–kinesthetic stimulation, three reports (Rice, 1977; Rosenfield, 1980; White & Labarba, 1976) of combined tactile and vestibular–kinesthetic stimulation, and two reports (Leib, Benfield, & Guidubaldi, 1980; Scarr-Salapatek & Williams, 1973) of multimodal sensory stimulation combining all four principal modalities (visual, auditory, tactile, vestibular–kinesthetic). As expected, the majority of acceptable studies, particularly prior to 1980, primarily examined infant-focused interventions, whereas more recent studies often included a parent-training component. The wide variability of both intervention modality and specific intervention parameters in terms of intensity, frequency, and duration among the infant-focused studies is also easily seen from the table. However, in only 3 of these 12 infant-focused reports (Powell, 1974; Rice, 1977; Scarr-Salapatek & Williams, 1973) were parents directly involved in administering the sensory stimulations. In most of the 17 studies, regardless of focus, the actual interventions occurred exclusively while the infant was hospitalized in the intensive care or intermediate care nursery. Only four of the studies (Bromwich & Parmelee, 1979; Field, Widmayer, Stringer, & Ignatoff, 1980; Rice, 1977; Scarr-Salapatek & Williams, 1973) investigated interventions that were partially or entirely home-based, by far the most extensive being the Bromwich and Parmelee study, which provided parent-focused home intervention to 2 years of age. The comprehensive nature and complex requirements of these home programs generally make them more difficult to perform adequately as individual, clinical research projects.

Premature/low birthweight infants recruited as subjects by the 17 studies

TABLE 4

Neonatal Developmental Intervention Studies

Reference	Nature of intervention	Intervention parameters	Setting	Role of parents
				I. Infant-focused,
A. Auditory stimulation only (2)				
Katz (1971)	Tape-recorded mother's voice via a speaker placed in the incubator	Tape recorder was activated for 5-minute segments, six times daily, at 2-hour intervals; regimen began on fifth day of life and continued until the infant's gestational age at the completion of the regimen was 36 weeks	Neonatal Intensive Care Unit	None, except for mother recording her voice
Segall (1972)	Tape-recorded mother's voice via a speaker placed in the incubator	Tape recorder played every day for a single period of 30 min until the infant reached 36 weeks gestational age	Neonatal Intensive Care Unit	None, except for mother recording her voice
B. Tactile stimulation only (1)				
Powell (1974)	Extra handling from simple touching to prolonged holding	Maternal handling began after 3 days of age at least 3 times weekly; nursing handling began after 3 days of age for a 20-min period twice daily until birthweight regained and then once daily until discharge	Neonatal Intensive Care Unit	Mothers provided the handling stimulation for one experimental group
C. Vestibular-kinesthetic stimulation only (1)				
Korner et al. (1975)	Oscillating waterbed which replaced the mattress conventionally used in incubators	Infants were placed on the waterbed on either the third, fourth, or fifth postnatal day and remained for 7 total days	Neonatal Intensive Care Unit	None
D. Auditory and vestibular-kinesthetic stimulation (3)				
Barnard (1973)	Oscillating bed plus tape recorded heart beat	Infants received both stimulations together during the 33rd and 34th weeks of gestational age for a 15-min period each hour	Neonatal Intensive Care Unit	None

Child characteristics	Experimental design	Outcome measures	Results
sensory stimulation interventions (12)[a]			
62 premature infants between 28–32 weeks gestational age; infants with severe neurological or physiologic disturbances excluded	Infants assigned on a sequential basis, according to birth order, into either an experimental group (31) or control group (31); post only comparisons	At 36 weeks gestational age, developmental level assessed by the Rosenblith Modified Graham Behavior Scale which measures general maturation, audiovisual response, muscle tension, and irritability	1. E Group scored significantly ($p <$ .01) higher than C Group in general maturation (including both motor and tactile-adaptive development), auditory and visual function, and optimal muscle tension 2. No group differences in irritability
60 premature infants between 28–32 weeks gestational age; infants with severe problems at birth excluded	Each infant randomly assigned to either experimental (30) or control (30) group and then paired with another infant of same sex and ethnicity, thus forming 30 pairs of infants; post only comparisons	At 36 weeks gestational age, heart rate measurements were recorded in response to a variety of auditory stimuli (white noise, mother's voice, unfamiliar female voice)	1. E Group demonstrated significantly ($p <$ .05) greater amount of increase in heart rate (suggesting increased autonomic responsivity) than C Group in response to white noise during quiescence 2. E Group responded with a significantly ($p <$ .01) greater decrease in heart rate during crying to both mother's voice and unfamiliar female voice 3. Nonsignificant trend to decelerate heart rate more to mother's voice than to unfamiliar female voice
36 black singleton infants between 1000 and 2000 g birthweight; severe problems excluded	Each infant randomly assigned to one of three groups: maternal experimental group (11), nurse experimental group (13), or control group (12); post only comparisons	Brazelton-Cambridge Newborn Scales administered between 4 and 12 days of age; Bayley Scales of Infant Development at 2, 4, and 6 months corrected age; Maternal Behavior Ratings of mother–child interaction	1. Handled infants regained birthweight faster (trend); no growth differences later 2. Handled infants scored higher on BSID at all follow-up visits, some significant at $p <$ .05 3. No differences in maternal behavior or infant development between maternal and nurse experimental groups
21 premature infants with gestational age ≤34 weeks and birthweight <2000 g; severe problems excluded	Random assignment to either experimental group (10) or control group (11); pre- and postcomparisons	Mean daily heart rate, respiratory rate, temperature, weight, incidence of vomiting, and incidence of apnea	1. Significantly ($p <$ .01) less apnea in experimental group 2. No other significant differences
15 premature infants between 28–32 weeks gestational age; severe problems excluded	Assignment to either experimental group (7) or control group (8); pre- and postcomparisons	Behavioral rating scale of activity to observe sleep/wake behavior; maturation on Dubowitz gestational age assessment; weight gain	1. E Group showed significantly ($p <$ .001) greater gain in quiet sleep, while C Group actually showed a decline 2. E Group showed significantly ($p <$ .01) greater drop in active awake state 3. E Group showed a trend of greater neurological maturation 4. No differences in corrected weight gain

(continued)

TABLE 4 (*Continued*)

Reference	Nature of intervention	Intervention parameters	Setting	Role of parents
				I. Infant-focused,
Burns et al. (1983)	Oscillating waterbed plus tape recorded intrauterine sounds of a pregnant woman	Infants received both of these stimulations on a continuous basis for 4 weeks beginning on the fourth postnatal day	Neonatal Intensive Care Unit	None
Kramer & Pierpoint (1976)	Rocking waterbed plus tape recorded simulated heartbeat and a female voice	Infants were placed on the waterbed at 2–7 postnatal days for the duration of stay in the incubator. Mechanical rocking of the waterbed occurred one hour prior to each feeding; playing of the recorded heartbeat and voice occurred during the rocking	Neonatal Intensive Care Unit	None
E. Tactile and vestibular-kinesthetic stimulation (3)				
Rice (1977)	Stroking and massaging plus rocking, holding, and cuddling	Structured, sequential, cephalocaudal progression of stroking and massaging the infant's nude body administered for 15min, 4 times daily for a total duration of 30 days, beginning the day the infants came home from the hospital; following each stroking treatment, infant was rocked, held, and cuddled for another 5 min; each infant had about 120 total treatments	Home	Mothers administered the intervention following training by nurses
Rosenfield (1980)	Stroking with a variety of textured materials plus stretching and folding of extremities, torsion of the trunk, and rocking	Intervention begun when infant clinically stable at an average of 2.5 weeks of age. Involved two 20-min periods daily and was administered inside the incubator	Neonatal Intensive Care Unit	None
White & Labarba (1976)	Rubbing plus flexing the arms and legs (passive kinesthetic stimulation)	Within 48 h after birth, infants received both stimulations in 15-min periods every hour for 4 consecutive hours; intervention continued through the end of the 11th day; rubbing included the infant's neck, shoulders, arms, legs, chest, and back; infants remained in incubators during stimulation	Neonatal Intensive Care	None

Child characteristics	Experimental design	Outcome measures	Results
sensory stimulation interventions (12)[a]			
22 premature infants between 28–32 weeks gestational age; severe problems excluded	Random assignment to either experimental group (11) or control group (11); pre- and postcomparisons	Growth parameters, state organization observations, and Brazelton Neonatal Behavioral Assessment Scale	1. E Group demonstrated significantly ($p < .05$) greater drop in active sleep 2. E Group scored significantly ($p < .05$) better in motoric organization and state organization on the Brazelton Scale 3. No differences in growth parameters
20 premature infants of <34 weeks gestational age; severe problems excluded	Random assignment to either experimental group (11) or control group (9); post only comparisons	Growth parameters, neurologic status, Brazelton Neonatal Behavioral Assessment Scale	1. E Group gained significantly ($p < .01$) more weight and increased their head circumference significantly ($p < .01$) greater 2. No significant differences in neurologic status or Brazelton Assessment
29 premature infants ≤37 weeks gestational age; severe problems excluded	Random assignment to either experimental group (15) or control group (14); pre- and postcomparisons	Assessment at 4 months age with growth parameters, neurological evaluation, and Bayley Scales of Infant Development	1. E Group showed significantly ($p < .05$) greater weight gain, but no differences on length or head circumference gains 2. E Group showed significantly ($p < .05$) more mature performance on certain neurological reflexes and reactions 3. E Group scored significantly ($p < .05$) higher on the Bayley Mental Scale, but not on the Motor Scale
78 premature infants of <1500 g birthweight	Random assignment to either experimental or control group; groups similar with respect to birthweight, gestational age, duration of hospitalization, race, sex, and maternal demographic variables; pre- and postcomparisons	State rating system and maternal visiting frequency	1. E Group demonstrated significantly ($p < .001$) more optimal, i.e., more awake and alert, state organization 2. E Group mothers demonstrated significantly ($p < .01$) higher visitation rates
12 premature infants ≤36 weeks gestational age and lowest SES group; severe problems excluded	Random assignment to either experimental group (6) or control group (6); pre- and postcomparisons	Weight gain, feeding volume, temperature, heart rate, respiratory rate, frequency of voiding and stooling	1. E Group demonstrated significantly ($p < .001$) greater rate of weight gain and volume of formula ingested 2. No significant differences in any other physiological measures

(*continued*)

TABLE 4 (*Continued*)

Reference	Nature of intervention	Intervention parameters	Setting	Role of parents
				I. Infant-focused,
F. Multimodal sensory stimulation (2)				
Leib et al. (1980)	Visual (mobile), tactile (rubbing, soothing), vestibular-kinesthetic (rocking), and auditory (talking, singing, music box)	Stimulations administered during feeding times; during intermediate care period, visual and tactile (5 min) procedures done inside incubator; during convalescent care period, all stimulations performed in open crib	Neonatal Intensive Care Unit	None
Scarr-Salapatek & Williams (1973)	Special room in the nursery. Visual (mobile, human faces), tactile (handling, patting), vestibular-kinesthetic (rocking), and auditory (talking)	Nursery staff in the special room is instructed to provide as much of these stimulations as possible to approximate optimal home care conditions; patterned visual experience included mobiles both inside and outside the incubator; as soon as possible, infants were removed from the incubator during feedings for rocking, talking, and "playing;" this consisted of eight ½-h stimulation sessions daily	Neonatal Intensive Care Unit with weekly home visitation throughout first year of life to encourage continuation of stimulation program	None during hospitalization; mediators of continued stimulation during infancy
				II. Parent-focused,
Bromwich & Parmelee (1979)	1. Free medical and nursing care including home visitation by nurses, and 2. Educational intervention by developmental home visitors to support and enhance the quality of parent–infant interactions and, indirectly, to positively impact the infants' social–affective, cognitive–motivational, and language development	Health care provided from birth to 2 years age; educational intervention provided in the home between the ages of 10 and 24 months; home visits were flexibly structured and timed according to the individual requirements of each parent–infant dyad; an individual intervention plan was made for each family	Home	Parents were the principal recipients of intervention efforts and were hoped to be the mediators of developmental change
Minde et al. (1980)	Parents of premature infants group with nurse coordinator	Parents met with coordinator during first hospital visit; groups met once weekly for 90–120 min and consisted of up to 10 parents; each group had a "veteran mother" of a premature baby; groups met for 7–12 weeks; objectives were to help parents cope with stresses, to recognize and meet the present and future needs of their infant, and to utilize supportive community resources	Neonatal Intensive Care Unit	Group involvement and interaction

Child characteristics	Experimental design	Outcome measures	Results
sensory stimulation interventions (12)[a]			
28 premature infants with birthweights between 1200 and 1800 g; severe problems excluded; all middle-class white	First 14 infants meeting selection criteria assigned to control group. Following discharge of last control infant, next 14 elligible infants assigned to experimental group; pre- and postcomparisons	Hospital weight gain; Brazelton Neonatal Behavior Assessment Scale prior to discharge; Bayley Scales of Infant Development at 6 months age	1. No significant differences in weight gain 2. No significant changes in neonatal behavioral assessment 3. E Group scored significantly ($p <$ .001) higher on both Bayley Mental and Motor Scales at 6 months
30 consecutively born premature infants with birthweights between 1300 and 1800 g; all lowest SES, black	Alternate assignment to either experimental group (15) or control group (15); pre- and postcomparisons	Brazelton Cambridge Newborn Scales before and after hospital stimulation phase; Cattell Infant Intelligence Scale at 1 year of age; weight gain	1. E Group showed significantly greater weight gain in the nursery 2. E Group showed significantly superior Brazelton performance after stimulation, whereas C Group had been somewhat superior before stimulation began 3. E Group showed significantly ($p <$ .05) higher Cattell scores at 1 year
training interventions (3)			
63 premature infants <37 weeks gestational age and <2500 g birthweight; infants ranged across social classes and across racial–ethnic groups	Infants divided into experimental (30) and control (33) groups; both groups received the health care component; only the experimental group received the education component; groups matched on SES, race, and severity of neonatal problems; pre- and postcomparisons	Parent Behavior Progression (PBP) and Play Interaction Measure (PIM) were developed as a by-product of the intervention program; Gesell Developmental Schedules, Bayley Scales of Infant Development, and Home Observation Scale at 24 months age	1. No group differences on any 2-year cognitive measures 2. Home Observation Scale at 2 years significantly ($p <$ .05) favored E Group in terms of mother–child interaction
57 premature infants with birthweights ≤1500 g and their parents; severe problems excluded	Four infants at a time were alternately assigned to either experimental group (28) or control group (29); pre- and postcomparisons	Continuous, observed characteristics of parent–child interactions both in the nursery and during home visits 1, 2, and 3 months after hospital discharge; semistructured parent interview with rating scales of attitudes, interaction with other parents, and general caretaking competence	1. E parents visited their infants in the nursery significantly ($p <$ .05) more often 2. E parents had significantly ($p <$ .01) better attitudes, interaction with their infants, and general competence prior to discharge 3. E parents at 3 months postdischarge talked to, looked at, and touched their infants significantly ($p <$ .001) more

(continued)

TABLE 4 (*Continued*)

Reference	Nature of intervention	Intervention parameters	Setting	Role of parents
				II. Parent-foc
Widmayer & Field (1981)	Mothers observed administration of Brazelton Neonatal Behavior Assessment Scale (NBAS) and then independently administered an adaptation, the Mother's Assessment of the Behavior of her Infant Scale (MABI)	Mothers administered the MABI at birth and at weekly intervals during the first month	Neonatal Intensive Care Unit	Mothers' involveme was the key inde dent variable
				III. Both infant-foct
Brown et al. (1980)	Infant stimulation with visual, auditory, tactile, and vestibular-kinesthetic protocols. Mother training by project nurse to (1) demonstrate stimulation program, (2) help mothers execute it themselves, and (3) help mothers monitor responses of their infants and become more sensitive to infant's cues	Infant stimulation began in nursery as soon as medically feasible. Stimulation sessions conducted twice daily (5 days/week) and lasted about 30 min each at feeding time; average total duration was 16 days; mothers met with project nurse while still hospitalized and during infant's continued hospitalization	Neonatal Intensive Care Unit	Mothers both receiv and provided inte vention
Field et al. (1980)	Home visitation by trained interventionists to (1) educate mothers on developmental milestones and child rearing practices, (2) teach mothers exercises and appropriate stimulation for facilitating infant development, and (3) facilitate mother–infant interactions; multimodal sensory stimulations included visual, auditory, tactile, and vestibular-kinesthetic modalities	Home visits after discharge biweekly for about ½-h per visit and continuing for 8 months; developmental milestone tables were provided; caretaking, sensorimotor, and interaction exercises were graded developmentally, and each 2-week period a group of these exercises was given to the mother; interventionists demonstrated each exercise and then invited mother to try; total exercise time per day was recommended to be 25–30 min; for most of the exercises special toys or objects were constructed	Home	Mothers were prima providers of intervention

[a] Numbers in parentheses indicate number of studies.

Child characteristics	Experimental design	Outcome measures	Results

Child characteristics	Experimental design	Outcome measures	Results
30 premature infants <37 weeks gestational age and their mothers; severe problems excluded; all teenage, lower SES, black	Random assignment to one of three groups: experimental₁ group (10) both observed NBAS and administered MABI, experimental₂ group (10) only administered MABI, and control group (10) did neither; pre- and postcomparisons	Brazelton NBAS and mother–infant interaction rating scale at 1 month; Denver Developmental Screening Test (DDST) and mother–infant interaction rating scale at 4 months; Bayley Scales of Infant Development at 12 months	1. Both E Groups showed significantly ($p < .05$) improved Brazelton scores over the first month; C Group did not 2. Both E Group mothers scored significantly ($p < .01$) higher than C Group mothers on mother–infant interaction ratings at 1 month 3. Both E Groups scored significantly ($p < .05$) higher on mother–infant interaction ratings and DDST at 4 months 4. Both E Groups scored significantly ($p < .05$) higher on the Bayley Mental Scale at 12 months 5. Few significant differences between the two E Groups

and parent-focused interventions (2)

Child characteristics	Experimental design	Outcome measures	Results
67 premature infants ≤37 weeks gestational age and birthweights between 1000 and 1750 g; all socially disadvantaged, black; severe problems excluded	Random assignment of 41 mother–infant dyads to one of three experimental groups: (1) E₁ infant stimulation only (13), (2) E₂ mother training only (14), and E₃ both (14); 26 premature infants assigned to control group; pre- and postcomparisons	Brazelton Neonatal Behavioral Assessment Scale (prior to discharge), weight gain, length of hospitalization. Frequency of maternal visits, mother–infant interaction during feeding prior to discharge and 3 months later, and mother–infant interaction at 1 year. Caldwell Home Scale at 9 months. Bayley Scales of Infant Development and growth parameters at 1 year	1. No group differences in initial weight gain, length of hospitalization, or Brazelton performance 2. Maternal visits while mothers were still hospitalized were significantly ($p < .05$) more for E₂ and E₃ mothers, but no group differences after mothers were home 3. No group differences in mother–infant interaction measures 4. No group differences on any mother or infant measures at 9 and 12 months age
60 premature infants <37 weeks gestational age and <2500 g birthweight and their teenage, lower SES, black mothers. Severe problems excluded. Also 30 term infants and their teenage mothers, 30 premature infants and their adult mothers, and 30 term infants and their adult mothers as contrast groups	Random assignment of the '60 premature/teenage dyads to either experimental group (30) or control group (30); pre- and postcomparisons	Four months: growth parameters, Denver Developmental Screening Test, Carey Infant Temperament Questionnaire, mother–infant interaction rating scale. Eight months: Bayley Scales of Infant Development, Caldwell Home Stimulation Inventory, Carey Questionnaire	1. E Group premature/teenage infants had significantly ($p < .001$) greater growth parameters and DDST scores than C Group premature/teenage infants at 4 months 2. E Group mothers rated their infants significantly ($p < .001$) less difficult and received significantly ($p < .001$) higher interaction ratings at 4 months 3. E Group scored significantly ($p < .001$) higher on Bayley Mental Scale at 8 months 4. E Group mothers received significantly ($p < .001$) higher Caldwell ratings and rated their infants significantly ($p < .001$) less difficult at 8 months 5. Experimental–control group differences greater than premature–term, teenage–adult, and premature/teenage–premature/adult group differences

tended to be between 1,000 and 2,000 g birthweight, between 28 and 34 weeks gestational age, predominantly of lower socioeconomic status (particularly in the parent-focused studies), and free from severe neonatal physiological or neurological problems. More specific information about neonatal course and complications was generally unavailable. Experimental design in all cases involved either random or sequential assignment to study groups, with two studies (Powell, 1974; Widmayer & Field, 1981) incorporating two different experimental groups and one study (Brown et al., 1980) analyzing three varying experimental groups. Group data comparisons were done with either a pretest–posttest or posttest-only design.

All 12 infant-focused studies reported at least one statistically significant group difference favoring the experimental group. All of the 12 also found an absence of significant group differences in numerous assessed outcome measures. However, after these superficial similarities, results dramatically diverge with the positive findings of one study often being the negative findings of another. Interpretation is rendered even more difficult, as previously discussed, by the great interstudy variability, which makes each individual investigation seem almost anecdotal in nature. For example, rapidity of weight gain is a desired medical outcome easily measured in many of these infant-focused studies. Kramer and Pierpont (1976), using a combination of auditory and vestibular–kinesthetic stimulations, reported improved growth parameters, particularly weight gain, as their only significant group difference attributable to this intervention program. In contrast, both Barnard (1973) and Burns et al. (1983), employing virtually the same intervention modalities 10 years apart, found no experimental–control group differences in weight gain as their major negative result. To complete this total disparity, Kramer and Pierpont found no significant group differences in newborn neurologic status or in standardized neonatal behavioral assessment, whereas again almost the exact opposite was reported by Barnard and Burns et al., who found very significant improvements for experimental group infants in these same developmental areas, specifically increased state stabilization and greater neuromotor maturation. Korner et al. (1975) reported no weight gain or other physiologic group differences following a study of solely vestibular–kinesthetic stimulation via oscillating waterbeds, with the single exception of a significant reduction of apnea in the experimental group. Even though this potentially important finding has not been reliably corroborated by other investigations, it has altered practices in a number of neonatal intensive care units.

Even the two studies utilizing similar multimodal sensory stimulations reported conflicting results. Scarr-Salapatek and Williams (1973), in a frequently cited study, found significantly greater weight gain and significantly superior performance on measures of neonatal behavior for experimental group infants receiving interventions in all four major sensory modalities. However, Leib et al. (1980), using the same modalities, reported no significant group differences in the identical outcome measures. The two studies did both report significantly higher scores on assessments of mental and motor development during the first year of life for experimental infants. But even this general agreement in findings must be cautiously interpreted in the light of its short-term nature (i.e., 1 year of age or less) and also in the light of other studies (e.g., Brown et al., 1980) with essentially no infant performance differences. It is particularly striking that two recent reviews of neonatal developmental interventions produced conclusions as disparate as the individual studies themselves. Cornell and Gottfried (1976) argued that the accumulated literature failed to substantiate convincing intervention effects on most outcome measures including weight gain, neonatal behavior, and mental development; only in the area of motor development could they detect a trend of positive influence. Nevertheless, Campbell (1983), referring to many of the same studies, summarized the effects of neonatal intervention programs as positively influencing weight gain and mental development during the first year of life but having no demonstrable influence on early motor development.

The most consistent finding of the five studies (Bromwich & Parmelee, 1979; Brown et al., 1980; Field et al., 1980; Minde, Shosenberg, Marton, Thompson, Ripley, & Burns, 1980; Widmayer & Field, 1981) that were partially or completely parent-focused in nature involved the positive facilitation of parent–infant interactions. Four of these five studies reported at least some significant, objective enhancement of the mother–infant relationship, with only Brown et al. (1980) failing to detect any group differences in interaction quantity or quality. However, clear documentation of other benefits of this practical, parent-training approach cannot be obtained from the results of these studies. The postulated parental outcome of increased frequency of hospital visitation was reported only by Minde et al. (1980); Brown et al. (1980) found that experimental group mothers, while they themselves were hospitalized, visited their infants in the neonatal intensive care unit significantly more often than control group mothers, but that this encouraging group difference rapidly disappeared once the mothers were discharged from the hospital and returned to their homes. No consistent group differences in weight gain, neonatal behavioral performance, or mental or motor development were apparent across the five studies.

Comparison of the two most rigorous, long-term parent-focused studies, both of which were conducted primarily in the infant's home following nursery discharge and utilized structured, educational home visitation as the principal intervention modality, highlights this dilemma. Field et al. (1980) reported numerous optimistic results from an 8-month home intervention program combining both parent-focused and infant-focused strategies. Significantly better outcomes for their experimental group premature infant–teenage mother dyads were realized for practically all dependent variables assessed (i.e., infant temperament ratings, mother–infant interaction ratings, weight gain, and mental development scores).

This study is the only one in which the authors expanded their investigation to include other demographic types of infant–mother pairs. Remarkably, they found that the premature infant–teenage mother experimental versus control group differences were greater than premature infant versus term infant, teenage mother versus adult mother, and premature infant–teenage mother versus premature infant–adult mother group differences. In contrast, Bromwich and Parmelee (1979) reported far more modest, almost discouraging, results from their highly individualized home intervention program between 10 and 24 months of age. This study was unique in that free, regular health care and supervision from birth to 2 years of age was provided to all participating families, and only the experimental group received the education component of the combined intervention effort. The only significant group difference discovered was enhanced mother–child interaction at 2 years of age for experimental group pairs. No group differences were apparent on any child developmental measures at the study conclusion. The authors suggested that possible interpretations for the failure to find cognitive group differences include the extensive health component available to both experimental and control groups and the temporal proximity of outcome measures to the intervention experience because there is evidence to indicate that parent-focused educational interventions may be anticipated to show greater effects over a period of time rather than immediately after program termination (Bronfenbrenner, 1975).

CONCLUSIONS AND RECOMMENDATIONS

How can we sort out and respond to these mixed effects, which occur within a framework of incredible interstudy variability? Following a thorough review of infant-focused, primarily hospital-based neonatal sensory stimulation interventions, one is almost forced to conclude that practically any early intervention protocol can be expected to yield at least some benefits in some measured area of performance. However, reported positive effects are generally very short-term, with significant developmental differences highly unusual even at 1 year of age and virtually no studies giving postinfancy data. Thus, the accumulated evidence hardly provides a convincing rationale on which to base specific nursery developmental intervention recommendations, nor does it seem, at this time, to justify the routine employment across multiple sites of such programs to normalize or facilitate the development of biologically vulnerable infants in the NICU environment.

There are several important reasons for this cautious, conservative interpretation. Too little evidence currently exists on how to achieve maximal and optimal effects from these types of intervention programs; the key variables responsible for success have not as yet been defined. Insufficient consideration and discussion of potential adverse side effects of neonatal developmental intervention is available in most individual studies or reviews of the field. The link between repeated, intrusive handling and disturbance of the physiologically fragile premature/low birthweight infant and such deleterious neonatal complications as hypoxia, acidosis, apnea, and bradycardia has been documented (Long, Philip, & Lucey, 1980). Increasing numbers of detailed investigations (Gorski, Hole, Leonard, & Martin, 1983; Lawson, Daum, & Turkewitz, 1977) into the typical "life" and ecology of the NICU emphasize both the autonomic nervous system instability of the immature newborn and the surprising ease of negatively exacerbating this individual instability by continual and unpredictable disruptions of quiet sleep. These observations confirm and partially explain long-standing anecdotal nursing descriptions of the seemingly paradoxical association between *decreased* neonatal physical examination and sensory stimulation and actual *increased* neurophysiological stability and readiness for nursery discharge.

Some of the most sustained neonatal intervention effects have been best demonstrated by those relatively few programs (e.g., Field et al., 1980; Scarr-Salapatek & Williams, 1973) that continued the stimulation design after hospital discharge into the infant's home with close and considerable parental involvement. Unfortunately, these very comprehensive programs would be sufficiently costly to be functionally prohibitive in many centers, but, more importantly, may actually owe the bulk of their apparent success to the extensive period of support for the mother rather than to the various stimulation modalities themselves. Certainly, the immense importance of parental involvement to the effectiveness of many different kinds of early intervention for both at-risk and handicapped children is evident from the developmental literature and repeatedly emphasized throughout this text. Another reason for cautious conclusions regarding exclusively infant-focused intervention approaches is that no evidence exists on the effectiveness or safety of intervention for those premature/low birthweight infants most at risk for developmental deviance because most available studies have dealt predominantly with relatively healthy premature newborns.

Finally, original theoretical bases for traditional neonatal developmental intervention, as described earlier in this chapter, have been found wanting in terms of appropriately conceptualizing the premature infant and the intensive care nursery environment. The majority of reported studies were designed around a model of the premature infant as an isolated, sensorially deprived organism in serious need of supplemental stimulation. This inadequate model led quite naturally to attempts to "train" immature, unready, disorganized preterm infants in behavior appropriate for mature full-term infants. More recent, complex models of premature infants and their parents and unique surroundings have suggested new intervention directions.

As has been discussed, the shift to more parent-focused, parent-training neonatal interventions based primarily on the "new" rationale of enhancement of the quality of parent–infant interactions also cannot be clearly and convincingly supported by the presently accumulated research evidence. Nevertheless, contemporary neonatal intervention programs that attempt to facilitate effective parenting strategies for immature, often unresponsive infants and that incorporate some type of extended home visitation plan appear to fit current child development models best, to be most acceptable and useful to families, and to have the greatest likelihood of achieving functional, meaningful results. Sufficient clinical experience in intervening with premature/low birthweight infants has been gathered to generate suggested practical guidelines (Campbell, 1983) for constructing neonatal intervention programs: (1) recognize the unusual physiological stresses being endured by the premature infant, (2) modify the environment to decrease overstimulation (specifically, screen out grossly bombarding and unnecessary sensory stimuli such as handling during periods of quiet sleep), (3) introduce diurnal rhythms to promote behavioral organization, (4) gradually facilitate reciprocal visual, auditory, tactile, vestibular–kinesthetic, and social feedback during alert periods, (5)immediately terminate or alter approaches that produce avoidance responses, and (6)educate and assist parents in reading, anticipating, and appropriately responding to their own infant's cues and signals.

This final programmatic recommendation is particularly important. Klaus and Kennel (1982) have emphasized the developmental utility of infant imitation rather than simple infant stimulation. That is, whereas normal morther–term infant dyads consist predominantly of the mother responding to and imitating the infant's behavioral leads, observed mother–premature infant dyads often primarily involve the mother actively attempting to stimulate and engage the relatively passive infant. Several investigators (Field, 1977; Trevarthen, 1977) have reported the unexpected observation that decreasing maternal activity level and substituting imitation for stimulation resulted in increased infant responsiveness and gaze time. Thus, early intervention programs should strive to help parents by interpreting the infant's behavior for them, by demonstrating how to handle the premature infant, and by fostering and reinforcing parental feelings of competence. The specific intervention plan chosen must be individualized, flexible, modifiable, and always sensitive to the changing, dynamic neurodevelopmental status of the particular infant.

The lack of definitive conclusions as to the effectiveness of early intervention on the behavior and development of the premature human infant should not be overly discouraging because this absence of clear consensus is certainly not unique to intervention for infants at increased biologic risk. Instead this current state of the art should be a strong, urgent stimulus to the planning, financing, and completion of new comprehensive, prospective, longitudinal investigations. With the increasing survival of ever smaller and sicker infants, early intervention studies must include these most vulnerable survivors as well as those infants with less complicated neonatal courses. New studies must attempt to differentiate intervention effectiveness and need for premature, middle and high socioeconomic status infants in comparison to premature, low socioeconomic status infants. Children "graduating" from intervention programs must be followed and assessed developmentally beyond 1 or even 2 years of age in search of long-term effects that might initially be obscured and inapparent.

Lastly, essentially negative studies should be critically analyzed in order to ascertain mitigating variables leading to program ineffectiveness. Brown et al. (1980), discussing their failure with a combined infant- and parent-focused approach to involve socially disadvantaged mothers with their babies and thereby enhance mother–infant interactions, enumerated such intervention impediments as mothers' lack of transportation to and from the hospital, mothers' need to care for older children at home, mothers' inability to leave the home because of cultural concerns of their own mothers, and crises of daily living (e.g., inadequate or no housing, lack of financial support). Brown et al. succinctly summarized this unfortunate reality: "Most of the mothers seemed so overwhelmed by the inadequacies of their social environments that no intervention short of massive environmental alteration was likely to have any lasting consequences" (p. 491). This sobering conclusion should serve both to keep individual, limited neonatal interventions in perspective but also to challenge us to develop innovative, broad-based approaches to the enormously complex task of optimizing the developmental and behavioral outcome of premature/low birthweight infants.

REFERENCES

Als, H., Lester, B. M., Tronick, E. C., & Brazelton, T. B. (1982). Towards a research instrument for the Assessment of Preterm Infants' Behavior (APIB). In H. E. Fitzgerald, B. M. Lester, & M. W. Yogman (Eds.), *Theory and research in behavioral pediatrics* (Vol. 1, pp. 1–35). New York: Plenum Press.

Barnard, K. E. (1973). The effect of stimulation on the sleep behavior of the premature infant. *Communicating Nursing Research, 6,* 12–40.

Bayley, N. (1969). Bayley Scales of Infant Development. The Psychological Corp., New York.

Bee, H. L., Barnard, K. E., Eyres, S. J., Gray, C. A., Hammond, M. A., Spietz, A. L., Snyder, C., & Clark, B. (1982). Prediction of IQ and language skill from perinatal status, child performance, family characteristics, and mother-infant interaction. *Child Development, 53,* 1134–1156.

Bennett, F. C. (1984). Neurodevelopmental outcome of low birthweight infants. In V. C. Kelley (Ed.), *Practice of pediatrics* (pp. 1–24). Philadelphia: Harper & Row.

Brazelton, T. B. (1973). Neonatal behavioral assessment scale. *Clinics in Development Medicine,* No. 50. Philadelphia: Lippincott.

Bromwich, R. M., & Parmelee, A. H. (1979). An intervention program for preterm infants. In T. M. Field (Ed.), *Infants born at risk* (pp. 389–411). New York: Spectrum Publications.

Bronfenbrenner, U. (1975). Is early intervention effective? In B. Z. Friedlander, G. M. Sterritt, & G. E. Kirk (Eds.), *Exceptional infant* (Vol. 3, pp. 449–475). New York: Brunner/Mazel.

Brown, J. V., LaRossa, M. M., Aylward, G. P., Davis, D. J., Rutherford, P. K., & Bakeman, R. (1980). Nursery-based intervention with prematurely born babies and their mothers: Are there effects? *Journal of Pediatrics, 97,* 487–491.

Burns, K. A., Deddish, R. B., Burns, W. J., & Hatcher, R. P. (1983). Use of oscillating waterbeds and rhythmic sounds for premature infant stimulation. *Developmental Psychology, 19,* 746–751.

Campbell, S. K. (1983). Effects of developmental intervention in the special care nursery. In M. Wolraich & D. K. Routh (Eds.), *Advances in developmental and behavioral pediatrics* (Vol. 4, pp. 165–179). Greenwich, CT: JAI Press.

Cattell, P. (1940). Infant Intelligence Scale. The Psychological Corp., New York.

Cornell, E. H., & Gottfried, A. W. (1976). Intervention with premature human infants. *Child Development, 47,* 32–39.

Drillien, C. M. (1972). Abnormal neurologic signs in the first year of life in low birthweight infants: Possible prognostic significance. *Developmental Medicine and Child Neurology, 14,* 575–584.

Drillien, C. M., Thomson, A. J. M., & Burgoyne, K. (1980). Low birthweight children at early school age: A longitudinal study. *Developmental Medicine and Child Neurology, 22,* 26–47.

Dunn, H. G., Crichton, J. U., Grunau, R. V. E., McBurney, A. K., McCormick, A. Q., Robertson, A. M., & Schulzer, M. (1980). Neurologocal, psychological and educational sequelae of low birthweight. *Brain and Development, 2,* 57–67.

Ehrlich, C. H., Shapiro, E., Kimball, B. D., & Huttner, M. (1973). Communication skills in five-year-old children with high risk neonatal histories. *Journal of Speech and Hearing Research, 16,* 522–529.

Field, T. M. (1977). Effects of early separation, interactive deficits and experimental manipulations on infant-mother face-to-face interaction. *Child Development, 48,* 763–771.

Field, T. M. (1980). Supplemental stimulation of preterm neonates. *Early Human Development, 4,* 301–314.

Field, T. M. (1983). High risk infants ''have less fun'' during early interactions. *Topics in Early Childhood Special Education, 3*(1), 77–87.

Field, T. M., Widmayer, S. M., Stringer, S., & Ignatoff, E. (1980). Teenage, lower class, black mothers and their preterm infants: An intervention and developmental follow-up. *Child Development, 51,* 426–436.

Fitzhardinge, P. M. (1975). Early growth and development in low birthweight infants following treatment in an intensive care nursery. *Pediatrics, 56,* 162–172.

Gorski, P. A., Hole, W. T., Leonard, C. H., & Martin, J. A. (1983). Direct computer recording of premature infants and nursery care: Distress following two interventions. *Pediatrics, 72,* 198–202.

Gottfried, A. W., & Gaiter, J. L. (Eds.). (1984). *Infant stress under intensive care: environmental neonatalogy.* Baltimore: University Park Press.

Gottfried, A. W., Hodgman, J. E., & Brown, K. W. (1984). How intensive is newborn intensive care? An environmental analysis. *Pediatrics, 74,* 292–294.

Gottfried, A. W., Wallace-Lande, P., & Sherman-Brown, S. (1981). Physical and social environment of newborn infants in special care units. *Science, 214,* 637–675.

Hack, M., Fanaroff, A. A., & Merkatz, I. R. (1979). The low birthweight infant—evolution of a changing outlook. *New England Journal of Medicine, 301,* 1162–1165.

Hagberg, B., Hagberg, G., & Olow, I. (1984). The changing panorama of cerebral palsy in Sweden, *Acta Pediatrica Scandinavia, 73,* 433–440.

Hirata, T., Epcar, J. T., Walsh, A., Mednick, J., Harris, M., McGinnis, M. S., Sehring, S., & Papedo, G. (1983). Survival and outcome of infants 501 to 750 grams: A six year experience. *Journal of Pediatrics, 102,* 741–748.

Katz, V. (1971). Auditory stimulation and developmental behavior of the premature infant. *Nursing Research, 20,* 196–201.

Klaus, M., & Kennell, J. (1982). Interventions in the premature nursery: Impact on development. *Pediatric Clinics of North America, 29,* 1263–1273.

Klein, N., Hack, M., Gallagher, J., & Fanaroff, A. A. (1985). Preschool performance of children with normal intelligence who were very low birthweight infants. *Pediatrics, 75,* 531–537.

Kopp, C. B. (1983). Risk factors in development. In M. M. Haith & J. J. Campos (Eds.), *Handbook of child psychology: Vol. 2. Infancy and developmental psychobiology* (pp. 1081–1188). New York: Wiley.

Korner, A. F., Kraemer, H. C., Haffner, M. E., & Cosper, L. M. (1975). Effects of waterbed flotation on premature infants: A pilot study. *Pediatrics, 56,* 361–367.

Kramer, L. I., & Pierpont, M. E. (1976). Rocking waterbeds and auditory stimuli to enhance growth of preterm infants. *Journal of Pediatrics, 88,* 297–299.

Kurtzberg, D., Vaughan, H. G., Daum, C., Grellong, B., Albin, S., & Rotkin, L. (1979). Neurobehavioral performance of low birthweight infants at 40 weeks conceptional age: Comparison with normal full-term infants. *Developmental Medicine and Child Neurology, 21,* 590–607.

Lawson, K., Daum, C., & Turkewitz, G. (1977). Environmental characteristics of a neonatal intensive care unit. *Child Development, 48,* 1633–1639.

Leib, S. A., Benfield, D. G., & Guidubaldi, J. (1980). Effects of early intervention and stimulation on the preterm infant. *Pediatrics, 66,* 83–90.

Long, J. G., Philip, A. G. S., & Lucey, J. F. (1980). Excessive handling as a cause of hypoxemia. *Pediatrics, 65,* 203–207.

Lucey, J. F. (1977). Is intensive care becoming too intensive? *Pediatrics, 59,* 1064–1065.

McCormick, M. C. (1985). The contribution of low birthweight to infant mortality and childhood morbidity. *New England Journal of Medicine, 312,* 82–90.

Meisels, S. J., Jones, S. N., & Stiefel, G. S. (1983). Neonatal intervention: Problem, purpose, and prospects. *Topics in Early Childhood Special Education, 3*(1), 1–13.

Minde, K., Shosenberg, N., Marton, P., Thompson, J., Ripley, J., & Burns, S. (1980). Self-help groups in a premature nursery—A controlled evaluation. *Journal of Pediatrics, 96,* 933–940.

Nickel, R. E., Bennett, F. C., & Lamson, F. N. (1982). School performance of children with birthweights of 1000 grams or less. *American Journal of Diseases of Children, 136,* 105–110.

Paneth, N., Kiely, J. L., Stein, Z., & Susser, M. (1981). Cerebral palsy and newborn care. III. Estimated prevalence rates of cerebral palsy under differing rates of mortality and impairment of low birthweight infants. *Developmental Medicine and Child Neurology, 23,* 801–807.

Paneth, N., Kiely, J. L., Wallenstein, S., Marcus, M., Pakter, J., & Susser, M. (1982). Newborn intensive care and neonatal mortality in low birthweight infants. *New England Journal of Medicine, 307,* 149–155.

Parmelee, A. H. (1981). Early intervention for preterm infants. In C. C. Brown (Ed.), *Infants at risk: Assessment and intervention* (pp. 82–89). Johnson & Johnson Baby Products Company.

Philip, A. G. S., Little, G. A., Polivy, D. R., & Lucey, J. F. (1981). Neonatal mortality risk for the '80s: The importance of birthweight/gestational age groups. *Pediatrics, 68,* 122–130.

Powell, L. F. (1974). The effect of extra stimulation and maternal involvement on the development of low birthweight infants and on maternal behavior. *Child Development, 45,* 106–113.

Ramey, C. T., Bryant, D. M., Sparling, J. J., & Wasik, B. H. (1984). A biosocial system perspective on environmental interventions for low birthweight infants. *Clinical Obstetrics and Gynecology, 27,* 672–692.

Rice, R. D. (1977). Neurophysiological development in premature infants following stimulation. *Developmental Psychology, 13,* 69–76.

Rosenfield, A. G. (1980). Visiting in the intensive care nursery. *Child Development, 51,* 939–941.

Saigal, S., Rosenbaum, P., Stoskopf, B., & Milner, R. (1982). Follow-up of infants 501 to 1500 grams birthweight delivered to residents of a geographically defined region with perinatal intensive care facilities. *Journal of Pediatrics, 100,* 606–613.

Scarr-Salapatek, S., & Williams, M. L. (1973). The effects of early stimulation on low birthweight infants. *Child Development, 44,* 94–101.

Scott, K. G., & Masi, W. (1979). The outcome from and utility of registers of risks. In T. M. Field (Ed.), *Infants born at risk* (pp. 485–496). New York: Spectrum Publications.

Segall, M. E. (1972). Cardiac responsivity to auditory stimulation in premature infants. *Nursing Research, 21,* 15–19.

Sparling, J., & Lewis, I. (Eds.). (1981). *Learning games for the first three years: A program for parent/center partnership.* New York: Walker Educational.

Sparling, J., & Lewis, I. (Eds.). (1985). *Partners for learning curriculum.* Chapel Hill, NC: Frank Porter Graham Child Development Center.

Stanley, F. J. (1979). An epidemiological study of cerebral palsy in western Australia, 1956–1975. I. Changes in total cerebral palsy incidence and associated factors. *Developmental Medicine and Child Neurology, 21,* 701–713.

Sweeney, J. K. (1983). Neonatal hydrotherapy: An adjunct to developmental intervention in an intensive care setting. *Physical and Occupational Therapy in Pediatrics, 3,* 1–6.

Trevarthen, C. (1977). Descriptive analysis of infant communicative behavior. In H. R. Schaffer (Ed.), *Studies in mother-infant interaction* (pp. 227–270). New York: Academic Press.

White, J. L., & Labarba, R. C. (1976). The effects of tactile and kinesthetic stimulation on neonatal development in the premature infant. *Developmental Psychobiology, 9,* 569–577.

Widmayer, S. M., & Field, T. M. (1981). Effects of Brazelton demonstrations for mothers on the development of preterm infants. *Pediatrics, 67,* 711–714.

Part III

Children with Documented Handicaps

Chapter 4

The Effectiveness of Early Intervention for Children with Cognitive and General Developmental Delays

MICHAEL J. GURALNICK

Child Development and Mental Retardation Center
University of Washington
Seattle, Washington 98195

DIANE BRICKER

Center on Human Development
University of Oregon
Eugene, Oregon 97403

INTRODUCTION

Young children who exhibit significantly delayed rates of cognitive development are the focus of this chapter. Despite wide variation in etiology (see Chapter 1 of this volume) and in course of development for this highly heterogeneous group of children, delays or impairments are apparent in virtually every facet of cognition, including information processing, problem solving, and especially the ability to apply information to new situations. Corresponding delays in motor, communication, language, and socioemotional development present a picture of global developmental delay for these youngsters. Although cognitive delays are the necessary condition for inclusion in this chapter, the term *general develop-*

115

THE EFFECTIVENESS OF EARLY INTERVENTION
FOR AT-RISK AND HANDICAPPED CHILDREN

mental delay or simply *developmental delay* will be primarily used as a means of underscoring the comprehensive delays common to these children and the corresponding need for comprehensive intervention.

In this chapter, we will explore and evaluate the impact of broad-based early intervention programs directed exclusively at children with these general developmental delays. The general characteristics of this population will be examined first with special emphasis placed on children with Down syndrome. This will be followed by a discussion of the nature of early intervention programs, including a brief history as well as descriptions of the various approaches and educational or developmental models applied to intervention programs that are commonly found in the field. With this information as background, the existing early intervention literature for young developmentally delayed children will be summarized and presented in a manner designed not only to yield a critical analysis of the effectiveness of these programs, but also to permit the detection of any meaningful and consistent outcome patterns that may exist. Based on this more comprehensive analysis, a number of recommendations for the practitioner and other professionals will be generated.

DEVELOPMENTAL CHARACTERISTICS OF DELAYED CHILDREN

In general, developmentally delayed children tend to reach developmental milestones in a manner that is generally similar to that of nondelayed children, but at a much slower rate. All children with significant delays are likely to reach a lower final level of cognitive development but, as will be described, the actual rate, limits on development, and other characteristics vary with the nature and severity of the disabling condition. Although a pattern of general developmental delay may exist, differences across one or more areas of development in comparison to that which is expected on the basis of a child's overall cognitive level are not uncommon. Moreover, as discussed later, a number of qualitative differences in developmental processes have been identified as well.

The children described in this chapter are likely to be labeled as mentally retarded at some point once the clinical picture stabilizes. For this to occur, two major criteria, as defined by the American Association on Mental Deficiency (Grossman, 1983), must be met. The first involves lowered intellectual functioning as assessed by standardized tests of intelligence. Currently, although flexibility is stressed in this determination, an IQ below 70 will satisfy this criterion. The second criterion reflects aspects of impaired adaptive behavior, with milestone measures of social, motor, and communicative development being used to assess this dimension during infancy and early childhood.

The psychometric assessment serves as the primary basis for the classification of the severity of the developmental delay. Children with IQs below 20–25 are classified as profoundly retarded, those between 20–25 and 35–40 as severely retarded, between 35–40 and 50–55 as moderately retarded, and those scoring between 50–55 and approximately 70 as mildly retarded. As a rough approximation, mildly delayed children develop at a rate about one half to two thirds that of normally developing children, and we can expect to see substantial developmental changes for the vast majority of these children, including walking and using language, during the early childhood period. In contrast, children with severe and profound delays make more limited progress toward major developmental milestones, with health, stimulation, and social interaction processes being primary concerns that extend throughout the first few years of life.

In practice and in the descriptive literature, this classification scheme for severity is often simplified by dividing delays into only two categories: those children with severe impairments (an IQ below 50) and those with mild delays (IQs 50–70). Despite the simplification, this distinction appears to be a useful one, with many important differences (apart from developmental rates and patterns) existing between children with severe and mild delays. From an etiological perspective, the cause for the conditions of approximately 50% of the more severely delayed children can be linked to identifiable prenatal problems in central nervous system development (Smith & Simons, 1975), with as many as a third of this group having chromosomal abnormalities. Although Down syndrome is the most prevalent chromosomal abnormality, the presumption that the vast majority of these children belong in the severely delayed category may no longer be valid (see later discussion).

Of the remaining 50%, approximately 10% of severe delays can be traced to problems during the perinatal and postnatal periods, with the final 40% falling into an undecided category in which no specific cause can be discerned. However, most of the difficulties for a considerable portion of the children in the undecided group can likely be attributed to prenatal defects in development because other evidence such as the abundance of certain major or minor anomolies that commonly co-occur are associated with prenatal onset (Smith & Simons, 1975). In fact, children with severe delays typically have a number of associated disabilities also, especially cerebral palsy and epilepsy (Jacobson & Janicki, 1983). Moreover, for the most part only isolated cases of severe delays within families are found; they are usually identified during the first 2 years and have a relatively small though noticeable association with socioeconomic status (Robinson & Robinson, 1976).

In contrast, mild developmental delay generally is confirmed later, accounts for as much as 60–75% of all instances of delays during infancy and early childhood, and has a much stronger association with socioeconomic status; its causes are less likely to be prenatal in origin, as few recognizable syndromes or related evidence are associated with these milder delays (Herbst & Baird, 1983;

Opitz, 1980). It is important to note that children identified as having mild delays in early childhood appear to differ from the mildly delayed population that is identified later, during the school years. Specifically, although the etiology for some proportion of the children in the mild group that is identified during early childhood may be associated with familial–environmental factors, it is much more likely that the majority of children for whom familial–environmental influences are primary ones will not be identified until they are of elementary school age. As such, they constitute part of a yet to-be-identified or at-risk group of youngsters, as described in Chapter 2. Those mildly delayed children who are actually identified during the preschool period tend to be those who have some clear biological basis for their delays or for whom a strong suspicion exists that implicates organic factors. In fact, a specific etiology can be identified for a substantial number of these children as early as 4 years of age (Herbst & Baird, 1983). This group of mildly delayed children may also manifest more prominent problems than those identified later, either behaviorally or developmentally, which are sufficient to set them apart from normal variations in growth and development. When school age is reached, however, large numbers of new mildly delayed children are identified, with relatively few having an established etiological basis, and the association with socioeconomic status increases.

These differences in the patterns of early identification for young developmentally delayed children have important implications for the evaluation of the effectiveness of early intervention because it is primarily this unique subgroup of mildly delayed children in conjunction with those with more severe delays that find their way into early intervention programs. Moreover, because so many children, especially those under 3 years of age, have a clear biological basis for their delays, early intervention research efforts have often been organized within etiologically homogenous groups. This is especially true for children with Down syndrome, as a substantial number of early intervention studies have focused on this subgroup. Accordingly, as background for the analysis of the effectiveness of early intervention, the general developmental course and characteristics of young Down syndrome children will be described in the following section.

Children with Down Syndrome

Since the mid-1970s, a more complete understanding of the character and expression of development of children with Down syndrome has been achieved through a series of extensive multidisciplinary studies. This examination of developmental characteristics has extended well beyond the traditional domains of cognitive and motor development, providing important insights into the social and emotional lives of these children as well as into underlying developmental processes. As a result, we now have a clearer appreciation of both the correspondence that exists between the developmental characteristics of Down syndrome and normally developing children as well as an appreciation of areas of difference.

At a descriptive level, the most straightforward and frequently used approach to gather information has been to track the developmental achievements of Down syndrome children through cross-sectional and longitudinal studies. For cognitive development, continued but gradual improvement occurs (measures of mental age increase). However, the rate of development slows progressively, resulting in a general decline of measured intelligence throughout infancy and early childhood (Carr, 1975; J. A. Connolly, 1978; Melyn & White, 1973; Morgan, 1979; Share, 1975). Although group differences between normally developing and Down syndrome children can be detected during the first year of life through assessments of cognitive functioning, there is, nevertheless, a substantial overlap in level of functioning at this early age. However, as the decline proceeds from an average IQ of 55–60 at 1 year of age toward a mean IQ of 40–50 by the fifth year, Down syndrome children become a clearly distinct subgroup, with only relatively rare instances of children scoring above the mildly delayed range. It is not clear why their test performances decline, but it does *not* appear to be a result of a progressive deterioration of these children (see Carr, 1975). To some extent it may reflect a greater reliance on language-based test items, but much of the measured decline may well be traced to the fact that cognitive tests increasingly tap more demanding and general aspects of competence, adaptive behavior, and problem solving, thereby enhancing developmental differences in overall cognitive functioning.

Accordingly, the majority of Down syndrome children, even by age 3 years, test at the mild, low mild, and high moderate range of intelligence. This is the case even for those studies whose testing procedures were such that relatively little decline was observed during this 3-year period (Reed, Pueschel, Schnell, & Cronk, 1980). Interestingly, many of the early studies had suggested far greater limits on the cognitive abilities of Down syndrome children (see Connolly, 1978, for discussion). It appears that these changes in cognitive development from the early to more current studies can be attributed to improved environmental conditions for Down syndrome children, including the positive effects resulting from less frequent institutionalization (see Centerwall & Centerwall, 1960) and the increased availability of a wide range of high-quality intervention services for handicapped children and their families.

Even with improved cognitive status, variability in terms of severity of delay for Down syndrome children as a group remains extensive (Connolly, 1978; LaVeck & Brehm, 1978). Although these individual differences have been found to be associated strongly with a number of biomedical factors (especially the correlations between the degree of hypotonia and severity of cardiac defects with lower intellectual performance [Cicchetti & Sroufe, 1978; Reed et al., 1980]), the factors contributing to these differences are not well understood. However, despite this variability within the group, there appears to be consistency in cognitive development over time for individual children. In one longitudinal study in which children were evaluated at 9-month intervals from birth to 3 years, considerable continuity was found (Reed et al., 1980). In particular, the shorter term correlation between 18 and 36 months on the Bayley Mental Scale was high ($r = .72$). Even the relationship between 6 and 36 months, a period of much less continuity for normally developing children (Honzik, 1976; Kopp & McCall, 1982), was unusually strong ($r = .53$). Overall, correlation coefficients remain especially high after 18 months of age (Kopp, 1983).

Corresponding delays also occur in other developmental domains, but the pattern varies from area to area. Motor development, although showing less of a difference from normal achievements during the first year, soon becomes similar to that of intellectual development (Carr, 1975; Reed et al., 1980). Feeding difficulties during the first 3 years also show a similar but less pronounced course, with delays of 10–33% occurring in gumming, chewing, finger feeding, food grasping, spoon grasping, and related milestones (Cullen, Cronk, Pueschel, Schnell, & Reed,1981). Aspects of social development, although having a less delayed onset and a less noticeable decline, do display significant lags (Cullen et al., 1981; Melyn & White, 1973; Morgan, 1979). For example, Vineland social quotients, which contain a substantial number of self-help items at lower age levels, decline from a mean of 71.4 at 1 year of age to 66.7 at 1–3 years, and then to an average quotient of 57.3 at 3–5 years of age (Morgan, 1979). Interestingly, not only do declines in these domains parallel one another on the average for the group, but, as might be expected, the domains themselves are interrelated for individual children. Specifically, the magnitude of the correlations among motor, cognitive, and language development (see subsequent discussion) range from .5 to .8 within the first 3 years of life (Reed et al., 1980).

The language development of Down syndrome children has been repeatedly found to lag considerably behind other developmental domains (e.g., Share, 1975). This discrepancy is apparent even in young children as measures of receptive and expressive language fall below that expected on the basis of their cognitive development and may be related to unusual deficits in vocal imitation skills (Mahoney, Glover, & Finger, 1981) or specific oral–motor dysfunctions. Observations by Greenwald and Leonard (1979) have also indicated that young Down syndrome children manifest substantial verbal language deficits in comparison to their level of cognitive (sensorimotor) development.

Taken together, as evaluated in terms of rate of achievement of developmental milestones, Down syndrome children manifest substantial lags in all domains. The typical pattern consists of the appearance of delays early within the first year and a progressive slowing of the rate of development during the later period of infancy and early childhood. Social development seems to be least affected during the first 3 years, whereas language development, especially expressive language, shows the most significant delays. For each child, progress across different developmental domains is significantly intercorrelated and most Down syndrome children fall within the mild and moderate ranges of cognitive functioning by age 5 years. Moreover, there is considerable individual consistency in relative rate of overall development across the early childhood period, and the degree of hypotonicity and severity of congenital heart disease are highly correlated with developmental progress.

Organization and Structure of Developmental Processes

An additional and important question regarding the developmental characteristics of Down syndrome children concerns the organization and structure of their cognitive processes as well as the relationship between cognition and other developmental domains. Correlations among different developmental areas have already been noted for milestone achievement, but information about interrelationships among processes and organizational features of development as compared to normally developing children has particularly important implications with regard to the design of early intervention programs.

These issues are not easily addressed but a number of creative research strategies have provided useful and important working hypotheses. In one study, the organization of sensorimotor skills of Down syndrome children (including object permanence, means–end, causality, etc.) was correlated with those of normally developing children matched in terms of mental age. Comparisons revealed a high correspondence in skills between these two groups (Mahoney et al., 1981). Morever, the organization of these sensorimotor domains for Down syndrome children has been found to be related to language and communicative development in a manner similar to that of normally developing children (Greenwald & Leonard, 1979; Mahoney et al., 1981).

A second line of research has focused on the correspondence between cognitive and affective development. In the field of child development, recent theoretical and empirical advances have improved our understanding of the important organizational processes of attachment, affiliation, fear/wariness, and exploration–curiosity, as well as their relationships to cognitive development (Sroufe, 1979). A large-scale longitudinal investigation (Cicchetti & Pogge-Hesse, 1982; Cicchetti & Sroufe, 1978) has examined these cognitive–affective systems in Down syndrome children. In an extensive series of analyses, affective and cognitive development were shown to have as close an association for Down syndrome children as they do for normally developing children. Emotional reactions producing smiling and laughter, negative affect (especially defensive reactions to perceptual stimuli), patterns of attachment, interrelationships among different systems (affiliation, fear/wariness,etc.), and a correspondence with levels of cognitive development were all similar in their sequence, organization, and relationships to those of normally developing children (Cicchetti & Pogge-Hesse, 1982). Other developmental patterns, such as the emergence of self-recognition, also appear to be similarly organized in Down syndrome children and to correspond to appropriate levels of cognitive development (Mans, Cicchetti, & Sroufe, 1978).

Although considerable evidence exists suggesting that the major developmental processes of Down syndrome children appear qualitatively similar to those of normally developing children, the limits of this generalization have yet to be established. Caution in extending these findings is certainly warranted because relatively few processes have been probed to date and little information is available regarding the organizational features of Down syndrome children's development beyond 3 years of age. Moreover, despite similarities in the structure or organization of developmental processes and the sequence of development, there are a number of characteristics of Down syndrome children that do appear to differ in important ways from nondelayed children. For example, although Down syndrome children's symbolic play correlates with mental age as expected (Hill & McCune-Nicolich, 1981; Odom, 1981), the characteristics of their spontaneous play with objects can be clearly distinguished from normally developing children matched in terms of developmental level. Even with appropriate toys and a supportive and attentive parent available, Down syndrome children are not as socially oriented nor do they use materials as effectively as nondelayed children. In particular, they are more likely to fail to monitor others, to fail to use opportunities to involve others in play adequately or initiate interactions, to have a more limited play repertoire, to fail to shift play activities readily, and to display frequent stereotypic and repetitive acts during play (Krakow & Kopp, 1982, 1983). Moreover, research focusing on the pretend play of Down syndrome children has revealed that these youngsters move through a somewhat different developmental sequence from that of nonhandicapped children, particularly in self-pretend play. In addition, Down syndrome children have unusual difficulty in progressing from single-scheme symbolic play (extending symbolism beyond themselves) to combinatorial symbolic play (combining single or multiple schemes), even though they appeared to be at the appropriate mental ages to do so (Hill & McCune-Nicolich, 1981).

Kopp (1983) suggested that these and other differences can be attributed to unusual deficits in information processing exhibited by Down syndrome children. In particular, problems in attending, discriminating, encoding, transforming, and transmitting complex or subtle stimuli may well underlie the failure of Down syndrome children to employ those interactive strategies necessary for appropriate developmental growth.

Another major difference is the apparent difficulty these children have in expressing affection and in modulating physiological arousal. Overall, children with Down syndrome manifest a lower level of affective expression than their normally developing counterparts, even when matched in terms of cognitive level (Cicchetti & Sroufe, 1978). It is generally more difficult to elicit both positive affective responses, such as laughter to incongruous stimuli, and negative reactions, such as distress to separation and stranger approaches (Cicchetti & Serafica, 1981; Cicchetti & Sroufe, 1978). Even the full form of the early social smile of Down syndrome children appears reduced (Emde, Katz, & Thorpe, 1978). This apparent inability to generate sufficient tension to create an affective response may be attributable to difficulties in processing the information provided by environmental stimuli as well as to specific deficits in physiological arousal.

These cognitive–affective deficits are also likely to influence parents' judgments of their infant's temperament. Despite many similarities in temperament to normally developing babies (although more Down syndrome children are considered ''difficult'' by parents), the reduced arousal capacities of these children may lead parents to rate their children as lower in approachability. Similarly, difficulties in modulating arousal once threshold has been reached or the active roles parents must adopt during infancy in order to establish an interactional exchange can also influence temperament ratings of activity level (Bridges & Cicchetti, 1982).

Emotional responses in infancy serve as a primary means of communication between caregivers and children. Absence of a normally differentiated and difficult-to-arouse (and settle) affective system in an infant can certainly have adverse effects on the nature of the caregiver–child relationship. As Cicchetti and Sroufe (1978) point out:

> It may be that parents of Down syndrome infants need to extend themselves much more than the typical caregiver, since they must assume more responsibility for helping the infant to generate tension and affect and to become emotionally engaged in the situation, and they must accept greater delays in the development of fully differentiated affective expression (e.g., laughter). Helping these infants sustain attention and build excitement is especially challenging. (p. 345)

Inadequate signaling by Down syndrome children and related characteristics are likely to require unusual parental adjustments in order to provide developmentally sound experiences and to establish synchronous and affectively warm interactions. Caregiver–child interactions that are associated with language and communicative development are perhaps most easily disrupted. Existing research suggests that, even at prelinguistic levels, Down syndrome children are much less interactive in parent–child communicative sequences than normally developing children at similar developmental levels. They tend to initiate far fewer interactions and are especially lacking in the use of eye contact to establish interactions, to ''ask questions,'' or to receive information or comments on their ongoing behavior. Moreover, in contrast to those of normally developing children, vocalization patterns of Down syndrome children are such that more vocal clashes with caregivers are likely to occur, proper turn-taking sequences are more difficult to establish, and parents are not able to expand upon their child's vocalizations and their intent as easily (Berger & Cunningham, 1983; Jones, 1980). As a consequence, much of the work of communication falls to parents, and a pattern that becomes more and more directive appears to be a common result. Although it is understandable how such a style of interaction can develop, it may be important to try to establish more mutual and synchronous interactive patterns at prelinguistic levels with the Down syndrome infant because these patterns appear to form a crucial foundation for later language development (Bruner, 1977). Of course, the problems parents may experience in adjusting communicative patterns in accord with the abilities of their Down syndrome infants and young children are far from universal phenomena (Crawley & Spiker, 1983; Rondal, 1978). Nevertheless, it is not surprising to find that many interaction difficulties persist. In fact, these problems may eventually be accompanied by a gradual decline in the amount of interaction between parents and children in the years ahead (Cheseldine & McConkey, 1979; see also Cunningham, Reuler, Blackwell, & Deck, 1981).

Children with Other Biologically Based Delays

The marked heterogeneity, in all respects, for children who have established or presumed biologically based developmental delays suggests that useful descriptive information on the course and characteristics of their development is not likely to extend meaningfully beyond generalities associated with severity of developmental delay. Given widely varying etiologies in particular, it would not be surprising to find that certain qualitative differences exist between this diverse group of children and more homogenous subgroups such as those with Down syndrome. An example of such a difference can be seen in a study on self-recognition. As discussed earlier, Down syndrome children show evidence of self-recognition when they reach appropriate developmental levels. However, when self-recognition tests are administered to a heterogeneous group of developmentally delayed children—children typical of those found in community based early intervention programs—responses are much more variable, with relatively few of these children showing any evidence of this cognitive achievement. This occurs even though assessed mental ages suggested that evidence for self-recognition should exist (Hill & Tomlin, 1981). Other research has also reported differences between Down syndrome children and a heterogeneous group of developmentally delayed children in their degree of social orientation and the extent to which they are engaged in interactions with toys (Krakow & Kopp, 1983).

Despite the fact that descriptions of the development and characteristics of children with other biologically based delays must remain general, some important patterns, many similar to those for children with Down syndrome, do nevertheless emerge. For example, difficulties in caregiver–child interactions can be detected early (e.g., Greenberg, 1971), mismatches between parental speech complexity and children's capacities are not uncommon (Cunningham et al., 1981), children fail to deploy their attention adequately and do not effectively use the social and physical environmental resources available to them during play (Krakow & Kopp, 1983), and highly directive and less responsive patterns of relating can develop (Terdal, Jackson, & Garner, 1976)—all in a manner similar to that of the Down syndrome subgroup. Not only does their toy play lack spontaneity and flexibility (Krakow & Kopp, 1983), but developmentally delayed children seem unusually deficient in adopting systematic strategies in problem-solving tasks (Goodman, 1981).

Moreover, the peer relationships of developmentally delayed children in general during the preschool years show unusual deficits—deficits that exceed those that would be expected on the basis of their levels of cognitive development (Guralnick & Weinhouse, 1984). Most developmentally delayed preschool-age children appear to have extraordinary difficulty in establishing more than simple social exchanges with their peers, a problem that can be traced in part to the directive pattern of caregiver–child relations, to unusual deficits in language development, to the existence of behavioral problems and to other aspects of the social environment (Guralnick, 1986). It may also be a reflection of the information-processing difficulties described earlier (Kopp, 1983), now applied to the problem of establishing social relationships with one's peers. Whatever the case may be, developmentally delayed children appear to be at risk for a host of developmental problems beyond cognitive delay.

At a more global level, families in which a handicapped child is a member also appear to be unusually vulnerable to developing numerous problems (Crnic, Friedrich, & Greenberg, 1983). Yet such outcomes are far from inevitable; many families draw upon their resources not only to cope with but also to be enriched by their relationships with their handicapped family member. The nature of the outcome depends on a complex set of forces. Characteristics of the child and family as well as the availability of social support networks have been found to be important in governing the adaptive abilities of families (Crnic et al., 1983; Gallagher, Beckman, & Cross, 1983).

Finally, the value of tracking the development of diagnostic subgroups of children should be emphasized. Despite even substantial within-group variability, the developmental characteristics of diagnostic subgroups do provide some measure of control and can serve as a useful baseline for evaluating the effects of early intervention. As we have seen for Down syndrome children, specific developmental patterns for this subgroup have been reliably identified. The discovery of the fragile-X syndrome (Carpenter, Leichtman, & Say, 1982) and fetal alcohol syndrome (Golden, Sokol, Kuhnert, & Bottoms, 1982; Steinhausen, Nestler, & Spohr, 1982) in recent years—syndromes involving relatively larger numbers of children—suggests the potential value of this strategy.

NATURE OF INTERVENTION PROGRAMS FOR CHILDREN WITH DEVELOPMENTAL DELAYS

The many problems likely to be encountered by young developmentally delayed children and their families provide an important framework for examining the effectiveness of early intervention efforts. Equally important, however, is an understanding of the nature, scope, and variations of the comprehensive intervention programs themselves. Accordingly, prior to our analyses of the effectiveness of intervention, a brief historical review of early intervention activities and a description of the major dimensions that characterize intervention programs will be presented.

Historical Background

Although prior to the 1900s a philosophical basis for the importance of the early childhood period existed (Lazerson, 1972), the actual catalyst for the development of educational programs may well have been the concern for children growing up in the squalid conditions of poverty. According to Maxim (1980), important educational reforms for young children were stimulated by a number of concerned individuals living in different countries. Programs for young children living in poverty were initiated in the late 1800s–early 1900s by such individuals as Owen in Scotland, Frobel in Germany, McMillan in England, and Montessori in Italy. In many respects, these programs were developed to offer poor children the opportunity to thrive in a more healthy and intellectually stimulating environment.

Concerns for the child from poverty circumstances were extended in this country to concerns for retarded and other children with handicapping conditions. There were two investigations conducted before the 1960s that offered promise for intervention with young developmentally delayed children through manipulation of the environmental context and/or the offering of educational programs during the early childhood period: the serendipitous but classic investigation conducted by Skeels (Skeels, 1966; Skeels & Dye, 1939) and the pioneer work of Kirk (1958).

The longitudinal study conducted by Skeels and his colleagues on two groups of infants placed in different environments produced remarkable findings. Initially both groups of infants were residents of an orphanage and were at first testing found to be comparable and functioning generally in the retarded or low normal range of intelligence. Thirteen of these infants were placed in an institution for the retarded as "house guests" of a group of retarded females and the ward staff (Skeels & Dye, 1939). These 13 children came to constitute the experimental group who, because of marked improvement in this actually more stimulating environment, were adopted and left the institution. The contrast group was composed of the children who remained wards of the state and resided in an institutional environment. Some 30 years later a follow-up study was completed, and as Skeels (1966) reports:

> All 13 children in the experimental group were self supporting and none was a ward of an institution, public or private. In the contrast group of 12 children, one had died in adolescence following continued residence in a state institution for the mentally retarded, and four were still wards of institutions, one in a mental hospital, and the other three in institutions for the mentally retarded. In education, the disparity between the two groups was striking. The contrast group completed a median of less than the third grade. The experimental group completed a median of the 12th grade. (p.55)

This investigation has been criticized on methodological grounds, especially with regard to the exact nature of the disabilities of the subjects as well as concerns about the attribution of the difference between groups solely to the children's early experiences (Clarke & Clarke, 1976; Ramey & Baker-Ward, 1982). However, the potential for substantially altering the rate of intellectual development through environmental manipulation was established.

In 1958, Kirk reported the first formal attempt at ameliorating delayed development through early education. His investigation included 81 preschool children between the ages of 3 and 6 years with IQs that ranged from 45 to 80. These children were classified as mentally retarded in line with the conventions of the time. The subjects were from four different groups: a community experimental group in which the children attended a community-based preschool program, a community contrast group who attended no preschool program, an institutional experimental group who attended an institutional preschool program, and an institutional contrast group who did not attend any preschool program. Upon completion of the preschool experience, the experimental subjects in both the community and institutional preschool groups out-performed the contrast subjects. A follow-up after the first year of elementary school found that the initial differences between contrast and experimental community subjects tended to disappear either through an acceleration of the contrast subjects and/or limited change for children in the experimental group. Nevertheless, according to Kirk (1977), "The conclusion we drew from this experiment was that intervention at the preschool level accelerates the rate of mental and social development, while no intervention at that age level tends to allow the rate of mental and social development to slow" (p. 7).

In 1970 an extremely interesting monograph was published by the State of California's Department of Mental Hygiene (Rhodes, Gooch, Siegelman, Behrns, & Metzger, 1970). This study was a follow-up of work completed by Stedman and Eichorn (1964) that compared the development of a group of 10 home-reared Down syndrome children with 10 institutionalized Down syndrome children. Most comparisons in the Stedman and Eichorn study favored the home-reared children and thus a further experiment was formulated to see if programmatic changes in an institutional environment could produce changes in the Down syndrome children.

Changes were made in the children's physical setting, staff were specially trained, and a comprehensive intervention program was initiated. Training language skills was the primary focus of the program. The reported result indicated that positive changes were seen in the language behavior, intellectual growth, and social skills of a population previously thought by many to be uneducable (Rhodes et al., 1970).

Taken together, the findings of these studies and a host of other factors suggesting that intervention during the first 5 years of life can have a significant impact on development (see Chapter 1 of this volume) set the stage for a major effort initiated at the federal level to foster the development of early intervention programs for developmentally delayed and other handicapped preschool children.

Handicapped Children's Early Education Program

In 1968 the United States Congress enacted the Handicapped Children's Early Education Program (HCEEP). The major purpose of this federal program for young handicapped children was to develop, demonstrate, and disseminate effective early intervention models. Until recently the appropriations for the HCEEP have steadily increased, resulting in a growing number of programs and children being served. An article by Swan (1980) describes the considerable success of this federal venture as measured by the number of programs that have been continued in communities using local and/or state funds. In addition, an evaluation report indicates the enormously positive impact of these programs (Littlejohn Associates, 1982). Although much work needs to be done, there seems little doubt that from both historical and contemporary perspectives the impact of this federal program on the development of early intervention programs for handicapped infants and preschool-age children has been significant.

The final link to contemporary programs can be found in a number of exemplary programs developed in the early 1970s, many of which were supported by HCEEP funds. Descriptions of many of the notable programs that formed the groundwork for many of today's programs can be found in the influential volumes edited by Friedlander, Sterritt, and Kirk (1975) and Tjossem (1976).

CONTEMPORARY EARLY INTERVENTION MODELS

Expectations of the effects of contemporary early intervention models can be conveniently divided into direct impact, indirect impact, and societal benefits. Direct impact refers to program goals and objectives designed to alter the behavior of the child and the immediate family. Most programs see changing the child's behavior and supporting the family as their primary objectives, and thus intervention strategies are developed to reflect this focus. Indirect impact refers to changes in the child and family members that permit maintenance of the child in the least restrictive setting in terms of educational placement. A second important indirect impact is the family's or community's willingness to maintain the child in the home and community.

Finally, many programs suggest that the impact of early intervention programs on the child and family produce benefits for society. In a state-of-the-art report compiled by Interact (Garland, Swanson, Stone, & Woodruff, 1981) it is argued that early intervention assists parents in maintaining their child at home, thus reducing the costs of institutionalization, which the community must bear. Similarly, by maintaining developmentally delayed and disabled children more in the mainstream of regular education, significant savings to the taxpayer result as well (Bricker, Bailey, & Bruder, 1984).

Early intervention services for developmentally delayed children from birth through 5 years of age are typically provided by community programs and include a range of children from those designated as at-risk to the most profoundly impaired child. According to Filler (1983), the three service delivery models used by early intervention programs to serve these children are home-based, center-based, and a combination of home- and center-based. Often programs for infants deliver services in the home setting. The target is the parent or caregiver who is helped to acquire effective intervention skills to use with the child.

As implied in the name, the center-based model requires that the child be brought to an educational setting on a regular basis. The setting might be a classroom, a hospital, or a more informal arrangement. The focus in the center-based models is usually the child; however, many center-based programs stress parental involvement and may even provide structured training for the parent.

Some programs have adopted a combined approach in one of two ways. First, there are programs that stress training both in the classroom and in the home. Second, there are programs that serve children initially employing a home-based model and, after children reach a certain age or developmental level, they are transferred to the center-based component of the program. However, within these three basic service delivery models considerable variability can be found in terms of philosophical/curricular emphasis, instructional approaches, staffing patterns, the nature of family involvement, the use of ancillary services, and assessment and evaluation strategies. These critical elements of early intervention programs are discussed in the following section.

Philosophical/Curricular Approach

An understanding of the philosophical orientation that underlies early intervention efforts is essential. Intervention decisions—including the choice of assessment and evaluation instruments, the determination of educational objectives, the selection of strategies for fostering development, and the construction or adaptation of curricular materials—should be governed by the program's philosophical orientation or approach.

Curricular approaches used by early intervention programs are distributed across a continuum from direct instruction (in which the child is given little choice over the nature of the instructional program) to those with an experiential emphasis (in which the child is free to choose from a variety of options throughout the instructional day). Harbin (1979) has suggested that current curricular models can be classified on the following continuum: experiential, Montessori, Piagetian, information-processing, diagnostic-prescriptive, or behavioral. As one moves away from the experiential end of the continuum the approach becomes increasingly teacher-directed. This is discussed in more detail in the section on instructional strategies.

The curricular emphasis chosen by a program not only guides its focus but should also dictate the content. The majority of programs providing services to developmentally delayed children tend to offer educational activities in a variety of developmental domains. The comprehensive nature of these programs is appropriate because by definition infants and young children with developmental dalays tend to show deficits in many critical areas of functioning. There is often a need to assist the child in gaining skills in cognitive, communicative, social, self-help, and motor areas, thus making mandatory a comprehensive curricular approach.

Although programs can and do operate using a variety of orientations, a general developmental perspective encompassing many different models is most prominent. This orientation assumes that several underlying principles govern the nature and cause of growth and change. In particular, this position assumes that important developmental changes are both hierarchical and sequential. Current developmental progress by a child involves the integration and reorganization of earlier acquired skills, and development occurs in a general, consistent sequential order. In addition, this position assumes that many important developmental changes result from the resolution of disequilibrium between the child's current level of development and the demands of his or her environment. The challenges posed by the environment must be neither too simple nor too difficult in relation to a child's developmental level in order for positive change to result (Hunt, 1961). The task of the interventionist within this model is to structure the environment in such a way as to place increasing demands on the delayed child's current level of functioning. By requiring the child to adapt actively to greater and greater environmental demands, growth and change are promoted. Finally, the approach assumes that what is critical to development may be specific behaviors in some cases, but often interventionists are addressing issues related to broad conceptual aspects of development, which require consideration of issues related to integration and interrelationships across behavioral domains.

Instructional Strategies

The instructional strategies adopted to present the curricular content often rely on some form of environmental programming, however implicit it may be according to varying curricular models. As articulated in behaviorally based strategies, the teaching staff arrange events to elicit and reinforce the occurrence of specific behaviors by the children. However, the rigor and rigidity with which the behavioral technology is employed varies considerably across programs. According to the Harbin (1979) continuum, a fair generalization might be that those programs reflecting the more teacher-directed approaches are the programs that tend to begin training focused on highly specific educational objectives using well-controlled presentation formats. As the child shows progress in the acquisition of the educational objective, the instructional presentation shifts to encourage generalization of the response to other settings and appropriate conditions. In contrast, those programs that are more child-directed tend to employ a more flexible use of this strategy. The child is encouraged to use a specific behavior in a variety of settings and conditions with the primary goal of making the response functional for the child. Once the response becomes functional, the use of well-controlled presentation formats is reduced. Application of an instructional technology requires that staff be skilled behavior managers and programmers if children are to make adequate progress.

Although the application of behaviorally based instructional strategies has been effective in many situations and for certain groups of children, researchers with a more cognitive orientation have questioned the utility and/or generalizability of the skills taught to children under such rigorously controlled and structured regimes. It is possible that these regimes tend to minimize flexibility and adaptability in that children are reinforced for careful adherence to an adult imposed structure. Flights of fancy, initiation of novel behavior, and variations in specified routines are not encouraged and may even be discouraged. Moreover, the technology often has been used to teach specific responses rather than to assist children in developing generative strategies that lead to problem solving and independence. Those favoring a behaviorally based technology argue that the general strategy is sound but rather the manner in which interventionists have applied it needs correction.

Contemporary views held by many interventionists tend to favor instructional approaches that specify the goals and objectives for the child but leave the implementation to be decided, in part, by events occurring in the environment and by the interests of the child. For example, an educational goal might be to assist the child to use more agent–action–object phrases. Rather than using specific drills on a set number of predetermined phrases, the interventionist capitalizes on opportunities that arise during the day to stimulate the use of the targeted language forms. Using such an approach requires careful attention to the daily activities to assure that each child is receiving adequate training on selected objectives. Often it is difficult to monitor the training of each objective, and successful employment of such a system requires systematic collection of data on the child's progress toward specified objectives.

Family Involvement

Increasing numbers of programs are considering the family to be an integral member of the intervention team. From the development of individualized educational plans (IEPs) to their implementation, parents in particular are consulted and involved in the decision making and participate in many aspects of the educational–therapeutic effort for their child. An underlying principle of family involvement is to begin intervention sufficiently early in order to prevent or minimize potentially difficult or distressing parent–child and/or child–family relationships from developing. A second principle of family involvement focuses on the need for an ecological approach to intervention in order to assure maximum development in the young delayed child. As Bronfenbrenner (1975) has suggested, all elements of a child's environment need to work in concert if maximum benefit from intervention is to occur. An exceptionally fine preschool program can probably offset the effects of a nonstimulating after-school environment only partially. There is a need to coordinate home and school expectations, which demands designing an intervention program that includes as many facets of the child's life as possible.

The family situation itself should dictate where, when, how, and in what areas to begin intervention. As is done when designing child-related programs, it is necessary to assess the family situation, select objectives, intervene, and then evaluate progress toward the established objectives. It is also essential that most intervention programs that involve families be based on a balanced blend of a family's emotional needs, on information and assistance within the community, and on skill development. Moreover, families included in programs often have widely disparate cultural backgrounds, availability of resources, demands on their time and energy, educational experiences, belief and value systems, and interests. Such divergence mandates program flexibility and individualization both in intervention objectives for families and in the method of reaching those objectives.

It is our contention, as well as that of many parents, that the professional should avoid becoming "the expert" and telling the parent what to do and how to do it (Roos, 1977; Sullivan, 1976). Rather, it is more helpful if a cooperative relationship evolves in which each individual contributes valuable information and skills. Becoming a member of the team is a responsibility that should be taken seriously be every parent and by every professional.

Training and Deployment of Staff

The professional staff is responsible for the shape and flavor of a program's content. The way in which the staff conducts the program is influenced by at least two important variables: the quality of their training and the fidelity with which they adhere to established program goals and objectives. No doubt other factors could be specified as well, but these two seem of overriding importance.

Personnel working in early intervention programs can be divided into two categories: direct service and support service. Direct service individuals are those interventionists, teaching aides, and/or parents who interact with the child on a regular and consistent basis; for example, the classroom teacher in a center-based program or a parent trainer in a home-based approach. Early interventionists and other direct service personnel are called on to fill a number of roles including developmental specialist, behavior manager, synthesizer, and evaluator. These roles have been discussed in detail by Iacino and Bricker (1978).

Support personnel include specialists such as physical therapists or communication specialists who have been trained in specific areas. The importance of obtaining the input and support of specialists from numerous health, educational, and social and behavioral disciplines is axiomatic for early intervention programs. In fact, prior to the initiation of a program a multidisciplinary diagnostic and assessment process should be conducted on each child. This often requires the participation of a physical therapist, occupational therapist, communication specialist, psychologist, medical personnel, and possibly others. Once a plan is developed on the basis of these assessments, the appropriate specialists should be available to formulate the daily intervention plan, to teach or supervise the direct intervention personnel in the delivery of the necessary therapeutic routines, to provide direct service as needed, and to evaluate the child's progress.

As indicated earlier, contributions from a variety of professionals are essential to the delivery of quality services to the delayed infant and young child. Because most programs cannot support a cadre of needed professionals on a full-time basis, specialists can be effectively used by adopting a consulting model. In such a model, the specialist functions primarily as an evaluator and consultant who

subsequently monitors the implementation of the developed program. The primary hands-on training of the child is provided by the classroom or home visitation
staff and parents, rather than by specialists.

The consulting model has been adopted by many programs, in part because of
financial exigencies; however, many staff, parents, and specialists have become
convinced that, despite limitations for certain complex procedures, this model
can be effective. Established training or therapeutic regimes can be employed
throughout the day rather than for only brief periods when the specialist works
directly with the child. Such practice increases total training time as well as
enhances generalization across settings, people, and events (Bricker, 1976).

Assessment and Evaluation

The development of an evaluation plan and its implementation are essential for
effective intervention. Evaluating individual change and programmatic impact
requires that intervention methods and systems have appropriate evaluation procedures. Evaluation techniques should be able to determine the format and degree of success of intervention for individual children as well as the impact of
programs on groups of children. Thus, evaluation serves three distinct but com-
plementary functions: It guides the development of individual programming, it
provides feedback about the success of individual programming, and it yields
information for determining the value of an intervention system designed to
benefit groups of children.

The need for a comprehensive evaluation of the child requires that the assessment battery be carefully constructed. This battery should tap the child's abilities
across a wide range of domains because educational plans will be constructed on
the basis of the initial assessment information. Second, assessment instruments
should be geared to the developmental age of the child. Third, the evaluation
instrument or format should be usable by available program personnel. Selection
of a sophisticated instrument that cannot be administered appropriately by program personnel is of no value. Fourth, at least some of the assessment/evaluation
tools should yield information that can be used to formulate educational objectives and related program plans. Finally, in addition to the more global assessments or evaluations that are administered at specific intervals, programs should
develop procedures for the collection of daily or weekly probe data that indicate a
child's progress towards established short-term educational or developmental
objectives (Guralnick, 1975).

A useful assessment/evaluation system is essential for monitoring the impact
of an intervention program. Accountability for all concerned is essential. Unfortunately, as will be seen, evaluation has not been given a high priority in many
programs because resources have been limited. Accordingly, programs have

differed widely in the comprehensiveness of the initial assessments as well as their monitoring and summary evaluation efforts.

OUTCOMES OF EARLY INTERVENTION FOR DEVELOPMENTALLY DELAYED CHILDREN

With this information as background, the remainder of the chapter will be devoted to an analysis of the effectiveness of early intervention efforts for children with developmental delays. Studies selected for this review consisted of those that were published in 1975 or later and were found in peer-reviewed journals or professionally edited book chapters. To be included, a study must have reported child change measures, not only parent-related outcomes. Of equal importance, each study selected must have been designed to provide a comprehensive, broad-based program and have attempted to evaluate systematically the impact of early intervention within that framework. To facilitate discussion of these outcomes, the analysis has been divided into programs that served only children with Down syndrome and those that served children with general biologically based delays. Within each group a detailed table is provided consisting of a study-by-study summary of information on the nature of the intervention, the intervention parameters, the setting of the intervention effort, the role of parents, characteristics of the participating children, the experimental design, the outcome measures, and the results. A discussion of the outcomes for each group follows in an effort to draw at least tentative conclusions from these investigations.

Outcomes for Children with Down Syndrome

Despite the importance of and enormous interest in an evaluation of the effectiveness of early intervention programs for children with Down syndrome, only 11 studies met the criteria for inclusion in this review. Nevertheless, as inspection of Table 1 will reveal, a number of important characteristics and patterns did emerge. Virtually without exception, these early intervention efforts reflected a very strong reliance on a developmental framework as the basis for setting educational goals and objectives, and progress was evaluated in terms of change in each of a variety of developmental domains. As noted, programs were comprehensive, attempting to influence the general course of development including cognitive, language and communicative, personal–social, and gross motor areas. However, some programs did provide a special emphasis that was consistent with the interests of the designers, such as specific feeding training (Connolly, Morgan, Russell, & Richardson, 1980), language development (Kysela, Hill-

TABLE 1

Summary of early intervention studies for children with Down Syndrome[a]

Reference	Nature of intervention	Intervention parameters	Setting	Role of parents
Aronson & Fallstrom (1977)	Institution-based program, implemented by a junior psychologist under guidance of authors; most training was individualized and formulated to stimulate sensory, self-help, cognitive, motor, memory, emotional, social, and attentional areas; normal developmental sequences provided the basis for systematic training	Intervention time span was 1½ years; training sessions twice a week for a period of between 15 min and 1 hr; journals kept for each child on a weekly basis for continuing training	Institutional-based, psychologist trainer with input from authors for continuing training programs	No children ever lived at home (all entered the nursing home between ages 4–10 months); Nursing home provided normal preschool program but no involvement with the specialized training program
Bidder, Bryant, & Gray (1975)	Mothers received training on behavior modification techniques as they related to delayed children; efforts designed to encourage increased verbal and social interactions with child at home and toward greater competence and independence; training focused on all developmental domains and was individualized for each child; mothers recorded data based on home-training sessions; a discussion group relating to family and personal problems was also part of the program	Mothers in treatment group received 12 training sessions over a 6-month period, 2 hr per session; more intense (weekly) at beginning of the 6-month period; 1 meeting for fathers and baby-sitters	Home-based for intervention but mothers received training at center	Mothers were recipients of training and counseling, and were the primary service providers; records and data were collected by parents over the 6-month period

yard, McDonald, & Ahlsten-Taylor, 1981; Rynders & Horrobin, 1980), or cognitive and language training (Clunies-Ross, 1979).

An additional characteristic of these programs was the structured and directive nature of the intervention activities. Many programs described highly specific objectives, often conducted on a one-to-one or small-group basis with careful monitoring of progress on each of the objectives. A considerable number of programs relied extensively and explicitly on behaviorally based teaching strat-

Child characteristics	Experimental design	Outcome measures	Results
16 Down syndrome children living in a nursing home; experimental group had mean CA = 52.7 (range 26–69); MA = 20.6 (range 19–34); DQ = 39.4 (range 24–49); control group had mean CA = 51.3 (range 21–68), MA = 20.6 (range 13–35), DQ = 40.5 (range 18–57)	Children matched by age and sex and divided into experimental and control groups; MAs and DQs were almost identical at beginning of study for groups established in this manner	Griffiths Mental Development Scales with the 6 subscales of motor function, personalsocial, hearing and speech, eye–hand coordination, performance, and practical judgment; both groups tested every 6 months; 12 months after training was completed retesting of both groups for follow-up was carried out	Intervention group showed greater increases in mental age (average gain = 10.5 months) and at a more rapid rate than control group (average rate = 3.5 months); held across all 6 subscales; All gains were progressive for all intervention children; during the 12-month follow-up, no statistically significant differences were found between the two groups in total test scores; note that 5 of 8 intervention and 3 control children were moved to other institutions during this no-treatment period
16 Down syndrome children ranging in age from 12 to 33 months participated in the study; experimental group mean CA = 23.8 months; control group 24.5 months; based on Griffiths Mental Development Scale, the mean MA of the experimental group was 16.6 months and the control 14.8 months at beginning of study	Children matched with regard to CA, MA, and sex were divided into two groups (N = 8 per group); experimental group mothers received training on behavioral techniques and counseling but controls only received typical interactions with health visitor and general practitioner; tester not aware of children's group membership	Griffiths Mental Development Scales; maternal reports	Significant differences in favor of the intervention group were found for language (mean gain 6.56 versus 2.56 months) and performance (mean gain 7 months versus 4.37 months) scales of the Griffiths; a strong trend also noted for the personal–social scale; the overall, locomotor, and eye–hand scales did not reveal any differences betwen the two groups; mothers reported increased knowledge and skills about their child's development and improved morale

(continued)

egies (e.g., Bidder, Bryant, & Gray, 1975; Hanson & Schwarz, 1978; Hayden & Haring, 1977; Kysela et al., 1981). Even when intervention was to be administered primarily by parents, detailed written materials and requests to collect progress data were considered vital aspects of the overall intervention strategy. Although there was an emphasis on behavioral objectives and goal setting, only about one third of the programs appeared to have a highly developed curriculum in a form that could be disseminated to others for replication.

TABLE 1 (*Continued*)

Reference	Nature of intervention	Intervention parameters	Setting	Role of parents
Clunies-Ross (1979)	Center-based and home-based instruction; Parent training provided in child management and home teaching; center-based program conducted by parents under staff supervision; curriculum consisted of comprehensive, structured programs in 6 developmental areas; 50% of instructional time focused on cognitive and language areas; normal developmental sequences provided guidelines for major objectives	3 intake groups (3 separate years); intervention time ranged from 4 months to 2 years; initial assessment occurred within 2 weeks of enrollment; children attended the intervention program 2–3 times per week (6 hr total time/week); prescribed instruction was conducted in small groups (1 staff to 2–3 children), or on a 1-to-1 staff–child basis; program objectives monitored each session, program reviews every 2 weeks; parent received 10-week training course; home teaching was conducted by parents 3 15-min sessions per day	Center-based for interdiciplinary team instruction, home-based parental instruction, parent training for implementation of home-based instruction	Provide generalization and consolidation of center-based programs; primary responsibility for self-care programs
Connolly, Morgan, Russell, & Richardson (1980)	Interdisciplinary program with professional teaching child and demonstrating techniques to parents for later home use; specific feeding training was singled out; general developmental model was basis with emphasis on intensive motor and sensory stimulation; group counseling and support for family was also provided	3-year program if enrolled early; maximum time, birth to 3 years; first 10 weeks in spring and fall, 1-hr group sessions, 1-hr individualized child teaching by professional alone, and 1 hr in group counseling with a professional to discuss issues and problems weekly; winter and summer, periodic follow-ups for evaluating and updating program; length of intervention varied for child but not continued after 3 years of age	Center-based for demonstration purposes but parents were expected to carry out home programs	Parents were primary service providers; instructed in general procedures and received counseling services

Child characteristics	Experimental design	Outcome measures	Results
36 Down syndrome children (35 trisomy 21, 1 translocation); average age at intake 14.3 months, age range 3–37 months	Pre–post without control or comparison group; progressive developmental achievements compared to initial assessment on Early Intervention Developmental Profile (EIDP); outcomes compared to normative patterns of Down syndrome children on existing developmental research (no systematic intervention)	EIDP administered at 4-month intervals following initial assessment; reported in mean developmental index scores	Progressive achievements of individuals ranged from large to moderate as measured by developmental index scores; continuous increments in developmental quotient were noted; for cognitive and language indices, children were developing at a rate of approximately 60% of CA; after 12–20 months of intervention, children scored at about 80% of CA; similar improvements occurred on other developmental domains; outcomes substantially replicated over 3 intake groups; younger groups began at higher developmental levels and maintained superiority over 12 months; also, the data suggested that rate of developmental progress was most rapid in 12–23-month age group
At age of intervention: Down syndrome, 0–2.5 years; 20 of original 40 children in group reassessed at 3.2–6.3 years ($\bar{X} = 4.5$)	Post-only comparisons with a specially constructed control group (no random assignment); matched on children referred to demonstration center but not enrolled in an EI program ($N = 53$); same CA and parental educational level as EI	Stanford–Binet or Cattell Infant Intelligence Scale, Vineland Social Maturity Scale	Statistically significant gains in IQ in favor of EI group ($\bar{X} = 54.7$ versus 42.9) and in SQ ($\bar{X} = 64.4$ versus 55.5); 65% of children in EI in mild AAMD level versus 24.5% in comparison group; no EI children classified as severe/profound for EI versus 19% for comparison

(continued)

TABLE 1 (*Continued*)

Reference	Nature of intervention	Intervention parameters	Setting	Role of parents
Hanson & Schwarz (1978)	Staff member visited homes weekly or biweekly, evaluated child's developmental status and established goals in conjunction with parent; detailed educational programs were provided as well as general recommendations for social and physical activities to promote development; normal developmental model with milestones as goals using behaviorally based teaching procedures	Average age of entry into program was 14 weeks, with average program involvement 24.4 months (range 15–30 months); parents were requested to carry out 4–5 different programs weekly with their child (10 trials per day per program)	Home-based program	Primary service providers with advice and teaching of staff home visitors
Hayden & Dmitriev (1975) Hayden & Haring (1977)	Interdisciplinary center-based model preschool program; structured program based on developmental sequences and behavioral objectives across all developmental domains; intensive, individualized program	Variable length of time spent in program; children in model preschool participated in intensive activities 1½–2 hr, 4 days per week	Center-based program	Active in all aspects of model program; parents trained to use strategies at home and participate in child's classrooms; attend parent meetings and group conferences

Parental involvement was a significant component in almost all 11 programs, and many were primarily home based. For infant and toddler programs, in particular, parents were either trained to be the primary service provider (e.g., Hanson & Schwarz, 1978; Rynders & Horrobin, 1980), or to provide additional programs at home, often reinforcing, supplementing, and generalizing lesson activities (e.g., Clunies-Ross, 1979; Kysela et al., 1981; Piper & Pless, 1980). Overall, the instructional burden for younger children was placed clearly on parents, with considerably less emphasis on counseling and support (but see

Child characteristics	Experimental design	Outcome measures	Results
12 Down syndrome children (11 trisomy 21, 1 mosaic), mixed socioeconomic backgrounds; included first 12 children referred from medical and social service agencies for intervention program; 4 children had significant cardiac defects	Post-only design with comparisons to published data on home-reared Down syndrome children's developmental milestones who were not enrolled in early intervention programs	Specific age of attainment of developmental milestones selected from different instruments; comparison data based on Share (1975), Share & French (1974), and Share & Veale (1974)	In comparison to "normative" group, children in the intervention program attained many motor and perceptual–motor milestones (e.g., rolls over, feeds with fingers, walks with no support) at an earlier age and with much less variability in time of attainment; delays in comparison to normal development were still apparent
94 Down syndrome children (95% trisomy 21, 3% mosaic, 2% translocation); analyses included children from model program now in public school ($N = 13$; median CA = 96 months); those currently enrolled in model preschool ($N = 53$; median CA = 42 months); and those enrolled in public school but no model preschool experience (contrast group: $N = 28$; median CA = 118 months)	Nonequivalent contrast group; the experimental group had attended the model preschool program while the control group, some of whom were matched for age with the experimental group, attended other programs; single scores taken from the child's performance on the Down's Syndrome Performance Inventory were used to examine the relationship between age and developmental level across children of different ages; both groups were similar on assessed demographic variables; data on children currently enrolled in the preschool were used for additional comparisons	Down's Syndrome Performance Inventory, Peabody Picture Vocabulary Test or Stanford–Binet; Denver Developmental Screening Test or Vineland Social Maturity Scale	Preliminary results suggest that model children do not show typical decline based on the Down's Syndrome Performance Inventory at certain ages; graduates of model program and control group show variable changes but model group at higher overall level

(continued)

center-based comprehensive programs, e.g., Hayden & Haring, 1977; Ludlow & Allen, 1979).

In contrast to the consistency of parental responsibilities, the intensity and duration of intervention programs varied widely. With regard to intensity, comprehensive center-based preschool programs for Down syndrome children typically ranged from 2 to 5 hr per day. During that time, extensive services were delivered within a model that usually designated certain portions of the day for different developmental domains. Although each developmental area presum-

TABLE 1 (*Continued*)

Reference	Nature of intervention	Intervention parameters	Setting	Role of parents
Kysela, Hillyard, McDonald, & Ahlsten-Taylor (1981)	Direct and incidental teaching methods used in recognition of deficits in attention, memory, and generalization within a behaviorally based model; emphasis on language, but teaching activities included cognition, motor, self-help, and play	2 groups of children (2½–6 years) attended half-day sessions 4–5 days per week in center-based program; daily individual language sessions and group activities; 1 day a week given to maintenance checks; no information provided on intensity or frequency for home-based programs; children in both center-based and home-based programs began at different times (home-based mean age at initiation 13.5 months, center-based mean age at initiation all under age 3) and moved through the program at differing rates; total length of program varied and was not specified clearly but intervals spanned a period of 6–8 months for some children and 12–14 months or longer for others	Home-based until 2½ years, then center-based	Implementation of home-based programs as primary teaching agents; collection of criterion data; provide parent-initiated situations and opportunities for generalization for children enrolled in center-based program
Ludlow & Allen (1979)	Center-based interdisciplinary program providing intervention and planned preschool activities; supportive counseling and training of mothers also offered; home-based program requested to be administered daily as a continuation of center-based program; program geared to individual needs and curriculum consisted of speech stimulation, self-help training, locomotor training, and social development; guidelines for teaching objectives provided by developmental charts and assessments	Intervention groups participated in a developmental clinic 2 hr, 2–3 times a week; some children attended play groups or nursery schools; Adult-to-child ratio was usually 1-to-1; duration of program varied with age of entry, but all children participated for at least 2 years prior to their 5th birthday	Center-based for interdisciplinary team instruction, parental counseling and support; home-based for continued stimulation; normal playgroup involvement when prescribed for specific children to futher independence and social acceptability	Parental participation in every area of center and home-based programs; supported by other parents; kept progress reports for home training

Child characteristics	Experimental design	Outcome measures	Results
Home-based program, 22 children (13 male, 9 female); birth to 2½ years of age; mean age intervention initiated was 13.5 months; program included 19 Down syndrome children, 3 undiagnosed; 64% had other serious medical problems; center-based program, 8 Down syndrome children, 3 with associated serious medical problems (intervention began at a mean of 28.4 months)	Pre–post only; comparisons based on normative test data in relation to the expected decline in test performance over time	Bayley Scales of Infant Development, Stanford–Binet Intelligence Scale, and Reynell Developmental Language Scales, but used developmental rates because norms often were below children's level	Children's rate of development increased significantly as measured by the Bayley or Binet during the first 6–8 months of intervention and was maintained during the subsequent 6–8 months for both home- and center-based programs; children in the home program maintained even progress in expressive language but those in the center program had accelerated development; Both center- and home-based groups had an increased comprehension ratio during the first 6–8 months and continued a positive trend from that point
72 Down syndrome children in intervention group, 79 in home-reared comparison, and 33 in institutional comparison group; followed until 10 years of age; groups similar in socioeconomic status, family size, and parental age	Pre–post with 2 comparison groups: (1) children living at home not receiving intervention and (2) children placed in residential care prior to their second birthday; no random assignment; portions were retrospective	Stanford–Binet and Griffiths Scale as well as school placement information	The intervention group scored higher on the standardized tests particularly on personal–social and speech development; school placement suggested that early intervention helped to integrate children into the normal community

(continued)

TABLE 1 (*Continued*)

Reference	Nature of intervention	Intervention parameters	Setting	Role of parents
Piper & Pless (1980)	Center-based program consisting of an interdisciplinary team with assignment of one staff member per child to be the primary therapist; Parent training provided in the form of demonstration and sets of written instructions. Normal developmental sequences provided guidelines for major objectives	Biweekly therapy sessions for 1 hr over a 6-month period; average CA for initiating treatment was about 9 months, but all children were below 2 years	Center-based for primary therapist intervention and parental demonstrations; home-based intervention between center-based sessions	Received training to provide additional and ongoing activities at home to stimulate development
Rynders & Horrobin (1980)	Center-based and home-based for preschool program; home-based only for infant program (0–30 months); center provided curriculum materials; home-based program conducted by parents using provided lesson plans, curriculum materials, and evaluation sheets; curriculum targeted concept utilization and communicative development within a developmental framework	3 intake groups; intervention duration was 5 years; age range of enrollment was 1–12 months; for infants, time spent on home lessons limited to 1 hr each day, 6 days per week; parent participants completed curriculum evaluation sheets daily; no lessons for preschool children at home except for 1 30-min reading session. Preschool consisted of a daily 5-hr program	Center-based for testing and home-based for implementation of lessons during infant program; center-based for preschool	Deliver lessons, collect evaluation data daily, help center to modify given lessons and develop new lessons for infant program; support program and provide reading experiences for 30–60-month-old children

a Abbreviations used in the table are as follows: AAMD, American Association on Mental Deficiency; CA, chronological age; DQ, developmental

ably supported and reinforced the other, the structured program and small group or one-to-one directive activities were most characteristic of these programs. For the birth–3 years age group, the intensity of the intervention was much less demanding. Although it was often difficult to determine all of the relevant intervention parameters from the descriptions provided by the authors, intervention ranged from 2 to 6 hr per week on the average, which included both staff training time and parent-teaching activities. In addition to variations in intensity, the average duration of involvement in the program also varied extensively. Some programs were designed to be very short term (e.g., 6 months in the Piper & Pless, 1980, study), but even programs beginning in infancy were as long as 2,

Child characteristics	Experimental design	Outcome measures	Results
37 Down syndrome infants (N = 21 treatment group; N = 16 control group); mean CA of treatment group was 9.33 months, control group was 8.43; mean birth weight for experimental 2,949 g, for control 2,990 g; mean number of siblings for treatment group 0.95, control group 0.81; mean number of children with congenital heart disease in treatment group was 1.33; control group 1.38; mean number in residential care for treatment group 1.14, control group 1.06	Pre–post using random assignment according to date of admission to the program; after admission, preassessments were made using the Home Observation for Measurement of the Environment Inventory (HOME), the Griffiths Mental Development Scales, and child and family variables; mean maternal age for treatment group, 30.43, control group 29.81; no initial differences on basis of any variable (with one exception on a HOME subscale)	Griffiths Mental Development Scales; Home Observation for Measurement of the Environment Inventory	Mean developmental quotient on the Griffiths Scales declined over the 6-month period; In 2 of the 6 subscales, treatment group decreased less than control group; on the remaining 4 subscales the control group decreased less than treatment group; no statistically significant differences between the 2 groups were found
35 Down syndrome children (all trisomy 21) enrolled prior to 12 months of age; no children suffering from any serious health problems; additional criteria: (1) parental decision to raise child at home for first 5 years of life; (2) family intact; (3) maternal IQ score 90 or above; (4) parents' educational level at least 10th grade; (5) total family income at least $6,000 (unless 1 or both parents were students); (6) parents used English as 1st language; and (7) family contained no more than 3 preschool-age children including the Down's syndrome child	Post-only (experimental N = 17) with specially formed distal control group (N = 18); all children enrolled on consecutive basis without exception if they met enrollment criteria stated earlier; comparisons on demographic, neurological, and psychometric variables at beginning of study indicated similar groups	Boehm Test of Basic Concepts; Stanford–Binet; Bruininks-Oseretsky; language samples	All children tested at 60 months; no statistically significant group differences appeared in the specified criterion variables (concept utilization and/or expressive language); however, significant differences did appear favoring treatment group in IQ score and in motor ability

quotient; MA, mental age; EI, early intervention; SQ, social quotient.

3, and 5 years (Connolly et al., 1980; Hanson & Schwarz, 1978; Rynders & Horrobin, 1980). For preschool programs, intervention typically ended at 5 years of age and rarely were any longer term follow-up efforts attempted (see Hayden & Haring, 1977; Ludlow & Allen, 1979).

It is important to note that virtually all of these "first generation" early intervention programs were experimental in nature. Services were often provided while curricula were being developed and modified continuously, and staff training and experience were very variable. In many respects, some of the more extensive intervention efforts were part of a series of demonstration projects with limited availability of well-tested instructional and curricular methods and materials. In fact, evaluation strategies and related research components were often superimposed on these demonstration programs. As a consequence, research and evaluation were not usually accorded a high priority, with limited resources being allocated to that component of the program.

Evaluation Efforts

In view of this, it is not surprising that efforts to evaluate the efficacy of these early intervention programs rarely conformed to usually accepted scientific standards. Testing and observations by independent staff, the establishment of interrater reliability, the development and use of instruments sensitive to and standardized for handicapped populations, and clear criteria for inclusion of subjects were not often found. Moreover, the random assignment of subjects to treatment conditions or the formation of appropriate contrast groups was extremely difficult to accomplish (see Chapter 1 of this volume for a discussion of these evaluation issues). As indicated in Table 1, with the possible exception of the Aronson and Fallstrom (1977), Bidder et al. (1975), and Piper and Pless (1980) investigations, most of the studies were forced to rely on means other than random assignment to determine whether their programs were effective. Often, decisions with regard to effectiveness were based upon comparisons with existing literature that traced the development of reasonably similar groups of Down syndrome children who had not received intervention. Another frequently used approach consisted of attempts to establish control groups by matching subjects in intervention and nonintervention groups on specific variables such as chronological age, developmental level, or socioeconomic status. However, in the absence of random assignment, the possibility of rival explanations accounting for any obtained differences other than those associated with intervention can never be entirely ruled out.

It is easy to be critical of the evaluation attempts of early childhood specialists, but it is far more difficult to suggest viable alternatives. Critics often belabor the point that suitable controls were not provided, thus rendering the reported outcome data uninterpretable as to program impact. Clearly the use of controls would be advantageous, but we cannot take lightly the impediments to establishing suitable comparison groups. Often ethical issues are involved. Can service legitimately be withheld from developmentally delayed or other handicapped children? The mandates of federal and state laws to identify and serve handicapped children have answered that question. Can we compare different approaches or strategies with matched groups of children? Often this is not possible because adequate numbers of similar children (e.g., same age, same family demographics, same handicapping conditions) are not available except perhaps in large metropolitan areas. Further, as noted earlier, most programs have not been provided with the necessary funds to conduct controlled evaluation in which independent testers assess the children with a variety of standardized and nonstandardized instruments. Nor do most early intervention program personnel have the necessary expertise to analyze and interpret quantitative outcomes. Finally, parents may offer barriers to the implementation of carefully controlled studies, for they may fail to appreciate encumbrances necessary for experimental research or strategies that do not appear to them to be of any immediate assistance to their child.

Without taking into account the many problems facing behavioral scientists interested in evaluating the outcomes of early intervention efforts for children with Down syndrome and those with cognitive delays in general, critics do children, parents, educators, other professionals, and the public a disservice. Unless there is some sense of rapprochement and compromise we will never move closer to the goal of achieving a meaningful evaluation of these early intervention programs. Moreover, as discussed next, despite research design limitations, a careful examination of existing studies has yielded certain consistencies and outcome patterns that allow us to establish what we believe is a strong working hypothesis with regard to the effectiveness of early intervention for children with Down syndrome. In particular, as we see it, the studies on early intervention for Down syndrome children conducted to date have provided sufficient information to enable us to provide strong recommendations on the specific issue relating to the prevention or amelioration of the reported decline in assessed cognitive ability of children with Down syndrome with increasing chronological age. Studies focusing on issues such as the relative significance of intervening during infancy in contrast to the preschool years and the importance of continuity in early intervention are unfortunately contradictory, but nevertheless provide some valuable directions for the future.

Analysis of Effectiveness

For children with Down syndrome, documentation of the decline, as well as possible explanations for the decline, in tested cognitive ability with increasing chronological age has been described in the first section of this chapter. Based on the findings of a substantial number of studies reviewed it now appears that this decline can be significantly reduced or entirely prevented during the period in which early intervention services are provided (Aronson & Fallstrom, 1977; Bidder et al., 1975; Clunies-Ross, 1979; Connolly et al., 1980; Hanson & Schwarz, 1978; Kysela et al., 1981; Ludlow & Allen, 1979; Rynders & Horrobin, 1980). This outcome held for studies that employed more global measures, such as standardized psychometric instruments, as well as more specific measures, such as achievement of specific developmental milestones or behavioral objectives. Moreover, these effects of early intervention were obtained not only for studies that were less well controlled in that only pre–post measures were obtained (e.g., Kysela et al., 1981) but were also obtained for (1) those studies with specially created control groups (e.g., Connolly et al., 1980); (2) a well-designed study in which a carefully developed distal control group was established for comparison (Rynders & Horrobin, 1980); and (3) a rare study based on children matched on age and sex and presumably unsystematically assigned to experimental and control conditions yielding identical groups on critical factors prior to intervention (Aronson & Fallstrom, 1977; see also Bidder et al., 1975). A similar pattern of outcomes was observed for other developmental domains as well, but less consistency in the measures and corresponding outcomes was obtained.

Certainly bias in different forms cannot be ruled out entirely in any of these studies, particularly bias related to the absence of independent testers, and not all studies found that the decline could be modified (e.g., Piper & Pless, 1980; but see Bricker, Carlson, & Schwarz, 1981). Moreover, certain studies did not achieve results that corresponded to the programmatic emphasis of their program (see absence of language effects in Rynders & Horrobin, 1980). Nevertheless, the consistency of reported results as well as corresponding progress on process variables such as achievement of specific educational and developmental objectives in many of the studies is impressive.

The contention that early intervention programs for children with Down syndrome can have the effect of preventing the typical decline in intellectual functioning has received additional support in a study by Berry, Gunn, and Andrews (1984). In an important longitudinal investigation, these researchers independently evaluated at periodic intervals the development of 39 home-reared Australian-born Down syndrome children during the first 5 years of their lives, using the Bayley Scales of Infant Development and the Merrill-Palmer Scale as outcome measures. All children in the sample were drawn from a variety of early intervention programs operated by public and private agencies, programs that were not under the authors' control. Assessments of this sample revealed that across the first 5 years of life, the Down syndrome children gained steadily in mental age—gains that remained proportional to chronological age, i.e., no decline or plateau was observed. The authors state, "Perhaps the main effects of better services, which have become more widely available in the 1970s and early 1980s, are to stabilize development in Down's syndrome infants and toddlers and to provide a paradigm for consistent progression for these young children whatever their levels of ability" (p. 176). Similar outcomes have been reported for a large sample of Down syndrome children from birth to age 3 in the northeastern United States (Reed et al., 1980).

In contrast to findings related to the prevention or even elimination of the decline in cognitive test scores, only limited information is available with regard to the issues of the continuity and timing of early intervention, and much of it is contradictory. Aronson and Fallstrom (1977) have provided evidence as to what happens when intervention is discontinued. Specifically, a 1-year follow-up of their successful intervention program suggested that differences between intervention and control children would be greatly diminished if the supportive environmental conditions were not maintained. In contrast, Connolly et al. (1980) reported that follow-up of children who had completed an early intervention program by 3 years of age still appeared to maintain most of their original gains approximately a 1½ years later and again 4 years later (Connolly, Morgan, & Russell, 1984). Because these studies differed on so many dimensions, including the potential for bias due to selective attrition of subjects, it is not possible to determine the sources of these contradictory findings.

The corollary issue of whether intervention is more effective if begun during infancy than if begun during the preschool period is equally contradictory. The Clunies-Ross (1979) data suggest that those children beginning intervention earlier are more likely to achieve higher developmental scores. Apparently what happens is that the younger children begin at an initially higher level (presumably prior to the usual declines) and whatever effects of early intervention that do occur remain proportional to that initial level. There were no indications, for example, that the development of children enrolled in early intervention after 2 years of age was accelerating at a level that would allow them to reach the same level as those beginning intervention earlier. These results are at best suggestive, as later enrollment may well be confounded with other factors such as parental motivations. Moreover, the absence of any effects of early intervention in the Piper and Pless (1980) study, which enrolled children at an average age of about 9 months, clearly suggests that the question of timing must await the findings of more extensive and more carefully designed systematic research.

OUTCOMES FOR CHILDREN WITH OTHER
BIOLOGICALLY BASED DELAYS

We now turn to an examination of the effects of early intervention for an etiologically heterogeneous group of developmentally delayed children whose delays have a clear or presumed biological basis. It should be observed at the outset that this heterogeneity adds additional complexity and variability to the analysis of the effects of early intervention. Nevertheless, a series of 14 studies have been conducted that met our criteria and are summarized in Table 2.

As might be expected, the addition of significant numbers of severely and even profoundly handicapped children to early intervention programs created new challenges in the areas of curriculum development and evaluation. Because so many of these children had associated disorders such as cerebral palsy and sensory handicaps, the problem of providing effective early intervention programs became extraordinarily demanding. The often minute, detailed, step-by-step procedures required for appropriate intervention for this population of handicapped children were rather remarkable. Moreover, many programs served an

TABLE 2

Summary of early intervention studies for children with other biologically based delays[a]

Reference	Nature of intervention	Intervention parameters	Setting	Role of parents
Barna, Bidder, Gray, Clements, & Gardner (1980)	Used adaptations of Portage Project materials as curriculum guide for home training (see Shearer & Shearer, 1976)	Home visits within the Portage model varied from 5 to 25 months (duration of intervention)	Home-based	Parents responsible for administering intervention program, data collection, and collaborating with home visitors
Barrera, Routh, Parr, Johnson, Ahrendhorst, Goolsby, & Schroeder (1976)	Interdisciplinary team approach; 5 areas of treatment were included: gross motor, fine motor, language, perceptual–cognitive, and personal–social; developmental activities were eclectic, drawn from diverse sources	Center program met twice weekly for 3 hr; approximately 30 min was scheduled for each of the specific intervention activities; 1-to-1 training with observer for recording; program was evaluated over a 3-month period	Center- and home-based	Recipients of counseling services and specific training to continue treatment programs at home
Brassell & Dunst (1978)	Home-based program providing infants with sequential intervention experiences; multidisciplinary instructional approach and interdisciplinary team recommendations used to implement the program. Object–concept curriculum was primary focus of study and covered 6 sequential levels of functioning paralleling Piaget's 6 ordinal stages of sensorimotor development	Length of total program 4–5 months; home training demonstrations by staff once per week (1½ hr)	Home-based	Implementation of the demonstrated programs; treatment procedures carried out within the context of play and with materials available at home

Child characteristics	Experimental design	Outcome measures	Results
Although many different groups were part of this study, the focus here was on the 15 children diagnosed as developmentally delayed (exclusive of Down syndrome); prior to intervention, mean monthly gains in mental age were 0.61; no other information available	Pre–post testing without a control group; estimates of impact based on rate of progress during time in program in comparison to rate prior to program	Griffiths Mental Development Scales assessed at entry into the program, during program midpoint, and latest scores available; scores based on mental age gains per month	Delayed children increased their mean monthly rates of mental age growth from .61 to .72 after intervention; greatest gains were noted in the hearing–speech and performance sections of the Griffiths; considerable variability among children noted; no relationship was obtained between age of entry into program and rate of development; no statistical analyses provided
Total of 10 moderately and severely delayed children with varying etiologies; CA range 13–48 months with mean of 26.82 months; average functioning levels of evaluated areas range from 10–14 months; 3 children had lowest area in gross motor, 3 in language, 3 in perceptual–cognitive, 1 in fine motor; all had additional handicapping conditions	Variation of multiple baseline design; each child received treatment in lowest area of development plus 2 randomly selected areas; comparisons made to untreated domains (control areas)	Memphis Comprehensive Developmental Scale	Seven children completed at least 15 sessions over a 2–3-month period; when reevaluated the children were found to have made 6.43 months of progress in the areas selected as the lowest level of functioning, 2.43 months of progress in the randomly selected treatment areas, and 1.68 months in control areas; differences were not statistically significant between experimental and control areas, but progress in the lowest area of functioning was reliably higher than the other 2
Total number of children 91 infants (52 males, 39 females); 24 in experimental group, 67 in control group; heterogeneous group ranging from normal to profoundly retarded and from no motor dysfunction to severe motor dysfunction (over 65% of the children were mildly, moderately, or severely delayed); mean age of mother 26.8 years, 28.9 years for father; mean years in school for mother 11.0, 10.9 years for father; mean monthly gross income $632	Pre–post with nonrandom controls; no differences between control and experimental groups on object–concept test prior to intervention; control group received general intervention but not object–concept curriculum	Scale I of the Uzgiris-Hunt Scales	Mean posttest scores for experimental group was significantly higher than control; pretest scores were used as a covariate

(continued)

TABLE 2 (*Continued*)

Reference	Nature of intervention	Intervention parameters	Setting	Role of parents
Bricker & Dow (1980)	Center-based model demonstration program; an interdisciplinary team approach was incorporated into the program; curricula areas included cognitive, communication, motor, and social/self-help; training lattices were constructed for first 3 domains by developmentally sequencing the instructional content based on order of acquisition; social/self-help behaviors incorporated into daily routine; instructional strategies were primarily behavioral in nature; strong emphasis on evaluation	Intervention began after the child entered program, was evaluated, and an IEP formulated; length of the total intervention program was 1 year, 5 days per week, 6 hr per day	Center-based, teaching staff and parents provided majority of direct instruction; support staff served as consultants; specialists conducted evaluations	Parents were involved in the areas of educational training, social services, and counseling; roles of both parents and program were specified in an individual contract
Bricker & Sheehan (1981)	Programs focused educationally on fine/gross motor, social/self-help, sensorimotor, and communication skills; large- and small-group instruction, individual intervention where necessary; interdisciplinary team approach; Center-based with home-based services to assist parents with moderately and severely handicapped children	Center-based instruction operated 5 days per week 2½ hr per day; 15–20 instructional activities initiated daily; home-based program consisted of weekly 1-hr visits to the home by interventionist; support specialists consulted as necessary; both programs began in the fall of the year and concluded in the spring (9-month span); overall 3-year project	Center-based (6 classrooms); all but 2 included at-risk and nonhandicapped peers in addition to handicapped children; home-based for children whose handicapping conditions ranged from moderate to severe	Individual instruction and/or participation in large and small groups (e.g., educational, social service, advocacy); parent implemented program activities, collected data, and developed skills to promote child's development

Child characteristics	Experimental design	Outcome measures	Results
Total number of children 50 (25 males, 25 females), age range for target population 7–54 months; mean age at program entry 27.6 months; 35 of 50 children severely or profoundly retarded, 13 moderately retarded, 1 each was mildly or not retarded; cultural, occupational, educational, and socioeconomic backgrounds varied widely	Pre–post with no controls; children were administered different numbers of performance tests dependent upon length of enrollment, at approximatey 3-month intervals; number of administrations 2–6; minimum enrollment in program per child 8 months	Uniform Performance Assessment System (UPAS)	A summary of results for 40 children enrolled at least 8 months showed statistically significant improvement in each of the 4 domains (see curricula areas) and in the overall score in terms of the percent of items passed on the UPAS; at termination of program 88% of the children were placed in public schools, 4% in group homes, 2% in Head Start programs, 6% in other programs within same school
91 children participated in the evaluation; Age range at start of program was 5 months to 7 years; heterogeneous population ranged from normal to severely handicapped; some children had more than one impairment and 10 were nonambulatory; level of education for mother and father ranged widely; annual income ranged from under $5,000 to over $26,000	Pre–post without control groups; formal assessments conducted on all children in center-based program who met a 7-month interval criterion between pre- and posttest	Uniform Performance Assessment System (UPAS), Student Progress Record (SPR), Bayley Scales of Infant Development, and McCarthy Scales of Children's Abilities	For Bayley scores (CA at initial administration was approximately 18 months, $N = 35$, for this young group), mental age and psychomotor equivalent scores increased significantly although mean developmental indexes did not; all subgroups did show change except for children with severe delays; McCarthy scores for 56 older children (mean CA approximately = 46 months) showed significant increases for both MA and the general cognitive index (GCI); Mildly and moderately delayed groups showed these changes in one year of the program but not in another for GCI; MA differences were statistically reliable in all instances; all children in all groups showed reliable progress on the UPAS

(*continued*)

TABLE 2 (*Continued*)

Reference	Nature of intervention	Intervention parameters	Setting	Role of parents
Goodman, Cecil, & Barker (1984)	Families in treatment group attended a hospital-affiliated program; teacher demonstrated techniques to parents; home visits provided by staff on as-needed basis; input received from different disciplines; educational program focused on broad developmental processes, such as imitation, sequential ordering, awareness of space, etc., but not specific skill acquisition; family counseling available	Families in treatment group attended programs between 2–5½ days per week; individualized lessons provided by staff; average length of program was 16 months	Center-based with occasional home visits	Received training but parents considered primary therapists
Moore, Fredericks, & Baldwin (1981)	Because study was retrospective, no details of the preschool intervention programs were provided; however, based on assessment instruments and prior work of the authors, programs were likely sequentially organized, directive, and behaviorally based	No details of preschool experience nor elementary school programs were provided	Center-based with an unspecified home component likely	Not specified

extensive range of developmentally delayed children in terms of both level of severity and chronological age, thereby creating a number of difficult organizational problems for interventionists.

Despite these increased demands, the curricular models were found to be highly similar to those for children with Down syndrome; that is, in utilizing a developmental framework to guide educational and developmental objectives in conjunction with a behavioral teaching technology. Some models even became standardized and were disseminated to other programs. For example, the studies by Revill and Blunden (1979) and Barna, Bidder, Gray, Clements, and Gardner (1980) used the Portage model (Shearer & Shearer, 1976). Others developed detailed training lattices linking one developmental objective to another, ensuring that the hierarchical and sequential nature of developmental processes were followed (Bricker & Dow, 1980). In contrast, some of the programs reviewed appeared to put together a loosely structured array of activities drawn from

Child characteristics	Experimental design	Outcome measures	Results
Children (treatment, $N = 35$; contrast, $N = 36$) had a wide range of confirmed or presumed biologically based delays; mean CA for all children was approximately 3 years (range 15 months to 5 years); families on welfare constituted 56% of the sample; mean IQ for treatment group was 55.6, for contrast group 59.3	Treatment group matched retrospectively to a contrast group selected on basis of initial age, IQ, and SES; treatment families must have been willing to participate and be included in program activities; however, 29 of the 36 contrast children did attend community programs that provided general support and care; testers not blind to group membership	Bayley Mental Scales of Infant Development or Stanford–Binet; ratio rather than deviation IQ scores used for Bayley	Treatment children significantly higher than contrast children during posttesting; mean gain was 8.1 versus 0.8 IQ points; 11 children in treatment group but only 2 in contrast group improved 15 points or more; children in particularly difficult home circumstances improved the most
Total number of children included was 151 (52 9-year-olds, mean age 103.6 months; 50 10-year-olds, mean age 119.8 months; and 49 11-year-olds, mean age 133.9 months); all children were moderately or severely retarded	Retrospective study comparing elementary age children (9-, 10-, 11-year-olds) who had 0, 1, or 2 or more years of preschool experience within a state-wide system; no control exerted over subjects who had different years of preschool experience; children were evaluated across three 1-year time periods	Student Progress Record	Results of students' performance indicated significant differences at ages 9, 10, and 11 in language, academic, self-help, and motor skill performance in favor of those who had at least 2 years of preschool experience

(*continued*)

numerous sources or failed to provide sufficient information with regard to the nature of those activities (e.g., Sandow, Clarke, Cox, & Stewart, 1981). Interestingly, most of the early intervention programs included in this analysis were part of larger scale systems providing services to a wide age range of children with widely varying levels of severity and etiologies. When studies did focus primarily on children with multiple handicaps (e.g., Barrera et al., 1976; Shapiro, Gordon, & Neiditch, 1977), the programmatic structure and goals were considerably different from those of the more broadly based intervention programs.

Parental involvement through home-based models was clearly a high priority for most of the studies, even for preschool-age children. Specialists were responsible for demonstrating techniques to parents and providing materials, suggestions, education, and support, but parents were often found to be the primary service providers. Models containing a strong center-based component (e.g.,

TABLE 2 (*Continued*)

Reference	Nature of intervention	Intervention parameters	Setting	Role of parents
Moxley-Haegert & Serbin (1983)	Home treatment of five skill-related exercises similar to those of Hanson & Schwarz (1978); developmental areas involved included fine and gross motor skills, language, spatial awareness, and object permanence; parents taught by therapist at pediatric service how to use materials and maintain records; developmental education group parents (see design section) also received special training to observe and detect progress of their child, to recognize the sequential nature of development, and to anticipate next milestones for their child	Materials supplied by program; parents were asked to carry out the exercises daily for one month; home visitors met once per week for first 3 weeks for all but control group	Home-based but training of parents took place at pediatric service	Primary service provider in home; parent used materials provided, maintained a journal, and recorded any developmental gains
Nielsen, Collins, Meisel, Lowry, Engh, & Johnson (1975)	Transdisciplinary approach; eclectic programming (primarily developmental in orientation) provided in area of sensory stimulation, language (encouraging vocalizations, imitation), motor development (neurodevelopmental methods), prespeech, and feeding domains	Varied with age of child; Home visits made once per week from birth to 3 years; occasional center-based individual sessions; parent–infant group children less than 1 year and new to program; Parents spent 1 hr per session with staff, child worked with other staff; group program: for CA 12–18 months, 3 hr, 4 mornings per week (attendance varied from 2 to 4 mornings per week with each child); total length of program 12 months	Home- and center-based	Primary change agent; support center-based programs

Child characteristics	Experimental design	Outcome measures	Results
39 children (mean CA = 21.5 months) scoring at least 1 standard deviation below the mean on either the Bayley Mental Development Index (MDI) or the Psychomotor Development Index (PDI) were included; the 13 children in each of three groups (see design section) consisted of 6 severely (Bayley score less than 50) and 7 moderate to mildly delayed (Bayley score 50–80) children; varied etiologies; mean age of parental education 11.33 years; all three groups were similar in the Home Observation for Measurement of the Environment Inventory (HOME) scores and parent education level	Children of parents in the home treatment program were matched according to severity of delay and assigned randomly to 1 of 3 treatment groups: (1) a developmental education group which parents received training to help them recognize small gains in their child's development; (2) an education in child management group providing general information and social reinforcement similar to the treatment group but not specific to delays; and (3) a control group not receiving any intervention	Bayley Scales of Infant Development, a developmental knowledge test for parents, parent participation measures in home program, and skills specified to be taught; the assessment schedule consisted of pretreatment, a 1-month posttreatment assessment carried out 9–15 months later; specific assessments varied at these three time periods; assessors were not aware of which experimental condition was assigned to each family	At the 1-month assessment, amount of participation, knowledge of development, and accuracy of recognizing developmental gains of their children by parents in the developmental education group was significantly greater than either of the other two groups on most measures; similarly, children in the developmental education group learned more of the prescribed skills than either of the other 2 groups; on the Bayley scales, the developmental education group made greater improvements on the motor scale but not the mental sclae; at follow-up, more parents in the developmental education group continued to be involved in their child's treatment program and significant gains in motor development were maintained at 1-year-follow-up; no group differences were obtained with regard to cognitive development at follow-up
Age range 0–3 years; 16 of 19 children participated in the evaluation using the Bayley; all 19 received The Denver Developmental Screening Test (DDST); varied etiologies and severity of developmental delay; mean CA at entry to program was 14.1 months (MA = 8.3 months)	Pre–post with no controls	Bayley Scales of Infant Development and Denver Developmental Screening Test (DDST)	Data showed a mean gain of 3.7 months in mental age and 3.9 months in motor age during the 5.4 mean months between first and second administration of the Bayley; no statistical tests provided; changes in mean age equivalents on DDST were statistically significant for the first 6 months but no further gains during the second 6 months

(continued)

TABLE 2 (*Continued*)

Reference	Nature of intervention	Intervention parameters	Setting	Role of parents
Revill & Blunden (1979)	The Portage Project model was applied (see Shearer & Shearer, 1976) involving weekly home visits and collaborative staff–parent goal setting and selection of educational activities	Weekly visits by home trainer for a period of 4 months	Home-based	Provide primary service, collect data, and monitor child's progress
Safford, Gregg, Schneider, & Sewell (1976)	Center-based program focusing on appropriate sensory experiences with minimal failure or frustration for both child and parent; interdisciplinary team approach and a 1-to-1 staff-to-child relationship was maintained; primary objective was to make child less irritable and easier for parent to manage; related objectives included increased verbal reactions, eye contact, and attending; relaxation, desensitization, feeding, and sensory stimulation activities were provided	One classroom with six children; five sessions (relaxation, sensory, relaxation, feeding, exploration) conducted each day; total length of program 6 months	Center-based	Facilitated carry-over of activities through staff offerings of specific suggestions mostly relating to positioning and feeding
Sandow, Clarke, Cox, & Stewart (1981)	Individualized learning programs were designed by experimenter and parents; no additional details were provided	Maximum program involvement over 3 years; for one intervention group, home visits occurred at 2-week intervals for 2–3 hr per visit; a second intervention group received a similar visit every 2 months; a matched distal control group did not receive any visits	Home-based	Primary service provider in conjunction with experimenter

Child characteristics	Experimental design	Outcome measures	Results
9 subjects from 2 geographic areas meeting the following criteria were included in the study: CA less than 4.5 years, child not attending nursery school more than 5 half-days per week, and child scored 78 or below on at least 2 subtests of the Griffiths Mental Development Scales; no other information provided	Pre–post without a control group; in addition, one of the two geographic groups entered the program with a planned delay of 2 months, allowing multiple baseline comparison of impact; baseline data were extensive	Pre–post measures taken weekly by home visitor for each designated skill; monthly recording of development on Portage checklist carried out in child's home; administration of the Griffiths Mental Development Scale at 2 months and again at 4 months	Both geographic groups completed nearly 90% of the tasks that were agreed on; Comparisons between pre-entry (baseline) and monthly assessments following entry into program on the number of Portage checklist skills gained per month revealed a substantial increase following program entry for each group; Griffiths scores showed limited and variable gains for either group; no statistical tests were presented
Total number of children 6 (5 male, 1 female); age range at onset of program was 20–45 months; IQs on Cattell Infant Intelligence Scale were 24, 28, 35, 40, 47, and 70; most children were irritable with poor eating and sleeping habits; Some rejected body contact, were self-stimulating, and self-abusive	Pre–post with no controls	Cattell Infant Intelligence Scale and Houston Test of Language Development	Gains across the 6-month period in assessed functional age equivalence in gross motor functioning occurred for all children (average age gain of 1.9 months); average gain in language age was 1.8 months; strong individual gains measured in perceptual and fine motor areas; no tests of statistical significance provided
2 severely delayed preschool children with a mean CA of 2 years 6 months and a mean MA of 1 year 3 months participated; wide range of SES and etiology; children remained in program until the age of 4 years 8 months; A matched group of 15 additional children were selected from a different community	2 matched intervention groups varying in frequency of home visits were evaluated on pre–post measures at annual intervals; a matched distal control group (no intervention) was also established	Assessments on the Cattell Infant Intelligence Scale occurred at program entry and at annual intervals thereafter; the Vineland Social Maturity Scale and specific criterion-referenced instruments were administered but not considered in the evaluation in detail	Both intervention groups gained in the Cattell at different rates but by the 3rd year both exceeded gains of the distal control. No differences were obtained between the 2 intervention groups on this measure

(continued)

TABLE 2 (*Continued*)

Reference	Nature of intervention	Intervention parameters	Setting	Role of parents
Shapiro, Gordon, & Nieditch (1977)	Program based on developmental–interaction approach involving cognitive and motivational components; measured 8 dimensions of behavior	Children and their families participated in intensive stimulation program for a period of approximately 3 months as in-patients in a rehabilitation center	Center-based (in-patients at medical center)	Required to spend 1 full day per week in active participation at the center
Shearer & Shearer (1976)	Emphasis on self-help, motor, socialization, cognitive, and language domains; interdisciplinary program staff (all home teachers); precision teaching model followed; goals are developmentally sequenced using detailed behavioral objectives; curriculum cards and manuals guide and suggest educational activities	All instruction took place in home; home teacher writes activity and data collection charts, and models activities once per week for 1.5 hr per child; up to 3 activity plans written or modified per week; no prescribed frequency or intensity for parental instruction noted but strong encouragement for parents; project evaluated children within an 8-month period	Home-based	Main change agent for child who also collects data and participates in selection of target behaviors

*a*Abbreviations used in the table are as follows: CA, chronological age; MA, mental age; SES, socioeconomic status.

Bricker & Dow, 1980) typically provided counseling in addition to working with parents to extend developmental programs to the home that were part of the center-based activities. For home-based programs, staff usually visited or consulted with parents on a weekly basis. During interim periods, parents were asked to carry out various activities as often as possible to try to meet certain mutually agreed-upon objectives prior to the next visit. Accordingly, the exact amount of intervention time that actually occurred could not be precisely determined in these models. In contrast, center-based models scheduled groups 2–5 times per week that ranged from 3 to 6 hr per day. Finally, the duration of early intervention programs was highly variable. Although some were evaluated across a relatively long intervention period of as much as 25 months (Barna et al., 1980), virtually all were shorter term programs, typically less than 12 months in duration.

Child characteristics	Experimental design	Outcome measures	Results
60 multiply handicapped children whose ages ranged from 18 to 36 months; medical diagnoses included cerebral palsy, spina bifida, and delayed development; no other information provided	Pre–post comparisons with no controls of coded anecdotal records maintained for each child	Anecdotal records by teachers written 3 times per week; logs coded on scales in the areas of interaction with materials, social responsiveness, expressive language, awareness of the environment, affect, gross and fine motor activity, and sensory responsiveness	Pre–post score differences indicated that the children were more responsive and functioning at a higher level in most areas coded than when they first entered the program; major areas not statistically significant included interaction with materials, fine motor activity, affect, and sensory responsiveness
Target population ranged from high risk to severe/multiply handicapped (birth to 6 years); average IQ 75; no other information available	Pre–post with no controls	Cattell Infant Intelligence Scale, Stanford–Binet Intelligence Test, Alpern-Boll Developmental Profile	Average child gained 13 months on developmental tests in the 8-month period; statistically significant gains were obtained on the Alpern-Boll (mean gain = 13.5); on the Stanford–Binet mean gain was 18.3 IQ points, also statistically significant

Analysis of Effectiveness

The difficulties in conducting meaningful evaluations that meet established scientific standards, discussed earlier in the section on children with Down syndrome, apply equally to early intervention programs for children with other biologically based delays. In fact, the group of studies that met the criteria for review in this section appeared to be much less sophisticated and less credible from a scientific perspective than those studies reviewed that focused exclusively on children with Down syndrome. With minor exceptions (e.g., Moxley-Haegert & Serbin, 1983) no effort was made to utilize independent observers or evaluators who were unaware of the intervention status of the children or families. Similarly, interrater reliability was rarely established, and many of the assessment instruments selected did not seem to have the capacity to be sufficiently sensitive to the range and complexity of delays exhibited by these children. Finally, as will be discussed, despite some creative efforts to establish control or contrast groups, the overwhelming majority of studies relied on the least sophisticated experimental designs in order to evaluate the impact of their program.

Certainly, as described in Chapter 1 of this volume, these problems are part of the larger methodological and ethical problems faced by investigators seeking to conduct intervention research for handicapped populations. However, difficulties in experimental design for this particular group of studies may also be a reflection of the added burden of providing intervention services and developing instrumentation for such a heterogeneous group of children. This drain on already scarce resources was likely to have left limited support available for research and evaluation. Moreover, it is important to note that, in contrast to the programs for children with Down syndrome, very few studies were available that had systematically traced the general course of development for this diverse group of children in a manner useful for evaluation. As described in the first sections of this chapter, documentation of changes in measured cognitive skills with increasing chronological age obtained for children with Down syndrome were simply not available for children with other biologically based delays to serve as a framework for interpreting the outcomes of early intervention programs. In particular, the absence of these developmental expectations makes any appeal for effectiveness based primarily on changes in rates of development subsequent to program services less compelling.

These difficulties are reflected in the finding that a substantial number of studies compared changes from pre- to post-intervention without the benefit of a control group (Barna et al., 1980; Bricker & Dow, 1980; Bricker & Sheehan, 1981; Nielsen et al., 1975; Safford, Gregg, Schneider, & Sewell, 1976; Shapiro et al., 1977; Shearer & Shearer, 1976). In essence, these programs had no other alternative but to appeal to changes in the rate of development (such as number of months in mental age gained per unit of time as reflected in proportion measures or more directly in IQ scores) that coincided with the provision of early intervention services. The outcomes of these studies ranged widely, with one (Barna et al., 1980) not reporting any statistical analyses of their data at all and one claiming rates of development for children in the program to be nearly twice that prior to entry (Shearer & Shearer, 1976). Findings of the remaining programs were more modest (see Table 2) but nevertheless did indicate an increase in the rate of development sufficient in many instances not only to prevent any further disparities with normally developing children but also to be capable of reducing the differences to some small extent. An interesting variation of this pre–post design was a study reported by Revill and Blunden (1979) in which a geographically matched group postponed entry into the program for 2 months. Rate changes in the number of curricular skills gained did coincide with entry into the program, but gains for both groups on a standardized intelligence test were minor.

Four studies did attempt to form contrast or control groups in some manner to enable them to make certain comparisons but random assignment was not possible. Goodman, Cecil, and Barker (1984) matched their treatment group retrospectively with children in community programs; Sandow et al. (1981) employed a distal control group presumably not receiving services; Brassell and Dunst (1978) compared the performance of experimental-group children to those not recommended for a specific form of intervention; and Barrera et al. (1976) used subjects as their own controls in a variation of a multiple-baseline design. Again, modifications in development as a result of early intervention were relatively modest, although Goodman et al. (1984) did report a mean gain of approximately 7 points on standardized intelligence tests above that of their contrast group. As noted earlier, each of these design strategies is fallible and their conclusions must be viewed accordingly.

The remaining prospective study was primarily concerned with evaluating the effectiveness of a particular type of parent education program utilizing both parent and child change measures (Moxley-Haegert & Serbin, 1983). This very well designed and executed study included a randomly assigned control group not receiving any intervention services. Comparisons on the Bayley Scales of Infant Development revealed reliabile differences in favor of the treatment group on the motor but not on the mental scale after 1 month (average increase over control group was approximately 6% above pretest level), which was maintained at a 1-year follow-up.

Although most of the early intervention programs served children with widely varying degrees of severity of developmental delay, it was not generally possible due to insufficient numbers of children to distinguish whether proportional gains were made by subgroups classified by level of severity. Data from Bricker and Sheehan (1981) did, however, suggest that where developmental gains did occur, groups of severely, moderately, and mildly delayed children all showed relative increments in development. Proportionally small gains were reported for programs specifically devoted to severely delayed and multihandicapped groups (Barrera et al., 1976; Bricker & Dow, 1980; Safford et al., 1976; Sandow et al., 1981; Shapiro et al., 1977). Moreover, Bricker and Dow (1980) found that for a group of predominantly severely and profoundly delayed children pretest scores were the best predictors of posttest scores. Similar correlations for a much more heterogeneous group were also high between pre- and posttests, but pretest scores were not correlated with change scores (Goodman et al., 1984). In addition, in this latter study greater improvement occurred for children who were in highly stressed home environments.

It should be noted that substantial gains in curriculum related skill areas as measured by corresponding criterion-referenced type instruments were reported by many programs—gains that seemed reliable and correlated with entry into the program (Bricker & Dow, 1980; Bricker & Sheehan, 1981; Moxley-Haegert & Serbin, 1983; Revill & Blunden, 1979; Shearer & Shearer, 1976). These changes should be considered important as they stand. At the same time, however, it is unclear whether the curriculum-based skills taught by prescribed instructional procedures produced generalized sets of skills and abilities. If standardized tests of general cognitive functioning reflect aspects of these generalized skills, then generalized gains must be considered modest. In fact, two studies found limited relationships between skill-related improvements and gains in general cognitive development (Moxley-Haegert & Serbin, 1983; Revill & Blunden, 1979).

It is certainly possible that the absence of these relationships and the modest gains found in the studies reviewed in this section in terms of standardized tests of general development may reflect an insensitivity of the instruments to detect important changes, as most of the tests were not designed for children with significant delays. In fact, the development of meaningful and appropriate evaluation instruments for many groups of handicapped children remains a major task for the future. It is also possible that important changes were occurring in domains not measured in the early intervention program evaluations. Improvements in social competence, emotional stability, motivational characteristics, parent–child relationships, and overall family functioning—all important potential outcomes of early intervention—were not systematically assessed (see Outcome Measures column in Table 2). Similarly, little is known about the longer term impact of early intervention. A retrospective analysis of children now of elementary school age comparing groups with varying degrees of preschool experience did yield positive relationships in support of the value of early intervention, but methodological problems make it very difficult to weigh this outcome strongly (Moore, Fredericks, & Baldwin, 1981). A 1-year reevaluation following termination of specific services did, however, indicate that gains could be maintained (Moxley-Haegert & Serbin, 1983).

Summary for Children with Other
Biologically Based Delays

In the studies meeting the criteria for inclusion in this section of the review, reports of successful efforts to teach curriculum specific skills were widely noted, and parents were relied upon to provide vital, direct intervention services in most instances. However, reported gains in more general areas of development, especially cognitive domains, were more modest and the studies yielded little information as to the specific characteristics of either programs or children that might produce the most substantial benefits. As noted earlier, the heterogeneity of developmental delays and accompanying disabilities for this group of children may well have been responsible for the unusual experimental design and curriculum development problems experienced by this group of early intervention programs. Although some investigators were extremely clever in developing designs that strengthened the link between programmatic efforts and developmental changes, a substantial proportion of programs were forced to rely on less sophisticated approaches. There were numerous signs from this literature that early intervention programs were having an impact but the difficulties noted earlier, the narrow focus of most outcome measures, the lack of follow-up, and the considerable instrumentation problems prevent us from going beyond these most tentative of statements.

Finally, the inclusion of a substantial number of children with severe and profound delays raises the issue as to what constitutes meaningful change for this subgroup of children. To some extent, of course, value judgments enter into all of our decision making in this field, but the impact and ultimate value of short-term changes in the development of severely and profoundly delayed young children occurring as a result of early intervention has been questioned in many quarters. Although it is beyond the scope of this chapter to discuss this issue in detail, it is important to note that a number of studies have reported benefits to these children that appear to have potentially important developmental and functional significance (Barrera et al., 1976; Bricker & Dow, 1980; Safford et al., 1976; Sandow et al., 1981). Follow-up studies of the long-term effects of early intervention efforts in relation to the impact of these programs on later life activities will be necessary to help evaluate this complex issue.

CONCLUSIONS AND RECOMMENDATIONS

Early intervention programs for children with general developmental delays are prominent features of contemporary service systems for young handicapped children. As we have seen (see Chapter 1 of this volume), there appears to be a logical and developmentally sound rationale for providing such services, but, of course, it is essential to examine empirically the extent to which the goals of early intervention programs have been accomplished. No attempt will be made in this section to summarize in any detail the numerous studies reviewed in this chapter, as summary statements have been presented at many points as part of the preceding analyses. However, we do feel that, despite the many problems associated with the evaluation of early intervention programs for developmentally delayed children, this review has many implications for the practitioner as well as for program and policy designers, researchers, parents, and evaluators.

Perhaps the most important implication these findings may have for health professionals, educators, parents, child development specialists, other practitioners, and policymakers, is the perspective they provide on early intervention issues. Specifically, this review has clearly not been an effort to arrive at a consensus opinion, as it would certainly result in oversimplifications and overextensions, given the nature of existing research. Nor has it been an effort to present a devastating critique of published work—a task all too easy to accomplish. Rather, this review may be of special value in providing a sense of what to expect realistically in terms of developmental gains from intensive and extensive involvement in early intervention programs.

In particular, claims of utter failure of early intervention as well as claims of incredible success for the group of children described in this chapter can now be more critically appraised. Neither is accurate. There is, however, reason to project confidence that the decline in measured intelligence with increasing chronological age common to children with Down syndrome can be prevented and to some extent reversed. As we have seen, this was a generally consistent finding, holding across many different types of experimental designs and programs. It was the convergence of different sources of information that was perhaps most convincing. Unfortunately, for children whose delays could be attributed to a biological basis other than Down syndrome, the evidence was less satisfactory. As noted, the heterogeneity of the population and other factors resulted in less sophisticated designs overall, raising important questions about both the internal and the external validity of the findings. Nevertheless, the consistency of the results, even for the better controlled investigations, suggests that early intervention programs for these children may well have an effect of about the same order of magnitude as those directed toward children with Down syndrome, but with much more variability in the possible outcomes.

To some readers of this review the range and magnitude of outcomes that can be realistically expected to occur due to systematic early intervention will be disappointing, as no evidence can be found to support expectations for radical and dramatic changes. To others, these results will suggest that promising but yet tentative optimism with regard to achieving a meaningful impact on the lives of young developmentally delayed children through early intervention programs is the most reasonable position to maintain. Still others perhaps may see these outcomes as a confirmation of the power of biological determinism or the ineffectiveness of intervention procedures that are experiential in nature.

In our view, the second position—that early intervention is indeed a promising strategy, one that has in fact demonstrated its ability to produce consistent positive changes in the development of young delayed children—is most compatible with the facts. Aligning ourselves with this position seems especially appropriate when the entire early intervention enterprise is placed in perspective. In essence, the evaluation of impact was based upon a series of "first generation" early intervention programs. Curricula were being written and tested, administrative procedures were being developed, techniques for incorporating the input from many disciplines were being refined, and team-process strategies were being explored; often while services were being delivered. Moreover, personnel preparation programs providing specialists to work with these children were limited, and many staffs were faced with a difficult on-the-job training experience. Finally, the measurement strategies were often questionable and restricted primarily to direct child change measures.

Whether better trained and experienced personnel, refined and well-tested curricula, as well as other strategies and resources designed to improve the quality of early intervention services will yield corresponding improvements in outcomes is a vital question for the future. Initial results suggest that this task should be actively encouraged. A fair appraisal for purposes of public policy as well as for individual decision making by professionals and parents regarding early intervention for developmentally delayed children must await the outcomes of a next generation of programs. In this next phase, researchers, evaluators, and program designers should seek to achieve a more enlightened family partnership and recognize more completely the implications of a broader ecological approach to intervention (Bronfenbrenner, 1977). It appears to be especially important to consider dimensions such as social support networks (Friedrich & Friedrich, 1981; O'Connor, 1983). Moreover, it may be helpful in subsequent programs to take a somewhat less directive and perhaps less artificial approach to intervention than that described in existing studies, relying more on the integration of intervention activities within the natural flow of family and school events. In addition, we recommend that measurement systems be expanded beyond primarily cognitive measures to assess potentially important outcomes of early intervention that have been generally excluded to date. Of particular importance are measures of social competence, motivation, family functioning, and problem-solving skills.

Of course, these recommendations do not resolve the basic difficulties inherent in conducting early intervention research for developmentally delayed children. The experimental design issues and strategies for extending evaluation beyond the short-term focus, characteristic of almost all the prospective studies reviewed, remain major barriers. Some suggestions for improving our experimental designs and establishing a meaningful data base for developmentally delayed and other groups of young handicapped children are described in the final chapter of this volume. Perhaps as these procedures are applied and additional studies are forthcoming more specific issues such as the relative value of early versus later intervention, the optimal intensity of programming, and determinations of which children are likely to benefit from specific early intervention approaches can be meaningfully addressed. Despite the fact that even tentative answers to these more detailed questions are not possible at this time, we are encouraged by the initial efforts of the studies analyzed in this review and look forward to the design and analysis of subsequent generations of early intervention programs for children with general developmental delays.

REFERENCES

Aronson, M., & Fallstrom, K. (1977). Immediate and long-term effects of developmental training in children with Down's syndrome. *Developmental Medicine and Child Neurology, 19,* 489–494.

Barna, S., Bidder, R. T., Gray, O. P., Clements, J., & Gardner, S. (1980). The progress of developmentally delayed pre-school children in a home-training scheme. *Child: Care, Health and Development, 6,* 157–164.

Barrera, M. E. C., Routh, D. K., Parr, C. A., Johnson, N. M., Arendshorst, D. S., Goolsby, E. L., & Schroeder, S. R. (1976). In T. D. Tjossem (Ed.), *Intervention strategies for high risk infants and young children* (pp. 609–627). Baltimore: University Park Press.

Berger, J., & Cunningham, C. C. (1983). Development of early vocal behaviors and interactions in Down syndrome and nonhandicapped infant-mother pairs. *Developmental Psychology, 19,* 322–331.

Berry, P., Gunn, V. P., & Andrews, R. J. (1984). Development of Down's syndrome children from birth to five years. In J. M. Berg (Ed.), *Perspectives and progress in mental retardation: Vol. 1. Social, psychological, and educational aspects* (pp. 167–177). Baltimore: University Park Press.

Bidder, R. T., Bryant, G., & Gray, O. P. (1975). Benefits to Down's syndrome children through training their mothers. *Archives of Disease in Childhood, 50,* 383–386.

Brassel, W. R., & Dunst, C. J. (1978). Fostering the object construct: Large-scale intervention with handicapped infants. *American Journal of Mental Deficiency, 82,* 507–510.

Bricker, D. (1976). Educational synthesizer. In M. A. Thomas (Ed.), *Hey, don't forget about me!* (pp. 85–97). Reston, VA: The Council for Exceptional Children.

Bricker, D., Bailey, E., & Bruder, M. B. (1984). The efficacy of early intervention and the handicapped infant: A wise or wasted resource. In M. Wolraich & D. K. Routh (Eds.), *Advances in developmental and behavioral pediatrics* (Vol. 5, pp. 373–423). Greenwich, CT: JAI Press.

Bricker, D., Carlson, L., & Schwarz, R. (1981). A discussion of early intervention for infants with Down syndrome. *Pediatrics, 67,* 45–46.

Bricker, D. D., & Dow, M. G. (1980). Early intervention with the young severely handicapped child. *Journal of the Association for the Severely Handicapped, 5,* 130–142.

Bricker, D., & Sheehan, R. (1981). Effectiveness of an early intervention program as indexed by measures of child change. *Journal of the Division for Early Childhood, 4,* 11–27.

Bridges, F. A., & Cicchetti, D. (1982). Mothers' ratings of the temperament characteristics of Down syndrome infants. *Developmental Psychology, 18,* 238–244.

Bronfenbrenner, U. (1975). Is early intervention effective? In B. Z. Friedlander, G. M. Sterritt, & G. E. Kirk (Eds.), *Exceptional infant: Vol. 3. Assessment & intervention* (pp. 449–475). New York: Brunner/Mazel.

Bronfenbrenner, U. (1977). Toward an experimental ecology of human development. *American Psychologist, 32,* 513–531.

Bruner, J. S. (1977). Early social interaction and language acquisition. In H. R. Schaffer (Ed.), *Studies in mother-infant interaction* (pp. 271–289). London: Academic Press.

Carpenter, N. J., Leichtman, L. G., & Say, B. (1982). Fragile X-linked mental retardation. *American Journal of Diseases of Children, 136,* 392–398.

Carr, J. (1975). *Young children with Down's syndrome.* London: Butterworth.

Centerwall, S. A., & Centerwall, W. R. (1960). A study of children with mongolism reared in the home compared to those reared away from the home. *Pediatrics, 25,* 678–685.

Cheseldine, S., & McConkey, R. (1979). Parental speech to young Down syndrome children: An intervention study. *American Journal of Mental Deficiency, 83,* 612–620.

Cicchetti, D., & Pogge-Hesse, P. (1982). Possible contributions of the study of organically retarded persons to developmental theory. In E. Zigler & D. Balla (Eds.), *Mental retardation: The developmental-difference controversy* (pp. 277–318). Hillsdale, NJ: Lawrence Erlbaum.

Cicchetti, D., & Serafica, F. C. (1981). Interplay among behavioral systems: Illustrations from the study of attachment, affiliation, and wariness in young children with Down's syndrome. *Developmental Psychology, 17,* 36–49.

Cicchetti, D., & Sroufe, L. A. (1978). An organizational view of affect: Illustration from the study of Down's syndrome infants. In M. Lewis & L. A. Rosenblum (Eds.), *The development of affect* (pp. 309–350). New York: Plenum Press.

Clarke, A. M., & Clarke, A. D. B. (1976). *Early experience: Myth and evidence.* New York: Free Press.

Clunies-Ross, G. G. (1979). Accelerating the development of Down's syndrome infants and young children. *The Journal of Special Education, 13,* 169–177.

Connolly, B. H., Morgan, S., & Russell, F. F. (1984). Evaluation of children with Down syndrome who participated in an early intervention program: Second follow-up study. *Physical Therapy, 64,* 1515–1519.

Connolly, B., Morgan, S., Russell, F. F., & Richardson, B. (1980). Early intervention with Down syndrome children: Follow-up report. *Physical Therapy, 60,* 1405–1408.

Connolly, J. A. (1978). Intelligence levels of Down's syndrome children. *American Journal of Mental Deficiency, 83,* 193–196.

Crawley, S. B., & Spiker, D. (1983). Mother-child interactions involving two-year-olds with Down syndrome: A look at individual differences. *Child Development, 54,* 1312–1323.

Crnic, K. A., Friedrich, W. N., & Greenberg, M. T. (1983). Adaptation of families with mentally retarded children: A model of stress, coping, and family ecology. *American Journal of Mental Deficiency, 88,* 125–138.

Cullen, S. M., Cronk, C. E., Pueschel, S. M., Schnell, R. R., & Reed, R. B. (1981). Social development and feeding milestones of young Down syndrome children. *American Journal of Mental Deficiency, 85,* 410–415.

Cunningham, C. E., Reuler, E., Blackwell, J., & Deck, J. (1981). Behavioral and linguistic developments in the interactions of normal and retarded children with their mothers. *Child Development, 52,* 62–70.

Emde, R. N., Katz, E. L., & Thorpe, J. K. (1978). Emotional expression in infancy: II. Early deviations in Down's syndrome. In M. Lewis & L. A. Rosenblum (Eds.), *The development of affect* (pp. 351–360). New York: Plenum Press.

Filler, J. W., Jr. (1983). Service models for handicapped infants. In S. G. Garwood & R. R. Fewell (Eds.), *Educating handicapped infants* (pp. 369–386). Rockville, MD: Aspen Systems.

Friedlander, B. Z., Sterritt, G. M., & Kirk, G. E. (Eds.). (1975). *Exceptional infant: Vol. 3. Assessment & intervention.* New York: Brunner/Mazel.

Friedrich, W. N., & Friedrich, W. L. (1981). Psychosocial assets of parents of handicapped and nonhandicapped children. *American Journal of Mental Deficiency, 85,* 551–553.

Gallagher, J. J., Beckman, P., & Cross, A. H. (1983). Families of handicapped children: Sources of stress and its amelioration. *Exceptional Children, 50,* 10–19.

Garland, C., Swanson, J., Stone, N., & Woodruff, G. (1981). *Early intervention for children with special needs and their families* (Series Paper No. 11). Seattle, WA: WESTAR.

Golden, N. L., Sokol, R. J., Kuhnert, B. R., & Bottoms, S. (1982). Maternal alcohol use and infant development. *Pediatrics, 70,* 931–934.

Goodman, J. F. (1981). The lock box: A measure of psychomotor competence and organized behavior in retarded and normal preschoolers. *Journal of Consulting and Clinical Psychology, 49,* 369–378.

Goodman, J. F., Cecil, H. S., & Barker, W. F. (1984). Early intervention with retarded children: Some encouraging results. *Developmental Medicine and Child Neurology, 26,* 47–55.

Greenberg, N. H. (1971). A comparison of infant-mother interactional behavior in infants with atypical behavior and normal infants. In J. Hellmuth (Ed.), *Exceptional infant: Vol. 2. Studies in abnormalities* (pp. 390–418). New York: Brunner/Mazel.

Greenwald, C. A., & Leonard, L. B. (1979). Communicative and sensorimotor development of Down's syndrome children. *American Journal of Mental Deficiency, 84,* 296–303.

Grossman, H. J. (Ed.). (1983). *Classification in mental retardation (rev. ed.)* Washington, DC: American Association on Mental Deficiency.

Guralnick, M. J. (1975). Early classroom-based intervention and the role of organizational structure. *Exceptional Children, 42,* 25–31.

Guralnick, M. J. (1986). The peer relations of young handicapped and nonhandicapped children. In P. S. Strain, M. J. Guralnick, & H. M. Walker (Eds.), *Children's social behavior: Development, assessment, and modification.* (pp. 93–140). New York: Academic Press.

Guralnick, M. J., & Weinhouse, E. M. (1984). Peer-related social interactions of developmentally delayed young children: Development and characteristics. *Developmental Psychology, 20,* 815–827.

Hanson, M. J., & Schwarz, R. H. (1978). Results of a longitudinal intervention program for Down's syndrome infants and their families. *Education and Training of the Mentally Retarded, 13,* 403–407.

Harbin, G. (1979). Mildly to moderately handicapped preschoolers: How do you select child assessment instruments? In T. Black (Ed.), *Perspectives on measurement: A collection of readings for educators of young handicapped children* (pp. 20–28). Chapel Hill, NC: The Technical Assistance Development System.

Hayden, A. H., & Dmitriev, V. (1975). The multidisciplinary preschool program for Down's syndrome children at the University of Washington model preschool center. In B. Z. Friedlander, G. M. Sterritt, & G. E. Kirk (Eds.), *Exceptional infant: Vol. 3 Assessment & intervention* (pp. 193–221). New York: Brunner/Mazel.

Hayden, A. H., & Haring, N. G. (1977). The acceleration and maintenance of developmental gains in Down's syndrome school-age children. In P. Mittler (Ed.), *Research to practice in mental retardation: Vol. 1. Care and intervention* (pp. 129–141). Baltimore: University Park Press.

Herbst, D. S., & Baird, P. A. (1983). Nonspecific mental retardation in British Columbia as ascertained through a registry. *American Journal of Mental Deficiency, 87,* 506–513.

Hill, P. M., & McCune-Nicolich, L. (1981). Pretend play and patterns of cognition in Down's syndrome children. *Child Development, 52,* 611–617.

Hill, S. D., & Tomlin, C. (1981). Self-recognition in retarded children. *Child Development, 52,* 145–150.

Honzik, M. P. (1976). Value and limitations of infant tests: An overview. In M. Lewis (Ed.), *Origins of intelligence: Infancy and early childhood* (pp. 59–95). New York: Plenum Press.

Hunt, J. M. (1961). *Intelligence and experience.* New York: Ronald Press.

Iacino, R., & Bricker, D. (1978). The generative teacher: A model for preparing personnel to work with the severely/profoundly handicapped. In N. Haring & D. Bricker (Eds.), *Teaching the severely handicapped* (Vol. 3, pp. 62–76). Columbus, OH: Special Press.

Jacobson, J. W., & Janicki, M. P. (1983). Observed prevalence of multiple developmental disabilities. *Mental Retardation, 21,* 87–94.

Jones, O. H. M. (1980). Prelinguistic communication skills in Down's syndrome and normal infants. In T. M. Field, S. Goldberg, D. Stern, & A. M. Sostek (Eds.), *High-risk infants and children: Adult and peer interactions* (pp. 205–225). New York: Academic Press.

Kirk, S. A. (1958). *Early education of the mentally retarded.* Urbana: University of Illinois Press.

Kirk, S. A. (1977). General and historical rationale for early education of the handicapped. In N. E. Ellis & L. Cross (Eds.), *Planning programs for early education of the handicapped* (pp. 3–15). New York: Walker,

Kopp, C. B. (1983). Risk factors in development. In M. M. Haith & J. J. Campos (Eds.), *Handbook of child psychology: Vol. 2. Infancy and developmental psychobiology* (pp. 1081–1188). New York: Wiley.

Kopp, C. B., & McCall, R. B. (1982). Predicting later mental performance for normal, at-risk, and handicapped infants. In P. B. Baltes & O. G. Brim, Jr. (Eds.), *Life-span development and behavior* (Vol. 4, pp. 33–61). New York: Academic Press.

Krakow, J. B., & Kopp, C. B. (1982). Sustained attention in young Down syndrome children. *Topics in Early Childhood Special Education, 2*(2), 32–42.

Krakow, J. B., & Kopp, C. B. (1983). The effects of developmental delay on sustained attention in young children. *Child Development, 54,* 1143–1155.

Kysela, G., Hillyard, A., McDonald, L., & Ahlsten-Taylor, J. (1981). Early intervention: Design and evaluation. In R. L. Schiefelbusch & D. D. Bricker (Eds.), *Language intervention series: Vol. 6. Early language: Acquisition and intervention* (pp. 341–388). Baltimore: University Park Press.

LaVeck, B., & Brehm, S. S. (1978). Individual variability among children with Down's syndrome. *Mental Retardation, 16,* 135–137.

Lazerson, M. (1972). The historical antecedents of early childhood education. *Education Digest, 38,* 20–23.

Littlejohn Associates, Inc. (1982). *An analysis of the impact of the Handicapped Children's Early Education Program.* Prepared for Special Education Programs, U.S. Department of Education.

Ludlow, J. R., & Allen, L. M. (1979). The effect of early intervention and pre-school stimulus on the development of the Down's syndrome child. *Journal of Mental Deficiency Research, 23*(1), 29–44.

Mahoney, G., Glover, A., & Finger, I. (1981). Relationship between language and sensorimotor development of Down syndrome and nonretarded children. *American Journal of Mental Deficiency, 86,* 21–27.

Mans, L., Cicchetti, D., & Sroufe, L. A. (1978). Mirror reactions of Down's syndrome infants and toddlers: Cognitive underpinnings of self-recognition. *Child Development, 49,* 1247–1250.

Maxim, G. (1980). *The very young: Guiding children from infancy through the early years.* Belmont, CA: Wadsworth.

Melyn, M. A., & White, D. T. (1973). Mental and developmental milestones of noninstitutionalized Down's syndrome children. *Pediatrics, 52,* 542–545.

Moore, M. G., Fredericks, H. D. B., & Baldwin, V. L. (1981). The long-range effects of early childhood education on a trainable mentally retarded population. *Journal of the Division for Early Childhood, 4,* 94–110.

Morgan, S. B. (1979). Development and distribution of intellectual and adaptive skills in Down syndrome children: Implications for early intervention. *Mental Retardation, 17,* 247–249.

Moxley-Haegert, L., & Serbin, L. A. (1983). Developmental education for parents of delayed infants: Effects on parental motivation and children's development. *Child Development, 54,* 1324–1331.

Nielsen, G., Collins, S., Meisel, J., Lowry, M., Engh, H., & Johnson, D. (1975). An intervention program for atypical infants. In B. Z. Friedlander, G. M. Sterritt, & G. E. Kirk (Eds.), *Exceptional infant: Vol. 3. Assessment & intervention* (pp. 222–246). New York: Brunner/Mazel.

O'Connor, G. (1983). Social support of mentally retarded persons. *Mental Retardation, 21,* 187–196.

Odom, S. L., Jr. (1981). The relationship of play to developmental level in mentally retarded, preschool children. *Education and Training of the Mentally Retarded, 2,* 136–141.

Opitz, J. M. (1980). Mental retardation: Biologic aspects of concern to pediatricians. *Pediatrics in Review, 2*(2), 41–50.

Piper, M. C., & Pless, I. B. (1980). Early intervention for infants with Down syndrome: A controlled trial. *Pediatrics, 65,* 463–468.

Ramey, C., & Baker-Ward, L. (1982). Psychosocial retardation and the early experience paradigm. In D. Bricker (Ed.), *Intervention with at-risk and handicapped infants* (pp. 269–289). Baltimore, MD: University Park Press.

Reed, R. B., Pueschel, S. M., Schnell, R. R., & Cronk, C. E. (1980). Interrelationships of biological, environmental and competency variables in young children with Down syndrome. *Applied Research in Mental Retardation, 1,* 161–174.

Revill, S., & Blunden, R. (1979). A home training service for pre-school developmentally handicapped children. *Behaviour Research and Therapy, 17,* 207–214.

Rhodes, L., Gooch, B., Siegelman, E., Behrns, C., & Metzger, R. (1970). A language stimulation and reading program for severely retarded mongoloid children. *California Mental Health Research Monograph, 11.*

Robinson, N. M., & Robinson, H. B. (1976). *The mentally retarded child: A psychological approach.* New York: McGraw-Hill.

Rondal, J. (1978). Maternal speech to normal and Down syndrome children matched for mean length of utterance. In C. E. Myers (Ed.), *Quality of life in severely and profoundly mentally retarded people: Research foundations for improvement* (Monograph No. 3). Washington, DC: American Association on Mental Deficiency.

Roos, P. (1977). A parent's view of what public education should accomplish. In E. Sontag, J. Smith, & N. Certo (Eds.), *Educational programming for the severely and profoundly handicapped* (pp. 72–83). Reston, VA: The Council for Exceptional Children.

Rynders, J. E., & Horrobin, J. M. (1980). Educational provisions for young children with Down's syndrome. In J. Gottlieb (Ed.), *Educating mentally retarded persons in the mainstream* (pp. 109–147). Baltimore: University Park Press.

Safford, P. L., Gregg, L. A., Schneider, G., & Sewell, J. M. (1976). A stimulation program for young sensory-imparied, multihandicapped children. *Education and Training of the Mentally Retarded, 11,* 12–17.

Sandow, S. A., Clarke, A. D. B., Cox, M. V., & Stewart, F. L. (1981). Home intervention with parents of severely subnormal pre-school children: A final report. *Child: Care, health and development, 7,* 135–144.

Shapiro, L. P., Gordon, R., & Neiditch, C. (1977). Documenting change in young multiply handicapped children in a rehabilitation center. *The Journal of Special Education, 11,* 243–257.

Share, J. B. (1975). Developmental progress in Down's syndrome. In R. Koch & F. De La Cruz (Eds.), *Down's syndrome (mongolism): Research, prevention and management.* New York: Brunner/Mazel.

Share, J. B., & French, R. W. (1974). Early motor development in Down's syndrome children. *Mental Retardation, 12,*(6), 23.

Share, J. B., & Veale, A. M. (1974). *Developmental landmarks for children with Down's syndrome (mongolism).* Dunedin, New Zeland: The University of Otago Press.

Shearer, D. E., & Shearer, M. S. (1976). The Portage Project: A model for early childhood intervention. In T. D. Tjossem (Ed.), *Intervention strategies for high risk infants and young children* (pp. 335–350). Baltimore: University Park Press.

Skeels, H. M. (1966). Adult status of children with contrasting early life experiences: A follow-up study. *Monographs of the Society for Research in Child Development, 31*(3, Serial No. 105).

Skeels, H. M., & Dye, H. E. (1939). A study of the effects of differential stimulation on mentally retarded children. *Proceedings of the American Association on Mental Deficiency, 44,* 114–136.

Smith, D. W., & Simons, F. E. R. (1975). Rational diagnostic evaluation of the child with mental deficiency. *American Journal of Diseases of Children, 129,* 1285–1290.

Sroufe, L. A. (1979). The coherence of individual development: Early care, attachment, and subsequent developmental issues. *American Psychologist, 34,* 834–841.

Stedman, D. J., & Eichorn, D. H. (1964). A comparison of the growth and development of institutionalized and home-reared mongoloids during infancy and early childhood. *American Journal of Mental Deficiency, 69,* 391–401.

Steinhausen, H., Nestler, V., & Spohr, H. (1982). Development and psychopathology of children with the fetal alcohol syndrome. *Developmental and Behavioral Pediatrics, 3,* 49–54.

Sullivan, R. (1976). The role of the parent. In A. Thomas (Ed.), *Hey, don't forget about me!* (pp. 36–45). Reston, VA: The Council for Exceptional Children.

Swan, W. W. (1980). The Handicapped Children's Early Education Program. *Exceptional Children, 47,* 12–16.

Terdal, L., Jackson, R. H., & Garner, A. M. (1976). Mother-child interactions: A comparison between normal and developmentally delayed groups. In E. J. Mash, L. A. Hamerlynck, & L. C. Handy (Eds.), *Behavior modification and families* (pp. 249–264). New York: Brunner/Mazel.

Tjossem, T. D. (Ed.). (1976). *Intervention strategies for high risk infants and young children.* Baltimore: University Park Press.

Chapter 5

Early Intervention for Children with Motor Handicaps

SUSAN R. HARRIS

Child Development and Mental Retardation Center
University of Washington
Seattle, Washington 98195

INTRODUCTION

The goal of this chapter is to present a summary of research findings examining the effectiveness of early intervention for children with motor handicaps. A motor handicap may result from specific damage to the central nervous system (CNS), as seen in cerebral palsy, or from a specific CNS malformation, such as myelomeningocele. Other causes include chromosomal disorders, such as Down syndrome, in which maldevelopment of the brain results in a combination of motor, cognitive, and language delays. The child with generalized developmental delay of unknown etiology also frequently exhibits a motor handicap manifested by delayed motor development, retention of primitive reflexes, and abnormalities in muscle tone.

The first section of this chapter will describe specific disabilities that are frequently accompanied by motor handicaps. It would be impossible to describe *every* disability that is accompanied by a motor handicap and is manifested during early childhood. Therefore, the author has chosen to highlight three major disabilities that are uniformly accompanied by motor handicaps: cerebral palsy, myelomeningocele, and Down syndrome. These disabilities are three of the most prevalent handicapping conditions affecting the motor development of young children. These are also the most common disabilities for which early intervention studies have been conducted in the recent research literature (particularly cerebral palsy and Down syndrome).

Readers may question the exclusion of Duchenne's muscular dystrophy as a disability that is fairly prevalent and is uniformly accompanied by a severe motor handicap, at least during the latter stages of the disease. The focus of this book is on early intervention, during infancy or preschool years, and thus it would not be relevant to include Duchenne's muscular dystrophy because intervention frequently does not begin until the child reaches school age and the motor symptoms are beginning to progress.

DESCRIPTION OF MAJOR DISABILITIES WITH MOTOR HANDICAPS

Cerebral Palsy

One of the most common causes of motor handicap in young children, cerebral palsy affects approximately 500,000 children in the United States (Batshaw, Perret, & Harryman, 1981) and occurs in about 2 of every 1,000 live births (Gordon, 1976). Cerebral palsy is a nonprogressive disorder of movement or posture that results from a lesion or maldevelopment in an immature brain (K. Bobath, 1966). The injury to the brain may be due either to extrinsic insult or to intrinsic developmental defect; it typically occurs during prenatal, perinatal, or early postnatal development (up to 3–5 years after birth) (Bennett, 1984). Delays in achieving age-appropriate motor milestones frequently result from the tone abnormalities as well as from retention of primitive reflexes and delayed development of postural reactions (K. Bobath & Bobath, 1972).

Types of Cerebral Palsy

Cerebral palsy is often described as a group of conditions that have in common the disorders of tone and movement. The different types of cerebral palsy are usually classified according to the nature of the tone abnormality and the distribution of that tone. The most common type of cerebral palsy, spastic cerebral palsy, accounts for between 40% (Courville, 1954) and 75% (Christensen & Melchior, 1967) of all reported cases. In a review of 142 cases of cerebral palsy, approximately 53% of the children had spastic cerebral palsy (Holm, 1982).

Spastic cerebral palsy is further classified by topographical distribution. Quadriplegia is defined as total body involvement with upper extremity involvement greater than or equal to lower extremity involvement. In spastic diplegia, the type of cerebral palsy most frequently associated with premature delivery, the lower extremities are more involved than the upper extremities. Hemiplegia denotes involvement of one side of the body (Harris, 1981a).

The second most common type of cerebral palsy is extrapyramidal (athetoid) cerebral palsy. Characterized by slow, involuntary, twisting movements of the extremities, hyperflexibility of the joints (Crill, 1976), and fluctuating muscle tone (K. Bobath & Bobath, 1972), athetosis usually involves the total body. Frequently rapid, involuntary, choreiform movements of the face and extremities may accompany athetosis (Courville, 1961; Ganong, 1977). It has been estimated that 50% of all individuals with cerebral palsy exhibit some type of athetotic or choreoathetotic movement, either in combination with spasticity (mixed cerebral palsy) or in isolation (Bakwin & Bakwin, 1951). In Holm's retrospective review, 10% of the cases were classified as athetoid cerebral palsy and an additional 18.3% were mixed cerebral palsy (Holm, 1982).

Two less common types of cerebral palsy are ataxia and rigidity. Although pure ataxic cerebral palsy is rare, ataxia may accompany spasticity, athetosis, or hypotonia (Carter & Gustafson, 1965). In rigidity, the clinical picture is similar to severe spasticity in that there is an excess of muscle cocontraction and a paucity of movement (Carter & Gustafson, 1965). Both ataxia and rigidity usually appear as quadriplegia.

The wide variety of types of cerebral palsy is an important consideration when evaluating early intervention research for children with cerebral palsy. Because of the extreme heterogeneity of symptomatology across the different types, it is difficult to create groups of children with similar involvement for conducting experimental group research (Martin & Epstein, 1976). This is an important variable to consider in evaluating the efficacy of early intervention for children with cerebral palsy.

Etiology of Cerebral Palsy

The causes of cerebral palsy are as complex and varied as the clinical types. In many cases, the etiology is unknown. It is estimated that 50% of cases result from brain damage acquired prenatally, 33% are due to perinatal factors, 10% are postnatally acquired during infancy or early childhood, and 7% are of mixed origin (Holm, 1982). Two common causes that frequently coexist are cerebral hemorrhage and cerebral hypoxia or asphyxia. Specific prenatal etiological factors include intrauterine hypoxia, intrauterine infection, toxemia, radiation exposure, and teratogenic drugs (Batshaw et al., 1981). Perinatal causes include asphyxia, prematurity with associated intraventricular hemorrhage, abruptio placentae, and mechanical birth injury (Abroms & Panagakos, 1980). Postnatally acquired cerebral palsy may result from meningitis, encephalitis, lead ingestion, or traumatic head injury (Hagberg, 1979).

Developmental Course of Cerebral Palsy in Early Childhood

Unlike myelomeningocele and Down syndrome, cerebral palsy is not always identifiable at birth and may not be diagnosed until as late as 2 years of age, particularly in mild cases. Early identification of cerebral palsy has gained increased attention since the 1960s, coincident with the advent of neonatal intensive care unit follow-up clinics. The goal of early identification is not only to establish a diagnosis but also to allow for the institution of early intervention efforts. The recent pediatric literature is replete with reports of longitudinal studies evaluating the predictive power of various high-risk infant evaluation protocols in identifying cerebral palsy (Drillien, 1972; Ellenberg & Nelson, 1981; Harris et al., 1984; Nelson & Ellenberg, 1979; Prechtl, 1972). A variety of assessment tools have been developed with this goal in mind (Capute, Accardo, Vining, Rubinstein, & Harryman, 1977; Chandler, Andrews, & Swanson, 1980; Milani-Comparetti & Gidoni, 1967).

Infants with severe forms of cerebral palsy are readily identifiable at birth or shortly thereafter because of obvious tone abnormalities and strong pathological patterns, such as opisthotonus. Frequently primitive reflexes are obligatory and interfere with normal movement patterns (K. Bobath & Bobath, 1975). Accompanying problems such as microcephaly, strabismus, and failure to thrive because of inadequate suck and swallow reflexes are frequently present.

In the infant with mild to moderate cerebral palsy, early diagnosis is more difficult due to symptomatology that may change as development progresses. According to the Bobaths (1975), infants with milder forms of spastic cerebral palsy may appear to have normal tone during the first few months of life. Hypertonus and increased tonic reflex activity begin to appear at about 4 months of age. Saint-Anne Dargassies (1977) also describes an initial "silent" or asymptomatic period, which may last for up to 8 to 10 months in some children who develop cerebral palsy.

Many infants with mild to moderate cerebral palsy go undiagnosed until they begin to show delays in some of the more important motor milestones such as sitting, creeping, and standing. With the advent of increasingly sophisticated neuromotor assessment tools, it is becoming possible to identify such infants before marked developmental motor delays are clearly apparent. In a high-risk infant follow-up study, 81% of children who went on to be diagnosed with cerebral palsy were retrospectively identified as abnormal or suspect at the 4-month evaluation based on scores on the Movement Assessment of Infants (Harris, et al., 1984).

Associated Handicaps

As the infant with cerebral palsy matures, other associated handicaps may become apparent. Intellectual delays (including mental retardation, borderline intelligence, or specific learning disabilities) are present in an estimated 60% (Batshaw et al., 1981) to 75% (McDonald & Chance, 1964) of children with cerebral palsy. Vision deficits are also common in cerebral palsy; these include strabismus, myopia, and homonymous hemianopsia (Gordon, 1976). More than 40% of children with cerebral palsy demonstrate some type of visual deficit (Black, 1980). Approximately 20% of children with cerebral palsy show hearing or language problems (Robinson, 1983). Seizure disorders are present in about one third of children (Jones, 1975). Other accompanying handicaps include feeding difficulties and orthopedic complications (Abroms & Panagakos, 1980). The presence of associated handicaps further confounds the difficulty of creating similar groups of children with cerebral palsy in conducting experimental group research.

Myelomeningocele

Myelomeningocele is a congenital defect of the central nervous system that results in a vareity of handicapping conditions including orthopedic deformities, sensory deficits, bowel and bladder problems, and learning difficulties ranging from severe mental retardation to visual–perceptual deficits. The degree of motor handicap associated with myelomeningocele is dependent, in part, upon the level of the spinal lesion. Except for children with very low sacral lesions, there is usually some degree of motor paralysis in the lower extremities ranging from loss of toe flexors to total paraplegia. Upper motor neuron signs are nearly always present also. These may include perceptual–motor deficits and fine motor coordination difficulties.

Myelomeningocele is readily apparent at birth and may also be detected prenatally, either through ultrasound scanning or amniocentesis to examine the level of alpha-fetoprotein (Gordon, 1976). Approximately 80% of infants display associated hydrocephalus secondary to the Arnold–Chiari malformation and aqueductal stenosis (Gordon, 1976). The first line of management for the neonate with myelomeningocele is to excise the sac surgically and close the lesion over the spine (Akins, Davidson, & Hopkins, 1980). If hydrocephalus appears, it is usually within the first 3 weeks of life. Immediate placement of a ventriculoperitoneal shunt is the preferred treatment for hydrocephalus (Akins et al., 1980). Recurrent shunt infection and obstruction are common early childhood problems that frequently persist throughout life.

Etiology of Myelomeningocele

Both genetic and environmental factors appear to play a role in the etiology of myelomeningocele (Thompson & Rudd, 1976). Resulting from failure of a portion of the neural tube to close posteriorly late in the first month of gestation, myelomeningocele occurs in 1 to 2 out of every 1,000 births in the United States (Janerich & Piper, 1978; Scarff & Fronczak, 1981). A much higher incidence is found in certain portions of Great Britain and a much lower incidence is reported in certain African countries (Haddow & Macri, 1979). There is a greatly increased risk of myelomeningocele when one or more older siblings have been born with a neural tube defect. For this reason, amniocentesis is offered for women who have previously given birth to an affected child.

The exact cause of myelomeningocele is unknown. It appears that certain environmental factors combine to act on a genetically predisposed embryo in a multifactorial mode. There is a slightly higher incidence of female infants born with myelomeningocele and there is a lower incidence among blacks (Scarff & Fronczak, 1981).

Developmental Course of Myelomeningocele in Early Childhood

Following the surgical closure of the open spine and implantation of the ventriculoperitoneal shunt during early infancy, other preventative and corrective measures must be taken in the management of other commonly associated problems. Careful urological management is extremely important because of the increased risk for urinary tract infections; 90% of children with myelomeningocele are incontinent because of lack of innervation to the bladder (Eckstein & MacNab, 1966).

The severity of associated orthopedic problems is largely dependent on the level of the spinal cord lesion. Foot deformities, such as talipes equinovarus, are common in infants with myelomeningocele and should be managed as early as possible with corrective splinting, bracing, and passive range of motion (Akins et al., 1980). Hip subluxation or dislocation is also frequently seen. In higher level sesions, spinal deformities such as kyphosis and scoliosis may develop as the child matures and often require later surgical management (Akins et al., 1980).

Delays in achieving developmental motor milestones are common during early childhood, due not only to the paralysis but also to delayed development of righting and equilibrium reactions (Wolf & McLaughlin, 1986). Early therapy should be aimed not only at minimizing contractures and deformities but also at facilitating the acquisition of age-appropriate postural reactions and motor milestones (Schafer & Dias, 1983). Early powered mobility has been recently recommended for very young children with myelomeningocele (Butler, Okamoto, & McKay, 1983).

Associated Handicaps

Loss of sensation below the level of the spinal lesion leads to a greater risk for burns and decubitus ulcers (Bleck, 1982). Bowel paralysis is also common in myelomeningocele; management includes a high-fiber diet and the use of rectal suppositories (Akins et al., 1980). Intellectual impairment is frequently seen in association with myelomeningocele, although a study of 100 school-aged children showed that 61 had IQs within the normal range (Hunt, 1981). Other frequent complications include visual deficits (particularly strabismus) and visual-perceptual disorders, seizure disorders, and obesity (Hunt, 1981). Because of the multiplicity of handicaps associated with myelomeningocele, its management involves an interdisciplinary team effort of medical, educational, and rehabilitation professionals.

Down Syndrome

Although the primary handicap usually associated with Down syndrome is mental retardation, it is important to recognize that infants and young children with Down syndrome frequently have delays in motor development as well as mental development (Harris, 1981c; LaVeck & LaVeck, 1977). Down syndrome is one of the most prevalent handicaps in early childhood, occurring in approximately 1.0 to 1.2 per 1,000 live births in the United States and Europe (Hook, 1981). It is the most common cause of moderate to severe mental retardation (N. M. Robinson & Robinson, 1976). Many of the early intervention studies that have been reported since the mid-1970s have included infants and young children with Down syndrome.

Etiology and Types of Down Syndrome

In the vast majority of cases of Down syndrome (approximately 93%), chromosome analysis reveals the presence of an extra small chromosome with the 21st pair (Kopp, 1983). Identified as trisomy-21, this abnormality occurs as a result of nondisjunction of two homologous chromosomes during either the first or second meiotic division (Novitski, 1977). A chromosomal abnormality known as translocation, in which there is a breakage of two nonhomologous chromosomes with subsequent reattachment of the broken pieces to other intact chromosome pairs, causes 3–4% of cases. Parents who are translocation carriers for this type of Down syndrome have a 2–10% risk that subsequent children will be similarly affected, a much higher recurrence risk than for the nondisjunction type (Novitski, 1977). The other 2–3% of cases of Down syndrome are mosaic disorders in which some of the cells of the individual are normal and some are trisomy-21.

Advanced maternal age has long been identified as a risk factor for giving birth to an infant with Down syndrome, with the risk increasing from 1 per 1,200 at age 25 to 1 per 100 at age 40 (Hook & Chambers, 1977). More recently, paternal origin of the extra chromosome has been suggested as a factor in 40–50% of trisomy-21 infants born to women under 30 (Holmes, 1978).

Developmental Course of Down Syndrome during Early Childhood

Clinical features that suggest the presence of Down syndrome at birth may include flat nasal bridge and facial profile, slanted palpebral fissures, abundant neck skin, malformed ears, and generalized hypotonia (Coleman, 1978). Hall (1964) has identified hypotonia as one of the most prevalent diagnostic signs; this is one of the factors contributing to the developmental motor delay typical of these infants.

Studies using standardized developmental tests, such as the Bayley Scales of Infant Development (Bayley, 1969), have shown a typical pattern of a decreasing *rate* of development during the early childhood years both in mental and in motor domains (Carr, 1970). Significant delays in the achievement of developmental milestones in cognitive, affective, language, and motor areas are characteristic of young children with Down syndrome, although wide variability exists in the degree of delay among different children.

Associated Handicaps

Associated handicaps are prevalent, the most serious of which are congenital heart defects such as atrioventricular canal defects and ventriculoseptal defects (Coleman, 1978). Visual impairments, such as strabismus, nystagmus, and cataracts, are also common (Jaeger, 1980). Binaural hearing loss and otitis media are typical audiologic problems found in this population (Balkany et al., 1979). Associated orthopedic handicaps include hip subluxation and dislocation, metatarsus primus varus, and pes planus (Diamond, Lynne, & Sigman, 1981). Potentially one of the most serious orthopedic problems is atlantoaxial dislocation, which in severe cases may result in spastic quadriplegia (Andrews, 1981). Many of these orthopedic problems result from the ligamentous laxity that is typical in Down syndrome.

Parent Concerns for the Young Child with Motor Handicap

It is clear from these brief descriptions of cerebral palsy, myelomeningocele, and Down syndrome that each of these disorders involves a multiplicity of associated handicaps in addition to the motor impairment. The parents of a young child with any of these handicapping conditions are faced with a complex set of medical, emotional, and financial problems.

The birth of a child with a congential handicap severely alters parental expectations of the hoped-for normal infant. Parents frequently progress through stages of grief parallel to those associated with the permanent loss of a loved one (Solnit & Stark, 1961). The realization that their child may never be able to live independently and will remain their responsibility throughout their own lives may result in feelings of "chronic sorrow" (Olshansky, 1962).

Professionals who work with families of young children with motor impairments and other associated handicaps must be fully cognizant of the emotional and financial burdens faced by these families when providing the necessary medical management. As Taft (1983) pointed out, in discussing early intervention for children with cerebral palsy, "The decision to support the use of early intervention for motor handicapped infants should not be solely based on its effect on motor performance. The nonmotor benefits of early intervention are considerable" (p. 221). Taft further suggested that the care of the child with a motor impairment should include "supportive counseling and educational programs for the parents as well as the more traditionally oriented 'medical' therapies" (p. 222). Such programs should include individual or group counseling; parental education on etiology, prognosis, and different therapeutic approaches for their child's disability; and an understanding of activities that are developmentally appropriate for their child rather than chronologically age-based (Taft, 1983).

Research on enhancing parent–child social interaction with children with physical handicaps further suggests that systematic parent instructional techniques can reduce stressful interactions between parents and their handicapped children (Kogan, 1980). Another positive approach to providing parental support is the recent development of "parent-to-parent" support groups in which parents of handicapped children are trained in active listening and other counseling skills and then are matched with parents of recently diagnosed children with similar handicaps. Parent-to-parent support groups are springing up across the United States frequently sponsored by local offices of the Association for Retarded Citizens (ARC) and other similar parent–professional organizations.

Relationship of Motor Development to Other Domains

The child with a motor handicap may also be compromised in other developmental domains. The ability to move freely and independently in one's environment enhances exploration and accompanied learning experiences. Piaget (1966) defined the first stage of cognitive development as the sensorimotor period, a time (during the first 2 years of life) when children learn through active exploration of themselves and their environment. It is hypothesized that the young child with a motor handicap will be hindered in this important period of exploration by virtue of his physical limitations. As the Bobaths (1972) stated in their description of the child with cerebral palsy: "A child, deprived by his motor handicap of touching and feeling his own body, of getting his hands or fingers to his mouth, of acquiring eye–hand coordination and the ability to grasp and manipulate objects, will not be able to develop a proper concept of his body, nor be able to explore his environment. His physical handicap alone may, therefore, result in a profound retardation of his mental and intellectual development" (p. 37).

Based on this suggested relationship between the motor impairment and other areas of development, it is theorized that amelioration of the motor handicap through early therapeutic intervention may also enhance gains in nonmotor domains of development. Consequently, several of the early intervention studies to be cited have looked at various nonmotor treatment outcomes in addition to evaluating specific motor performance changes (Carlsen, 1975; Harris, 1981a; Scherzer, Miké, & Ilson, 1976).

Summary

Young children with motor impairments frequently present with a variety of associated handicaps also. The three disabilities highlighted in this chapter—cerebral palsy, myelomeningocele, and Down syndrome—are three of the most prevalent disabilities of early childhood that are characterized by motor deficits, frequently in conjunction with deficits in learning, perception, and social–emotional development. Health professionals must be aware of the problems faced by the families of these children in seeking medical and educational intervention as well as the medical problems faced by the children themselves. The next section of this chapter will focus on early intervention strategies commonly used in dealing with children with motor handicaps.

EARLY INTERVENTION STRATEGIES FOR CHILDREN WITH MOTOR HANDICAPS

The purpose of this section is to describe specific modes of therapy which have been standard practice in the treatment of young children with motor handicaps. In addition to looking at typical forms of intervention, this section will also describe assessment procedures which have been used to evaluate the effects of treatment. Finally, some different models for service delivery will be presented, including the roles of parents and teachers in the various forms of service delivery.

Therapy Intervention Strategies

The pediatric physical or occupational therapist traditionally has been the primary service provider in dealing with motor handicaps in young children. The term *developmental therapist* has been used to describe the pediatric physical therapist (PT) or occupational therapist (OT) who specializes in the evaluation and management of children with developmental disabilities (Tyler & Chandler, 1978). Typically, the developmental therapist has acquired advanced knowledge or training in one or more theoretical approaches to providing therapy. The three approaches most commonly used in the United States in treatment of young children are the neurodevelopmental treatment approach (Bobath & Bobath, 1972), the sensorimotor approach (Rood, 1962; Stockmeyer, 1972), and proprioceptive neuromuscular facilitation (Knott & Voss, 1968). In addition, three other therapeutic approaches—passive range of motion, vestibular stimulation, and the Vojta approach—will be briefly described.

Neurodevelopmental Treatment Approach

Neurodevelopmental treatment (NDT) is probably the most widely used developmental therapy approach in the United States. Developed in England more than 30 years ago for treatment of children with cerebral palsy (B. Bobath, 1963, 1967), NDT has also been advocated for use with infants with Down syndrome (Harris, 1981a). Facilitation of normal postural tone is one of the goals of NDT (K. Bobath & Bobath, 1964). In the case of a child with spastic cerebral palsy, the aim is to reduce tone in an effort to achieve more normal movement patterns. In the hypotonic child, such as the child with ataxic cerebral palsy or the child with Down syndrome, the aim is to increase or build up postural tone.

Following the normalization of tone, a secondary goal is to facilitate automatic reactions such as righting, equilibrium, and protective extension responses (K. Bobath & Bobath, 1964). The Bobaths hypothesize that automatic reactions serve as a necessary base for the achievement of developmental motor milestones, such as sitting, creeping, and walking. Facilitation of automatic reactions also has been suggested in the treatment of severely retarded children (Ellis, 1967).

Because NDT involves careful handling of the child aimed at inhibiting abnormal tone and abnormal reflex patterns and subsequently facilitating normal movement patterns, it is imperative that the developmental therapist be skilled in these strategies. Teaching parents and other care providers to handle and position the child properly with these goals in mind is another important role of the developmental therapist in carrying out NDT. By allowing the child to experience normal movement with normalized tone as a basis for that movement, the Bobaths suggest that this type of sensory input will maximize the young child's ability to develop functional motor skills later on.

Early identification of cerebral palsy is crucial to the provision of early NDT therapy. If treatment can begin prior to the age of 1 year, when the normal infant would be acquiring automatic reactions and key motor milestones, it is presumed that treatment goals can be optimized (B. Bobath, 1967; Köng, 1966).

Sensorimotor Approach to Treatment

Initially described by Rood (1954, 1956, 1962), the sensorimotor approach to treatment also involves careful sensory input aimed at achieving normal patterns of movement (Stockmeyer, 1972). It is postulated that the additional sensory feedback that results from the child's active motor responses continues to reinforce the acquisition of normal movement patterns. As in NDT, treatment is aimed at following the normal developmental sequence.

Rood's theory describes the interaction of two systems: mobility and stability. Mobility is provided by phasic muscle groups whereas stability depends on the action of tonic muscle groups. The combination of mobility superimposed upon a stable postural background allows for progression through advanced stages of motor development.

The goal of the carefully tuned sensory input is to facilitate an active and automatic motor response on the part of the child. This is analogous to the goals of NDT, which also are aimed at facilitating a subconscious movement response in the child. Whereas the primary sensory input in NDT involves the careful handling of the child by the therapist or trained caregiver, a variety of different sensory stimulation techniques are advocated in the sensorimotor approach. These include stretch, vibration and tapping, joint compression, and cutaneous stimulation, such as brushing and icing (Stockmeyer, 1972).

Proprioceptive Neuromuscular Facilitation

A treatment approach that has been advocated for use with both children and adults with neuromotor handicaps, proprioceptive neuromuscular facilitation (PNF) utilizes spiral and diagonal components of movement rather than the traditional cardinal planes of motion used in passive range of motion (Knott & Voss, 1968). The goal is to facilitate movement patterns that will have more functional relevance for the individual rather than the more traditional approach of strengthening individual muscle groups. These movement patterns are developmentally sequenced, a concept somewhat analogous to the other two developmental approaches previously described. Another similarity is the use of sensory stimulation, such as proprioception, touch, stretch, and pressure, to promote movement. It is theorized that resistance throughout the spiral and diagonal patterns may be used to facilitate irradiation of impulses to other body parts associated with carrying out that particular movement.

Auditory stimulation is also used in PNF (Voss, 1972). The tone of the therapist's voice in giving movement commands is modulated with the goal of louder tones being used to facilitate movement and softer tones to facilitate stability. The interaction of mobility and stability components is similar to the concepts expressed by Rood (Stockmeyer, 1972). In actual practice within the United States, PNF is used much more with adult neurological populations than in the treatment of children with developmental disabilities.

Passive Range of Motion

One of the more traditional therapeutic exercise approaches in physical therapy is passive range of motion. Although seldom used in isolation when treating a child with motor impairment, passive range of motion may be used in conjunction with other forms of developmental therapy. The goals of providing passive range of motion exercises are to maintain joint range of motion and to prevent muscle contractures. Exercise is carried out passively by the therapist through the cardinal ranges of motion for the neck, trunk, and extremities. There is little or no active participation by the child.

Passive range of motion is probably most important for the child with myelomeningocele. Passive stretching and appropriate splinting are particularly important in early management of the infant with lower extremity flaccid paralysis (Akins et al., 1980). The use of passive stretch for the child with cerebral palsy is controversial, particularly in spastic cerebral palsy. Because spasticity is due, in part, to hyperactivity of the gamma motor neuron system (Bishop, 1977), passive stretch to spastic muscles (especially quick stretch) may serve to increase rather than decrease the hypertonus (K. Bobath & Bobath, 1972). Because the child with Down syndrome usually has excessive range of motion due to hypotonia and ligamentous laxity, passive range of motion is an inappropriate mode of therapeutic exercise for children with this type of disability.

Vestibular Stimulation

Stimulation of the vestibular system through activities such as rocking, swinging, and spinning is one aspect of a therapeutic approach known as sensory integration or sensory integrative therapy (Ayres, 1972b). Although Ayres's early research focused on the effects of sensory integration for children with learning disorders (1972a), more recently proponents of her approach have focused on examining the effects of vestibular stimulation on improving motor performance in young children with developmental disabilities (Chee, Kreutzberg, & Clark, 1978; Kantner, Clark, Allen, & Chase, 1976; MacLean & Baumeister, 1982; Sellick & Over, 1980). In clinical therapy practice, vestibular stimulation may take many forms, such as swinging in prone on an overhead net swing, forward acceleration down a ramp on a scooter board in prone, or spinning in a swing or on a scooter board. Clinical research, however, has focused primarily on the efficacy of one form of vestibular stimulation, spinning or rotation, in improving motor performance (Chee et al., 1978; Kantner et al., 1976; MacLean & Baumeister, 1982; Sellick & Over, 1980). Studies that have looked at the effects of a more generic program of sensory integrative therapy tend to use school-aged children rather than preschoolers or infants because of the hypothesized effects of this type of therapy on academic performance (Carte, Morrison, Sublett, Uemura, & Setrakian, 1984).

Vojta Approach to Treatment

The Vojta method of intervention for cerebral palsy is a prophylactic approach in which an early diagnosis is made according to a series of standardized postural reflexes and early treatment is initiated to "prevent" the development of cerebral palsy (Brandt et al., 1980). This treatment approach is popular in Europe but seldom used in the United States.

Vojta uses seven postural reflexes in the assessment of an infant's neuromotor development. By his definition, an infant is considered at risk for cerebral palsy is she shows deviations in six of the postural reactions or if she shows deviations in five reactions plus evidence of asymmetries or retained primitive reflexes (d'Avignon, Norén, & Arman, 1981). Treatment involves systematic exercises known as reflex creeping and reflex turning, which are carried out daily by the parents for a minimum period of 6 months following early identification of the abnormal postural reflexes at 4–6 months (Brandt et al., 1980).

Although Vojta does not purport to be able to prevent the development of complicated cerebral palsy (cerebral palsy combined with severe mental retardation or severe seizure disorder), he does claim that his approach will prevent the development of uncomplicated cerebral palsy if treatment is initiated before the age of 6 months (d'Avignon et al., 1981).

Assessment Procedures

In order to evaluate the efficacy of any treatment strategy for young children with motor handicaps, some type of assessment procedure must be conducted. In clinical practice and in the early intervention research literature, a variety of assessment approaches have been utilized. These have included standardized motor assessment tools, nonstandardized instruments, and behavioral observation measures (Harris & Tada, 1983).

Standardized Motor Assessment Tools

A standardized assessment tool is one for which normative data have been systematically collected on a broad, representative sample of children of varying ages, sexes, ethnic and sociocultural backgrounds. Standardized materials, equipment, and test administration procedures must be used.

Two standardized assessment tools that have been widely used with young handicapped children, both in research and in clinical practice, are the Bayley Scales of Infant Development (Bayley, 1969) and the Gesell Developmental Schedules (Knobloch, Stevens, & Malone, 1980). The Bayley Scales comprise two parts, the Mental Scale and the Motor Scale, whereas the Gesell provides for behavioral assessment in five areas: adaptive, gross motor, fine motor, language, and personal–social.

Another tool familiar to physicians is the Denver Developmental Screening Test (Frankenburg, Dodds, & Fandal, 1973). Unlike the Bayley and Gesell tests, the Denver is a screening test that samples a broad spectrum of behaviors in four areas: gross motor, fine motor–adaptive, language, and personal–social. A child who is identified as questionable or abnormal on the Denver test should then be referred for a more detailed assessment, such as the Bayley or Gesell tests.

Nonstandardized Instruments

There are a number of tools used in evaluating infants and young children with motor handicaps for which normative data are not available. These instruments tend to assess qualitative aspects of motor behavior such as muscle tone, primitive reflexes, and automatic reactions. Two examples are the Movement Assessment of Infants (Chandler et al., 1980) and the Primitive Reflex Profile (Capute et al., 1977). Although both of these tools were designed with the primary goal of early identification of cerebral palsy, they each have application for use in documenting qualitative motor changes in children with identified motor handicaps. The Movement Assessment of Infants has been used to document changes in motor development in infants with Down syndrome (Lydic, Short, & Nelson, 1983) and in infants with myelomeningocele (Wolf & McLaughlin, 1986).

Behavioral Observation Measures

A third means of assessing motor changes as a result of early intervention is the use of systematic behavioral observation. By evaluating the frequency or duration of certain motor behaviors prior to initiating treatment, the developmental therapist can establish specific objectives aimed at modifying those behaviors and can monitor the child's progress and subsequently alter the treatment plan if necessary. For example, a therapist may note that a child with cerebral palsy exhibits a pathological asymmetrical tonic reflex each time he looks to the left during feeding. The therapist would document the frequency of that behavior during mealtime (baseline) and then institute a specific treatment plan to minimize the occurrence of the interfering behavior. If the initial treatment plan is not successful in minimizing the behavior, an alternative treatment strategy should be attempted.

The use of behavioral observational measures is a key component of single-subject research design, a relatively new research strategy for examining the efficacy of treatment for children with motor handicaps (Martin & Epstein, 1976).

Developmental Therapy Service Delivery Models

There are two primary models for the delivery of developmental therapy services: the direct service model and the consultation model (Harris & Tada, 1983). The direct service model may occur as part of a global early intervention program or as an individualized direct therapy program in a child's home. The therapist serves as both the evaluator and interventionist in carrying out direct, hands-on treatment.

For the child who has multiple handicaps, such as the child with Down syndrome who typically shows a combination of cognitive, language, *and* motor delays, a center-based early intervention program may be more appropriate. In this instance, the PT or OT will be serving as one member on an intervention team that might also include a speech therapist and an early childhood special educator. For a child with cerebral palsy or myelomeningocele who has age-appropriate cognitive and language abilities, a specific developmental therapy program carried out in the home may be the most appropriate type of direct service.

In the consultation model, the developmental therapist's role is to provide indirect services such as periodic monitoring of the child's motor development and specific motor programming suggestions to other intervention staff. This type of model may be used for children with mild motor handicaps who have more severe deficits in other areas.

Parents, teachers, and other caregivers also play an important role in meeting the therapy needs of the child with a motor handicap in either service delivery model. Finnie (1975) has expressed the importance of training parents and other caregivers in the correct positioning and handling of the young child with cerebral palsy. It is the developmental therapist's role to train others in these management techniques (Harris & Tada, 1983).

A recent concept in the care of young handicapped children is the transdisciplinary approach to treatment (Haynes, 1976). In order to reduce the number of adult handlers of the young child, one professional member of the team is designated as the team facilitator. The team facilitator utilizes evaluation data collected by other team members in developing the intervention strategies for the child. The parent then serves as the primary caregiver in implementing these strategies, under the advice and direction of the team facilitator. This approach has been advocated for use with infants with cerebral palsy (Haynes, 1976) as well as for infants with Down syndrome (Harris, 1980).

Nontraditional Intervention Strategies: Patterning Therapy

One very controversial therapeutic approach for children with brain damage is patterning therapy or the Doman–Delacato approach to treatment. Based on the early work of Temple Fay, a neurosurgeon, patterning involves passive manipulation of the head and extremities through primitive movement patterns for the purpose of bring about "neurological organization" (Fay, 1948; Chapanis, 1981). In addition to the patterning, other treatment strategies include rebreathing techniques, restriction of fluid intake and diet, and visual, tactile, and sensory stimulation (Chapanis, 1981).

The proponents of patterning, Doman and Delacato, founded the Institutes for the Achievement of Human Potential in Philadelphia for evaluating children with severe brain damage and planning treatment programs. Parents are required to provide treatment during most of the child's waking hours every day of the year. Because a minimum of three people are required to carry out the patterning treatment, countless volunteers or family members are needed to assist in the program. Any failure to progress on the part of the child is usually blamed on parental inadequacy in providing the demanding day-to-day treatment regime.

There is no valid scientific basis for the concept of enhancing "neurological organization" through passive manipulation of the extremities and head (Zigler, 1981). Although there are many zealous and vocal proponents of the benefits of patterning therapy, its efficacy is not supported by clinical research. In a study conducted by investigators at Yale University, 45 seriously retarded youngsters were assigned to one of three treatment groups: a group that received a modified sensorimotor patterning treatment, a comparison group that received additional individualized attention from foster grandparents, and a no-treatment control group (Sparrow & Zigler, 1978). The authors used 22 different dependent measures to analyze possible treatment effects, including scores on the neurologic profile developed at the Institutes for the Achievement of Human Potential. No significant between-group differences were found for the two treatment groups following a 1-year intervention period, leading the authors to conclude: "No evidence was found that the treatment resulted in an improvement of the children's performance over what would be expected on the basis of attention (as assessed by the performance of the motivational group) and maturation" (Sparrow & Zigler, 1978, p. 148).

Physicians and other health professionals must be aware of the shortcomings of this approach—the lack of scientific support, the emotional and financial drain it creates on families, and the unrealistic promises it makes in offering parents hope of "neurological organization" for severely damaged brains. Two excellent resources that provide further information on this controversial therapeutic approach are those by Zigler (1981) and Chapanis (1981), included in the reference list at the end of this chapter.

REVIEW OF EARLY INTERVENTION RESEARCH FOR CHILDREN WITH MOTOR HANDICAPS

The following section will provide a brief summary of 13 early intervention studies published since 1973. Studies were selected that utilized samples of children with cerebral palsy, myelomeningocele, or Down syndrome. The intervention programs used in these reported studies were clinically based and represented standard therapeutic regimens aimed at improving some aspect of sensorimotor performance. Each study cited was included also because at least one of the outcome measures evaluated motor development or attainment of motor skills. Thus only studies were chosen in which *both* the independent and dependent variables were motor related.

Other selection criteria for the studies reviewed included the use of subject samples in which all of the children were less than 6 years of age when the studies began. One exception to this criterion was the Gluckman and Barling (1980) study of children with myelomeningocele, because this was the *only* experimental study reported in the literature using children in this population. However, 15 of the 36 children in this study were, in fact, preschoolers. Finally, only studies that used experimental or quasi-experimental designs were selected. Descriptive studies were omitted from this review.

Studies will be briefly described for each of the three disability areas. In addition, a study that examined the comparative effects of two different motor programs on a sample of children with mild motor handicaps will be discussed. A detailed description of each of the studies can be found in the tables.

Cerebral Palsy

There were eight studies selected that examined the effects of early intervention for young children with cerebral palsy (see Table 1). Six of the studies were prospective (Brandt, et al., 1980; Carlsen, 1975; Chee et al., 1978; Scherzer et al., 1976; Sellick & Over, 1980; Wright & Nicholson, 1973) and two were retrospective (Kanda, Yuge, Yamori, Suzuki, & Fusake, 1984; Soboloff, 1981). Each of the studies consisted of at least two groups of children whose performance was compared on a variety of outcome measures; either a control or a contrast group was include in each study.

Four of the studies employed a pre–post test design with random assignment to groups (Carlsen, 1975; Scherzer et al., 1976; Sellick & Over, 1980; Wright & Nicholson, 1973). Random assignment is the safest way to control for systematic bias in an experimental design by minimizing the effects of extraneous variables. Thus, the results of these four studies have greater internal validity than the other four studies, which did not employ random assignment (Brandt et al., 1980; Chee et al., 1978; Kanda et al., 1984; Soboloff, 1981).

Four of the studies reviewed demonstrated positive changes in favor of the experimental group. Scherzer and colleagues (1976) compared a neurophysiologic, developmental physical therapy program combined with home treatment (experimental group) to a treatment regime consisting of passive range of motion (contrast group) in a sample of infants with cerebral palsy. Children in the experimental group showed greater improvement in both motor status and social maturation. In a study examining the effects of semicircular canal stimulation in children with cerebral palsy, Chee and colleagues (1978) showed significant improvement on tests of gross motor skills and reflex integration for the group receiving the stimulation. In a retrospective study of 100 young children with cerebral palsy, Soboloff (1981) reported earlier achievement of mobility milestones for children who had received early intervention and greater acceptance and understanding by their families than a group of children who did not receive early intervention. Similarly, Kanda and colleagues (1984) found that children with spastic diplegia in an early treatment group (before 9 months of age) walked earlier and more steadily than children for whom treatment was initiated between 9 months and 3 years of age.

Three studies reported failed to detect significant differences between experimental and control groups. Wright and Nicholson (1973) examined the effects of physical therapy (NDT) on children with spastic cerebral palsy and found no significant differences between treated and untreated groups. Sellick and Over (1980) evaluated the effects of vestibular stimulation on motor and mental development in children with a variety of types of cerebral palsy using an experimental–control group design; no significant between-group differences were noted. Finally, Brandt and colleagues examined the incidence of cerebral palsy among infants who had received the Vojta method of treatment and infants who had not. Their results—an incidence of 27.3% in the first group vs. 33.3% in the second group—were not significantly different.

The last study reviewed involving children with cerebral palsy (Carlsen, 1975) compared two different treatment approaches, facilitation techniques versus functional skill training. Carlsen found significantly greater motor gains in children in the facilitation group.

There were a number of limitations across many of the studies cited. As mentioned previously, four of the studies failed to use random assignment. Most of the studies failed to employ blindness in the posttest assessments, thus introducing threats of examiner bias. Heterogeneity of the subject samples was a potential problem in all but one of the seven studies (Kanda et al., 1984) because a variety of different types of cerebral palsy were included (and a range of intellectual levels). None of the seven studies cited reported specific reliability data for their outcome measures, a problem discussed by Taft (1983).

Group size in at least one of the studies (Carlsen, 1975) was too small to examine statistically significant differences. Even in those studies where group size was large enough to show statistically significant between-group differences, it is possible that such differences would fail to be clinically significant.

In an attempt to counter many of the limitations just listed, single-subject experimental designs have been proposed as a more viable alternative to experimental–control group studies for evaluating treatment efficacy for children with cerebral palsy (Martin & Epstein, 1976). In assessing the value of early therapy for children with cerebral palsy, it is important also to examine the contributions made to family support and acceptance as well as any motor gains. As Wright and Nicholson (1973) have suggested, the role of the therapist in teaching the

TABLE 1

Summary of early intervention studies for children with cerebral palsy[a]

Reference	Nature of intervention	Intervention parameters	Setting	Role of parents
Brandt, Lonstrup, Marner, Rump, Selmar, & Schack, (1980)	The Vojta method of treatment, which recommends daily systematic exercises in prone including reflex creeping and reflex turning	One group of infants (N = 15) received Vojta treatment at home by a parent; second group (N = 19) apparently received an alternate form of treatment, most frequently NDT; infants were assessed every 3 months; treatment continued until infants were either neurologically asymptomatic or diagnosed as having CP	Home-based for Vojta group; not specified for "control" group	Intervention for infants in Vojta group was administered by a close relative; role of parents or relatives in "control" group was not specified
Carlsen (1975)	Two types of OT approaches were compared; children in facilitation group (N = 6) received a program emphasizing normalization of postural tone, sensory integration, and sensorimotor interaction with the environment; children in functional group (N = 6) received training in fine motor, adaptive, and self-care skills	Therapy sessions lasted 1 hr and took place twice weekly; duration of intervention was 6 weeks	Center-based program plus written home programs	Parents were primary treatment providers under supervision of OT; parents provided center-based and home-based treatment
Chee, Kreutzberg, & Clark (1978)	Children in the experimental group (T) received horizontal and vertical semicircular canal stimulation; children in Control Group 1 (CH) received the handling associated with the treatments; children in Control Group 2 (CNH) received no handling or any other type of intervention	There were 16 sessions of semicircular canal stimulation during a 4-week period for the T group; pretesting occurred 4 days prior to intervention and posttesting 4 days after; length of treatment sessions was not reported; the CH group received handling but no semicircular canal stimulation	Center-based (assumed based on type of intervention but not specifically reported)	Mothers, unaware of the group assignment, were interviewed at the end of the intervention period (as were the therapists)

Child characteristics	Experimental design	Outcome measures	Results
34 infants identified at motor risk at 4–6 months because of the presence of at least 4 abnormal reflexes (according to Vojta's standardized reflexes); Vojta group began treatment between 4 and 6½ months; "control" group began treatment between 4 and 7 months	Posttest only without random assignment; all infants reassessed every 3 months	Diagnosis of CP or "neurologically asymptomatic"	11 infants in Vojta group completed the study (3 had diagnoses of cerebral palsy, 8 were neurologically asymptomatic); 18 infants in "control" group completed the study (6 had diagnoses of CP, 12 developed normally)
12 children with CP (mild to moderate athetoids and spastics); age range, 1–5 years	Pre–post design with random assignment of matched pairs (matched according to mean developmental age on retests); pairs were cross-checked for type and degree of CP	Bayley Motor Scale, Denver Developmental Screening Test (all 4 areas)	Statistically significant gains ($p = .05$) in favor of facilitation group on Bayley Motor Scale and in Gross Motor subsection of Denver; higher achievements, although not statistically significant, for the other 3 Denver subtests for the facilitation group
23 preambulatory children with CP (of mixed types and severity); age range, 2–6 years; 12 children in the T group, 6 children in CH group, and 5 children in CNH group	Pre–post without random assignment; children were assigned to "equated groups" based on pretest scores on the motor skills test and reflex test	*Quantitative:* Scores on a motor skills test (gross motor skills) and a reflex test (17 elicited reflexes) *Qualitative:* Subjective evaluation by mothers and therapists on a variety of motor and social–emotional behaviors	Significant differences ($p < .01$) on motor skills posttest between T and CH groups and T and CNH groups; significant differences ($p < .001$) on reflex test posttesting between T and CH groups and T and CNH groups; no significant differences on either test between CH and CNH groups Some mothers reported some improvements in motor and social–emotional behavior for each of the children in the T group; some improvements were reported for 3 children in the CH group and 1 child in the CNH group

(continued)

TABLE 1 (*Continued*)

Reference	Nature of intervention	Intervention parameters	Setting	Role of parents
Kanda, Yuge, Yamori, Suzuki, & Fusake (1984)	The Vojta method of treatment applied either early (before 9 months of age) or late (between 9 months and 3 years of age) to children with spastic diplegia	There were 8 children in the early treatment group who received treatment for a 6-month period within 1 month following their first exam (before 9 months); there were 21 children in the late treatment group who received treatment for a 6-month period within 1 month following their first exam	Home-based	Parents provided treatment for all children in the study
Scherzer, Miké, & Ilson (1976)	Experimental group ($N = 14$) received a neurophysiologic PT approach representing a combination of Rood, PNF, and NDT; parents were also trained in home therapy; the contrast group ($N = 8$) received traditional passive range-of-motion exercises	Treatment took place twice weekly and continued until the child reached the age of 2; 11 children were treated for longer than 12 months; the length of each individual treatment session was not reported	Center-based with additional home program by parents for experimental group	Parents of experimental group children were trained to provide therapy at home in addition to center-based treatment; parents of children in contrast group were asked *not* to provide therapy at home
Sellick & Over (1980)	Experimental group ($N = 10$) received stimulation in a hand-operated rotating chair with child seated upright (2 spins) and in side-lying on either side (4 spins on left and 4 on right); children in control group ($N = 10$) were handled in the treatment room for the same length of time but no vestibular stimulation was provided; all children continued regular outside programs	There were two sessions of vestibular stimulation a day, twice weekly for 4 weeks (16 sessions)	Center-based	No parent involvement in intervention

parents how to handle the child with cerebral palsy skillfully is probably a major contribution of therapy.

Myelomeningocele

In spite of the fact that myelomeningocele is one of the more prevalent motor handicaps found during early childhood, there have been *no* studies reported in

Child characteristics	Experimental design	Outcome measures	Results
29 children with spastic diplegia: 8 children in early treatment group and 21 children in late treatment group; children were selected as "motor-risk" infants based on Vojta's assessment protocol of postural reflexes; complications found in both groups included abnormal computerized tomography findings, epilepsy, visual impairment, and DQ less than 75	Posttest only without random assignment	Age at time of starting to sit, crawl, and walk; percentage of children in each group who became ambulatory and who could walk steadily for more than 30 min	$\bar{X}$ age of sitting: early group, 19.8 months; late group, 15.2 months $\bar{X}$ age of crawling: Early group, 12.0 months; late group, 15.5 months $\bar{X}$ age of walking: early group, 22.4 months; late group, 30.8 months Percent walking steadily (30 min): early group, 62.5%; late group, 33.3%
22 infants with CP who ranged in age from 5 to 17 months when intervention began; types of CP included spastic hemiplegia, spastic quadriplegia, athetosis, and ataxia; degree of involvement ranged from mild to severe	Pre–post design with random assignment	Response categories labeled motor status, social maturation, and home management; these were derived from prepost data from the Gesell Developmental Schedules, the Vineland Social Maturity Scale, and a motor development evaluation form constructed for the study	Experimental group showed greater improvement (percentage of change) in all 3 categories; when controlling for age and mental development, there was a clear trend in favor of the experimental group; children with normal intelligence made strong gains regardless of treatment group
20 children with CP ranging in age from 8 to 56 months; types of CP included spastic hemiplegia and diplegia, ataxia, athetosis, and hypotonia	Pre–post with random assignment of matched pairs (matched for chronological age, psychomotor developmental score, mental developmental score, and diagnostic category)	Five indices (physical development, mental development, gross motor skills, fine motor skills, eye–hand coordination) derived from scores on the Bayley; Pre-, post-, and follow-up data (12 weeks later) were collected	No significant between-group differences on any of the 5 measures; however, significant improvement in mean performance over the 18 weeks was shown for all children in the study; these gains may have been due to maturation or to other aspects of the child's regular ongoing program

(continued)

the scientific literature that have attempted to evaluate the efficacy of *early* developmental therapy for children with this disorder. Although there are a number of articles that describe "early treatment," these generally refer to the surgical closure of the open spine and implantation of the shunt for controlling hydrocephalus.

Rosenbaum, Barnitt, and Brand (1975) presented a developmental program emphasizing the importance of early mobility and visual–motor training for

TABLE 1 (*Continued*)

Reference	Nature of intervention	Intervention parameters	Setting	Role of parents
Soboloff (1981)	Developmental therapy with parent training of appropriate exercises and positioning was provided to 50 children with CP from 1965 to 1978; data from these children were compared to data of 50 children (control group) who had attended the same center from 1952 to 1965 but had not received early intervention	Children in early intervention group began treatment at an average age of 19.2 months; they received 2 hr of direct therapy each week and additional treatment from their mothers; children in the earlier group (1952–1965) began receiving treatment at an average age of 5.6 years	Center-based program	Parents of children in early intervention group were trained in appropriate exercises and positioning by the developmental therapist
Wright & Nicholson (1973)	Intervention identified as NDT (Bobath method) although some aims of treatment presented were incongruent with stated goals of NDT; treatment was individualized and aimed at reducing spasm, encouraging assumption of near-normal postures, improving strength of weak and hypotonic muscle groups, and progressing through normal sequence of locomotion	Children in Group A (N = 7) received PT for 12 months; Group B children (N = 9) got no treatment for the first 6 months; Group C (N = 10) was a pure control group; frequency of treatment and length of treatment sessions was not reported	Center-based	No direct parent role

[a]NDT, neurodevelopmental treatment; OT, occupational therapy or therapist; PT, physical therapy; CP, cerebral palsy; PNF, proprioceptive

infants with myelomeningocele, but this is merely a descriptive study and thus not included in the tables. Gluckman and Barling (1980) conducted a controlled experimental study examining the efficacy of a remedial program on visual–motor perception in children with myelomeningocele (see Table 2). Although the mean age of the 36 children in the study was 6.9 years, there were 15 preschoolers in the sample. Because there were some young children in this study, it has been included in the tables. Significant improvements in visual–perceptual functioning were noted for the experimental group with no significant changes found in the attention-placebo and control groups.

Limitations in this study include the small group size ($n = 12$) and the heterogeneity of the sample (18 were independently mobile and 18 were in wheelchairs; 24 had shunts and 10 had ocular defects). No reliability data were reported for the dependent measures used not was it stated that the examiners were blind to the subjects' group assignment.

Child characteristics	Experimental design	Outcome measures	Results
)0 children with CP (spastic diplegia, hemiplegia, and quadriplegia; athetosis); $\bar{X}$ age of first attendance for EI group was 19.2 months; $\bar{X}$ age of first attendance for nonintervention group was 5.6 years	Retrospective study comparing data from 2 groups enrolled in a center during 2 different time periods, 1952–1965 and 1965–1978	Dependent measures included number of children who had received surgery, age of attainment of early motor milestones, ability to walk independently or with mechanical aids, family reaction to the child, and presence or absence of mainstreaming in the educational setting	More surgery performed and at earlier ages on children in EI group; earlier achievement of motor milestones and greater ability to ambulate with mechanical aids were also characteristic of EI group; greater parental acceptance found among EI group; no between group difference in mainstreaming
f 47 children in the study originally, only 26 completed the study; all had spastic CP with varying distributions (diplegia, hemiplegia, quadriplegia); 19 of original 47 were mentally retarded; 12 had epilepsy; all children were less than 6 years of age when the study began	Pre–post design with random assignment following division into groups stratified by developmental age (as measured by IQ, neurological, and physical assessments)	Function, as measured by achievement of developmental motor milestones; passive range of motion as measured by dorsiflexion of ankle and hip abduction; presence or absence of primary automatic reflexes (primitive reflexes)	No significant differences between treated and untreated groups (A and C) on any of the measure; no significant difference between first 6 months (no treatment) and latter 6 months (treatment) for Group B; overall progress made by children with all types of spasticity in function and disappearance of primitive reflexes, regardless of treatment group

euromuscular facilitation; EI, early intervention.

The absence of any controlled studies in the literature examining the efficacy of early intervention for young children with myelomeningocele is disheartening. Because of the many upper motor neuron problems associated with myelomeningocele, such as abnormalities in muscle tone and upper extremity coordination (Wolf & McLaughlin, 1986), developmental therapy approaches similar to those being used for children with cerebral palsy should be implemented and systematically evaluated. This is certainly a population for whom single-subject research designs would also be appropriate in examining the efficacy of clinical intervention strategies.

Down Syndrome

Three studies in the recent literature have examined the effects of early treatment on motor development in young children with Down syndrome (see Table

TABLE 2

Summary of early intervention study for children with myelomeningocele

Reference	Nature of intervention	Intervention parameters	Setting	Role of parents
Gluckman & Barling (1980)	Frostig Program for the Development of Visual Perception (Frostig & Horne, 1964), consisting of 5 sets of worksheets divided into a series of 3 books graded according to difficulty	Intervention lasted 6 months with children in experimental group ($N = 12$) receiving two 30-min sessions per week of an individualized remedial program; the attention-placebo group ($N = 12$) carried out activities such as puzzles, coloring, drawing, and cutting for a similar time period; the control group attended regular classes	School-based program	No parent involvement

3). These studies are included in this chapter because of their emphasis on providing improvements in the motor domain through the use of motor intervention strategies. Readers are referred to the chapter by Guralnick and Bricker (Chapter 4, this volume) for a discussion of studies aimed at making changes in cognitive development for children with Down syndrome. The study by Piper and Pless (1980), reviewed in their chapter, used developmental therapy as the intervention strategy but measured treatment outcome primarily in terms of mental development. Thus, although the independent variable was motor oriented, the major dependent variable assessed was a measure of mental development.

Two of the studies examing the effects of early therapy intervention on motor performance in children with Down syndrome were prospective (Harris, 1981a; MacLean & Baumeister, 1982). Harris's study, examining the effects of NDT on improving motor performance in infants with Down syndrome, included both experimental and control groups that had been randomly assigned. MacLean and Baumeister (1982) used a single-subject withdrawal (ABA) design to examine the effects of vestibular stimulation on motor development of four infants with developmental delay (two of whom had Down syndrome). In single-subject research such as this, each subject serves as his or her own control.

Connolly and Russell (1976) carried out a retrospective study in which they compared the motor performance of a group of 40 children with Down syndrome who had received early intervention to previously published data on a group of 71 children who had not received early intervention (Fishler, Share, & Koch, 1964). The lack of using a randomly assigned control group in this study limits the assurance that extraneous variables did not systematically bias the results.

Child characteristics	Experimental design	Outcome measures	Results
36 children with myelomeningocele, ranging from preschool through fifth grade; $\bar{X}$ age was 82.87 months; 18 children were ambulatory with crutches and/or braces; 18 were in wheelchairs; 10 had ocular defects; 24 had been shunted for hydrocephalus	Pre–post with random assignment to 1 of 3 groups: experimental, attention-placebo, and control	Frostig Developmental Test of Visual Perception, which includes 5 subtests: visual coordination, figure–ground perception, form constancy, perception of position in space, and spatial relations	Significant differences in favor of experimental group compared to control group and attention-placebo group on all 5 subtests and on global perceptual score at posttesting

Although all three of these studies showed trends in favor of early intervention, a number of limitations exist in each of them. The small group size ($n = 10$) in the Harris (1981a) study as well as the relatively brief duration of the intervention period (9 weeks) are limitations that are unfortunately typical in studies of children with developmental disabilities. The use of preset time periods in the three phases of the MacLean and Baumeister study (1 week–2 weeks–1 week) contradicts the more acceptable practice in single-subject research of making phase changes based on changes in levels or trends of the data (Wolery & Harris, 1982). As mentioned earlier, the lack of a randomly assigned control group in the Connolly and Russell study introduces a number of threats to the internal validity of this study, including history, maturation, and selection biases.

Strengths of two of these studies include the use of blindness and reliability testing in assessing the dependent measures (Harris, 1981a; MacLean & Baumeister, 1982). Another strength is the homogeneity of using only subjects with Down syndrome in the studies by Connolly and Russell (1976) and Harris (1981a). Because MacLean and Baumeister (1982) used a single-subject research design in which each subject served as his or her own control, the lack of homogeneity of their sample (two subjects with Down syndrome and two with severe developmental delay) is not considered to be an important limitation. Although the treatment strategies in each of these three studies was markedly different, they each lend preliminary support to the possibility of enhancing motor performance in children with Down syndrome through early intervention.

A fourth study, which utilized vestibular stimulation to effect motor performance and nystagmus response in infants with Down syndrome (Kantner, Clark,

TABLE 3

Summary of early intervention studies for children with Down syndrome[a]

Reference	Nature of intervention	Intervention parameters	Setting	Role of parents
Connolly & Russell (1976)	Interdisciplinary program with professionals teaching the child and demonstrating techniques to parents; developmentally oriented, individualized intervention focusing on gross motor activities and sensory stimulation (proprioceptive, tactile, auditory, and olfactory)	3-year program if enrolled early (birth to 3 years); first 10 weeks in spring and fall; 1-hr group sessions, 1-hr individualized treatment by professionals, and 1 hr in group counseling to discuss issues and problems; periodic follow-ups in winter and summer for evaluation and updating program	Center-based for demonstration with expected parent carry-over at home	Parents were primary interventionists following instruction from professionals; parents also received general counseling services
MacLean & Baumeister (1982)	Semicircular canal stimulation via rotation in a motor-driven chair in a semidarkened room; child positioned in a car seat and rotated for 10 consecutive 1-min periods; 2 rotations in upright sitting and 4 each with child positioned on right and left sides	10 sessions of 10-min semicircular canal stimulation over a 2-week period	Center-based	Parents were present during treatment to observe any emotional changes in the child
Harris (1981a)	NDT program aimed at increasing postural tone, facilitating righting, equilibrium, and protective reactions, and encouraging developmentally appropriate movement patterns and motor milestones	Infants aged 2.7–21.5 months at pretesting; intervention occurred 3 times per week for 40-min sessions over 9 weeks	Treatment was provided by physical therapists in the infants' homes; 1 infant's treatment was center-based	No specific parent training, although parent observation was allowed

[a]NDT, neurodevelopmental treatment; EI, early intervention.

Allen, & Chase, 1976), has not been included in the tables because of serious methodological problems. Although it was a prospective study with random assignment, there was only one child in the experimental group and two in the control group who were actually posttested. Thus, the attempt by the authors to look at changes in mean scores between these two extremely small "groups" must be questioned. With such small numbers, a single-subject research design would have been more appropriate.

Child characteristics	Experimental design	Outcome measures	Results
0 children with Down syndrome entolled between birth and 3 years of age; comparison group of 71 children with Down syndrome followed from infancy who did not receive early intervention (Fishler, Share, & Koch, 1964)	Retrospective comparisons with previously published data for a group of infants (N = 71) who did not receive early intervention	Age of achievement of gross motor milestones (Gesell Developmental Schedules)	Early intervention group achieved all gross motor milestones at an earlier age ($\bar{X}$) than comparison group; Infants in EI group who received intervention before 6 months of age achieved milestones earlier than those enrolled after 6 months
male infants with developmental delay; 2 subjects (42 months and 34 months old) were severely delayed with several congenital disorders including growth deficiency and visual deficits; 2 subjects (17 months and 30 months old) had Down syndrome and moderate delay; all had abnormal stereotyped body movements	Single-subject design (ABA) with observational data taken during base-line (1 week), treatment (2 weeks), and a follow-up period (1 week); additional follow-up data collected 4 weeks after treatment	Motor scale (sequential stages of motor development) and reflex inventory (Clark, Chee, Kantner, & Kreutzberg, 1980); parent questionnaires recording types and amounts of stereotyped behavior	3 of the 4 subjects (including the 2 with Down syndrome) showed improvement in motor performance at posttreatment and 1-month follow-up; 3 of 4 subjects showed increase in maturity of reflex behavior at posttreatment; the fourth subject (with Down syndrome) had a maximum score on this scale at all 3 testings; both Down-syndrome children showed decreases in stereotyped behavior, and the 17-month-old's changes were significant
) infants with Down syndrome, aged 2.7–21.5 months; experimental group (N = 10): $\bar{X}$ age = 10.91 months; control group (N = 10): $\bar{X}$ age = 9.45 months	Pre–post with random assignment; posttesters blinded to group assignment of each child	Bayley Scales of Infant Development (Mental and Motor Scales), Peabody Developmental Motor Scales (Folio & DuBose, 1974), individualized therapy objectives	No significant between group differences on Bayley or Peabody tests; significant (p = .05) difference in favor of experimental group on achievement of individualized therapy objectives

Additional Research

In a pre–post study (see Table 4) that examined the relative effects of two types of motor intervention programs for preschool children with mild to moderate motor delays (Jenkins, Fewell, & Harris, 1983), 44 preschool children, ages 3–5 years, were randomly assigned to two treatment groups. One group received individualized sensory integrative therapy (Ayres, 1972b) twice weekly for 25-min sessions. Children in the comparison group received gross motor program-

TABLE 4

Summary of early intervention studies for mild to moderately motor delayed children

Reference	Nature of intervention	Intervention parameters	Setting	Role of parents
Jenkins, Fewell, & Harris (1983)	Children in Group 1 received individualized sensory integrative therapy from an occupational therapist; vestibular and proprioceptive stimulation activities were provided using scooter boards, swings, and hammocks; children in Group 2 received a small-group developmental gross motor program including activities such as catching and throwing balls, hopping, and jumping	Duration of intervention period was 17 weeks; children in Group 1 received 1-to-1 sensory integrative therapy 2 times weekly in 25-min sessions; children in Group 2 received gross motor programming in groups of 3–4, 4 times weekly in 25-min sessions	Experimental preschool	No parent involvement other than signed consent for participation

ming four times weekly for 25-min sessions in small groups of 3–4 children. Although there were no significant between-group differences, motor gains were observed for both groups during the 17-week intervention period.

The results of this study suggest that *both* types of motor intervention programs may have some effect in facilitating motor gains, although the absence of an untreated control group limits the assurance with which this conclusion can be made.

Conducting well-controlled experimental research on children with motor impairments is extremely difficult. Each of the studies cited suffers from one or more methodological limitations. In an editorial examining the lack of submitted manuscripts attempting to assess systematically the value of treatment programs for handicapped children, Bax (1984) discussed the fact that many researchers and practitioners feel that the use of a control group is unethical and that this problem is a stumbling block for conducting research with handicapped children. Again, the use of single-subject research designs as proposed by Martin and Epstein (1976) would help to solve this problem because each child serves as his or her own control and thus receives the treatment for at least some period of time. Single-subject research for children with motor handicaps is beginning to become an accepted research practice and promises hope for the future in evaluating specific treatment strategies (Harris & Riffle, 1986; Laskas, Mullen, Nelson, & Willson-Broyles, 1985).

Child characteristics	Experimental design	Outcome measures	Results
44 subjects from 3–5 years of age $\bar{X}$ = 50.9 months); handicaps included behavior disorders, communication disorders, health impairments, and mild to moderate mental retardation; 4 subjects had Down syndrome	Pre–post with random assignment to one of 2 treatment groups; no untreated control group.	Scores on Peabody Developmental Motor Scales (Folio & DuBose, 1974) and on Assessment of Sensorimotor Integration in Preschool Children (DeGangi, 1979)	No significant between group differences on either pre–post measure; trends in favor of Peabody gains for the sensory integration group and in Assessment of Sensorimotor Integration in Preschool Children gains for children in motor programming group; pre–post gains on both measures for both groups

CONCLUSIONS

The foregoing studies represent the various types of clinically based intervention strategies commonly used for young children with motor handicaps. Of the eight studies reviewed in the area of cerebral palsy, five are supportive of the effects of early intervention on enhancing the children's motor progress and encouraging parental support and acceptance. The sole study reported on myelomeningocele, although not exclusively involving young children, lends some support for therapeutic remediation of visual–perceptual deficits. The three studies cited in the area of Down syndrome are supportive of early intervention for improving motor performance.

There are obvious strengths and weaknesses in each of the study designs, but the difficulties inherent in conducting experimental studies with young handicapped children are many (Simeonsson, Cooper, & Scheiner, 1982). The choice of appropriate and reliable dependent measures for evaluating the efficacy of treatment is a particularly difficult issue. Although positive changes in the child's motor handicap may be difficult to document or to measure objectively, the contributions made to the family's ease in handling and physically caring for the child may be one of the most important outcome measures—but one that is seldom evaluated.

Several of the studies reviewed suggest that the child's intellectual level is an important correlate of progress, regardless of the mode of intervention. Although this information should not be used to suggest that children with more severe levels of retardation should be excluded from early motor intervention programs, it is an important variable to consider in estimating the child's overall prognosis as a result of treatment.

Although supportive data on the efficacy of early intervention for children with motor handicaps are scarce, Lawrence Taft, a child neurologist who has published extensively on the importance of early intervention, provides this rationale:

> Clinical observation has shown me that intervention programs have the following benefits for motor-handicapped children and their families: (1) better parent–child relationships; (2) child more strongly motivated to try new motor tasks; (3) less parental "shopping"; (4) quicker and less painful adaptation by parents to child's handicaps; and (5) a happier child. Some people might consider these results insignificant for, say, a child who cannot walk independently. I disagree! Growing up without depression, well-motivated, and socially competent in spite of a serious handicap, meets my criteria for a positive outcome. (Taft, 1981, p. 74).

Taft's clinical observations suggest trends for future research on the efficacy of early intervention for children with motor handicaps. Whereas most previous studies have examined effects of treatment on improvement in various motor variables, future research should be directed at evaluating the effects of early intervention on such dependent variables as parental and child adaptation to the disability, parent–child interaction, and the child's degree of motivation and self-esteem. Such research is desperately needed to document the variety of positive effects that can be made through early intervention. Without early identification and referral by health practitioners, it is impossible for researchers to be able to document such changes. Together, through clinical practice and improved research strategies, we must strive to improve the quality of life for children with motor handicaps and their families.

REFERENCES

Abroms, I. F., & Panagakos, P. G. (1980). The child with significant developmental motor disability (cerebral palsy). In A. P. Scheiner & I. F. Abroms (Eds.), *The practical management of the developmentally disabled child* (pp. 145–166). St. Louis: Mosby.

Akins, C., Davidson, R., & Hopkins, T. (1980). The child with myelodysplasia. In A. P. Scheiner & I. F. Abroms (Eds.), *The practical management of the developmentally disabled child* (pp. 116–144). St. Louis: Mosby.

Andrews, L. G. (1981). Myelopathy due to atlanto-axial dislocation in a patient with Down's syndrome and rheumatoid arthritis. *Developmental Medicine and Child Neurology, 23,* 356–360.

Ayres, A. J. (1972a). Improving academic scores through sensory integration. *Journal of Learning Disabilities, 5,* 336–343.

Ayres, A. J. (1972b). *Sensory integration and learning disorders.* Los Angeles: Western Psychological Services.

Bakwin, R. M., & Bakwin, H. (1951). Cerebral palsy in children. *Journal of Pediatrics, 39,* 113–122.

Balkany, T. J., Downs, M. P., Balkany, D. J., Blager, D. B., Krajicek, M. J., & Fanning, P. L. (1979). Hearing problems in children with Down syndrome. *Down's Syndrome Papers and Abstracts for Professionals, 2,* 5.

Batshaw, M. L., Perret, Y. M., & Harryman, S. (1981). Cerebral palsy. In M. L. Batshaw & Y. M. Perret (Eds.), *Children with handicaps* (pp. 191–212). Baltimore: Brookes.

Bax, M. (1984). Criticism, contact, and control. *Developmental Medicine and Child Neurology, 26,* 423–424.

Bayley, N. (1969). *Bayley Scales of Infant Development.* New York: Psychological Corporation.

Bennett, F. C. (1984). Cerebral palsy: The why and how of early diagnosis. *Consultant, 24,* 151–173.

Bishop, B. (1977). Spasticity: Its physiology and management. Part I, Neurophysiology of spasticity: Classical concepts. *Physical Therapy, 57,* 371–377.

Black, P. D. (1980). Ocular defects in children with cerebral palsy. *British Medical Journal, 281,* 487–488.

Bleck, E. E. (1982). Myelomeningocele, meningocele, spina bifida. In E. E. Bleck & D. A. Nagel (Eds.), *Physically handicapped children: A medical atlas for teachers* (pp. 345–362). New York: Grune & Stratton.

Bobath, B. (1963). Treatment principles and planning in cerebral palsy. *Physiotherapy, 49,* 122–124.

Bobath, B. (1967). The very early treatment of cerebral palsy. *Developmental Medicine and Child Neurology, 9,* 373–390.

Bobath, K. (1966). *The motor deficit in patients with cerebral palsy* (Clinics in Developmental Medicine No. 23). London: Spastics International Medical Publications/Heinemann.

Bobath, K., & Bobath, B. (1964). The facilitation of normal postural reactions and movements in cerebral palsy. *Physiotherapy, 50,* 246–252.

Bobath, K., & Bobath, B. (1972). Cerebral palsy. In P. H. Pearson & C. E. Williams (Eds.), *Physical therapy services in the developmental disabilities* (pp. 28–185). Springfield, IL: Thomas.

Bobath, K., & Bobath, B. (1975). *Motor development in the different types of cerebral palsy.* London: Heinemann.

Brandt, S., Lonstrup, H. V., Marner, T., Rump, K. J., Selmar, P., & Schack, L. K. (1980). Prevention of cerebral palsy in motor-risk infants by treatment ad modum Vojta. *Acta Paediatrica Scandinavica, 69,* 283–286.

Butler, C., Okamoto, G. A., & McKay, T. M. (1983). Powered mobility for very young disabled children. *Developmental Medicine and Child Neurology, 25,* 472–474.

Capute, A. J., Accardo, P. J., Vining, E. P., Rubinstein, J. E., & Harryman, S. (1977). *Primitive reflex profile.* Baltimore: University Park Press.

Carlsen, P. N. (1975). Comparison of two occupational therapy approaches for treating the young cerebral palsied child. *American Journal of Occupational Therapy, 29,* 267–272.

Carr, J. (1970). Mental and motor development in young mongol children. *Journal of Mental Deficiency Research, 14,* 205–220.

Carte, E., Morrison, D., Sublett, J., Uemura, A., & Setrakian, W. (1984). Sensory integration therapy: A trial of a specific neurodevelopmental therapy for the remediation of learning disabilities. *Journal of Developmental and Behavioral Pediatrics, 5,* 189–194.

Carter, C. H., & Gustafson, S. R. (1965). *Drugs in neurospastic disorders.* Springfield, IL: Thomas.

Chapanis, N. P. (1981). The patterning method of therapy: A critique. In P. Black (Ed.), *Brain dysfunction in children: Etiology, diagnosis, and management* (pp. 265–280). New York: Raven Press.

Chandler, L. S., Andrews, M. S., & Swanson, M. W. (1980). *Movement assessment of infants: A manual.* Rolling Bay, WA: Authors.

Chee, F. K. W., Kreutzberg, J. R., & Clark, D. L. (1978). Semicircular canal stimulation in cerebral palsied children. *Physical Therapy, 58,* 1071–1075.

Christensen, E., & Melchior, J. (1967). *Cerebral palsy—A clinical and neuropathological study* (Clinics in Developmental Medicine No. 25). London: Spastics International Medical Publications/Heinemann.

Clark, D. L., Chee, F. K. W., Kantner, R. M., & Kreutzberg, J. R. (1980). *Evaluation of motor skills in preambulatory children.* Unpublished manuscript, Ohio State University.

Coleman, M. (1978). Down's syndrome. *Pediatric Annals, 7,* 90–103.

Connolly, B., & Russell, F. (1976). Interdisciplinary early intervention program. *Physical Therapy, 56,* 155–158.

Courville, C. B. (1954). *Cerebral palsy.* Los Angeles: San Lucas Press.

Courville, C. B. (1961). Clinical evaluation of brain damage in cases of cerebral palsy. *Archives of Pediatrics, 78,* 127–142.

Crill, W. E. (1976). The cerebellum. In H. D. Patton, J. W. Sundsten, W. E. Crill, & P. D. Swanson (Eds.), *Introduction to basic neurology* (pp. 289–300). Philadelphia: Saunders.

d'Avignon, M., Norén, L. Arman, R. (1981). Early physiotherapy ad modum Vojta or Bobath in infants with suspected neuromotor disturbance. *Neuropediatrics, 12,* 232–241.

DeGangi, G. A. (1979). *Assessment of sensorimotor integration in preschool children.* Baltimore: Johns Hopkins University Press.

Diamond, L. S., Lynne, D., & Sigman, B. (1981). Orthopedic disorders in patients with Down's syndrome. *Orthopedic Clinics of North America, 12,* 57–71.

Drillien, C. M. (1972). Abnormal neurologic signs in the first year of life in low birthweight infants: Possible prognostic significance. *Developmental Medicine and Child Neurology, 14,* 575–584.

Eckstein, H. B., & MacNab, J. N. (1966). Myelomeningocele and hydrocephalus: The impact of moderate treatment. *Lancet, 1*(2), 842–845.

Ellenberg, J., & Nelson, K. (1981). Early recognition of infants at risk for cerebral palsy. *Developmental Medicine and Child Neurology, 23,* 705–716.

Ellis, E. (1967). *Physical management of developmental disorders* (Clinics in Developmental Medicine No. 26). London: Spastics International Medical Publications/Heinemann.

Fay, T. (1948). Neurophysical aspects of therapy in cerebral palsy. *Archives of Physical Medicine, 29,* 327–334.

Finnie, N. R. (1975). *Handling the young cerebral palsied child at home* (2nd ed.). New York: Dutton.

Fishler, K., Share, J., & Koch, R. (1964). Adaptation of Gesell developmental scales for the development of children with Down's syndrome. *American Journal of Mental Deficiency, 68,* 642–646.

Folio, R., & DuBose, R. F. (1974). *Peabody developmental motor scales* (IMRID Behavioral Science Monograph No. 25). Nashville: George Peabody College.

Frankenburg, W., Dodds, J. B., & Fandal, A. W. (1973). *Denver developmental screening test—Manual/workbook for nursing and paramedical personnel.* Denver: LADOCA Project and Publishing Foundation.

Frostig, M., & Horne, D. (1964). *The Frostig program for development of visual perception: Teacher's guide.* Chicago: Follett.

Ganong, W. F. (1977). *The nervous system.* Los Altos, CA: Lange Medical Publications.

Gluckman, S., & Barling, J. (1980). Effects of a remedial program on visual-motor perception in spina bifida children. *Journal of Genetic Psychology, 136,* 195–202.

Gordon, N. (1976). *Paediatric neurology for the clinician* (Clinics in Developmental Medicine Nos. 59/60). London: Spastics International Medical Publications/Heinemann.

Haddow, J. E., & Macri, J. N. (1979). Prenatal screening for neural tube defects. *Journal of the American Medical Association, 242,* 515–516.

Hagberg, B. (1979). Epidemiological and preventative aspects of cerebral palsy and severe mental retardation in Sweden. *European Journal of Pediatrics, 130,* 71–78.

Hall, B. (1964). Mongolism in newborns: A clinical and cytogenetic study. *Acta Paediatrica Scandinavica* (Suppl. 154), 1–95.

Harris, S. R. (1980). Transdisciplinary therapy model for the infant with Down's syndrome. *Physical Therapy, 60,* 420–423.

Harris, S. R. (1981a). Effects of neurodevelopmental therapy on improving motor performance in Down's syndrome infants. *Developmental Medicine and Child Neurology, 23,* 477–483.

Harris, S. R. (1981b). Neuropathology in cerebral palsy. *Physical and Occupational Therapy in Pediatrics, 1,* 45–52.

Harris, S. R. (1981c). Relationship of mental and motor development in Down's syndrome infants. *Physical and Occupational Therapy in Pediatrics, 1,* 13–18.

Harris, S. R., & Riffle, K. (1986). *Effects of ankle-foot orthoses on standing balance in a child with cerebral palsy. Physical Therapy, 66,* 663–667.

Harris, S. R., Swanson, M. W., Andrews, M. A., Sells, C. J., Robinson, N. M., Bennett, F. C., & Chandler, L. S. (1984). Predictive validity of the Movement Assessment of Infants. *Journal of Developmental and Behavioral Pediatrics, 5,* 336–342.

Harris, S. R., & Tada, W. L. (1983). Providing developmental therapy services. In S. G. Garwood & R. F. Fewell (Eds.), *Educating handicapped infants* (pp. 343–368). Rockville, MD: Aspen Systems Corporation.

Haynes, U. E. (1976). The national collaborative infant project. In T. D. Tjossem (Ed.), *Intervention strategies for high-risk infants and young children* (pp. 509–534). Baltimore: University Park Press.

Holm, V. A. (1982). The causes of cerebral palsy: A contemporary perspective. *Journal of American Medical Association, 247,* 1473–1477.

Holmes, L. B. (1978). Genetic counseling for the older pregnant woman: New data and suggestions. *New England Journal of Medicine, 298,* 1419–1421.

Hook, E. B. (1981). Down syndrome: Its frequency in human populations and some factors pertinent to variation in rates. In F. F. de la Cruz & P. S. Gerald (Eds.), *Trisomy 21 (Down syndrome): Research perspectives* (pp. 3–67). Baltimore: University Park Press.

Hook, E. B., & Chambers, G. M. (1977). Estimated rates of Down syndrome in live births by one year maternal age intervals for mothers aged 20–49 in a New York State study. *Birth Defects, 13,* 123–141.

Hunt, G. M. (1981). Spina bifida: Implications for 100 children at school. *Developmental Medicine and Child Neurology, 23,* 160–172.

Jaeger, E. A. (1980). Ocular findings in Down syndrome. *Trans American Ophthalmologic Society, 78,* 808–845.

Janerich, D. T., & Piper, J. (1978). Shifting genetic patterns in anencephaly and spina bifida. *Journal of Medical Genetics, 15,* 101–105.

Jenkins, J. R., Fewell, R. R., & Harris, S. R. (1983). Comparison of sensory integrative therapy and motor programming. *American Journal of Mental Deficiency, 88,* 221–224.

Jones, M. H. (1975). Differential diagnosis and natural history of the cerebral palsied child. In R. L. Samilson (Ed.), *Orthopedic aspects of cerebral palsy* (pp. 5–25). Philadelphia: Lipincott.

Kanda, T., Yuge, M., Yamori, Y., Suzuki, J., & Fusake, H. (1984). Early physiotherapy in the treatment of spastic diplegia. *Developmental Medicine and Child Neurology, 26,* 438–444.

Kantner, R. M., Clark, D. L., Allen, L. C., & Chase, M. F. (1976). Effects of vestibular stimulation on nystagmus response and motor performance in the developmentally delayed infant. *Physical Therapy, 56,* 414–421.

Knobloch, H., Stevens, F., & Malone, A. F. (1980). *Manual of developmental diagnosis: The administration and interpretation of the revised Gesell and Amatruda developmental and neurologic examination.* Hagerstown, MD: Harper & Row.

Knott, M., & Voss, D. E. (1968). *Proprioceptive neuromuscular facilitation: Patterns and techniques* (2nd ed.). New York: Harper & Row.

Kogan, K. L. (1980). Interaction systems between preschool handicapped or developmentally delayed children and their parents. In T. M. Field, S. Goldberg, D. Stern, & A. M. Sostek (Eds.), *High-risk infants and children: Adult and peer interactions* (pp. 227–247). New York: Academic Press.

Köng, E. (1966). Very early treatment of cerebral palsy. *Developmental Medicine and Child Neurology, 8,* 198–202.

Kopp, C. B. (1983). Risk factors in development. In M. M. Haith & J. J. Campos (Eds.), *Handbook of child psychology: Volume 2. Infancy and developmental psychobiology* (p. 1090). New York: Wiley.

Laskas, C. A., Mullen, S. L., Nelson, D. L., & Willson-Broyles, M. (1985). Enhancement of two motor functions of the lower extremity in a child with spastic quadriplegia. *Physical Therapy, 65,* 11–16.

LaVeck, B., & LaVeck, G. D. (1977). Sex differences in development among young children with Down's syndrome. *Journal of Pediatrics, 90,* 767–769.

Lydic, J. S., Short, M. A., & Nelson, D. L. (1983). Comparison of two scales for assessing motor development in infants with Down's syndrome. *The Occupational Therapy Journal of Research, 3,* 213–221.

MacLean, W. E., & Baumeister, A. A. (1982). Effects of vestibular stimulation on motor development and stereotyped behavior of developmentally delayed children. *Journal of Abnormal Child Psychology, 10,* 229–245.

Martin, J. E., & Epstein, L.H. (1976). Evaluating treatment effectiveness in cerebral palsy: Single-subject designs. *Physical Therapy, 53,* 285–294.

McDonald, E. T., & Chance, B. (1964). *Cerebral palsy.* Englewood Cliffs, NJ: Prentice-Hall.

Milani-Comparetti, A., & Gidoni, E. A. (1967). Routine developmental examination in normal and retarded children. *Developmental Medicine and Child Neurology, 9,* 631–638.

Nelson, K., & Ellenberg, J. (1979). Neonatal signs as predictors of cerebral palsy. *Pediatrics, 64,* 225–232.

Novitski, E. (1977). *Human genetics.* New York: Macmillan.

Olshansky, S. (1962). Chronic sorrow: A response to having a mentally defective child. *Social Casework, 43,* 190–194.

Piaget, J. (1966). *The origins of intelligence in children.* New York: International Universities Press.

Piper, M. C., & Pless, I. B. (1980). Early intervention for infants with Down syndrome: A controlled trial. *Pediatrics, 65,* 463–468.

Prechtl, H. F. R. (1972). Strategy and validity of early detection of early detection of neurological dysfunction. In C. P. Douglas & K. S. Holt (Eds.), *Mental retardation: Prenatal diagnosis and infant assessment* (pp. 41–46). London: Butterworth.

Robinson, R. O. (1983). The frequency of other handicaps in children with cerebral palsy. *Developmental Medicine and Child Neurology, 15,* 305–312.

Robinson, N. M., & Robinson, H. B. (1976). *The mentally retarded child: A psychological approach.* New York: McGraw-Hill.

Rood, M. S. (1954). Neurophysiological reactions as a basis for physical therapy. *Physical Therapy Review, 34,* 444–449.

Rood, M. S. (1956). Neurophysiological mechanisms utilized in the treatment of neuromuscular dysfunction. *American Journal of Occupational Therapy, 10,* 220–225.

Rood, M. S. (1962). The use of sensory receptors to activate, facilitate, and inhibit motor response, automatic and somatic in developmental sequence. In C. Sattely (Ed.), *Approaches to treatment of patients with neuromuscular dysfunction* (Study Course VI, Third International Congress, World Federation of Occupational Therapists, pp. 26–37). Dubuque, IA: Brown.

Rosenbaum, P., Barnitt, R., & Brand, H. L. (1975). A developmental intervention programme designed to overcome the effects of impaired movement in spina bifida infants. In K. Holt (Ed.), *Movement and child development* (Clinics in Developmental Medicine No. 55, pp. 145–156). London: Spastics International Medical Publications/Heinemann.

Saint-Anne Dargassies, S. (1977). Long-term neurological follow-up study of 286 truly premature infants. I: Neurological sequelae. *Developmental Medicine and Child Neurology, 19,* 462–478.

Scarff, T. B., & Fronczak, S. (1981). Myelomeningocele: A review and update. *Rehabilitation Literature, 42,* 143–146.

Schafer, M. F., & Dias, L. S. (1983). Physical therapy intervention. In M. F. Schafer & L. S. Dias (Eds.), *Myelomeningocele: Orthopedic treatment.* Williams & Wilkins.

Scherzer, A. L., Miké, V., & Ilson, M. A. (1976). Physical therapy as a determinant of change in the cerebral palsied infant. *Pediatrics, 58,* 47–52.

Sellick, K. J., & Over, R. (1980). Effects of vestibular stimulation on motor development of cerebral palsied children. *Developmental Medicine and Child Neurology, 22,* 476–483.

Simeonsson, R. J., Cooper, D. H., & Scheiner, A. P. (1982). A review and analysis of the effectiveness of early intervention programs. *Pediatrics, 69,* 635–641.

Soboloff, H. R. (1981). Early intervention—fact or fiction? *Developmental Medicine and Child Neurology, 23,* 261–266.

Solnit, A. J., & Stark, M. H. (1961). Mourning and the birth of a defective child. *Psychoanalytic Study of the Child, 16,* 523–537.

Sparrow, S., & Zigler, E. (1978). Evaluation of a patterning treatment for retarded children. *Pediatrics, 62,* 137–150.

Stockmeyer, S. A. (1972). A sensorimotor approach to treatment. In P. H. Pearson & C. E. Williams (Eds.), *Physical therapy services in the developmental disabilities* (pp. 186–222). Springfield, IL: Thomas.

Taft, L. A. (1981). Intervention programs for infants with cerebral palsy. In C. E. Brown (Ed.), *Infants at risk: Assessment and intervention* (pp. 73–82). Boston: Johnson & Johnson Baby Products.

Taft, L. A. (1983). Critique of early intervention for cerebral palsy. In T. B. Brazelton & B. M. Lester (Eds.), *New approaches to developmental screening of infants* (pp. 219–228). New York: Elsevier.

Thompson, M. W., & Rudd, N. L. (1976). The genetics and treatment of spinal dysraphism. In T. P. Morley (Ed.), *Current controversies in neurosurgery* (pp. 126–146). Philadelphia: Saunders.

Tyler, N. B., & Chandler, L. S. (1978). The developmental therapists: The occupational therapist and physical therapist. In K. E. Allen, V. A. Holm, & R. L. Schiefelbusch (Eds.), *Early intervention—A team approach* (pp. 169–197). Baltimore: University Park Press.

Vojta, V. (1973). Frühbehandlung der CP—Risikokinder. Analyse der Endresultate. *Monatsschrift Kinderheilkd, 121,* 271–273.

Voss, D. E. (1972). Proprioceptive neuromuscular facilitation: The PNF method. In P. H. Pearson & C. E. Williams (Eds.), *Physical therapy services in the developmental disabilities* (pp. 223–282). Springfield, IL: Thomas.

Wolery, M., & Harris, S. R. (1982). Interpreting results of single subject research designs. *Physical Therapy, 62,* 445–452.

Wolf, L. S., & McLaughlin, J. F. (1986). *Early motor development in children with myelomeningo-cele.* Manuscript submitted for publication to *Developmental Medicine and Child Neurology.*

Wright, R., & Nicholson, J. (1973). Physiotherapy for the spastic child: An evaluation. *Developmental Medicine and Child Neurology, 15,* 146–163.

Zigler, E. (1981). A plea to end the use of the patterning treatment for retarded children. *American Journal of Orthopsychiatry, 51,* 388–390.

Chapter 6

Effectiveness of Early Intervention for Children with Language and Communication Disorders

LEE SNYDER-MCLEAN
JAMES E. MCLEAN

Parsons Research Center
Bureau of Child Research
University of Kansas
Parsons, Kansas 67357

INTRODUCTION

The young child's early years are replete with critical milestones and achievements, but perhaps the single most celebrated event in the child's first 2 years is the production of baby's first word—a mandatory entry in any baby book! The child's progress in mastering the complexities of our spoken language system is monitored by parents and professionals alike as an index to the child's overall cognitive and social maturation. However, the system is a complex and demanding one, vulnerable to many types of disorder. Thus, it is not surprising that a large proportion of the preschool-aged children referred to early intervention programs are referred on the basis of family or physician concern regarding the child's speech or language development. In fact, the U.S. Department of Education reported that children with speech/language impairments represented 71% of the total number of 3–5-year-old handicapped children who received special education services in the 1982–1983 school year (Karr & Punch, 1984).

213

THE EFFECTIVENESS OF EARLY INTERVENTION
FOR AT-RISK AND HANDICAPPED CHILDREN

DISORDERS OF COMMUNICATION IN PRESCHOOL-
AGED CHILDREN

Speech Disorders versus Language Disorders

Any meaningful treatment of the topic of early intervention for children with communication disorders must begin with some clarification and delineation of the different types of specific disability subsumed within this general rubric. Traditionally, communication disorders are described in three broad categories: hearing disorders, speech disorders, and language disorders. Because hearing disorders, and the disorders of speech and language associated with hearing impairment, are the specific focus of Kathryn Meadow-Orlans's chapter (Chapter 9 in this volume), this chapter will concentrate on disorders of speech and language.

Speech Disorders

Speech disorders encompass those disorders affecting the actual mechanics of speech production. The production of speech sounds requires the control and coordination of two basic processes: *phonation,* the volitional movement of air from the lungs through the larynx and into the oral cavity; and *articulation,* the formation of specific, discrete speech sounds or phones through manipulation of this moving air. More specifically, phonation requires adequate breath control, an intact respiratory tract, and control of the laryngeal folds. The interaction of these elements produces the voice qualities of pitch, intensity, resonance, and smoothness that are characteristic of normal speech. Similarly, coordinated control of the movable articulators—the lips and tongue—is necessary to create the distinctive features that are characteristic of each of the 36 different sound families, or phonemes, used in speaking English. Speech disorders are traditionally divided into three classes, reflecting different aspects of this overall production process: *articulation disorders* (e.g., substitution of /th/ for /s/), *fluency disorders* (e.g., repetition of sounds or syllables), and *voice disorders* (e.g., inappropriate high pitch, breathiness). Each of these major types of speech disorder will be discussed in more detail later in this chapter.

Language Disorders

Language is most broadly defined as a rule-governed system of arbitrary symbols used to convey meaning within a particular culture. Language disorders, then, are those that affect the child's ability to encode or decode meaning in ways that are consistent with the rules of that child's linguistic community. The language system is actually composed of several major subsystems, each with its own set of culture-specific rules. These subsystems are: *pragmatics,* rules governing the appropriate forms and functions of communication in interpersonal contexts; *semantics,* rules governing the relationship of specific symbols to specific meanings; and *syntactics,* rules governing the arrangement of specific words and parts of words in different linguistic contexts. It should be noted that a fourth component of the overall language system is its *phonology.* However, in this chapter phonological disorders will be discussed in the context of articulation/speech disorders.

Until very recently, the diagnosis and treatment of language disorders focused exclusively on the phonological and syntactic aspects of a child's language system. Increasingly, however, therapy is being expanded to include consideration of the pragmatic and semantic components of disordered language, particularly in children with more pervasive handicaps. This chapter will address three major types of language disorder: specific language disorders or disabilities, language delays, and communication deficits associated with pervasive handicapping conditions.

Disorders of Speech: Prevalence, Subclassifications, and Associated Etiologies

Articulation Disorders

According to the American Speech-Language-Hearing Association (Fein, 1983), disorders of speech and language affect approximately 4.2% of the general population, with higher incidence rates among very young children. This estimate is based on statistics from the National Health Interview Survey and on actual prevalence figures from direct evaluation of school-aged child population samples. The most common types of speech/language disorder reported by the National Advisory Neurological Diseases and Stroke Council (Perkins, 1971) were articulatory disorders, representing 64% of the total disordered population. Although separate incidence figures for articulation disorders among preschool-aged children are not available, it is safe to conclude that they represent a significant portion of the communication disorders found among this age group.

Disorders of articulation are commonly differentiated as being either *organic* or *functional* in etiology. Examples of organic causes of articulation disorders observed in young children include oral–facial clefts, abnormal tongue size (often associated with Down syndrome), and *dysarthria* (a lack of control over the motor articulatory mechanism due to specific neurological damage, often associated with various forms of cerebral palsy). By far, however, the great majority of articulation disorders seen in children are classified as functional— that is, not organic in origin and apparently the result of learning and habituating incorrect articulatory patterns or of more general developmental delay and immaturity.

Beyond the distinction between organic and functional disorders, articulation disorders are generally also described in terms of degree of severity, although no standardized severity rating system exists. These disorders occur along a continuum ranging from very mild (e.g., the child who substitutes a /w/ for an /l/ or an /f/ for a /th/ sound, errors which still allow most of the child's speech to be understood) to severe. Severe articulation disorders affect a large number of phonemes and typically involve highly deviant production of the phoneme system required by a language system. In this disorder, children may substitute one sound for another, distort sounds, or omit required sounds, rendering the child's speech wholly or partially unintelligible.

Because the development of a full and correct phonological system requires a considerable length of time, all young children learning to talk manifest a deviant phonological system during the developmental period. Children acquiring speech generally simplify the phonological system of their language in rather systematic and predictable ways. The product of these simplifying "phonological processes" (Ingram, 1976) is the type of speech generally referred to as baby talk. In some cases, however, the simplification processes children use may deviate from the more-or-less standard ones, and such deviance signals a potential for problems continuing beyond the developmental period. Other young children may initially exhibit rather standard simplification patterns but, for many reasons, may fail to develop the subsequent more correct patterns. In these cases, the problems are most often relatively mild, but there are children with no identifiable organic involvement who manifest highly aberrant phonological systems that severely reduce the intelligibility of their speech. The consequences of such a disorder are not to be taken lightly.

The classification *apraxia* or *developmental verbal apraxia* (Aram, 1984) has been applied to those children who demonstrate severe and persistent articulatory disorders, usually accompanied by language/syntactic disorders, that are particularly resistant to therapy. Associated with this classification is the presumption of a specific neurological base for the disorder, similar to the lesions associated with dysarthria. However, even those who use this classification point out that there is no empirical support for considering apraxia a discrete medical entity (Aram, 1984; Perkins, 1984). Further, and critically, there is as yet no consensus among practitioners or researchers as to the exact definition or criterion for applying this classification. Perhaps Aram's recent suggestion (1984) that developmental apraxia be viewed as a syndrome (i.e., a cluster of symptoms that, when present in a constellation, characterize a particular clinical population) will ultimately result in more widespread use of this classification.

Fluency Disorders

It is estimated that fluency disorders represent about 11% of all speech/language disorders, affect slightly less than 1% of the general population, and are about three times more prevalent in boys than girls (Curlee, 1984; Perkins, 1971).

Because of continuing controversy regarding the identification of this type of disorder in early childhood (to be discussed further), it is difficult to obtain specific incidence figures for the preschool-age population. However, it seems reasonable to assume that the 1% figure represents at least a conservative estimate of the prevalence of fluency disorders in preschool-aged children, for whom incidence reports are generally higher than for older age groups (Curlee, 1984).

Generally, three types of fluency disorder are recognized by speech pathologists: *cluttering, neurological disorders,* and *stuttering.* Cluttering, as defined by Weiss in 1964, is a manifestation of a central language imbalance and differs from stuttering in that the speaker is unaware of the disorder. Further, cluttering is associated with such traits as excessive speed, hyperactivity, linguistic and articulatory disorders, and a high rate of dysfluency. This diagnostic category has not been widely used in this country, and there has been little systematic study of it as a clinical phenomenon or of effective treatment procedures that might differ from those prescribed for stuttering. Therefore, it will not be addressed separately in this chapter. Neurological fluency disorders are those that occur as associated symptoms with a range of neurologic disorders, including parkinsonism, brain damage resulting from head injury, and true apraxia. However, again there is little research literature available regarding this type of fluency disorder, or any unique treatment considerations associated with it, in young children. Therefore, this chapter will concentrate on the most common type of fluency disorder: stuttering.

There is one subclassification system in stuttering that has been in use for some time: that which differentiates *primary stuttering* from *secondary stuttering.* A classification of primary stuttering is reserved for dysfluency patterns that are characterized by repetitions of syllables or words at higher than normal rates and consistency, but in which there is no evidence that the speaker is making special attempts to control these episodes of nonfluency. There is a hypothesis that when speakers begin to try to ''stop'' or ''control'' this dysfluency characterized by repetitions, they begin to do such things as take breaths when they anticipate stuttering, alter their words in midsentence, blink their eyes, and use many other behaviors that they think will avoid the repetition episodes. The assumption is further made that when these additional mechanisms fail to prevent a dysfluent episode, speakers begin to exaggerate them. These attempts to avoid stuttering are thought to be responsible for the behaviors that characterize severe stuttering: struggles for breath, facial grimaces, and blocks in initiating speech. These additional mechanisms have been classified as secondary symptoms of stuttering and those speakers whose dysfluency patterns demonstrate these characteristics have been historically classified as *secondary stutterers.*

There is no further subclassification system of different types of stuttering, although one may evolve as research produces more conclusive evidence regarding the causes of stuttering. As with articulation, stuttering is often differentiated by degrees of severity, in terms of the number of stuttered words or syllables produced per minute, percent of words/syllables stuttered, number of repetitions per sound, and/or amount of struggle behavior associated with blocks, but again no standardized severity rating system exists.

Much work in recent years has recast the historical *primary* versus *secondary* dichotomy. This work is focused on identifying quantifiable differences that might exist between stuttering and normal dysfluencies. Freeman (1982) cited a number of studies indicating that stuttered speech is perceived by listeners as different from normally dysfluent speech. The primary difference is that normal dysfluencies tend to involve breaks between words, whereas stuttering involves sound and syllable repetitions and prolongations that fragment words themselves. There also seems to be a consensus that stuttering is associated with high levels of tension and normal dysfluencies are not.

It should be emphasized that these descriptions of phonatory and auditory characteristics of stuttering do not resolve the issue of underlying etiology. Traditional theories have tended to concentrate on *psychodynamic* accounts of etiology, pointing to excessive stress associated with speech production, due either to parental or child personality characteristics or to interaction patterns. More recent *behavioral* accounts of stuttering etiology implicate speaking habits shaped and reinforced through specific patterns of environmental consequences for dysfluent speech produced under certain stimulus conditions. At the other extreme, studies of genetic patterns associated with stuttering are argued to support an underlying, inherited organic etiology. In addition, some experts suggest that the perception of *blocking* (the temporary inability to control the speech mechanism) that is reported by stutterers to be the most pervasive and frightening symptom of their stuttering might be physiologically based in the vocal tract, most likely in the laryngeal folds. Thus, these reports offer the hypothesis that the stutterer actually experiences episodes of phonatory blockage originating in the larynx. As a consequence, some therapy approaches for stuttering are increasingly focused on the structures and processes of phonation (Freeman, 1982; Perkins, 1983). In the face of these continuing unknowns, most authorities in the field today seem to agree only that the manifestation of true stuttering by any one child may represent some combination or interaction of genetic/organic, psychogenic, and/or environmental/behavioral causes.

Voice Disorders

Within the broad category of voice disorders we will include those disorders affecting the processes of *phonation* and *resonance*. Thus, this type of disorder is reflected in a voice that is perceptibly abnormal in terms of its pitch (too high or too low), its loudness (too soft or too loud), its nasality (too much or too little), and/or its overall quality (e.g., breathiness or hoarseness). Prevalence estimates for voice disorders range from 1% to over 20% of the school-aged population, with conservative estimates suggesting that 3–5% of all children have some type of voice disorder, with about 1% of these being severe and chronic enough to merit voice therapy (Murry, 1982). Again, no separate prevalence figures are available for preschool-aged children although, as with fluency disorders, disorders of voice are reported to be more prevalent among boys than girls at all ages.

In addition to being characterized in terms of which of the four major features of voice are affected, voice disorders are sometimes also classified as being either *hyperfunctional* or *hypofunctional,* depending on whether the child demonstrates too much or too little of the affected feature(s) and/or demonstrates a disorder resulting from too much or too little tension and pressure in the phonation process.

It is possible to distinguish two broad types of etiology: *organic* and *functional.* In reality, however, there is generally an interaction of both types of etiological factors associated with any one case of observed voice disorder. Organic factors include any condition that affects the functioning of the respiratory system, the larynx, and/or the intactness of the resonance cavities. Within this broad grouping are such cases as acute laryngitis, cleft palate or other types of velopharyngeal insufficiency, neuromuscular disease and disorders, tracheotomies, and ulcers, tumors, or nodules on the laryngeal folds themselves.

Functional etiological factors are those associated with the habitual patterns and conditions under which the child vocalizes. Many environmental pollutants are included within this general category because they may affect the health of the larynx. However, by far the greatest cause of voice disorder among children is vocal abuse. *Vocal abuse* refers to any habitual voicing process that places abnormal stress on the larynx. In young children, this most often means habitual shouting or screaming, which may be due to emotional/behavioral problems, the need to communicate in very noisy environments, or simply the development of unhealthy vocalization habits. Functional and organic etiological factors interact in many ways. A history of chronic vocal abuse will often result in the development of vocal nodules on the larynx, which will require medical consultation in conjunction with vocal reeducation to reduce the original vocal abuse problems.

Disorders of Language: Prevalence, Subclassification, and Associated Etiologies

The second major category of communication disorder that we will address in this chapter involves disorders of *language.* We noted earlier that that the language system can be described in terms of three different but closely interrelated and interdependent rule systems: pragmatics, semantics, and syntactics. It will be seen that different types of language disorder may affect the child's performance and competence in one or all of these rule systems. Although there is no universally accepted subclassification system for differentiating specific types of language disorder, we will divide this population into three major subgroups, which are at least consistent with the types of broad distinctions generally made by researchers and clinicians who work with language disordered children today. These subgroups are specific language disabilities or disorders, general language delays, and language communication deficits associated with pervasive handicapping conditions.

Prevalence

It has only been in recent years that language disorders have been identified and classified separately from speech disorders. Therefore, in many prevalence studies, it is difficult to determine whether the figures given for speech disorders subsume or exclude those disorders that we would now include under the heading of language disorders. The few studies that have treated disorders of language separately have generally treated this as a unitary phenomenon. Thus, although we will discriminate among several major types of language disorder, we cannot, at this time, provide separate prevalence figures for each.

It has been estimated that 16% of all expressive communication disorders are disorders of language (National Advisory Neurological Diseases and Stroke Council, 1969). If we accept a prevalence estimate for communication disorders of 4–5% of the preschool-aged population, we would conclude that the prevalence for disorders of language within that population should be slightly less than 1%. However, data from studies analyzed by Marge in 1972 indicated a 6.5% prevalence of language disorders among children below the age of 4 years. It seems likely that the true prevalence figure lies somewhere between these two estimates. (The authors' own experience in clinical and preschool settings tends to support a figure closer to the 6.5% estimate.)

Before moving on to discuss the three major types of language disorder that we will be considering in this chapter, it is important to note who we are *not* talking about. In this context of language *disorders*, we are not talking about children whose language is *different* from that of our predominant linguistic community. It may be argued that children who speak English only as a second language or who speak some nonstandard dialect of English (e.g., Black English) are at a disadvantage when they enter public school. However, this type of language difference does not, in itself, qualify a child as having a language disorder. Of course, such a child may also have a true language disorder that is manifested within the child's dominant language or dialect. However, the mere existence of a language difference is not considered a language disorder.

Specific Language Disabilities or Disorders

The classification of *specific* language disability or disorder is generally only applied to children who have reached a level of development characterized by the production of multiword utterances—in other words, children at or above the age of 3 years—and who manifest very specific discrepancies within their overall linguistic performance level. Thus, this applies to the 4-year-old child who demonstrates language comprehension at the 4-year level, but produces sentences characteristic of 3-year-old development. Or this may include the 5-year-old child who comprehends and produces many linguistic structures characteristic of 5-year-old development, but concurrently fails to comprehend or produce language rules that are generally demonstrated by much younger children. Most typically, these children manifest disorders in the area of syntax and are often reported to have attentional and auditory processing deficits, as well as poor short-term memory for language stimuli.

It is commonly presumed that this type of specific language disorder is symptomatic of some underlying neurological damage or dysfunction, although there are very rarely any hard signs of such neurological involvement. Etiologies associated with specific language disorders include a broad spectrum of prenatal and perinatal complications that place an infant at risk for brain damage, as well as rare instances of postnatal traumatic brain injury or disease. However, of all the children diagnosed as having a specific language disorder, only a small percentage can be attributed to such specific etiological factors. For most such children, etiology remains unknown and is assumed to be some interaction of genetic/biological predisposition and environmental factors.

General Language Delays

In contrast to the specific language disorder, which is diagnosed on the basis of intralinguistic performance discrepancy, the diagnosis of general language *delay* is made on the basis of a discrepancy between overall level of language development and overall level of cognitive or mental development. This diagnosis is generally not made until a child reaches the age at which at least some language production is normally expected, at least 2 years of age. Language delayed children, then, are those whose measured levels of language performance are consistent across receptive and expressive measures and across different aspects of the language system, but for whom this language level is significantly below that which would be expected on the basis of their mental ages.

Language delays range from *mild* (e.g., the 4-year-old child functioning at a $3\frac{1}{2}$-year language level) to *severe* (e.g., the 6-year-old functioning at a 2-year language level). It should be noted that this diagnosis may be applied to mentally retarded children, whose mental ages are significantly below their chronological ages. However, to be classified as language delayed, such children must demonstrate a level of language delay even greater than their general developmental or cognitive delay. For example, a 6-year-old child with Down syndrome whose general mental age is 3 years but whose overall language age is only 18 months would be considered multiply handicapped, being both mentally retarded and language delayed.

Like the specific language disorder, language delays usually cannot be clearly attributed to any single causative factor. In general, this type of language disorder seems more likely to be associated with environmental factors (such as lack of appropriate language models or opportunities and/or requirements to use language) than does the specific language disorder. However, in many cases there is reason to believe that pre- or perinatal complications may have adversely affected the child's neurological development specifically in the areas critical to cognitive and linguistic functioning. Finally, the prevalence of language delays appears to be considerably higher among groups of children who are affected by other handicapping conditions, especially mental retardation, again pointing to a biological basis for the language delay.

Language and Communication Deficits Associated with Pervasive Handicapping Conditions

Finally, in this chapter we will be discussing early intervention aimed at the language disorders of children for whom these disorders are secondary to some more pervasive handicapping condition. These are children who can not be accurately diagnosed as having either a specific language disorder or even a general language delay, as these two diagnostic categories were defined earlier. Thus, these are children whose level of communication and language functioning may, in fact, be commensurate with their overall level of development. However, the resulting deficits in communication skills are so significant and compelling that they demand direct intervention and require the specialized input of a speech/language pathologist.

This group includes children whose primary handicaps are mental retardation, cerebral palsy, severe behavior disorders, and autism. Within each of these specific populations, the prevalence of communication deficits is very high, with the severity of the communication deficit generally commensurate with the pervasiveness and severity of the primary handicapping condition. This group, then, includes children who demonstrate no intentional communicative behavior at all, children who communicate only nonverbally, children who demonstrate very deviant linguistic behavior, and children who demonstrate only very limited language use. Because this type of language disorder is secondary to the specific pervasive handicapping conditions just listed (which are addressed in other chapters in this volume), we will not attempt to discuss the prevalence and etiological considerations associated with each type of primary handicap in this chapter.

The major types of early childhood speech and language disorders described in the preceding pages are summarized in Table 1. If a child is suspected of demonstrating a communication disorder, it is suggested that the child be referred to a speech/language pathologist for screening or full evaluation. Now we are ready to consider the nature and demonstrated efficacy of early intervention efforts aimed at these major types of communication disorder.

TABLE 1

Major types of communication disorders affecting young children[a]

Speech disorders	Language disorders
Articulation disorders	*Specific language disability*
Functional articulation disorders	*General language delay*
Developmental verbal apraxia[b]	*Language and communication deficits associated with pervasive handicapping conditions*
Dysarthria	
Fluency disorders	Mental retardation/developmental delay
Stuttering	Autism and severe behavior disorders
Cluttering	
Neurological disorders	
Voice disorders	
Hyperfunctional disorders	
Pitch	
Nasality	
Loudness	
Quality	
Hypofunctional disorders	
Pitch	
Nasality	
Loudness	
Quality	

[a]Types of disorder shown in italics are those for which efficacy studies with preschool-aged children are reported in this chapter.

[b]See comments in text regarding controversy surrounding use of this classification

EARLY INTERVENTION FOR COMMUNICATION DISORDERS

Organizing Perspectives

In most of the chapters in this volume and in common usage, the term *early intervention* is associated with a constellation of procedures designed to foster development and/or remediate deficits in multiple skill domains. Further, this term is generally applied to educational or school-sponsored programs in which the child (and his or her family) participates for a relatively long period of time—at least 1 school year. Thus, it seems important to note that many of the intervention procedures we will describe in this chapter are neither broad in their scope nor extensive in their duration. Rather, early intervention for many types of communication disorders is more narrowly clinical in nature because it is designed to remediate a very specific skill deficit within a finite time period.

Although such procedures may not conform to our common usage of the term *early intervention,* they do in fact conform to the technical meaning of this phrase. All of the approaches and programs we will describe involve some procedure for *intervening* in a child's disordered communication skill system during the period of *early* skill development (i.e., before the age of 6 years). We might note here that the American Heritage Dictionary defines intervention as the process of "coming between so as to modify." It is this intent to modify—and specifically to remediate or at least ameliorate—deficient or disordered patterns of communicative performance in the early years of a child's life, before these patterns become further ingrained and compounded by interaction effects on subsequent communication skill development, that defines early intervention as we will use the term in this chapter.

In the pages that follow, we will address three major questions concerning early intervention for children with communication disorders:

1. What are the major approaches to intervention for these various types of communication disorder and what are the issues surrounding use of these approaches?

2. What data are available concerning the effectiveness of these approaches in achieving their stated intervention aims?

3. What conclusions can we draw about the merits and potential benefits of these approaches for young children with communication disorders?

In addressing these questions, we will focus on those types of disorder that are well represented in the literature on communication intervention for very young children and on those procedures that are best documented in that literature. Our aim, then, is to provide a report on the state of the art in this area that is representative of current practice and wisdom and thus has generality to most intervention settings, at least in the United States. Toward this end we have searched the literature on early intervention for communication disorders to identify published reports that describe the procedures and results of such intervention. The information and conclusions presented on the following pages are based entirely on that literature search. Therefore, a few words about the parameters and organization of this literature review are merited.

Our first task was to identify those articles and chapters that described some actual *intervention* for an identified *communication disorder* in children who were below mandatory school age (i.e., children below the age of 6 years). This initial filter eliminated three large and otherwise relevant bodies of literature: (1) reports that simply described the nature and sequelae of communication disorders in early childhood, (2) reports of general language stimulation programs designed for use in preschool programs that were not designed to remediate specific communication disorders, and (3) reports of intervention procedures and effectiveness with school-aged children. The resulting collection of books, chapters, and articles was reviewed and is reflected in the following discussion of current early intervention approaches and issues.

To address the question of effectiveness, we applied one more filter to this body of literature: the requirement that some actual data be presented documenting the effects of the intervention on the targeted communication skill area. (Additional requirements, in terms of experimental design and overall reliability of findings, were also applied and will be explained in a later section.) This filtering process eliminated from further review a large number of clinical reports and case studies that provided only descriptive or anecdotal support for the efficacy of various procedures. Our discussion of the effectiveness of early intervention for communication disorders is based on the 30 published studies we found that passed this final test. Although we made every effort to conduct a thorough review of the literature, we cannot guarantee that we succeeded in identifying every relevant study. If we have failed to include a study that meets all of these criteria, it is an omission due to oversight and human error, not reviewer bias. We believe that the following review reflects current practice and empirical evidence in the area of early intervention for communication disorders.

The 30 studies that are presented in our discussion of intervention effectiveness are summarized in six different tables according to the nature of the communication disorder addressed. These tables, found at the end of this chapter, are organized as follows:

Table number and title	Earliest Publication	Number of studies	Number of children
2. Speech Disorders: Articulation	1970	8	55
3. Speech Disorders: Stuttering	1972	3	18
4. Language Disorders: Specific Language Delay or Disorder	1978	8	185
5. Communication & Language Deficits Associated with Pervasive Handicapping Conditions: Retardation/Developmental Delay	1974	5	56
6. Communication & Language Deficits Associated with Pervasive Handicapping Conditions: Autism and Severe Behavior Disorders	1979	3	34
7. Communication & Language Deficits Associated with Pervasive Handicapping Conditions: Augmentative Modes	1980	3	40

It can be seen that all of this literature is relatively recent, with the earliest publication dates found for studies involving speech disorders. This seems to reflect a relative recency of experimental interest in the effects of early intervention, particularly in the area of language disorders. It should also be noted that no studies are reported in the area of voice disorders and that the separate classifications of specific language disorder versus general language delay are combined in Table 4, because the studies reported generally did not treat these groups differentially.

With these organizational perspectives established regarding the scope and content of the literature reviewed we are ready to begin our discussion of current approaches to early intervention for communication disorders. Following this discussion, we will examine the data concerning effectiveness of these approaches, as documented in the 30 studies summarized in Tables 2–7.

Some Generic Issues

Before going on to describe the specific therapeutic procedures currently advocated for different types of speech and language disorder, we would like to identify and discuss some generic issues that seem to cut across early intervention efforts for all such disorders. These issues revolve around the five critical questions of *what, who, where, when,* and *how.* Let us discuss these briefly in order.

The issue of *what* is the goal of an intervention related specifically to two major types of treatment outcome: (1) initial acquisition of the target skill and (2) subsequent generalization of that skill to the real-world situations in which the child must actually use it. It is commonly agreed that the ultimate goal of any intervention is that training on a few exemplars in any one problem area will produce effects that extend beyond the specific exemplars trained. In the area of communication disorders there are three major types of response generalization that are of concern: generalization to novel physical and interpersonal contexts (e.g., a different room or a different conversational partner), generalization to novel linguistic contexts (e.g., producing a newly learned sound in untrained words or word positions or producing a newly learned syntactic rule in untrained sentences), and generalization effects that are realized in intralinguistic contexts in which one specific change effects changes in another untrained element of the linguistic system (e.g., training on copular *is/are* may result in correct use of auxiliary *is/are*). In assessing and comparing the relative effectiveness and efficiency of any intervention approach, we must ask how successful that approach is in achieving all of these types of generalization.

The question of *who* implements the intervention program actually subsumes two issues. The first of these involves the role of the child's family, most often the primary caregiver, in the intervention. Programs vary along a continuum on this issue, from programs at one extreme in which a speech/language clinician conducts all of the programming specifying no role at all for the family to programs at the other extreme that stipulate that the child's parent(s) serve as the primary change agents and actually implement all direct programming. Although there is much emotion and rhetoric currently surrounding this issue, it seems important that we examine the available data in an attempt to gain some empirical perspective on the appropriate role of parents in communication-disorder remediation. A related issue concerns the role of the speech/language clinician vis-à-vis other professionals, most notably the classroom teacher. Again, current practice varies along a continuum, ranging from programs in which the clinician alone works on the child's speech and language intervention goals to those in which the clinician serves only a consulting role (or no role at all), with the special education teacher carrying responsibility for implementing the child's communication intervention program.

A closely related question concerns *where* communication intervention programs should be implemented. Traditionally, speech/language clinicians have conducted therapy in isolated therapy rooms or designated therapy corners in classrooms. Similarly, special education teachers implementing remedial speech or language programs have also traditionally conducted such programs in some quiet corner removed from the ebb and flow of ongoing classroom activities. Recently, however, the emphasis on pragmatics (i.e., the actual communicative and conversational use of speech and language skills) and concerns about skill generalization have led many professionals to suggest that communication programming should generally not be conducted in settings isolated from the child's daily activities and interactions. Recent literature reflects a trend toward conducting many types of communication intervention programs in the context of more "natural" interactive routines. With very young children there is one further question concerning the locus of intervention: the issue of home versus center-based programming. Proponents of home-based intervention point both to practical factors (primarily in transporting and managing very young children in center-based contexts) and to arguments that home-based programming is more likely to result in generalization and maintenance of treatment effects because family members and routine family events are involved in the initial treatment process. In reviewing the studies of early communication intervention, then, we will look for data concerning effects of programming conducted in isolated versus in situ contexts and those conducted in home versus center or clinic settings.

Our fourth generic issue concerns the question of *when* intervention should be started for the child with an apparent communication disorder. Underlying this question is concern regarding the reliability with which different types of communication disorder can be identified in children of very young ages. One practical problem has been that of how to identify communication-skill deficits in children who are not yet talking. In recent years, however, improved knowledge bases regarding the course of prelinguistic oral–motor and communication/-language development have allowed the identification of even very young infants who are failing to develop appropriate prelinguistic skills in the standard manner or time frame and who are, thus, very likely to demonstrate subsequent speech and/or language disorders. However, judging these early prelinguistic deficits is still problematic because there is great variability in the rates at which children develop communication skills and achieve specific communication developmental milestones. Further, many characteristics of disordered speech and language in older children and adults might be quite acceptable in early developmental stages. Think, for example, of the young child who says *wabbit* for *rabbit* or *he runned* instead of *he ran* and of the normal dysfluencies that characterize the speech of many young children during the period of rapid linguistic development at around 3–4 years. At what point are such error patterns appropriately labeled as communication disorders? Additionally, the question arises whether it is possible or efficient to intervene in a child's speech or language development at a stage when that child's level of cognitive development and/or neuromotor maturation may not be sufficient to support more advanced skills. At this point, it appears that the only way to address these issues is through controlled studies of the effectiveness and efficiency of direct intervention procedures as these have actually been applied to very young children with apparent communication deficits or deviant developmental patterns.

Finally, the last question that arises in our review of early intervention procedures in the area of communication disorders is that of *how* the intervention is implemented. Clearly, each type of disorder has associated with it a unique set of procedural issues. However, we can identify one generic issue that is reflected in the literature on all types of early childhood communication therapy, and that concerns the use of highly structured "behavioral" procedures versus more loosely structured and "naturalistic" procedures. Typically, behavioral methodology is associated with the use of massed trials and a set of tightly controlled antecedent stimuli and contingent consequences. More naturalistic procedures generally involve dispersing learning trials throughout an interactive session in which the child's immediate interests and behaviors will, to some extent, determine the specific stimuli and consequences for that session. Proponents of the behavioral approach point to the demonstrated effectiveness and efficiency of these procedures for many types of specific response acquisition treatment goals. Conversely, proponents of the naturalistic approach point to the problems of response maintenance and carryover that have frequently plagued behavioral programs. We will see that many of today's intervention programs are attempting to combine the best features of both these approaches, and we will look at the results of several early intervention studies in an attempt to gain some empirical perspective on this issue.

Having identified these five issues as generic to all types of early childhood communication disorder, we should now caution that the specific parameters and shadings of these issues vary slightly with each type of disorder. Further, we are certain that there is no simple or single resolution to any of these issues. Rather, it seems more realistic to seek to identify specific constellations of factors—including child characteristics, nature and severity of disorder, and type of intervention outcome sought—that would suggest the way we should answer the questions of what, who, where, when, and how for any one child and treatment goal. We will return to these issues when we review a number of studies regarding the efficacy of specific treatment programs for different types of early childhood communication disorder. First, however, let us briefly describe the major treatment approaches and associated procedural issues for the types of speech and language disorder most commonly observed in young children.

Early Intervention Procedures for Speech Disorders

Articulation

The way in which a clinician assesses and describes a child's specific articulation disorder directly reflects the particular theoretical model followed by that clinician. In this chapter, we will discuss three dominant models or approaches which can be identified as (1) a traditional approach, (2) a distinctive feature approach, and (3) a phonological process approach. As will become evident, these models impact primarily on the selection and clustering of sounds to be targeted in a child's therapy program, and only secondarily on the actual procedures used to foster production of those sounds.

The *traditional approach* seeks to identify errors in a child's repertoire of the speech sounds required by his or her particular language system. These error patterns are identified and analyzed at several levels. First, an inventory of the child's phonemic repertoire is taken by having a child produce a collection of words that contain a robust sample of the various consonant phonemes of the target language. Such samples are usually collected in a picture or object-naming format with young children. Spontaneous (nonimitative) naming responses to the stimuli are most desirable. However, with many young children prompts are often needed and, thus, children's responses are often deferred imitations. When errors of production occur in these sampling tasks they are classified as to type (e.g., omission, substitution, or distortion). Each error, then, is further tested to determine its relative extent in terms of the different word and sentence contexts in which it occurs. When the extent of the error production has been determined, the child's ability to respond to imitative models and verbal and tactile cues about how to produce the desired sound are sampled.

Depending on the specific sound being trained, therapy procedures may include direct modeling, verbal instruction, tactile cues, and, perhaps, direct manipulation of the movable elements of the articulatory mechanism (i.e., tongue and lips). Such procedures in the development of an appropriate articulatory response are applied in a basic trial-and-error process in which the clinician provides auditory and visually observable models and instructional activities and children receive rewarding and instructional feedback after their production attempts.

When a target phone has finally been attained under these instructional conditions, therapy shifts to procedures designed to extend the correct production of the sound into more and more complex phonemic and linguistic contexts. Gradually, the modified sound is extended into linguistic contexts that match the complexity of the child's current expressive language.

The decision to initiate intervention on a particular sound generally reflects two considerations. With very young children, often the first consideration is the normal age at which the sound is acquired and its relative place in the developmental sequence. Some sounds (e.g., /b/ and /g/) are relatively easy to produce and are clearly articulated by most 2-year-olds, whereas other sounds (e.g., /s/ and /l/) are more difficult and are not usually articulated correctly until children are 4 years or older. A second consideration, if the clinician must choose between several sounds that might be appropriate therapy goals for a particular child, is that of the relative contribution each might make to the child's overall intelligibility.

The *distinctive feature approach,* derived from the distinctive feature theory of phonology proposed by Jakobson, Fant, and Halle (1963), analyzes children's sound production errors in terms of specific distinctive features shared by the sounds that are correctly and incorrectly produced by the child. Each phoneme is characterized by the presence or absence of each of 11 distinctive features. For example, the sounds /m/, /n/, and /ng/ share the feature of nasality, /s/, /f/, and /v/ share the feature of continuance, and /n/, /v/, and /b/ share the feature of being voiced. The implications of this model for selecting intervention targets lie in the expectation that features learned in one sound should generalize and thus facilitate acquisition of other sounds that share those features. Also, in order to facilitate a child's discovery and ability to recognize his or her own correct production of such distinctive features, target sounds are paired and contrasted with sounds containing the opposite feature. The studies by Costello and Onstine (1976) and Ruder and Bunce (1981) listed in Table 2 both employed a distinctive features approach.

Most recently, many clinicians have adopted a *phonological processes approach,* following the model proposed by Ingram in 1976. This approach focuses on the predictable patterns of phonological errors or processes that characterize early sound development and that may affect the production of several different sounds. For example, the process of "stopping" results in a child's saying /t/ for

/s/ and /p/ for /f/; the process of "fronting" (consistent placement of the tongue at points in the front of the mouth) are demonstrated in a child's saying /d/ for /g/ and /t/ for /k/. In this approach, then, treatment targets are grouped on the basis of underlying phonological processes and there is an expectation that correction of the process will result in generalized production of all sounds affected by that process. As with the distinctive feature approach, this type of programming often involves pairing together words containing contrasting sounds. Here, however, the contrast is in terms of the sound as it is correctly produced versus the sound that is produced in error. Thus, if a child is fronting, his or her program might involve production alternately of such minimal pairs of *d*ate (fronted sound) and *g*ate (target sound). An example of such programming is found in the study by Weiner (1981) listed in Table 2.

It should be noted here that the distinctive feature and the phonological process approaches are currently used widely to organize and direct articulation therapy. However, most of the studies of early intervention discussed in this chapter (see Table 2) used the traditional approach to the assessment and prescription of articulation treatment targets. Essentially, the procedures for specific response development training remain the same for all three approaches.

Although the approaches described so far focus on the way in which treatment targets are identified and clustered, they do not actually specify the types of therapy procedures that are used to achieve those therapy goals. Many of the studies summarized in Table 2 can be characterized as using behavioral intervention procedures. In this context, we are deliberately oversimplifying and stereotyping the term *behavioral* and have applied it to intervention programs that share the following characteristics: (1) treatment follows a prescribed series of program steps or phases with each continued to some prespecified criterion performance level, (2) sessions are usually conducted in a massed-trial format, and (3) contingent consequences are prescribed for correct and incorrect responses. Further, the first four studies shown in Table 2 all follow a specific behavioral methodology for achieving a "shift of stimulus control" (McLean, 1970). This procedure meets the criteria just listed for any behavioral procedure and specifically involves a series of program steps that are designed to increase systematically the child's ability to produce a target sound in multiple linguistic contexts and under different stimulus conditions, beginning with imitation and advancing to picture labeling and finally to spontaneous use.

In recent years there has been some movement away from tightly structured behavioral approaches to articulation therapy toward more naturalistic approaches, in which correct target sound production is modeled and reinforced by natural consequences in the context of interactive dialogue between child and teacher or clinician. The article by Kupperman, Bligh, and Goodban (1980), however, is the only study in Table 2 that involves this type of procedure. There is considerable debate among clinicians today about the appropriateness and overall efficacy of such procedures for treatment of articulation disorders and we may expect to see more studies on this issue in the coming years.

Although all of the these approaches involve some direct treatment of the specific articulation error of concern, we will note that there are some cases in which more indirect approaches are used, usually in concert with one of these direct types of therapy. The indirect types of articulation therapy focus on either auditory discrimination processes or oral–motor control processes that are assumed to be related to, and to some degree responsible for, the child's sound production errors. The study by Christensen and Hanson (1981) listed in Table 2, which included oral myofunctional therapy for tongue thrust as a procedure in treatment of an articulatory disorder, is an example of such an indirect approach to specific sound modification. Unfortunately, there seem to be very few data regarding the effectiveness of such approaches with preschool-aged children.

Stuttering

Of the three types of fluency disorder identified earlier in this chapter (see Table 1), stuttering is by far the most common and the best represented in the literature. Although there are many specific treatment programs and procedures in use with older stutterers and considerable controversy regarding the effectiveness of those procedures, there are two basic approaches to working with very young stutterers: *indirect management* and *direct fluency shaping*. The indirect approach is typically associated with one or both of two basic assumptions about early childhood stuttering. Perhaps most widely accepted is the assumption that most children go through a period of normal dysfluency, which will be outgrown as the child's linguistic skills mature unless too much attention and stress is placed on these initial dysfluencies, thus setting the stage for the child to become a true stutterer. The second assumption underlying an indirect approach is that the child's stuttering is an outward manifestation of some internal stress associated with speaking and the interactive contexts in which the child is expected to speak. Both assumptions then lead to an indirect intervention approach that minimizes any focusing of attention on the child's episodes of dysfluency. In this approach, the clinician usually works primarily with the child's caregivers toward the goal of reducing any stress associated with speaking situations and attenuating corrective consequences to dysfluent speech. The emphasis is on creating a more relaxed communicative atmosphere in which the child has ample time and opportunity to formulate his or her utterances and in which any stuttering episodes that may occur are treated as "no big deal."

In contrast, proponents of direct fluency shaping argue that stuttering and fluent speaking are behaviors that are amenable to direct intervention. Further, clinicians who use this approach argue that directing attention to the child's stuttering early in life prevents the pattern of dysfluent speech from becoming more ingrained and intractable in later childhood. Thus, this type of approach usually involves the types of behavioral procedures already described, with specific emphasis on differential feedback and consequences for episodes of fluent versus dysfluent speech. All three of the studies of stuttering treatment listed in Table 3 represent this latter approach of direct fluency shaping.

Voice

We noted earlier in this chapter that voice disorders may be associated with specific organic/anatomical anomalies or with functional etiologies, most notably poor voicing habits. The former category includes children with tracheotomies and cleft palates who thus have special problems in producing and controlling the airflow necessary to produce intelligible speech sounds. Early intervention for such children generally involves the interaction of a speech/language clinician with the child's physician or specialized interdisciplinary team to prescribe any needed surgery or prosthesis and provide appropriate therapy for the production of speech with or without corrective surgery and/or prosthetic devices.

The majority of voice disorders in young children are functional in nature. In some cases, vocal abuse has resulted in edema or the development of nodules on the vocal folds and, in consultation with a physician, therapy is most often directed toward vocal reeducation. When a child's vocal habits have been altered, the abuse-caused edema or nodules can disappear with no additional medical therapy. There is little controversy associated with the treatment of such disorders and early intervention takes the form of teaching the child to use a soft glottal attack and talk at an appropriate pitch if the disorder is due to vocal abuse in the form of constant shrieking or yelling, or to use a stronger glottal attack if the child whispers chronically. As with articulation response development, such therapy may involve some combination of verbal instruction and direct monitoring and feedback of the child's own vocal output. Again, the argument for early intervention rests on the assumption that it is easier and more efficient to modify maladaptive speech patterns in early childhood, before they have become habituated, than in later childhood when they are more resistant to modification.

Although case studies regarding early intervention for both organic and functional voice disorders are frequently reported in the speech pathology literature, we found no controlled *experimental* studies of the effectiveness of such intervention. Therefore, the reader will note that there is no table of efficacy studies for the area of voice disorders.

Early Intervention Procedures for Language Disorders

For this chapter, we have divided the broad category of language disorders into three major subcategories: specific language disorders or disabilities, general language delays, and communication/language deficits associated with pervasive handicapping conditions. When we turn to the topic of intervention procedures for language disorders, however, we generally do not find differential procedures associated with these different types of disorder. (There is one exception to this statement; we will discuss this later.) Therefore, we will describe here the general approaches that are most commonly used in early intervention programs for all of these types of language disorder. The reader will find these, then, represented in the studies on effectiveness of intervention for the different types of disorder summarized in Tables 4 through 7.

Assessment Procedures and Measures

Any attempt to assess and describe a child's language development must begin with the basic distinction between *language comprehension* (or *receptive language*) and *language production* (or *expressive language*). Although these two aspects of language are closely related, they are not isomorphic and must be assessed separately. It is not uncommon to find significant discrepancies between receptive and expressive skill levels among disordered populations. For example, the specific language-disabled child may receptively understand and discriminate between present and past tense forms, but not use those forms discriminatively in expressive language. Similarly, the child with autism may produce very long and complex sentence constructions, but only comprehend single word utterances. Further, training in one modality does not necessarily result in acquisition in the other. For example, teaching a child to mark plurals correctly and differentially by adding /s/, /z/, or /ez/ to singular nouns may not generalize to that same child's being able to respond correctly to a receptive language task in which the child is shown a picture of one book and several books and is asked "Show me the book*s*." For this reason, most standardized language tests consist of two major subscales, receptive language and expressive language; results of performance on the two subscales are usually reported separately.

Much language assessment, particularly when conducted as part of a study of intervention effectiveness, is done with norm-referenced tests. Whereas speech disorders are more typically assessed and described in terms of a child's characteristic error patterns (e.g., omissions, stopping, or syllable prolongations), language disorders are often reported in terms of relative developmental status of the child's receptive and expressive language skills. Thus, most widely used standardized language tests produce a score that is reported in terms of receptive and/or expressive language age; that is, the age at which most normally developing children demonstrate the highest level skills demonstrated by this particular child. For example, it may be reported that a 5-year-old language-disordered child has a Receptive Language Age (RLA) of 4 years, 6 months, and an Expressive Language Age (ELA) of 2 years, 6 months. These ages can then be converted to developmental rates or quotients by dividing them by the child's chronological age and multiplying by 100. In the example above, the child would be said to have a Receptive Language Quotient (RLQ) of 90 and an Expressive Language Quotient (ELQ) of 50. The goal of intervention is to modify not just the child's language age, which usually increases somewhat simply through maturation, but also, more critically, his or her developmental status in relation to current chronological age, as indicated by this developmental quotient. Three widely used instruments are the Sequenced Inventory of Communication Development or SICD (Hedrick, Prather, & Tobin, 1975), the Reynell Developmental Scales of Language (Reynell, 1969), and the Receptive-Expressive Emergent Language Scale or REEL (Bzoch & League, 1970). Although they differ in the range of developmental levels covered and methods of administration, these instruments are all standardized, norm-referenced, and composed of discrete receptive and expressive scales.

Beyond such norm-referenced measures, probably the next most common type of language assessment is the *language sample*. The language sample is a procedure for assessing a child's expressive language skills as they are demonstrated under conditions of actual conversational use. A language sample session typically involves the child in an interaction with one other person (most often the therapist or a familiar adult) and is usually audiotape-recorded, although with very young or severely handicapped children videotape may be used to capture more information regarding the nonverbal aspects of the communicative interaction. The interaction is then transcribed and a core sample of 50 or 100 child utterances is used in the actual analysis.

A language sample can be analyzed in many different ways, depending on the primary focus of clinical or research interest. In this chapter we will describe only those procedures most commonly used for analyzing linguistic structure as a measure of language intervention effectiveness. For such an analysis, each child utterance is described in terms of its constituent morphemes and overall structure. (Morphemes are the smallest units of meaning in a language. In English, these include both root words and meaningful suffixes such as +*ing* or +*es*, *which modify the meaning of the root word. For example, the word book*s is credited as two morphemes: the root word *book* and the plurality marker *s*.) Following this analysis of each utterance in a sample, the child's expressive language performance is summarized, usually in terms of three types of measure: total lexicon, use of specific morphemes in obligatory contexts, and mean length of utterance (MLU).

Total lexicon refers to the number of different words that the child uses in spontaneous language and is often reported in terms of a type-token ratio (TTR, Templin, 1957)—that is, the number of different words used as a proportion of the total number of words produced by the child in the entire sample. Thus, a child who has a very small speaking vocabulary or lexicon and uses those few words over and over to produce a large number of utterances will have a very small TTR, whereas a child with a larger lexicon, and thus more diverse lan-

guage sample, will have a TTR that more closely approaches 1.00. Data presented by Templin in 1957 suggest that a normal TTR for young children (3–8 years)
is between .40 and .50. Measures of lexicon size are generally only of clinical
concern with children at the earliest stages of expressive language development
and are rarely reported for children past the stage of one- and two-word utterances. None of the studies reported in Tables 4–7 used the TTR as an outcome
measure, although it would have been appropriate in those that specifically
targeted lexicon training (see, for example, Barrera, Lobato-Barrera, & Sulzer-
Azaroff, 1980, and Jago, Jago, & Hart, 1984, in Table 7).

The concept of *obligatory contexts* is an important one in analyzing a child's
expressive language performance. An obligatory context is one in which standards of normal, mature usage require the use of a particular morpheme. For
example, in the sentence "They're eating lunch," the auxiliary or contracted
auxiliary *are* is obligatory and the sentence is incorrect if it is omitted (as in
"they eating"). Clearly, it would be meaningless to look for use of every
morpheme in every child utterance. Instead, morpheme usage is typically analyzed and reported in terms of percentage of obligatory contexts in which the
morpheme is appropriately used or, alternatively, is omitted. (Additionally, use
of morphemes when they should not be used may also occur—e.g., "He
went*ed*.") If a child consistently omits or inappropriately uses a morpheme, her
performance can be compared to developmental data regarding the normal sequence and time frame for emergence of appropriate and consistent use of that
particular morpheme (e.g., Brown, 1973). If such a comparison indicates that
the morpheme is one this particular child should be expected to use appropriately, then it will be identified as a target for direct intervention. For such
intervention, then, an appropriate outcome measure is the change in percentage
of obligatory contexts in which the child correctly uses that morpheme (see, for
example, Culatta & Horn, 1982, in Table 4.)

One final type of language measure that merits explanation is that of MLU.
MLU is calculated by dividing the total number of utterances in a sample by the
total number of morphemes in that sample, thus yielding a figure that represents
the average length of that child's utterances in morphemes. Some investigators
prefer to report MLU in words. However, it is much more common today to
report MLU in morphemes; all of the MLU data reported in the studies reviewed
here were of this type. The reader will realize that the MLU-morpheme measure
thus reflects information about both the length and the grammatical sophistication of a child's spontaneous utterances. Not surprisingly, then, it correlates
quite highly with chronological age in normally developing children and approximate age norms for different MLUs are often used in interpreting MLU data in
clinical application (Miller, 1981). In interpreting the MLU results summarized
in studies such as Warren, McQuarter, and Rogers-Warren, 1984 (Table 4) or
Snyder-McLean, Solomonson, McLean and Sack, 1984 (Table 5), the reader

should be cautioned that MLUs in young children are small numbers and that increases are measured in small increments. This is so because of the large number of one- and two-word utterances that occur in any conversational language sample. (Even with normal adult speakers, many conversational turns take the form of one- or two-word answers or replies.) In normal development, MLU typically increases from 1.00 at approximately 1 year of age to only 4.00 at about 4 years of age.

Treatment Approaches

The studies summarized in Tables 4–7 reflect the great diversity of approaches characterizing the field of early language intervention. Approaches range from highly behavioral to highly naturalistic, from narrowly focused and short-duration interventions to others that are broad in scope and longer in duration, and from isolated therapy to total program curriculum models.

The most common set of procedures found in the studies reviewed for this chapter, though by no means in all of them, are those described earlier as behavioral. The reader will recall that we are applying this descriptor to intervention approaches that are characterized by a specified sequence of program steps, specified arrangements of antecedent stimuli, and, most critically, specified and manipulated consequence contingencies for responses to those stimulus conditions. Most of the programs that employed such systematic behavioral procedures also used a massed-trial approach, but this is not always the case. For example, the study by Warren et al. (1984; see Table 4) applies behavioral procedures but on a dispersed-trial schedule in the context of free-play activities. With children who have pervasive handicapping conditions, behavioral language intervention programs typically include multiple steps beginning with such nonverbal behaviors as attending, giving eye-contact, and motor imitation. This approach is exemplified by the Kysela, Hillyard, McDonald, and Ahlsten-Taylor (1981) program for developmentally delayed/Down syndrome children (see Table 5) and the Bloch, Gersten, and Kornblum (1980) program for young children with autism (see Table 6). Such behavioral language programs are typically implemented as one component of a school program for such children, with sessions conducted daily throughout the school year.

In recent years, there has been a growing concern with generalization of language skills to conversational use and a concomitant move towards treatment procedures that emphasize language in the context of its social use—defined earlier in this chapter as the pragmatics of language. In our summary tables, we have characterized programs of this type as representing a *conversational* approach to intervention. These procedures typically emphasize the design of interactive or conversational situations in which use of specific words, morphemes, and/or syntactic structures is obligatory. If the child fails to produce the appropriate linguistic structure(s) in such obligatory conversational contexts, their use is modeled and prompted by the adult. Usually, the consequences for correct or incorrect child responding in a conversational intervention program are those that might be expected to obtain naturally. Thus, a correctly formed question or request will be responded to by the requested information or event, whereas an incorrect form will be responded to by a request for repetition or clarification of the request. Examples of programs using this approach include those of Culatta and Horn (1982; see Table 4), Snyder-McLean et al. (1984; see Table 5), and Beisler and Tsai (1983; see Table 6).

Beyond the behavioral and conversational approaches, there are a number of intervention programs that incorporate some combination of these procedures. For example, the Environmental Language Intervention Program (ELI; MacDonald, 1978), is a structured program designed to teach spontaneous production of two- and three-word utterances. This program involves a sequence of teaching procedures for each target construction that begins with direct imitation and progresses to conversation and, finally, to spontaneous use in play contexts. The systematic structure and initial imitation training phases of the ELI are reminiscent of many behavioral programs; however, the final conversation and play phases more closely resemble what we have characterized as a conversational approach.

Perhaps the best example of an intervention method that combines the features of both behavioral and conversational approaches is that of incidental teaching (Hart & Risley, 1974, 1975). Incidental teaching is typically conducted in a classroom setting and involves teaching a targeted language structure in situations in which the child is spontaneously producing an utterance in which that structure is appropriate or obligatory. The incidental teaching procedure was developed for use with children with mild language disorders who initiate spontaneous utterances at a rate high enough to assure adequate learning opportunities. A variation of that procedure has been developed for children with more severe language delays and is called the mand-model procedure (Rogers-Warren & Warren, 1980; see Warren et al., 1984 in Table 4). This procedure differs from the original in its inclusion of antecedent verbal stimuli from the teacher in the form of questions or "mands," demands for verbalizations from the child (e.g., "Tell me what you are doing."). The mand-model procedure allows the teacher to control the number and types of learning opportunities that will occur for a particular child in the interactive context. This procedure also calls for the teacher to model the requested utterance if the child does not respond to the mand or question. In other respects, this procedure is just like the incidental teaching procedure. Thus, both of these approaches involve teaching language structures in the context of their conversational use and teach these structures with utterances that correspond to the particular materials and activities with which the child is engaged at the moment.

The approaches we have described thus far are relatively circumscribed and specific in terms of treatment targets and procedures. However, a large proportion of early language intervention is conducted in the context of broader and more comprehensive language programs. These programs typically involve a central curriculum that includes sequences of both receptive and expressive language skills. These curricula may also include other related but nonlinguistic skill areas such as imitation and attending or concept development. These curricula generally reflect the developmental skills and sequences observed in normal development. Children are assessed on a curriculum-referenced instrument, and intervention is then directed towards attainment of specific curriculum objectives based on that initial assessment. The intervention usually involves a combination of several different treatment procedures and may combine both home-based and center-based activities. Children are typically enrolled in such programs for at least 1 school year, and progress is reported in terms of gains or changes from the start of the school year to the end. Examples of such programs include the Language Assessment, Remediation and Screening Procedure (LARSP; Christie, 1979; see Table 4), and the Developmental Language Program (DLP; Cooper, Moodley, & Reynell, 1979; see Table 4).

The final approach to early language intervention that we will discuss differs dramatically from all the approaches described thus far and is only used with certain types of language disorder. This approach is the use of *augmentative modes* for language production. We have treated augmentative modes as a separate approach and presented studies concerning the use of augmentative modes with young children in a separate table (Table 7). Augmentative modes are nonoral (usually visual) modes that can be used to express symbolic language. Since the 1960s, a growing body of empirical literature has emerged documenting the use of such modes with children who have normal hearing but who are nonverbal or have severely limited productive language. For some individuals, particularly those with severe neuromotor disorders that preclude intelligible speech production, these modes actually take the place of speech and have thus been referred to as ''alternative modes.'' However, such modes are also prescribed for children who may, in fact, be capable of producing intelligible speech but are not yet doing so, or who are producing so little functional oral language that their continuing cognitive, linguistic, and social development is jeopardized. Some data indicate that the introduction of a nonoral mode (most frequently manual signing) with such children can result not only in an increase in their nonoral expressive language skills, but also in the intelligibility and productivity of their spoken language. Because of this potential for facilitating speech, and because vocal production can continue to carry important inflectional meaning even for individuals whose speech is not intelligible, the American Speech-Language-Hearing Association has recently adopted a position urging that such modes be considered when prescribing treatment for severely language deficient clients, and that they be referred to as *augmentative* and not alternative modes (American Speech-Language-Hearing Association. 1981).

The most common use of augmentative modes with young children, and the use reflected in the studies summarized in Table 7, is with individuals who have expressive language deficits associated with autism or mental retardation. Recently, there has also been interest in the potential of this approach with children who have specific language disorders associated with underlying CNS pathology (Johnston, 1982). For all of these populations, the speculation is that nonoral modes are effective because they do not present the types of demands for auditory (and general perceptual) information processing that are presented by spoken language. Specifically, it is thought that the more static and tangible nature of most visual modes allow them to be processed by children who cannot process the fleeting and intangible stimuli provided by speech. Most of the studies involving augmentative modes with such populations have involved school-aged children and adults. However, the use of this approach with very young children is increasing, and Table 7 summarizes three studies involving the use of manual signs with young children with autism and Down syndrome. The reader will realize that the use of an augmentative mode does not prescribe the actual types of treatment procedure used to teach language in that mode. In fact, Table 7 illustrates that augmentative modes can be implemented with a behavioral approach, a conversational approach, or other approaches that combine features of these two.

Effectiveness of Early Intervention for Communication Disorders

General Considerations

Having described the many approaches and procedures associated with early intervention for these various types of communication disorder, we must now address the critical question: Is such early intervention effective? One global response to that question can be found in the report on effectiveness of early special education commissioned by the Colorado General Assembly (Colorado Department of Education, 1982). This report includes retrospective data on 71 children from three different counties who received early intervention services for diagnosed speech and/or language handicaps. At school entry, 52% of these children were able to enter regular classrooms with no additional intervention or therapy services required, another 35% entered regular classrooms with some support therapy or special education services, and only 13% required special education placement. Although data such as these are encouraging, they clearly leave many critical questions unanswered. They provide us with no detailed information regarding the nature and severity of the children's disorders or the nature and duration of the intervention provided. More critically, they leave us to wonder whether other factors, such as maturation or environmental pressures, might have accounted for the results reported. Thus, to obtain a more satisfying answer to the question of effectiveness of early intervention, we must turn to reports that adhere to the standards of experimental research, including replicability, reliability, generality, and, ultimately, something called believability.

The 30 studies highlighted in the summary tables provided at the end of this chapter were included because they satisfied these basic requirements—some better than others, but all to a minimally acceptable degree. One type of experimental design that appears frequently throughout the summary tables is the $N = 1$ design, demonstrating experimental control through some type of intrasubject replication—most often with a multiple-baseline or reversal design. Reports that did not include such a demonstration of experimental control were considered to be case studies and not included in these tables. Further, $N = 1$ studies were usually not included if they did not involve replication of effects with at least two different subjects. The other most commonly occurring experimental design is the pretest–posttest design. Some of these studies demonstrated experimental control through random assignment to control and experimental groups or the use of a planned comparison group. Others, however, offered no formal evidence of experimental control. The ultimate judgment that must be made in weighing the results of any treatment research is that of believability: Is there good reason to believe that the results reported are reliable and are, in fact, attributable to the experimental intervention rather than some other uncontrolled factor? In the absence of adequate assurances of experimental control, then, we need to consider such factors as severity and stability of the disorder prior to intervention, as well as the relative amount of time that intervened between pretest or baseline measures and final outcome measures, in order to address this issue of believability.

A few additional points should be made regarding the presentation of studies in Tables 2–7. Although our criteria for inclusion specified studies involving children below the age of 6 years, the reader will note that a few of the group studies include children above this age. Such studies were included if the majority of children studied were within our target age range and none was past primary school age (8 years). Whenever possible, we have summarized all relevant quantitative data (e.g., chronological ages, language ages, and test scores) by presenting both the mean and range for those data. Where this information is not provided, it could not be derived from the data provided in the original reference. Most of these studies were published as journal articles. In a few instances, we have included book chapters where these provided adequate procedural information to satisfy our criteria of replicability, reliability, generality, and believability. It should be noted that most of these studies were designed to demonstrate the relative efficacy of a particular approach or to compare two different approaches to treatment of a specific type of disorder. Very few of these studies were conducted to test the benefits of early intervention in general. Therefore, in many cases the basic effectiveness data that are summarized in the tables represent only a small part of the results reported by the investigators, and the interested reader is strongly urged to read these studies in their entirety.

For ease of reference, we have located all of the summary tables at the very end of this chapter. For each study listed, the tables provide a synopsis of the subjects, setting, procedures, measures, experimental design, and outcome. In the remaining pages of this chapter, then, we will not reiterate this descriptive information. Rather, we will summarize the conclusions that can be drawn about effectiveness of early intervention for the various types of communication disorder represented in these tables.

Effectiveness of Intervention for Articulation Disorders

A review of the eight studies summarized in Table 2 provides strong evidence that early intervention for articulation disorders can be effective. Further, we see that most of the children involved in these therapy programs were between 4 and 6 years of age, that the therapy was typically directed at a limited number of phones (usually three or fewer), and that the therapy was effective in modifying the children's articulation performance.

More specifically, several of the studies provided convincing evidence that correction of articulation errors did not occur in these children unless and until intervention was initiated (see Costello & Onstine, 1976; Ruder & Bunce, 1981; Shelton, Johnson, Willis, & Arndt, 1975; Weiner, 1981). There is also evidence that sound training alone will not result in response carryover or generalization (Carrier, 1970; Shelton et al., 1975). However, programs that included specific procedures to promote generalization were effective in achieving this outcome. Generalization to novel linguistic contexts was reported in several studies using the shift-of-stimulus-control procedure (Carrier, 1970; Costello & Onstine, 1976; Shelton et al., 1975). Generalization to untrained sounds sharing common distinctive features was reported in both studies that used a distinctive features approach (Costello & Onstine, 1976; Ruder & Bunce, 1981) and in Weiner's (1981) study, which used a phonological processes approach. Finally, Costello and Bosler (1976) reported high rates of setting generalization, although it should be noted that this was not a measure of spontaneous use.

All of these studies involved direct therapy provided in a clinical setting. In addition, four studies included the parents in a home-based component. In all four of these studies, the parents were involved in conducting sessions only after the child had learned to produce the target response(s) in the clinic setting; then the parents' role was to conduct generalization or carryover sessions. Parents in these studies did not conduct any response development training.

It can be seen that there is considerable variability in the relative efficiency of the different intervention programs represented in Table 2. For example, Weiner reported successful modification of three different phonological processes in an intervention period spanning just 2–3 weeks and a total of 6–14 sessions, whereas Ruder and Bunce report modification of two and three individual sounds after an intervention period involving daily sessions for 4 and 8 months, respectively. It is tempting to note that this latter study is one of the few that did not report use of highly systematic, behavioral procedures and to speculate that this may have contributed to the difference in apparent intervention efficiency. However, it must also be realized that differences in subject characteristics, difficulty of target sounds, and measurement procedures could also account for the differences in relative efficiency of the intervention programs summarized in Table 2.

Finally, a comparison of the different approaches reflected in these studies suggests, most basically, that there is evidence of effectiveness for many different approaches. Certainly the most commonly reported and documented are the behavioral approaches. However, the data provided by Kupperman et al. (1980) suggest that a conversational approach, as embodied in their theraplay procedure, may also be effective for some children. And the study by Christensen and Hanson (1981) gives indication that modification of related oral–motor processes can be an effective way to intervene in certain sound production disorders.

Effectiveness of Early Intervention for Stuttering

The three studies summarized in Table 3 all involved behavioral, direct fluency-shaping types of intervention, with subjects ranging in age from $3\frac{1}{2}$ to 8 years. As in the articulation studies, intervention was provided primarily in a clinic, with parents involved only in carryover sessions (Shine, 1980) or in generalization probes. Although none of these three studies employed a research design demonstrating levels of experimental control that one might like to see, all presented powerful evidence that the stuttering behaviors observed in these children were significant and were not likely to have attenuated without some intervention.

The studies by Martin, Kuhl, and Haroldson (1972) and Reed and Godden (1977) included measures of generalization of fluent speech to spontaneous conversations in the home setting, with results indicating a generalized level of fluency only slightly less than that achieved in the clinic. One of the most striking features of all these studies is the inclusion of follow-up data, documenting the maintenance of intervention effects over periods ranging from 8 months to 5 years.

The weight of evidence from these three studies would seem to support the effectiveness and efficiency, in terms of long-term benefits, of early intervention for stuttering, at least when a direct, fluency-shaping approach is used. However, we must note that we did not locate any comparable studies reporting the effects of a more indirect approach (e.g., stress reduction or parental counseling). Because these indirect approaches are widely used and advocated, generally on the basis of clinical experience, it is unfortunate that we did not find data to document the effectiveness of such approaches. It certainly seems very possible that such an approach can be equally effective in attenuating stuttering in the early childhood years, and we caution against discounting such an approach unless and until future research demonstrates that it is any less effective than direct fluency shaping.

Effectiveness of Early Intervention for Language Delays and Specific Disorders

Table 4 presents summaries of eight studies that involved young children with general language delays and/or specific language disorders. Because many studies involved both types of disorder or did not clearly indicate which classification would best describe their subjects, we have combined them in this table. Several of these studies reported the effects of narrowly focused and short-term clinical procedures on the acquisition of specific expressive language skills by 3–5-year-old children with specific expressive language disorders. These include the studies by Wilcox and Leonard (1978), Hegde, Noll, and Pecora (1979), Olswang, Bain, Dunn, and Cooper (1983), and Culatta and Horn (1982). The first three of these employed behavioral procedures, whereas the Culatta and Horn intervention can be characterized as conversational in approach (although very structured and systematic). All of these reports include convincing documentation of effectiveness in terms of initial acquisition of the target language forms and generalization of those forms to untrained linguistic contexts. Further, based on the results of these studies, it seems reasonable to conclude that a systematic intervention effort should produce this type of achievement, with this type of child, in about 1–2 months of therapy. However, these studies provide little documentation of any generalization of the trained language structures into spontaneous conversational use outside the training settings. This is a critical issue that needs to be addressed in future research.

Two more general center-based programs are those described by Christie (1979) and by Warren et al. (1984). Both of these interventions sought to increase overall levels of expressive language skill through the application of structured intervention procedures over time spans of approximately 3 months. The summary data provided by these studies indicate that they were effective in increasing ELAs and MLUs, respectively, to higher levels than would be expected for these children after 3 months without intervention. Given the short duration of these interventions and the nature of the outcome measures reported, the issue of maintenance of treatment effects seems critical and cannot be addressed from the data provided.

Only two of the studies summarized in Table 4 involved parents in any home-based intervention. Cooper et al. (1979) specifically addressed the issue of home-based versus center-based intervention by comparing effects of the same intervention procedures implemented under both conditions. Stevenson, Box, and Stevenson (1982) compared an experimental group of children who received therapy from a clinician in their homes with a control group who did not receive any individual therapy, but whose mothers were given some general information about language development and stimulation. Results from these studies indicate that children who received intervention did, in fact, demonstrate gains in overall language ages and quotients. However, in the Cooper et al. study, children who received center-based intervention made greater gains than those on home-based programs; and in the Stevenson et al. study, posttest results showed no significant differences between the experimental and control groups with the control making significant, albeit not as extensive, gains from pretest to posttest. We should note that in the Cooper et al. study, the parents were actually responsible for implementing the intervention program on a daily basis; in the Stevenson et al. program, the experimental group of parents were not responsible for intervention but were present at the sessions and were encouraged to participate and improve their general skills for interacting with their children. The results of these two studies suggest the need for further research into the relative efficacy of home-based early language intervention and the factors that might be associated with greater or lesser effectiveness of such intervention.

Finally, one additional aspect of the results from these same two studies merit special mention. Both of these studies employed control groups. As already explained, the Stevenson control group received no intervention other than some general information given to the mothers at the start of the study. Cooper et al. studied four different subject groups, one of which was a control group that received no intervention at all. Although in both studies the control groups made smaller gains than the experimental groups, it is important to note that both control groups did, in fact, demonstrate gains that would not be predicted on the basis of pretest performance levels. (Note that the outcome data for Cooper et al. are based on language development quotients. Such quotients should, theoretically, remain stable with increasing chronological age, yet they reportedly increased for 30% of the control group subjects.) These findings underscore the importance of adequate experimental control in research of this type and the need to be cautious in interpreting the results of efficacy studies that report gains in developmental ages or even quotients.

In sum, then, the published data on early intervention for children with general language delays and specific language disorders support the conclusion that such intervention can be effective in remediating specific language skill deficits and producing general gains in developmental language levels. However, several critical questions are not fully answered by the studies reported here: the generalization of treatment effects into everyday language use, the maintenance of treatment effects over time, and the factors (including measurement or diagnostic error) as evidenced by the results from two control groups. Clearly, further controlled research is needed in this area.

Effectiveness of Early Intervention for Language Disorders Associated with Pervasive Conditions

Finally, in Tables 5–7 we have summarized a number of studies of early intervention efforts directed at the language and communication deficits associated with more pervasive handicapping conditions. Clearly there are important differences in the nature and severity of problems associated with the different subgroups represented in these different tables. However, we will discuss them here in the composite because, as a group, these intervention programs differ from the types of intervention we have discussed thus far and share a number of common features. In reviewing the studies in all of these tables, it is important to recognize that language and communication deficits represent only one aspect of the overall intervention needs presented by these children. In all of the previous speech and language disability groupings, we have been describing interventions for children who generally bring normal levels of cognitive and sociobehavioral functioning to the intervention process. Now, however, we will be examining language intervention with children who bring to the intervention effort a set of confounding problems that can be expected to have deleterious effects not only on the natural rate and course of language development, but also on the effectiveness and efficiency of any treatment procedure designed to modify that development.

The nature of this last group of language disorders, then, has some important implications for our analysis of the studies summarized in Tables 5–7. First, it becomes apparent that the absolute size of intervention effects will typically be much smaller and the rate of demonstrated gain slower than in studies involving other types of communication disorder. Also, we may be more tolerant about weak demonstrations of experimental control when an intervention involves children who have a severe and pervasive handicapping condition that is historically associated with continuing language deficits and lack of spontaneous improvement. In fact, clinical experience and observation suggest that the relative language development status of many such children may actually decrease with increasing chronological age if no intervention is provided. With such children, then, it may be justifiable to view any change in a positive direction as evidence that an intervention has been effective.

This general concern with mitigating the negative effects of more pervasive handicapping conditions on children's communication and language development is reflected in the types of outcome measures most commonly used to assess the effectiveness of early language intervention for such children. Generally, the focus of such intervention is quite broad, including multiple aspects of language skill development and usage, with the ultimate goal of increasing the child's overall rate and level of language development. To measure the success of such efforts, then, outcomes are generally measured in terms of net changes over time on various global measures of language development. Most of the studies summarized in Tables 5–7 take this approach to assessing effectiveness. Among the most commonly used measures in these studies are ELA and RLA, associated language development quotients, and MLU. Three studies in this group focused on interventions that were designed to modify very specific aspects of language performance and, therefore, used direct measures of the targeted skills as their outcome measures. These three are the Salzberg and Villani (1983; see Table 5) study of procedures to increase verbal imitation in young children with Down syndrome; the Palyo, Cooke, Schuler, and Apolloni (1979; see Table 6) study of procedures to decrease rates of echolalia and increase rates of appropriate answering in young children with autism; and the study by Barrera et al. (1980; see Table 7), which compared the effects of two different procedures for teaching single word production to a mute autistic child (see also Chapter 7 by Simeonsson, Olley, & Rosenthal, focusing on children with autism, in this volume).

This last group of disorders also differs from the more specific speech and language disorders in terms of the setting for intervention. Not surprisingly, because most of these children are receiving some type of general early intervention for their primary handicapping condition, most of the programs summarized in these three tables were implemented in school settings. A review of these tables will show that only two of these interventions were conducted in hospital or clinic settings; one of these (MacDonald, Blott, Gordon, Spiegel, & Hartmann, 1974; Table 5) represented only the first phase in a predominantly home-based program.

A total of four studies, all involving children with Down syndrome, were partially or totally home based. Two of these studies (Clements, Evans, Jones, Osborne, & Upton, 1982; see Table 5; Kysela et al., 1981) reported results suggesting that the home-based intervention was relatively ineffective. The Kysela et al. study used a behavioral approach and compared a home-based with a center-based version of this program and found that the center-based children made significant gains in both ELA and RLA, whereas the home-based group made no significant gains in ELA. However, gains in RLA were significant at the .05 level. The Clements et al. study compared a home-based treatment group with a control group that received general, home-based early intervention but no specific language intervention and found no significant differences between the two groups. In both of these studies, the parents had primary responsibility for implementing language intervention and there is no indication that any special training was provided to the parents, although a teacher did make weekly home visits to review program progress and consult with parents in the Clements et al. study.

The other two home-based procedures were more structured and provided more support to the parents. In MacDonald et al.'s study (1974; see Table 5), parents and children participated in clinic sessions twice a week for the first 7 weeks of a 5-month home-based intervention. Weller and Mahoney (1983; see Table 7) provided parents with 4–8 hours of training before expecting them to implement a home-based expressive language intervention program. Both of these studies employed the highly structured and focused ELI program described earlier; both of these studies report significant gains made by the children on all outcome measures.

Finally, in reviewing the studies in Tables 5–7, we must again raise the dual question concerning demonstration of both maintenance and generalization of treatment effects. Like the studies of more specific language delays/disorders, these studies tended not to report data relevant to either of these questions. The only study in these three tables that included any type of follow-up was that by Palyo et al. (1979; see Table 6), who report that the effects of their intervention to decrease echolalic responding did maintain 1 year after treatment. Generalization was addressed in only one study (Salzberg & Villani, 1983; Table 5) and their training to increase rates of verbal imitation did not generalize to the home setting until training was introduced into that setting. We note that studies that report MLU as one of their outcome measures do provide at least an indirect measure of generalization, because MLU is calculated on the basis of spontaneous, conversational language produced in an interactive context. Clearly, however, there is a need for future research in this area to address the issues of both maintenance and generalization of intervention effects.

In sum, the data provided by these studies seems to indicate that early intervention for language disorders can be effective with these special populations. It is also clear that some intervention efforts are more effective than others, and it will be important in the years ahead to attempt to identify those factors that increase the effectiveness and efficiency of such intervention. In doing so, we will need to scrutinize closely the role of home and family vis-à-vis the center and professional staff, and also expand our evaluations of effectiveness to more routinely include measures of maintenance and generalization of treatment effects.

SUMMARY AND CONCLUSIONS

In this chapter, we have reviewed current practices, issues, and data bases in order to draw some conclusions about the state of the art in the area of early intervention for communication disorders and specifically to look for evidence regarding the effectiveness of such intervention. What have we learned? Certainly we have found this to be a field characterized by much activity and debate, with many different schools of thought concerning the best and most appropriate approaches to assessment, diagnosis, and treatment for various types of speech and language disorder. But the most basic conclusion we must draw, in view of the weight of the evidence offered by the 30 studies reviewed in this chapter, is that early intervention for communication disorders can be effective in modifying the course and impact of those disorders.

Beyond this very global conclusion about the potential benefits of early intervention for communication disorders, can we identify specific practices that seem to be related to the relative effectiveness and efficiency of intervention programs and thus merit closer consideration and further research? To begin to answer this question, we can at least point out some trends in the cumulative data from these 30 studies that seem to have important implications for future clinical and research programs.

On the issue of direct versus indirect approaches to intervention, the studies reviewed here suggest that direct therapeutic interventions focused on very specific deficient or deviant speech and language behaviors tended to be both effective and efficient. Similarly, highly systematic behavioral approaches to remediation of specific skill deficits also tended to be effective in achieving the stated goals of therapy in a relatively short time.

Unfortunately, few of the studies reviewed, especially among those involving language disorders, provided data regarding the maintenance or generalization of treatment effects to the real-world communicative contexts in which newly acquired skills must ultimately be used by children. The current trend among many practitioners to adopt more conversational or interactive approaches to language, and even speech therapy, reflects the expectation that such approaches will be more likely to result in this type of generalization. However, although clinical wisdom and many anecdotes tend to support this expectation, there was little empirical support for it in the studies reviewed here. Clearly, this is an important issue that should be addressed in future efficacy studies.

The data from these studies raise some provocative questions regarding the effectiveness of home-based intervention. We found good evidence supporting the value of parent and home involvement at the level of extending newly acquired skills into daily use (i.e., response generalization or carryover). More specifically, a number of studies reported intervention efforts that involved initial systematic intervention by a professional therapist or teacher in a clinic or school setting provided in combination with a structured series of home practice or generalization activities implemented by the parents at home, under the guidance of the professional. Programs that thus involved both professionals and parents, differentially assigning responsibility for actual response training to the professional and response generalization to the parents. tended to achieve initial skill development quite efficiently and also to document effectiveness in terms of response generalization. However, the results from programs that were more totally home based, in which the parents assumed primary responsibility for actually implementing all phases of training, tended to report equivocal data regarding the effectiveness of their intervention. Although this pattern seems to have clear implications regarding the appropriate (and inappropriate) role of parents in early intervention programs for communication disorders, we must note that many other factors could have accounted for the differences in relative effectiveness of programs reviewed here. This is a question that will require intensive investigation under controlled conditions before we can determine whether this apparent trend is a real or illusory phenomenon.

Finally, what advice would we offer to the practitioner or parent who is concerned about the speech or language development of a particular child? First, we would strongly urge that the child be evaluated by a certified speech/language pathologist to determine whether the child does have a communication disorder. (We might note that many school districts now provide early intervention services for infants and young children and that speech/language evaluation is often available at no charge through such school-sponsored programs.) If the evaluation indicates that the child's speech and language development are occurring within normal boundaries, this information in itself should be worth the effort to the concerned parents.

If a communication disorder is diagnosed, the data available to date suggest that direct intervention should be initiated as soon as the disorder is identified. In

TABLE 2

Speech disorders: articulation

Reference	Nature of intervention	Intervention parameters	Setting	Role of parents
Carrier, 1970	Behavioral; systematic program for shift of stimulus control from imitation to picture name to conversational use; speech therapist completed response development training for the target sound before stimulus-shift procedure was started; response development involved imitation training of the target sound in isolation; a control group was given general instructions on how to prompt correct sound use but did not use the stimulus shift procedure	Duration not specified; stimulus shift procedure involved 2 short (5–10 min) sessions per day; program consists of 6 lessons, each of which was repeated until child reached a specified criterion level	Initial response development was done at clinic; carryover and stimlus shift training were done at home	Mothers were responsible for implementing the stimulus-shift procedure (experimental group) or general carryover procedure (control group)

selecting an intervention program, the parent or referring professional should probably look for a program that is structured towards attainment of specific intervention targets and that will provide documentation of the child's progress towards achievement of those target skills. Further, it is important to look for evidence that a program has procedures to assess and promote generalization and maintenance of newly acquired skills, including some plans for home involvement in carryover or practice activities. The extent to which such generalization will be achieved is also likely to be directly related to the degree to which parents are willing and able to work cooperatively with professional staff in providing such home carryover experiences for the child.

Expectations, in terms of outcomes from intervention for any particular child, must reflect the initial severity of the child's communication disorder. The studies reviewed here suggest that it is reasonable to expect remediation of many specific speech or language skill deficits to be achieved in a short period of time—a matter of a few weeks or months. However, as the severity and pervasiveness of the disorder increase, so does the time required for effective intervention. Also, it must be recognized that not every child is able to acquire a fully intelligible speech system or sophisticated linguistic system. However, every child with a diagnosed communication disorder should be able to benefit from early intervention and should be able to become a more effective and efficient communicator as a result of that intervention.

Child characteristics	Experimental design	Outcome measures	Results
20 children with articulation disorders ranging from mild to severe and CAs between 4 and 7 years; 10 children were assigned to experimental and 10 to control groups; subjects were matched for CA, type of articulation error, and specific articulation target	Pre–posttest with planned comparison group; tests were administered at 4 points: prior to isolated sound training, immediately after isolated sound training, at the mid point of stimulus-shift program, and at end of stimulus-shift program	Program Word Test including words taught in stimulus-shift program, Developmental Articulation Test (Hejne, 1959), and Deep Test of Articulation (McDonald, 1964) for both the target sound and its cognate (voiced or unvoiced counterpart)	No subject improved on any of the measures after only the clinical sound-in-isolation imitation training; after the home carryover/stimulus-shift phase, the experimental group showed greater improvement than the control group on all measures; author states difference was statistically significant, but does not give significance level

(continued)

TABLE 2 (*Continued*)

Reference	Nature of intervention	Intervention parameters	Setting	Role of parents
Christensen & Hanson, 1981	Oral myofunctional therapy for tongue thrust in addition to traditional articulation therapy for specific misarticulated sounds (/s/ and /z/); control group received only the articulation therapy	22 sessions, 30 min each over 14 weeks; experimental group: 14 sessions oral myofunctional therapy, 8 sessions articulation therapy; control group: 22 sessions articulation therapy	Clinic for therapy sessions, with carryover activities in the home	Conducted daily home "practice" sessions for both types of therapy
Costello & Bosler, 1976	Behavioral; systematic programming for shift of stimulus control (same as Carrier, 1970; see above); subjects first taught to imitate sound in isolation by speech therapist; target sound was /v/ for all subjects	Parent stimulus-shift program required 2 sessions per day; each session involved 60 trials; subjects completed the 8-step program in a mean of 13 sessions over a mean of 9½ calendar days	Initial training at clinic; stimulus shift at home	Primary responsibility for implementing stimulus-shift program
Costello & Onstine, 1976	Behavioral and distinctive feature; 9-step program with systematic shift of stimulus control from imitation of sounds in release and arrest positions to conversational contexts; feature targeted was continuancy and sounds were /s/ and /θ/ (e.g., *th*ank) with /t/ used for contrasting (stop) feature	4 sessions per week, 30 min each; total number of sessions was 32 for Subject 1 and 50 for Subject 2, a total of 8 and 12 weeks, respectively	Clinic	None specified
Kupperman, Bligh, & Goodban, 1980	Theraplay; clinician engaged child in intensive play session, focused on interaction and sound/word games; words and sounds used in each child's session were selected to maximize experience with sounds child misarticulated on pretest; no differential or corrective feedback was provided	2 sessions per week, 30 min for 6 weeks (total of 12 sessions)	Clinic	None specified

Child characteristics	Experimental design	Outcome measures	Results
N = 10; CA: $\bar{X}$ = 6,2[a] (range: 5,8–6,9); all had tongue thrust and severe frontal lisp; all had normal hearing and cognitive development	Pre–posttest with random assignment of subjects to experimental (N = 5) and control (N = 5) groups	An experimenter-designed word repetition test, A clinician-designed picture articulation test, Goldman–Fristoe Test of Articulation (Goldman and Fristoe, 1969), and a tongue-thrust evaluation	Both groups showed "significant" improvement (level not specified) on all articulation measures and on tongue-tip sound placement; experimental group also showed improvement on tongue thrust; control group showed no change on tongue thrust; anecdotal reports suggest that experimental group generalized correct sound production to conversational use more rapidly than control group
N = 3; mean CA = 5,8 (range: 4,11–6,2); all had functional articulation errors and normal hearing	Quasi-pre–posttest with no control (different measures were used for pre- and posttest)	Generalization probes for target sound production in untrained settings and in untrained words; pretest measures: Goldman–Fristoe Test of Articulation and Deep Test of Articulation	All subjects successfully completed the training program (criterion for completion was correct production of target sound in both initial and final position in 20 training words in story-telling context); mean percent correct productions on generalization tasks were 90.5% for setting generalization and 71.7% for word generalization
N = 2; CA = 4,2 and 4,5; both in clinic for multiple phoneme errors	Pre–posttest with control sound /r/, that was tested but not trained; test for generalization to untrained sounds sharing target distinctive feature	Two Pre–posttest measures: specific sound production tasks (imitative production in multiple sound contexts) and Deep Test of Articulation (spontaneous production of sound in 2-word utterances); also, probes were administered at the end of each program phase	Both subjects successfully completed program; test scores (reported as percent correct) on trained sounds improved from pretest means of 0.25% (Deep Test of Articulation) and 1.5% (sound production tasks) to 98.25% and 92.5%, respectively; training generalized to untrained sounds with same (continuant) distinctive feature, but not to untrained and unrelated control sound, /r/ (mean pretest of 20% and posttest of 21.5% correct on sound production task)
N = 6; CA range: 3,2–6; all enrolled for articulation remediation	Pre–posttest, with no control	Number of misarticulated items on the Fisher–Logeman Test (Fisher and Logeman, 1971)	Range of number of errors: 13–67 on pretest, 5–56 on posttest; mean decrease in number of errors per subject was 10.8 (range: 5–18)

(continued)

TABLE 2 (*Continued*)

Reference	Nature of intervention	Intervention parameters	Setting	Role of parents
Ruder & Bunce, 1981	Distinctive feature; articulation therapy procedures reportedly included use of social reinforcement and manipulation of objects; eclectic approach to therapeutic procedures; target sounds identified on basis of distinctive feature analysis; target sounds for Subject 1 were /s/ and /k/ with generalization predicted for /t/; training for Subject 2 provided for /b/; /k/ and /s/ sequentially	Subject 1: 5 sessions per week, 30–45 min each, total of 68 sessions (approximately 4 months); Subject 2: 5 sessions per week for 8 months	Clinic	None specified
Shelton, Johnson, Willis, & Arndt, 1975	Behavioral; systematic program for shift of stimulus control and sound automatization; target sound (/l/, /r/, or /s/) was first trained in isolation by speech therapist until child could produce correctly; stimulus control was then shifted from an imitative model to a picture; when criterion reached for picture naming, the home program for automatization of the sound was begun; the home program required the parent to listen for 30 spontaneous productions of the target sound each day; parents were trained to differentially respond to correct and incorrect productions and to record data on each target sound production	Response training and stimulus-shift procedure (clinical training) required a mean of 6.8 lessons per child (range: 3–13 lessons); home carryover program lasted 5 weeks and involved 30 responses per day, 5 days per week	Clinic (initial training) and home (carryover)	Identify and provide differential consequences for correct production of target sound in daily conversations
Weiner, 1981	Behavioral and phonological process approach; treatment provided for three phonological processes: deletion of final consonant, stopping, and fronting; procedure involved using minimal contrast pairs in a meaningful communication task; corrective feedback and differential reinforcement (verbal and token) procedures were used to respond to child productions	3 sessions per week, 1 hr each: Subject 1, total of 6 sessions (2 weeks); Subject 2, 14 sessions (3 weeks)	Clinic	None specified

[a]Chronological ages given in years and months.

Child characteristics	Experimental design	Outcome measures	Results
$N = 2$; CA = 4,0 and 5,5; Subject 1 had severe articulation disorder and language delay; Subject 2 had severe articulation disorder	$N = 1$; untrained control sounds for Subject 1; multiple probe across responses for Subject 2	Subject 1: University of Kansas articulation test (imitative production of sounds in initial, medial and final positions); Subject 2: Deep Test of Articulation	Both subjects demonstrated acquisition of the trained sounds and some generalization to untrained sounds that shared multiple distinctive features with trained sounds; no generalization to untrained sounds with very different features; for Subject 2, data show no improvement on successive sounds until training was provided
$N = 10$; mean CA = 5,6 (range: 4,6–5,7); articulation skills at least 1 standard deviation below mean for CA; normal hearing	Pre–posttest without control for all subjects; $N = 1$ with control (quasi-multiple baseline across sounds for 6 of the subjects; second control sound was probed but not trained)	Talking task probes analyzed for number of correct sound productions out of 30 responses in spontaneous, conversational use	At end of first phase of sound training in the clinic, no significant improvement was found in talking task sound productions ($\bar{X}$ for pretest = 3.5 and $\bar{X}$ for posttest = 5.5 correct out of 30 productions); at conclusion of 5-week home program, $\bar{X}$ was 11.7 correct out of 30 productions (significant at .01 level); control sound data reported for 6 of the subjects showed no significant improvement over this same period
$N = 2$; CA = 4,10 and 4,4, both with severe articulation disorders; unintelligible	$N = 1$; multiple baseline across responses	Training response and generalization probe data on targeted processes	Subjects successfully acquired trained rules with posttraining correct production rates 60–80%; untrained rules stayed at baseline levels until training was initiated; acquired rules did generalize to untrained words, although rates of correct sound production were lower than for words used in training

TABLE 3

Speech disorders: stuttering

Reference	Nature of intervention	Intervention parameters	Setting	Role of parents
Martin, Kuhl, & Haroldson, 1972	Behavioral; direct fluency shaping; 10 sec of time out from conversation with a puppet was delivered contingent on occurrence of stuttering episode	1 session per week, 20 min each; baseline (no treatment) phases lasted 3–4 sessions; treatment lasted 27 sessions for Subject 1 and 10 sessions for Subject 2; withdrawal/ maintenance sessions (no treatment) lasted another 12–13 sessions	Clinic with home carryover probes after treatment phase	Participated in posttreatment home-carryover probes; Subject 2's mother also participated in daily generalization probes
Reed & Godden, 1977	Behavioral; direct fluency shaping; delivery of verbal consequence, "slow down," contingent on each episode	2 sessions per week, 20 min each; total of 10 weeks. Subject 1: baseline = 5 sessions, treatment = 15 sessions; Subject 2: baseline = 10 sessions, treatment = 10 sessions)	Clinic with home carryover probes	Participated in 4 home carryover probes
Shine, 1980/1984	Behavioral; direct fluency shaping; program consists of 5 phases that progress from picture labeling to conversational speech; focus is on slowing speech rate and decreasing vocal intensity; length and complexity of utterances are systematically increased over duration of program; responses are responded to contingently with token reinforcement or corrective feedback	Minimum of 2 sessions per week, 40–50 min each; $\bar{X}$ number of sessions = 56.7 (range: 16–133); $\bar{X}$ duration = 10.4 months (range: 1–28)	Clinic and home or school	Parents collect home carryover data and conduct carryover training for each program step after child achieves fluency on that step in clinic

Child characteristics	Experimental design	Outcome measures	Results
$N = 2$; CA = 3.5 and 4.5, Subject 1 was a severe stutterer (baseline rate approximately 60 stutterings per 20-min session); Subject 2 was a mild–moderate stutterer (baseline rate approximately 15 stutterings per 20-min session with accompanying face/neck muscle tension)	$N = 1$; ABA design (second A phase did not return behavior to initial baseline rate; However, baseline data support claim that stuttering rates were stable and were not declining without intervention)	Number of words spoken and number of stutterings per 20-min session; generalization session involved 20-min conversation with clinician (Subject 1) or mother (Subject 2); 4 home conversations were recorded and analyzed after training phase completed; follow-up session with clinician after 1 year	For both subjects, stuttering reduced to zero and near-zero rates during training phase and remained stable after withdrawal of the time-out contingency; generalization probes also declined to zero and near-zero rates during the training and withdrawal phases; home carryover data showed range of 0–3 stutterings in conversations of 10–40-min length; after 1 year, Subject 1 produced 7 stutterings in 20 min and Subject 2 produced 4 stutterings in 20 min
$N = 2$; CA = 5,10 and 3,9; Subject 1 demonstrated sound and syllable repetition accompanied by facial tension, mean baseline stuttering rate of 7%; Subject 2 was a severe stutterer with repetitions and prolongations accompanied by muscle tension, mean baseline stuttering rate of 18%	$N = 1$; multiple baseline across subjects; also, one session on ABA schedule within session (i.e., 10-min baseline, 20-min treatment, 10-min baseline)	Percent of words stuttered during sessions and in 4 home carryover probes.	In ABA design session, mean rate of stuttering reduced from 8% during 10-min baseline to 4% during 20-min treatment; At end of 10-min return to baseline, rate increased to 11%; stuttering reduced over course of treatment to a rate of 1% of words by session 20; home carryover probes also showed reducing frequency over course of treatment with final rates of 3% and 2%; follow-up probe 8 months after treatment showed rates of 1% and 0.6%; extended baseline rate of stuttering for Subject 2 remained stable until treatment was initiated
$N = 14$; Mean CA = 4,9 (range = 2,9–8,0)	Retrospective and pre–posttest with no control (author is summarizing clinical data collected over 7 years)	Stuttered words per minute (SW/M); author does not specify conditions under which this was sampled—may have differed for different subjects over the 7 years of this research	Pretest mean SW/M = 13.9 (range 4–22); posttest (mean SW/M = 1.7 (range 0–8.4); 1 year after therapy, only 1 subject was stuttering (reinstituted therapy for that subject and achieved fluency in 18 sessions); long-term follow-up (up to 5 years): subjects have maintained fluency (mean SW/M = 3.2, range = 0.2–7.5)

TABLE 4

Language disorders: specific language delay or disorder

Reference	Nature of intervention	Intervention parameters	Setting	Role of parents
Christie, 1979	Structured program, the Language Assessment, Remediation and Screening Procedure (LARSP); program combines developmental and behavioral approaches; highly structured therapy focused on treatment targets identified as deficient based on initial assessment; specific procedure used was forced alternative questioning ("Is it a ____ or a ____?")	20 sessions, 30 min each; total of 8–15 weeks	Clinic	None specified
Cooper, Moodley, & Reynell, 1979	Structured program, Developmental Language Program; program curriculum targeted 12 developmental areas, including receptive and expressive language and related areas; training targeted specific deficits identified for each child on basis of initial assessment; procedures include both 1-to-1 therapy and group training; had both a home-based and a center-based version of program	Total duration approximately 1 year: center-based, 2 hr per day, 5 days per week; home-based, daily work with child by parent, contact with therapist once every 6 weeks	Either clinical center *or* home	Center-based: observe sessions and meet with staff once per semester or term; home-based: conduct daily training
Culatta & Horn, 1982	Conversational/dispersed trials; systematic strategy for promoting generalization by modeling and evoking target linguistic structures in role-play contexts; density of modeling and structure occurrences systematically faded through 4 phases to normal rate of occurrence for structure in natural interactions (target structures included copulas, auxiliaries, pronouns, modals, and irregular past tense)	2 sessions per week, 45 min each; trained to criterion; total number of sessions 8–16	Clinic	None specified

258

Child characteristics	Experimental design	Outcome measures	Results
$N = 6$; mean CA $= 3,6^a$ (range: 3,0–3.10); mean expressive language age: 2,6; all diagnosed as having expressive language impairment	Pre–posttest with no control	LARSP profile, based on analysis of 30-min language sample	Mean gain of 1 year in expressive language age from pretest to posttest (8–15 week interval, mean of 3 months)
Center-based: $N = 50$; CA $= 3,0$–4,6; Home-based: $N = 69$; CA $= 2,0$–4,6; all had language age $\leq \frac{2}{3}$ of nonverbal performance age	Pre–posttest with comparison groups: Control Group 1: 20 subjects, received no treatment; Control Group 2: 39 subjects, received conventional speech therapy	Reynell Develomental Language Scales (reported only "better," "same," or "worse," on posttest in comparison to pretest measure of developmental rate/quotient; no actual scores are reported)	In terms of percentage of subjects whose developmental rates on comprehension and expressive measures improved; best results were for center-based group (82% and 86%), compared to home-based group (72% and 72%); fewer control subjects showed improvements, with more improvement by those receiving conventional therapy (53% and 54%) than no treatment at all (30% and 30%); follow-up of experimental subjects after 6 months showed treatment gains maintained
$N = 4$; Mean CA $= 6,6$ (range: 4,6–9,2); all demonstrated specific grammatical deficits in expressive language, but normal/near-normal development in receptive language	$N = 1$ with control: Multiple baseline across two responses (grammatical rules)	Training data: percent of obligatory utterances in which subject correctly used target structure	All subjects achieved criterion levels on all rules trained (criterion = correct spontaneous use in 9 out of the first 10 obligatory discourse contexts; 2 consecutive sessions); target responses in second baseline remained at baseline levels (range: 30–60% correct spontaneous production) until training procedure initiated; 1-month follow-up showed rules taught in first baseline maintained at 100% level for all subjects

(*continued*)

TABLE 4 (*Continued*)

Reference	Nature of intervention	Intervention parameters	Setting	Role of parents
Study A: Hegde & Gierut, 1979; Study B: Hegde, Noll, & Pecora, 1979	Behavioral; massed-trial format; procedures included presentation of picture stimulus, modeling, differential reinforcement, and corrective feedback; training targets were specific grammatical structures (Study A: pronouns and auxiliaries; Study B: auxilliaries, copulas, and possessives); training continued on each structure until subject showed generalization to untrained examples	4–5 sessions per week 30 min (A) and 45 min (B); Total of 15–18 sessions over 4 weeks	Clinic	Study A: none specified; Study B: observed sessions and conducted home generalization probes
Olswang, Bain, Dunn, & Cooper 1983	Behavioral; massed-trial format; followed 6-step program to teach production of a total of 10 nouns and 10 verbs; compared 2 stimulus conditions: picture identification versus object manipulation	2 therapy sessions and 1 probe session per week, 30 min each; total of about 20 therapy sessions	Clinic	None specified
Stevenson, Box, & Stevenson, 1982	Structured therapy conducted in home; therapy individualized on basis of child's deficits in language structure and phonology; control group mothers received information on general language stimulation, but no structured therapy was provided to children	22 home visits by therapist to experimental group subjects over approximately 6 months	Home	Experimental group mothers were encouraged to observe and participate in therapy sessions; aim was to help mothers improve quality of teaching

Child characteristics	Experimental design	Outcome measures	Results
Total $N = 3$; Study A: $N = 1$; CA = 4,9; Study B: $N = 2$; CAs = 3,9 and 4,0; all subjects had expressive language delays with multiple grammatical and articulation errors	$N = 1$ with controls: multiple baseline across responses, with generalization probes to untrained exemplars and, for 1 subject, to probe session in home setting	Percent correct responses on baseline, training, and generalization probes	Specific structures remained at zero-correct baseline levels until systematic training was initiated; all trained structures reached criterion level of 100% correct production in all training and generalization probe contexts
$N = 4$; Mean CA = 33 months (range: 23–40 months); all language impaired and functioning at 1-word expressive level; expressive language ages were 10–20 months below CA	$N = 1$ with controls: Alternating treatment with set of control (untrained) words	Spontaneous production on target words in elicited language production probes conducted weekly throughout baseline and training phases	At end of training program, subjects spontaneously produced a mean of 14.7 (range: 9–20) of the trained words, compared to 5.7 (range: 2–10) of the control/untrained words; comparison of two stimulus conditions revealed individual differences: 2 subjects did best in object manipulation, 1 in picture identification and one did equally well in both; pictures evoked a higher rate of responding for all subjects
$N = 22$; all with expressive language delay (mean = -2.67 standard score on Reynell); low-income families; assigned to 2 groups: experimental: $N = 12$, mean CA = 35.5 months; Control: $N = 10$; mean CA = 36.1 months; not randomly assigned, but matched control group subjects to experimental group subjects on demographic factors and nonverbal IQ	Pre–posttest with comparison group; quasi-matched pairs design	Reynell Developmental Language Scales, English Picture Vocabulary Test (receptive language, Brimer and Dunn, 1962), and Griffiths Mental Developmental Scales: nonverbal subscales (Griffiths, 1970)	No significant differences between experimental and control groups at posttest; both groups made significant gains ($p < .001$ for experimental group and $p < .05$ for control group) on Reynell (mean posttest standard score for experimental group was -1.73 and for control group was -1.85); 4 control group subjects regressed on Reynell; no E group Ss showed regression

(*continued*)

TABLE 4 (*Continued*)

Reference	Nature of intervention	Intervention parameters	Setting	Role of parents
Warren, McQuarter, & Rogers-Warren, 1984	Behavioral and conversational/ dispersed trials; mand-model procedure in which child was required to produce 1-word (phase 1) or 2-word (phase 2) utterances in response to teacher questions or mands (e.g., "Tell me what you're doing") in free-play context; appropriate verbal responses were responded to by positive feedback and continued attention; inappropriate or no responses were responded to with a modeling procedure	Daily, in context of 45–min free-play sessions; total number of intervention sessions: 36–54	Preschool classroom for language-delayed children	None specified
Wilcox & Leonard, 1978	Behavioral; massed-trial format; procedures included modeling, corrective feedback, and differential reinforcement; treatment targets were specific grammatical forms (6 different *wh* + auxiliary question types—e.g., "What is . . . What does . . . Who is . . .")	Not specified; each subject participated until criterion (20 consecutive correct responses) was reached on specific structure targeted for that subject	Clinic	None specified

[a]Chronological ages given in years and months.
[b]MLU, mean length of utterance.

Child characteristics	Experimental design	Outcome measures	Results
$N = 3$; CA = 2,11, 3,2, and 3,7; language ages and MLUs[b] were below age expectancy for all subjects; receptive skills higher than expressive skills for all subjects	$N = 1$; with controls: multiple baseline across subjects, with maintenance phase	Number of verbalizations, percent responsiveness to teacher mands, and MLU in 15-min samples recorded during each intervention session	Total verbalizations and responsiveness increased for all subjects; MLUs increased from a baseline mean of 1.5 to a maintenance phase mean of 2.16; Baseline rates for Subjects 2 and 3 remained low and stable until intervention was initiated; rates attained in training did maintain when formal use of mand-model procedure was withdrawn
$N = 24$; mean CA = 5,3 (range: 3,8–8,2); all diagnosed as language disordered and scored below 10th percentile on standardized test of expressive language; subjects randomly assigned to experimental ($N = 12$) or control group ($N = 12$)	Pre–posttest with random assignment	Number of correct productions in response to 30 novel test items; test items included specific structures on which subject received training, as well as related but untrained grammatical structures; score assigned was gain from pretest to posttest	Experimental group had a mean gain score at posttesting of 9.5, compared to 0.08 for control group (difference significant at $p < .001$ level); greatest gains were on specifically trained constructions with generalization to other structures with the same auxiliary verb

TABLE 5

Communication language deficits associated with pervasive handicapping conditions: mental retardation/developmental delay

Reference	Nature of intervention	Intervention parameters	Setting	Role of parents
Clements, Evans, Jones, Osborne, & Upton, 1982	Portage curriculum and procedures (see Chapter 4, this volume), supplemented by a specially designed communication skills sequence, with activity cards for each goal in that sequence; a comparison group received Standard Portage program/general early intervention only	1 home visit per week by home teacher for total of 16 months; parents conducted daily training sessions; mean number of tasks targeted for each child over 16-month period was 113.4	Home	Primary trainers; responsible for conducting daily sessions
Kysela, Hillyard, McDonald, & Ahlsten-Taylor, 1981	Behavioral; direct teaching methods in massed trial format; both receptive and expressive language programs consisted of 5 steps and child had to achieve preset criterion at each step before moving to next step; expressive program extends from attending (step 1) to "labeling" (step 5); receptive program extends from "responds to name" (step 1) to "operations with distractions" (step 5); 2 groups reported: school and home	Total duration approximately 1½ years School group: 1 individual language therapy session per day in context of half-day preschool program, 4–5 days per week Home group: daily individual language therapy session	School and home	School group participated in maintenance and generalization phases Home group conducted daily sessions
MacDonald, Blott, Gordon, Spiegel, & Hartmann, 1974	Structured program: environmental language intervention (ELI), uses sequential imitation–conversation–play procedure to train generalized use of 2-word semantic–grammatical utterances (e.g., agent + action; action + object); primarily parent/home implemented	19 weeks (5 months); weeks 1–7: 2 sessions per week at clinic and daily sessions at home; weeks 8–19: sessions at home only; minimum of 3 sessions per week	Clinic (weeks 1–7) and home (weeks 1–19)	Primary trainers, responsible for conducting all home sessions

Child characteristics	Experimental design	Outcome measures	Results
Total $N = 11$, all "mentally handicapped" Experimental Group: $N = 6$, mean CA = 14.25 months, mean IQ = 78.23 Comparison Group mean CA = 6.5 months, mean IQ = 76	Pre–posttest, with comparison group (groups determined on de facto basis: Experimental group subjects were children on waiting list for preschool program; comparison group subjects were already enrolled in Portage model preschool program; author notes difference in CA between groups approached significance ($p < .10$)	Griffiths Scales of Mental Development: Individual subscale scores and overall derived mental age results reported in net change in developmental ages, not quotients	No significant differences between groups; both groups showed gains; language age scores increased by 6.67 months for the experimental group and 9.5 months for the comparison group; note: from data provided, the reader can compute developmental rates or quotients on language scale; this computation reveals that language quotients for both groups declined from pretest mean of .72 to posttest mean of .56 (net change = $-.16$) for experimental group and from .86 to .67 (net change of $-.19$) for control group
Total $N = 30$; all developmentally delayed and all but 3 with Down syndrome School group: $N = 8$, all younger than 3 years, all had "some" speech Home group: $N = 22$; mean CA = $13\frac{1}{2}$ months (range: 1–30 months); all had no speech	Pre–posttest with no control	Reynell Developmental Language Scales, both receptive and expressive; data reported in terms of language development ratios (i.e., language age to chronological age)	School group: expressive language age (ELA) ratio increased significantly ($p < .001$) as did receptive language age (RLA) ratio ($p < .01$); home group: no significant change in ELA ratio, RLA ratio showed significant ($p < .05$) improvement
$N = 6$ (3 experimental and 3 control); CA = 3–5 years; all had Down syndrome and were functioning at 1-word utterance stage at start of intervention	Pre–posttest with control group (authors do not specify how subjects were assigned to groups)	ELI prescriptive assessment instrument used for program placement; MLUs[a] calculated from language samples	Experimental group showed greater increase in MLUs (range: 57–191% increase) than control group (range: -15–73% change); posttest on ELI showed experimental group subjects had acquired spontaneous use of 5 types of grammatical 2-word utterance; control group subjects "made negligible gains" on this measure

(continued)

TABLE 5 (*Continued*)

Reference	Nature of intervention	Intervention parameters	Setting	Role of parents
Salzberg & Villani, 1983	Behavioral program to increase frequency of vocal imitation and spontaneous vocalizations; procedures included modeling, mand for imitation, 5-sec delay, differential reinforcement, and a correction procedure	3–4 20-trial sessions per week, 5–20 min each; total of approximately 3 months	Training conducted in preschool; generalization data collected in home	Conducted training sessions at school with own children
Snyder-McLean, Solomonson, McLean, & Sack, 1984	Conversational/dispersed trials: structured interactive routines implemented throughout school day; specific receptive, expressive, and discourse language targets identified from initial assessment on project-developed curriculum; additional massed-trial articulation therapy was provided to some children for 20 min per day	3 hours per day, 4 days per week; 3–7 months; Mean length of enrollment 4.7 months	Preschool	None specified

[a]MLU, mean length of utterance.
[b]Chronological ages given in years and months.

Child characteristics	Experimental design	Outcome measures	Results
$N = 2$; CAs for both: 3–5 years; both had Down syndrome; both nonverbal; DQs of 52 and 64	$N = 1$ with controls: multiple-baseline across subjects and settings	Rate of occurrence of target behaviors in school training sessions, in home generalization/play sessions, and at 1-month follow-up session	Rates of vocal imitation increased for both children under training conditions from baseline rates of approximately 10% of all trials to approximately 50%; rates did not increase for the second subject or in the second setting (home) until training procedure was initiated; when training initiated in home setting, rates of spontaneous vocalizations increase from baseline mean of .5 per min to mean of 1.1 per min
$N = 7$; Mean CA = $3,8^b$ (range: 3,2–4,0); primary handicapping conditions: mental retardation/Down syndrome (2), emotional/behavior disorder (1), and communication disorder (4)	Pre–posttests; no controls	Sequenced Inventory of Communication Development (SICD); Developmental Profile: Communication subscale (Alpern and Boll, 1972); spontaneous language sample: MLU and total number of intelligible utterances	Net changes from pre- to posttest on the SICD: +6.86 months in receptive communication age (RCA) and +5.14 months in expressive communication age (ECA), and +10.5 months on the developmental profile communication age (DPCA); to allow for differing lengths of program participation, results also reported in terms of months gain for each month of participation, as follows: RCA: 1.41; ECA: 1.12; DPCA: 2.24 Language sample analyses are reported as pre- and posttest means on 3 measures: total number of utterances produced (pre = 58.43, post = 71.71); total number intelligible morphemes produced (pre = 86.71, post = 144.57); and MLU in morphemes (pre = 1.49; post = 1.88)

TABLE 6

Communication language deficits associated with pervasive handicapping conditions: autism and severe behavior disorders

Reference	Nature of intervention	Intervention parameters	Setting	Role of parents
Beisler & Tsai, 1983	Pragmatic/conversational approach; targeted individually prescribed communication skills in context of interactive therapy sessions that involved turn-taking routines in which therapist initially modeled appropriate communicative responses for child; a delay procedure was introduced when child was consistently imitating response to evoke spontaneous conversational responding	15–30 min sessions over 6 weeks; number/frequency of sessions not specified	Hospital (short-term inpatient placement)	None specified
Bloch, Gersten, & Kornblum, 1980	Individualized language remediation programs focusing on specific skill targets in 7 curriculum areas (eye contact, auditory comprehension, nonverbal imitation, vocal play, vocal imitation; expressive speech, and communicative speech); activities integrated throughout classroom day in addition to individual therapy sessions; comparison group participated in preschool program but did not get specific language intervention	Daily preschool program for duration of 2 school years (20 months); experimental group children also received individual therapy from speech/language clinician in 2 sessions per week, 30 min each	Preschool	Authors indicate parent involvement was a basic component of this program, but do not describe this involvement
Palyo, Cooke, Schuler, & Apolloni, 1979	Behavioral treatment to reduce echolalic speech; differential consequences and audiotape modeling; echolalic responses to questions were punished by saying "no" and removing reinforcer; correct responses were reinforced with praise and edibles	90 to 118 sessions, 10 trials per session	Enclosed therapy booth within preschool for handicapped children	None specified

[a]Chronological ages given in years and months.
[b]MLU, mean length of utterance.

268

Child characteristics	Experimental design	Outcome measures	Results
$N = 5$; mean CA: 4,6[a] (range: 3,1–5,0); all diagnosed autistic and all with normal hearing; IQs in normal range for 4 subjects; IQ of 1 subject was 65	Pre–posttest with no control	Sequenced Inventory of Communication Development (SICD) and MLU[b] calculated from language sample	Significant gains on all language measures: *SICD* Receptive Scale: pretest $\bar{X}$: 28 months, posttest $\bar{X}$: 33.6 months ($p < .05$) *SICD* Expressive Scale: pretest $\bar{X}$: 25.6 months, posttest $\bar{X}$: 31.2 months ($p < .01$) MLU: pretest $\bar{X}$: 2.12, posttest $\bar{X}$: 2.63 ($p < .01$)
$N = 26$; all diagnosed with early infantile autism and all nonverbal at program entry Experimental group ($n = 12$): mean CA = 3,9; mean IQ = 43 Comparison group ($n = 14$): mean CA = 4,2; mean IQ = 49 No significant differences between groups on baseline/Time 1 scores	Retrospective analysis of triannual reports completed by teachers; comparison group were children enrolled in this preschool during 3-year period prior to introduction of language curriculum and therapy procedures; reports analyzed by 2 independent raters, with reported interrater reliability $>.90$	Teacher reports analyzed for evidence of criterion-level behavior in each of the 7 target curriculum areas; data reported in terms of percent of subjects in each group demonstrating criterion behaviors at start of program (Time 1) and end of second year (Time 3)	Overall, experimental group achieved criterion levels on more skills in less time than comparison group; At Time 3, 58.3% of experimental group passed all 7 items, compared to 14.3% of comparison group; also, at Time 3, 75% of experimental group passed "expressive speech," compared to 43% of comparison group, and 67% of experimental group passed "communicative speech," compared to 14% of comparison group (difference significant at $p < .01$)
$N = 3$; CA = 3,8, 4,2, and 5,7; all echolalic and developmentally delayed	$N = 1$ with controls: multiple baseline across 4 responses (different questions)	Frequency of appropriate and echolalic responses (out of 10 trials) in each session and at 12-month follow-up session	All subjects decreased rate of echolalic responses to trained questions from 100% to 0% and increased rates of appropriate responses from 0% to 100% over course of training phase; the decrease in rate of echolalia generalized across baselines to untrained questions; however, rates of appropriate responses remained at 0 until training was initiated; 2 subjects followed up after 12 months showed no echolalic responses, but some decrease in appropriate responses

269

TABLE 7

Communication language deficits associated with pervasive handicapping conditions: use of augmentative modes

Reference	Nature of intervention	Intervention parameters	Setting	Role of parents
Barrera, Lobato-Barrera, Sulzer-Azaroff, 1980	Behavioral procedures to teach production of single words; comparison of 3 modes: oral only, manual sign only, and TC[a] (oral and sign, simultaneous)	3 sessions daily (1 per condition), 20 min each; total length of intervention was 17 days	Communication disorders preschool	None specified
Jago, Jago, & Hart, 1984	Experimental group: manual sign training provided in context of TC classroom program; signs were modeled and reinforced in structured and exploratory play activities dispersed throughout day; emphasis on parent involvement Comparison group: received sign training in separate session; massed-trial format	Total intervention: 7 months Experimental group: 2 sessions per week, 3½ hr each Comparison group: Home-based: 1 session per week, 1 hr each; Center program: 1 session per week, 4 hr each	Preschool	In experimental group, parents participated in class 1 day per week In home-based comparison group, parents participated in sessions with teacher; parents were not involved in center-based comparison program
Weller & Mahoney, 1983	Environmental Language Intervention program (ELI; see MacDonald et al., 1974, in Table 5) implemented by parents assigned to 1 of 2 conditions, oral only (no manual signs used) or TC (manual signs paired with spoken words); training sessions with both groups included receptive language, imitation, conversation, structured play, and generalization	1 training session, 20–30 min each, per day, with generalization activities dispersed throughout the day, for a total of 5 months; During first 2 months, home teachers visited home once a week; for last 3 months, visits made once a month	Homes	Conduct all training sessions (parents received 4–8 hr of formal instruction in procedures to be used prior to start of intervention)

[a]TC, total communication.
[b]Chronological ages given in years and months.

Child characteristics	Experimental design	Outcome measures	Results
$N = 1$; CA $= 4,6$;[b] mute; diagnosis of autism	$N = 1$ with controls: alternating treatments design with 1 within-subject replication of effects	Number of words per training set and condition to pass criterion of 30 correct productions (in either mode)	TC produced learning of most words on both the first and second training sets; after 14 days, subject met criterion on all 10 words taught with TC, and only 4 of 10 in both sign-only and oral-only condition. On first set, responses in TC were just signs; on second set, subject paired vocalization with his signs on 47% of trials.
$N = 24$; of these, 20 had Down syndrome Experimenal group: $n = 11$; mean CA $= 28.16$ months Comparison group: $n = 13$; mean CA $= 27.96$ months Comparison subjects were matched to experimental subjects on the basis of CA and etiology; differences in initial communication skill levels were controlled statistically	Pre–posttest with planned comparison group	Gesell Developmental Schedules, Receptive-Expressive Emergent Language Scale (REEL), and Sequenced Inventory of Communication Development (SCID)	Experimental group made significantly greater gains ($p < .01$) than comparison group on 2 measures: REEL/Expressive Language Age and total number of signs acquired; groups did not differ significantly on any other measures
$N = 15$ (oral only, $n = 7$; TC, $n = 8$); CA $= 18–36$ months; all had Down syndrome and all were at or below 1-word production stage; no severe sensory or motor impairments; no significant differences between groups in CA, DA, or DQ	Pre–posttest with planned comparison group (children were enrolled in 2 different infant stimulation programs)	Bayley Scales of Infant Development, Uzgiris and Hunt Ordinal Scales of Psychological Development, REEL, and Environmental Pre-Language Battery (assessment instrument used in prescribing treatment goals in ELI program)	No significant difference between groups, although TC group produced more different words ($\bar{X}$: 66.5 words spoken or signed) than oral group ($\bar{X}$: 37.71 words spoken) at posttest; both groups made significant gains ($p < .01$) on all cognitive and language measures; language quotients (developmental rates) also increased for both groups

REFERENCES

Alpern, G. D., & Boll, T. J. (1972). *Developmental Profile*. Aspen, CO: Psychological Development Publications.

American Speech-Language-Hearing Association (1981). Position statement on nonspeech communication. *ASHA, 23* 577–581.

Aram, D. M. (Guest Ed.). (1984). Assessment and treatment of developmental apraxia. *Seminars in Speech and Language, 5*(2).

Barrera, R. D., Lobato-Barrera, D., & Sulzer-Azaroff, B. (1980). A simultaneous treatment comparison of three expressive language training programs with a mute, autistic child. *Journal of Autism and Developmental Disorders, 10,* 21–37.

Beisler, J. M., & Tsai, L. Y. (1983). A pragmatic approach to increase language skills in young autistic children. *Journal of Autism and Developmental Disorders, 13,* 287–303.

Bloch, J., Gersten, E., & Kornblum, S. (1980). Evaluation of a language program for young autistic children. *Journal of Speech and Hearing Disorders, 45,* 76–89.

Brimer, M. A., & Dunn, L. M. (1962). *The English Picture Vocabulary Test Manual*. Bristo, UK: Education Evaluation Enterprises.

Brown, R. (1973). *A first language: The early stages*. Cambridge, MA: Harvard University Press.

Bzoch, K. R., & League, R. (1970). *Receptive-Expressive Emergent Language Scale*. Gainesville, FL: Anhinga Press.

Carrier, J. K. (1970). A program of articulation therapy administered by mothers. *Journal of Speech and Hearing Disorders, 35,* 344–353.

Christensen, M., & Hanson, M. (1981). An investigation of the efficacy of oral myofunctional therapy as a precursor to articulation therapy for pre-first grade children. *Journal of Speech and Hearing Disorders, 46,* 160–165.

Christie, B. (1979). A clinical evaluation of an approach to language assessment and remediation with six language-impaired children. *The South African Journal of Communication Disorders, 26,* 46–61.

Clements, J., Evans, C., Jones, C., Osborne, K., & Upton, G. (1982). Evaluation of a home-based language training programme with severely mentally handicapped children. *Behavior Research and Therapy, 20,* 243–249.

Colorado Department of Education (1982). *Effectiveness of early special education for handicapped children* (Report commissioned by the Colorado General Assembly).

Cooper, J., Moodley, M., & Reynell, J. (1979). The developmental language programme. Results from a five year study. *British Journal of Disorders of Communication, 14,* 57–69.

Costello, J., & Bosler, S. (1976). Generalization and articulation instruction. *Journal of Speech and Hearing Disorders, 41,* 359–373.

Costello, J., & Onstine, J. (1976). The modification of multiple articulation errors based on distinctive feature theory. *Journal of Speech and Hearing Disorders, 41,* 199–215.

Culatta, B., & Horn, D. (1982). A program for achieving generalization of grammatical rules to spontaneous discourse. *Journal of Speech and Hearing Disorders, 47,* 174–180.

Curlee, R. F. (1984). A case selection strategy for young disfluent children. In W. H. Perkins (Ed.), *Current therapy of communication disorders: Stuttering disorders*. New York: Thieme-Stratton.

Fein, D. J., (1983). The prevalence of speech and language impairments. *ASHA, 25,* 37.

Fisher, H. B., & Logemann, J. A. (1971). *The Fisher-Logemann Test of Articulation Competence*. Boston: Houghton-Mifflin.

Freeman, F. J. (1982). Stuttering. In N. J. Lass, L. V. McReynolds, J. L. Northern, and D. E. Yoder (Eds.), *Speech, language and hearing: Volume II: Pathologies of speech and language*. Philadelphia: Saunders.

Goldman, R., & Fristoe, M. (1969). *Goldman-Fristoe Test of Articulation*. Circle Pines, MN: American Guidance Service.

Griffiths, R. (1970). *The Abilities of Young Children*. London: Child Development Research Center.
Hart, B. M., & Risley, T. R. (1974). Using preschool materials to modify the language of disadvantaged children. *Journal of Applied Behavior Analysis, 7*, 243–256.
Hart, B., & Risley, T. R. (1975). Incidental teaching of language in the preschool. *Journal of Applied Behavior Analysis, 8*, 411–420.
Hedrick, D. L., Prather, E. M., & Tobin, A. R. (1975). *Sequenced Inventory of Communication Development*. Seattle: University of Washington Press.
Hegde, M. N., & Gierut, J. (1979). The operant training and generalization of pronouns and a verb form in a language delayed child. *Journal of Communication Disorders, 12*, 23–34.
Hegde, M. N., Noll, M. J., & Pecora, R. (1979). A study of some factors affecting generalization of language training. *Journal of Speech and Hearing Disorders, 44*, 301–320.
Hejne, R. F. (1959). *Developmental Articulation Test*. Madison, WI: R. F. Hejne & College Typing Co.
Ingram, D. (1976). *Phonological disability in children*. New York: Elsevier.
Jago, J. L., Jago, A. G., & Hart, M. (1984). An evaluation of the total communication approach for teaching language to developmentally delayed preschool children. *Education and Training of the Mentally Retarded, 19*, 175–182.
Jakobson, R., Fant, C. G. M., & Halle, M. (1963). *Preliminaries to speech analysis: The distinctive features and their correlates* (2nd ed.). Cambridge, MA: MIT. Press.
Johnston, J. R. (1982). The language disordered child. In N. J. Lass, L. V. McReynolds, J. L. Northern, and D. E. Yoder (Eds.), *Speech, language and hearing: Volume II: Pathologies of speech and language*. Philadelphia: Saunders.
Karr, S., & Punch, J. (1984). PL 94-142 state child counts. *ASHA, 26*, 33.
Kupperman, P., Bligh, S., & Goodban, M. (1980). Activating articulation skills through theraplay. *Journal of Speech and Hearing Disorders, 45*, 540–548.
Kysela, G., Hillyard, A., McDonald, L., & Ahlsten-Taylor, J. (1981). Early intervention: design and evaluation. In R. L. Schiefelbusch and D. D. Bricker (Eds.), *Early language: Acquisition and intervention*. Baltimore: University Park Press.
McDonald, E. T. (1964). *A Deep Test of Articulation*. Pittsburgh: Stanwix House.
MacDonald, J. D. (1978). *Environmental Language Inventory: A semantic-based assessment and treatment model for generalized communication*. Columbus, OH: Merrill.
MacDonald, J. D., Blott, J. P., Gordon, K., Spiegel, B., & Hartmann, M. (1974). An experimental parent-assisted treatment program for preschool language-delayed children. *Journal of Speech and Hearing Disorders, 39*, 395–415.
Marge, M. (1972). The general problem of language disabilities in children. In J. V. Irvin and M. Marge (Eds.), *Principles of childhood language disorders*. New York: Appleton-Century-Crofts.
Martin, R., Kuhl, P., & Haroldson, S. (1972). An experimental treatment with two preschool stuttering children. *Journal of Speech and Hearing Research, 15*, 743–752.
McLean, J. E. (1970). Extending stimulus control of phoneme articulation by operant techniques. In F. L. Girardeau & J. E. Spradlin (Eds.), *A functional analysis approach to speech and language behavior* (ASHA Monograph 14). Washington, DC: American Speech-Language-Hearing Association.
Miller, J. F. (1981). *Assessing language production in children: Experimental procedures*. Baltimore: University Park Press.
Murry, T. (1982). Phonation: Assessment. In N. J. Lass, L. V. McReynolds, J. L. Northern, and D. E. Yoder (Eds.), *Speech, language and hearing: Volume II: Pathologies of speech and language*. Philadelphia: Saunders.
National Advisory Neurological Diseases and Stroke Council. (1969). *Human communication and its disorders—An overview*. Bethesda, MD: National Institute of Neurological Diseases and Stroke.

Olswang, L., Bain, B., Dunn, C., & Cooper, J. (1983). The effect of stimulus variation on lexical learning. *Journal of Speech and Hearing Disorders, 48,* 192–201.

Palyo, W. J., Cooke, T. P., Schuler, A. L., & Apolloni, T. (1979). Modifying echolalic speech in preschool children: Training and generalization. *American Journal of Mental Deficiency, 83,* 480–489.

Perkins, W. H. (1971). *Speech pathology: An applied behavioral science.* St. Louis: Mosby.

Perkins, W. H. (1983). Onset of stuttering: The case of the missing block. In D. Prins and R. J. Ingham (Eds.), *Treatment of stuttering in early childhood: Methods and issues.* San Diego: College-Hill Press.

Perkins, W. H. (1984). Foreword to special issue: Assessment and treatment of developmental apraxia. *Seminars in Speech and Language, 5*(2).

Reed, C. G., & Godden, A. L. (1977). An experimental treatment using verbal punishment with two preschool stutterers. *Journal of Fluency Disorders, 2,* 225–233.

Reynell, J. K. (1969). *Reynell Developmental Language Scales: Experimental edition.* Windsor, UK: N.F.E.R. Publishing.

Rogers-Warren, A. K., & Warren, S. F. (1980). Mands for verbalization: Facilitating the generalization of newly trained language in children. *Behavior Modification, 4,* 230–245.

Ruder, K., & Bunce, B. (1981). Articulation therapy using distinctive feature analysis to structure the training program: Two case studies. *Journal of Speech and Hearing Disorders, 46,* 59–65.

Salzberg, C. L., & Villani, J. V. (1983). Speech training by parents of Down syndrome toddlers: Generalization across settings and instructional contexts. *American Journal of Mental Deficiency, 87,* 403–413.

Shelton, R. L., Johnson, A. F., Willis, V., & Arndt, W. B. (1975). Monitoring and reinforcement by parents as a means of automating articulation response: II. Study of preschool children. *Perceptual and Motor Skills, 40,* 599–610.

Shine, R. E. (1984). Direct management of the beginning stutterer. In W. H. Perkins (Ed.), *Current therapy of communication disorders.* New York: Thieme-Stratton. (Original work published 1980)

Synder-McLean, L., Solomonson, B., McLean, J., & Sack, S. (1984). Structuring joint action routines: A strategy for facilitating communication and language development in the classroom. *Seminars in Speech and Language, 5*(3), 213–228.

Stevenson, P., Box, M., & Stevenson, J. (1982). The evaluation of home-based speech therapy for language delayed preschool children in an inner city area. *British Journal of Disorders of Communication, 17,* 141–148.

Templin, M. C. (1957). *Certain language skills in children.* Minneapolis: University of Minnesota Press.

Warren, S. F., McQuarter, R. J., & Rogers-Warren, A. K. (1984). The effects of mands and models on the speech of unresponsive language-delayed preschool children. *Journal of Speech and Hearing Disorders, 49,* 43–52.

Weiner, S. (1981). Treatment of phonological disability using the method of meaningful minimal contrast: Two case studies. *Journal of Speech and Hearing Disorders, 46,* 97–103.

Weiss, D. A. (1964). *Cluttering.* Englewood Cliffs, NJ: Prentice-Hall.

Weller, E. L., & Mahoney, G. J. (1983). Comparison of oral and total communication modalities on the language training of young mentally handicapped children. *Education and Training of the Mentally Retarded, 18,* 103–110.

Wilcox, M. J., & Leonard, L. B. (1978). Experimental acquisition of wh-questions in language-disordered children. *Journal of Speech and Hearing Research, 21,* 220–239.

Chapter 7

Early Intervention for Children with Autism

RUNE J. SIMEONSSON

*School of Education and Carolina Institute for Research
on Early Education of the Handicapped
University of North Carolina
Chapel Hill, North Carolina 27514*

J. GREGORY OLLEY

*Division TEACCH
Department of Psychiatry
University of North Carolina
Chapel Hill, North Carolina 27514*

SUSAN L. ROSENTHAL

*School of Education
University of North Carolina
Chapel Hill, North Carolina 27514*

INTRODUCTION

Autism is a disorder that has been widely misunderstood and frequently debated since it was first labeled by Leo Kanner in 1943. It is also one of the most difficult and controversial of childhood disorders to diagnose. But there has been progress in recent years, and substantial agreement now exists regarding many aspects of the syndrome. Rather than being viewed as an emotional disorder caused by cold, unresponsive parents (Bettelheim, 1950, 1967), autism is now seen as a developmental disability of multiple and usually unknown but biologically based etiologies, characterized by severe cognitive, communication, and social deficits (Ritvo & Freeman, 1984). Similarly, although the treatment of

275

THE EFFECTIVENESS OF EARLY INTERVENTION
FOR AT-RISK AND HANDICAPPED CHILDREN

children with autism has received relatively little systematic study, progress in early intervention has occurred in recent years.

In this chapter we will review the nature of autism as it is currently understood with an emphasis on those characteristics that can be identified in children 5 years of age and below. In addition, we will review the recent research on early intervention by focusing on the dominant intervention approaches, their theoretical emphases, and their effectiveness. On the basis of this review, recommendations for best practices for young children with autism will be presented.

INCIDENCE, ETIOLOGY, CLASSIFICATION SYSTEMS, AND DEFINITION

Autism in its classical form occurs in approximately 4 or 5 cases in 10,000 live births (National Society for Autistic Children [NSAC], 1978), and it may coexist with other disorders. In fact, about 80% of children with autism also function at a mentally retarded level of development. Wing and Gould's (1979) epidemiological study found cases of autism and related disorders associated with congenital rubella syndrome, encephalitis/meningitis, infantile spasms, epilepsy, severe perinatal asphyxia, phenylketonuria, and tuberous sclerosis. Although specific factors have not been isolated at this time, atuism appears to be a disorder with multiple organic etiologies, primarily prenatal in origin (Coleman & Gillberg, 1985).

Kanner's (1943) original description of autism and other early work supported the belief that autism is primarily a disorder of upper-middle-class, well-educated families. However, more recent data (Schopler, Andrews, & Strupp, 1979) have indicated no social class bias in the prevalence of autism. Ritvo and Freeman (1984) concluded that "autism occurs with the same incidence throughout the world, in all social classes, in all types of families, and in remarkably similar clinical form" (p. 298). Autism is also more prevalent in boys than girls by a ratio of about 4 to 1.

Unlike other disorders, there have been few extensive efforts to classify children with autism into subtypes or to relate such groupings to outcome. Rutter, Shaffer, and Sheperd (1975) and Wing and Gould (1979) have taken some initial steps, but no subtypes are widely accepted at this time. Diagnostic instruments such as the Childhood Autism Rating Scale (Schopler, Reichler, DeVellis, & Daly, 1980; Schopler, Reichler, & Renner, 1985) have provided objective data to indicate that autistic characteristics do appear in different degrees. Children thus classified as *severely autistic* have a poorer prognosis than those with milder problems.

The Childhood Autism Rating Scale (CARS) is useful in rating the degree of autism because its items represent various diagnostic criteria and allow the rater to indicate severity of each item on a 7-point scale. The diagnostic criteria are those associated most commonly with autism (e.g., relationships with people, relations to objects, and consistency of intellectual skills).

Because autism overlaps greatly with mental retardation, the degree of retardation is also an important consideration in prognosis. Rutter's (1983) review of such research highlighted two factors as the *best* predictors of adult outcome: higher intellectual functioning (i.e., IQ above 50) and development of effective speech before age 5.

There are several current definitions of autism. Rutter (1978) emphasized difficulties in social relationships and language as well as evidence of compulsive, ritualistic behaviors as essential to autism. The NSAC (now the National Society for Children and Adults with Autism) definition (NSAC, 1978) includes disturbances in four areas, all of which must occur in the first 30 months of life. They are disturbances of (1) developmental rates and sequences, (2) responses to sensory stimuli, (3) speech, language-cognition, and nonverbal communication, and (4) the capacity to relate appropriately to people, events, and objects. Although there are other current and similar definitions (e.g., American Psychiatric Association [APA], 1980), as listed in the following the NSAC definition provides a useful framework in which to consider characteristics to be found in young autistic children.

Disturbances of Developmental Rates and Sequences

These involve three developmental pathways: motor, social/adaptive, and cognitive. Development may be normal for age in one area but delayed, arrested, or atypical in other areas, even within the same skill domain.

1. Good gross motor skills, but poor fine motor skills
2. Normal motor development until a certain age, then development stops or markedly slows
3. Normal cognitive development until a certain age: subsequent slowing down or stopping
4. Crucial cognitive skills delayed or absent
5. Poor imitation skills, e.g., not repeating words, waving bye-bye, or playing patty-cake
6. Sleep–wake cycle problems

Disturbances of Responses to Sensory Stimuli

1. Hyperactivity, hypoactivity, or alternation between the two
2. Visual symptoms, e.g., close visual examination of objects, avoiding eye contact, staring at hands, switching lights on and off, staring vacantly, or looking at things out of the corner of the eyes rather than directly

3. Auditory symptoms, e.g., close attention to self-produced sounds, inappropriate response to level of sound, ignoring speech or communication of others, or fear of certain sounds
4. Tactile symptoms, e.g., inappropriate response to touch, pain, or temperature, or rubbing objects
5. Vestibular symptoms, e.g., preoccupation with rocking, whirling self, or spinning objects
6. Olfactory and gustatory symptoms, e.g., smelling or licking inappropriate objects or odd food preferences
7. Proprioceptive symptoms, e.g., posturing, lunging, hand flapping, or grimacing

Disturbances of Speech, Language, Cognition, and Nonverbal Communication

1. No speech, delayed speech, poor syntax or articulation, echolalia, repeating meaningless words or phrases, speaking for several months then stopping, or pronoun reversal
2. Limited symbolic skills
3. Poor nonverbal communication, e.g., gestures

Disturbances of the Capacity to Relate Appropriately to People, Events, and Objects

1. Delay or absence of smiling response and/or fear of strangers or extreme fear of strangers
2. Appearing withdrawn
3. No anticipation of being picked up
4. Resistance to being held or cuddled
5. No interest in peek-a-boo, patty-cake, etc.
6. Lack of relationship with parents or caregivers
7. No development of cooperative play and friendships
8. Inappropriate use of play materials; no symbolic use of toys
9. Idiosyncratic, stereotypic, repetitive use of objects
10. Resistance to change in routine
11. No response to danger
12. Inappropriate laughing, giggling, or crying

COURSE OF DEVELOPMENT

This section provides a brief overview of the early course of development and a list of problems often associated with autism in young children. These problems are often hard to identify or to differentiate from other developmental problems during infancy. Pediatricians and other professionals must often rely upon parent report, and because some of these characteristics can be found for brief periods in normally developing infants, parents are often advised to wait and observe. In autistic infants, of course, the problems do not go away and are likely to become worse. When told to wait or told that there is no problem, parents may blame themselves, making later treatment more difficult. At best, such a delay means lost time in initiating treatment. Accordingly, if parents describe such problems or if the problems are readily observable, a thorough assessment should be undertaken. Formal scales for the diagnosis of autism have been reviewed by Parks (1983), and detailed information on the assessment of children with autism can be found in Baker (1983), Marcus and Baker (1986), and Olley and Marcus (1984).

The general developmental picture for young children with autism may be quite variable across children as well as within the individual. Some of the characteristics usually associated with autism may be present, whereas others may not be. Each of the characteristics may be found in mentally retarded and other handicapped children who are not diagnosed as autistic. Characteristics may be present from early infancy, or development may follow normal milestones for many months with the child slowly or suddenly regressing in skills and developing the pathological signs of autism. In all cases, however, autism is characterized by significant problems of communication and social interaction (Rutter, 1983).

Earliest Characteristics

The most recognizable characteristic of autism in very young children and the one that gave the disorder its name is the inability to relate to others. Rutter contrasted the normal baby's "responsive, reciprocal social dialogues" (1983, p. 525) with the autistic infant's lack of interaction and failure to seek comfort from others. In later life, these characteristics are manifested in social problems ranging from active avoidance of others to great difficulty in making and maintaining friendships.

Early recognition of autism is a very difficult task. Prior and Gajzago (1974, p. 183) identified five early signs of autism but cautioned that they do not predict autism in all cases. These early signs are:

1. Resistance to being held or nursed
2. Behaving as if deaf
3. Overreaction to sensory stimuli
4. Failure to assume the normal anticipatory or body-molding posture when being picked up
5. A persistent failure to imitate toward the end of the first year

TABLE 1

Early problems associated with autism[a]

Ages	Sensorimotor	Speech/language	Relating to people, objects and events
Birth: 0–6 months	Quiet or fussy Persistent rocking Startled and/or nonresponsive to stimuli Unusual sleep cycles	No vocalizing Crying not related to needs	No anticipatory social responses (absent or delayed smiling response) Poor or absent eye-to-eye contact Fails to respond to mother's attention and crib toys
6–12 months	Sleeping and eating cycles fail to develop Uneven motor development Difficulty with transition to table foods Failure to hold objects and/or attachment to unusual objects Appears to be deaf Preoccupation with fingers Over and/or underreaction to sensory stimuli	Babbling may stop Does not imitate sounds, gestures or expressions	Unaffectionate; difficult to engage in baby games Does not wave bye-bye No interest in toys Flicks objects away
12–24 months	Sleep cycle problems Loss of previously acquired skills Sensitivity to stimuli Seeks repetitive stimulation Repetitive motor mannerisms appear, e.g., handflapping, whirling	No speech or occasional words Stops talking Gestures do not develop Repeats sounds noncommunicatively	Withdrawn No separation distress Unusual use of toys; e.g., spins, flicks, lines up objects

More recently Freeman and Ritvo (1984) suggested a developmental progression of autism in the first 5 years in three areas: sensorimotor, speech/language, and relating to people, objects, and events. Their list of characteristics appears in Table 1. This list is a clinical description rather than the result of an empirical study of early characteristics, but it may be useful in considering the range of

TABLE 1 (*Continued*)

Ages	Sensorimotor	Speech/language	Relating to people, objects and events
24–36 months	Sleep cycle problems continue Appears to be able to do things but refuses Delay in self-care skills Unusual sensitivity to stimuli and repetitive motor mannerisms continue Hyperactivity and/or hypoactivity	Mute or intermittent talking Echolalia; e.g., repeats TV commercials Specific cognitive abilities, e.g., good rote memory, superior puzzle skills Leads adult by hand to communicate needs	Does not play with others Prefers to be alone Unusual use of toys continues
36–60 months	Above problems continue; sensitivity to stimuli and motor mannerisms may decrease	No speech Echolalia Pronoun reversal Abnormal tone and rhythm in speech Unusual thoughts	Above problems continue but may become social Upset by changes in environment

*a*Adapted from "The Syndrome of Autism: Establishing the Diagnosis and Principles of Management" by B. J. Freeman and E. R. Ritvo, 1984, *Pediatric Annals, 13*, p. 286. Copyright 1984 by Charles D. Slack, Inc. Reprinted by permission.

associated problems. Wing (1985) has also provided a very readable clinical description of autism during the preschool years.

Effective early intervention depends upon our knowledge of the early course of the disorder in two ways. First, an improved recognition of early signs of autism is important for early identification. Second, treatment programs for young children must use knowledge of the early course of autism in order to determine the success of efforts to alter that course.

Until recent years, the developmental course of autism into adulthood had not been extensively studied. It is now clear that autism is a severe and almost always lifelong disorder (Schopler & Mesibov, 1983). Changes do occur in adolescence and adulthood, but the passage of time alone will not result in significant developmental improvements.

FAMILY STRESS

The presence of a child with autism in a family is often associated with many severe stresses for that family. Schopler and Mesibov's (1984) book on this topic covered a broad range of family issues and illustrated that there is an increasing interest among professionals in identifying and solving problems affecting the whole family. Bristol and Schopler (1983) noted that these stresses change over the lifetime of the handicapped person. Although autism is typically identified in the preschool period and results in the stress of coping with an apparent tragedy, stresses continue and change throughout the child's development. Further research (Bristol, 1984) has shown that the services provided by professionals can complement natural support systems (e.g., family, friends, religious beliefs) in order to help families to cope with these stresses.

APPROACHES TO EARLY INTERVENTION

As is the case for most severe and chronic disorders, treatment of autism has ranged from the highly scientific and objective to the subjective and even mystical. During the 1950s and early 1960s, autism was usually regarded as an emotional problem, and treatment focused on psychodynamic aspects of the children and their parents. For instance, Bettleheim's (1950, 1967) approach to treatment of autistic children emphasized separating them from their parents, and Speers and Lansing's (1965) approach provided both play therapy for the children and group therapy for the parents. None of the approaches of this type yielded data supporting their effectiveness.

The 1960s brought a growing diversity of approaches. Behavioral principles of learning were applied to the treatment of autistic children (Wolf, Risely, & Mees, 1964), and parents were taught to use these procedures at home (Nordquist & Wahler, 1973). Educational approaches grew and specific classroom procedures for autistic children were tried and evaluated (e.g., Hewett, 1964).

The 1970s and 1980s saw an increase of specific research studies as well as extensive programs for autistic children. Behavioral approaches flourished during this time (e.g., Koegel, Rincover, & Egel, 1982), whereas psychoanalytic applications in this country were few and lacking data to support their effectiveness. In some instances various approaches have been integrated and unique service models implemented (Bachrach, Mosley, Swindle, & Wood, 1978; Knobloch, 1982; Reichler & Schopler, 1976; Schopler & Reichler, 1971). Several quite unorthodox approaches to treatment also have appeared (e.g., Kaufman, 1976; Tinbergen & Tinbergen, 1983). In the review that follows, however, only published research with some attempt at empirical evaluation will be included.

The various approaches to experiential treatment of autistic children have been implemented in several types of settings. As will be seen, some interventions took place in well-controlled experimental settings. Others were carried out in schools, homes, or other natural environments of children. In some instances, treatment was initiated in a clinic and extended to the home or school, often with the parent(s) serving as the primary therapist. Treatments have taken place with one individual at a time, with a group of autistic children, or in programs with other handicapped or nonhandicapped children. The treatment setting and its effect are major factors to be considered in this review.

Comprehensiveness is also an important factor in considering the effectiveness of intervention. In this review only three comprehensive programs for young autistic children were found that had strong empirical evaluations of their effects. As will be discussed, the approaches were similar in emphasizing a structured behavioral model to treatment but varied along many dimensions including the use of formal preschool classrooms, the extent to which individual treatment was provided, and the training of parents, teachers, and community members to teach the children.

CRITERIA FOR INCLUSION OF STUDIES

In this chapter, certain criteria were specified for reviewing the research on early intervention with autistic children. Until recent years, this research took a traditional therapeutic approach and yielded no evidence for effectiveness (e.g., Brown, 1960). Thus, the scope of this review encompasses only the recent (since 1975) research on interventions with autistic children 5 years of age and younger. In order for a study to be included for review, it had to involve continuing intervention of children over two or more sessions and document the effects of the treatment on children.

As has already been emphasized in this book, early intervention should reflect some definable strategy that has developmental change as its primary aim. This is in contrast to many studies in which the purpose of intervention is primarily to demonstrate the effects of a therapeutic or educational procedure on a narrow range of behaviors. Illustrative of this latter form of intervention study are comparisons of three procedures to suppress self-stimulation (Harris & Wolchik, 1979) and a comparison of the effects of two methods of presenting a discrimination task (Dunlap & Koegel, 1980). Although it could be argued that such interventions may in some broader sense influence development, the focus of the research was clearly methodological. Studies of this type were thus excluded from review in this chapter. Because intervention during the early years is the emphasis of this book, a further criterion was that the intervention program should be restricted to children 5 years of age or younger. Studies that included children in this age range as well as older children but failed to present findings in such a way that separate conclusions could be drawn about treatment effects of intervention for the 0–5-year age group were also excluded (e.g., Hemsley et al., 1978; Schopler, Mesibov, & Baker, 1982; Short, 1984).

Pharmacological treatment of young autistic children is a common intervention that often occurs in combination with other forms of treatment. As noted, this chapter considers only experiential approaches; pharmacological treatments have been reviewed elsewhere (Campbell, Anderson, Deutsch, & Green, 1984; Campbell, Cohen, & Anderson, 1981; Campbell, Geller, & Cohen, 1977). General issues in the use of medication with handicapped preschool-aged children have been reviewed by Simeonsson and Simeonsson (1981), and the conclusions and cautions expressed in these reviews should be considered carefully.

Also beyond the scope of this review is an analysis of other biomedical or neurophysiologically based interventions such as megavitamins, the Feingold diet, and the Doman–Delacato patterning approaches. Although these approaches are sometimes extolled in the popular press, a scholarly review by Coleman and Gillberg (1985) revealed no approach of this type that was universally effective in treating autism. Geller, Ritvo, Freeman, and Yuwiler (1982), however, have reported favorable effects for three preschool-aged autistic children who were administered fenfluramine, a mild appetite suppressant that has the effect of lowering blood serotonin levels. Later studies of children from a broad age range (Ritvo, Freeman, Geller, & Yuwiler, 1983; Ritvo et al., 1984) found general improvement primarily in children with low initial serum serotonin levels and higher IQs. More recently, August, Raz, and Baird (1985) studied a somewhat lower-functioning group and found fenfluramine to reduce whole blood serotonin and to affect activity level, attention, and motor disturbance. However, measured intelligence was not affected. Further studies are currently being carried out in an attempt to verify these preliminary findings, but at this time fenfluramine should be considered an experimental drug when used with autistic children.

A final criterion applied to the selection of studies for review pertained to the nature of the evidence regarding the effectiveness of early intervention. Studies that lacked some form of evaluation and appropriate measurement were excluded. Group designs usually involved a comparison of pre- and postintervention performance. In single-subject studies, the experimental design needed to involve at least a comparison of baseline versus a treatment phase. Multiple baseline procedures also provided results from which inferences about intervention could be drawn. However, interventions in the form of case studies without experimental control or objective developmental measures, such as a detailed description of the course of treatment using melodic intonation therapy (Miller & Toca, 1979), were not included. Also not included were interventions such as that reported by Ayers and Tickle (1980) on sensory integration therapy in which analyses did not address developmental change or include control or comparison groups. To put the review into context, the criteria applied to the selection of studies for review are summarized in Table 2. These criteria provide a frame of reference defining and qualifying the conclusions drawn.

TABLE 2

Criteria for review of studies on early intervention with autistic children

Criteria	Defining dimensions
Date of publication	1975 to present
Age of children studied	5 years or younger
Intervention focus	Promote development of children
Definition of intervention	Experimental treatment, 2 or more sessions of same treatment
Outcome documentation	Objective measures
Analysis of change	Experimental or methodological means to analyze change

REVIEW OF THE EFFECTIVENESS
OF INTERVENTION

Although there is a sizable literature on intevention with autistic children, few studies met all of the criteria in Table 2. Many reports of traditional therapeutic approaches have been published, but none met the standards for measurem∋nt or research design, and they were thus excluded. Ten studies did meet the criteria. Of these, seven were not comprehensive, having a limited focus (see Table 3). Each of these seven studies focused on changing discrete behaviors, usually including language skills, and used behavioral procedures such as reinforcement to bring about learning (see also chapter on communication disorders, Chapter 6 in this volume). In contrast to the more comprehensive programs described in a later section, the programs summarized in Table 3 were relatively brief, lasting from 10 weeks to 20 months. In addition, these studies usually consisted of short training sessions, often as adjuncts to other programs.

All of the studies but one described in Table 3 have some limitations in design or procedure in addition to limited scope that make it difficult to draw definitive conclusions about their overall effectiveness. This problem is certainly not unique to interventions with autistic children, as has been found in earlier reviews of interventions with handicapped young children (Simeonsson, Cooper, & Scheiner, 1982). Nevertheless, a brief review of some of the studies in Table 3 will serve to identify their findings and limitations with implications for the development of more comprehensive programs.

In the study by Salvin, Routh, Foster, and Lovejoy (1977), a mute 5-year-old boy was taught sign language. Signs were used continuously at home and at school, and the child participated in 20 twice-weekly 45-min structured teaching sessions using physical prompts and natural reinforcers (e.g., child was shown a

TABLE 3

Selected characteristics of noncomprehensive early intervention studies with autistic children

References	Nature of intervention	Intensity of intervention	Sample size
Beisler & Tsai, 1983	Language training as part of an inpatient program	15–30-min sessions of individual and group communication therapy of unstated frequency over 6 weeks	5
Bloch, Gersten, & Kornblum, 1980	Language component in traditional preschool	A mean of 20.6 months of a therapeutic nursery/kindergarten with additional language training	26
Cohen, 1981	Language stimulation/behavioral	20-min sessions, 3 times weekly for a total of 20 sessions	1
Groden, Domingue, Chesnick, Groden, & Baron, 1983	Behavioral preschool program with parent training	2 sessions a week in addition to a half-day nursery program for 1 year	1
Harris, Wolchik, & Milch, 1982	Parent training in language and behavior modification	Weekly parent training sessions for 13 weeks	9
Johnson, Whiteman, & Barloon-Noble, 1978	Behavioral training of parents in the home	30-min sessions for 103 days	1
Salvin, Routh, Foster, & Lovejoy, 1977	Behavioral methods to teach signing	45-min sessions, 2 times a week for a total of 20 sessions	1

cookie, prompted to sign *cookie,* then received cookie). After 3 months the child had mastered 12 signs, used them spontaneously, and made 6 months progress on the Communication Scale of the Alpern–Boll Developmental Profile (Alpern & Boll, 1972). While this study was limited to the acquisition of signs for one child, it demonstrated that spontaneous communication can be improved.

Another example in the communication area can be found in the study by Beisler and Tsai (1983) in which five children received communication training as part of a 6-week inpatient program. The training was intended to establish reciprocal communication through modeling and the use of natural reinforcers. Following this training period, the children gained in their understanding and use of language on standardized measures as well as in spontaneous speech. Although this report was a demonstration, rather than an experimental study, and the confounding effects of the inpatient program further limited its power, it provides another illustration of possible methods for teaching communication skills.

Similarly, in a study of 26 children, Bloch, Gersten, and Kornblum (1980) concluded that the addition of a language component to a traditional preschool program led to greater language gains. However, the retrospective design and subjective measures employed in the study limit the strength of the findings.

As a final example from Table 3, Harris, Wolchik, and Milch (1982) provided services to young autistic children by teaching behavioral techniques to their parents. In a multiple baseline design, parents received 6 weeks of training in behavior modification principles and 7 weeks of instruction on behaviorally oriented speech training. Child language was found not to be affected by the behavior modification training but did improve when the parents were taught to to carry out speech training. Harris, Wolchik, and Weitz (1981) described a similar program, and Harris's (1983) book includes many of the clinical details of this approach, such as the manner in which concepts derived from family systems theory and structural family therapy were applied to address broad family issues. The Harris et al. (1982) study was the only one in Table 3 that employed a design with adequate experimental control.

Although all of the studies in Table 3 are limited in scope and/or method, three studies were identified which were sufficiently comprehensive and well carried out to allow at least some guarded conclusions to be drawn. These are reviewed in the following section.

Characteristics of Comprehensive Programs

The three comprehensive research projects identified all reported positive outcomes for children with autism, although the extent of behavior change varied (see Table 4 for details). The first project, that of Ivar Lovaas of the University of California at Los Angeles, is an extension of a behavioral treatment and research program on autism that has been operating since the mid-1960s. Lovaas (1980) noted that in his earlier treatment programs children did not maintain or generalize new skills, and some even regressed in their abilities. In his current project, Lovaas (1980, 1982) has shifted his emphasis to treatment of *younger* children (typically less than $3\frac{1}{2}$ years of age) and emphasized opportunities to generalize skills and involve parents in treatment. This very intensive and structured approach, described in detail by Lovaas (1981), begins with individual treatment sessions emphasizing orienting to others, compliance with instructions and elimination of idiosyncratic, repetitive behaviors. Later stages include intensive language instruction. As treatment continues, the children are required to respond in new and appropriate natural settings, in the presence of their families and others, and eventually in regular preschool or kindergarten settings. As the parents and

TABLE 4

Characteristics of four comprehensive studies of early intervention

Reference	Nature of intervention	Intervention parameters	Setting	Role of parents
Fenske, Zalenski, Krantz, & McClannahan (in press)	Comprehensive behavioral intervention program for autistic children; a day school and treatment program; parent-training services; teaching–family model group home treatment; individualized transition programs for children approaching readiness for discharge; follow-up services	5½ hours a day, 5 days per week, for a mean length of 45.9 months for children in younger group and 72.4 months for children in older group; for children unable to remain with their own families, group home treatment was available; children participating in individualized transition programs attended local preschools, after school recreation activities and/or regular public school classrooms	Day school program; children who required residential intervention lived with professional teaching parents (a married couple) in family-style, community-based homes	Individualized parent-training services were delivered in children's own homes at least monthly; the home programmer modeled instruction and intervention strategies, taught observation and behavioral measurement, and provided hands-on training enabling parents to serve as home tutors and therapists for their own children; parents participated in the selection of treatment goals and collected performance data that they submitted to their home programmer on a weekly basis
Hoyson, Jamieson, & Strain (1984); Strain, Hoyson, & Jamieson (1985); Strain, Jamieson, & Hoyson (1985)	Developmentally oriented curriculum goals based on the Learning Accomplishment Profile (LAP; LeMay, Griffin, & Sanford, 1977) using a behavioral approach; peer-mediated behavioral intervention involving 10 nonhandicapped preschoolers (3–5 years of age) and 6 autistic-like children in an integrated classroom emphasizing social skills; parents of the autistic children received intensive training	3 hr a day, 5 days per week, 12 months school program for 2 years; 12 hr a week for parent training	Preschool classroom	Parents supported and extended preschool program
Lovaas (1980, 1982)	Student therapists worked directly with children and trained parents as cotherapists to reduce psychotic behavior and promote appropriate social behavior; children taught in home, then community settings, then in regular preschools or kindergartens	Intensive treatment group received 40 hr or more 1-to-1 treatment per week by therapists, 12 months of the year; less intensive treatment group received 10 hr or less 1-to-1 treatment per week; treatment lasted 2 years or more for both groups	Home, community, and regular classrooms	Cotherapists

Child characteristics	Experimental design	Outcome measures	Results
18 subjects (16 boys and 2 girls), all diagnosed as autistic by outside referral agencies and accepted for enrollment because behavioral observation indicated that they met the diagnostic criteria specified by the National Society for Autistic Children (NSAC, 1978); the children's mean age at program entry was 48.9 months for younger group and 101.2 months for older group	A correlational design, static group comparisons of treatment outcomes for children who entered the comprehensive intervention program before 60 months of age and after 60 months of age	Positive outcome was considered to have been achieved when a child lived with his or her natural parents and was enrolled full-time in a public school classroom; annual follow-up established whether these arrangements were maintained	During the 9-year period 1975–1984, 7 of the 18 children (6 boys and 1 girl) achieved positive treatment outcomes, i.e., they continued to live with parents and to be enrolled full-time in public school classrooms, either at grade level or in special education classrooms, but "mainstreamed" for some classes; of the 9 children in the younger group, 6 achieved positive treatment outcome; of 9 children in older group, only 1 child attained a positive treatment outcome; alternatively, these findings may be stated as follows: of 7 children in the sample who achieved positive treatment outcomes, 6 children entered the comprehensive intervention program prior to 60 months of age
6 children diagnosed as autistic or autistic-like based on DSM-III (APA, 1980); age range 30–53 months at beginning of the program; all children showed marked problems in functional speech, tantrums, and social interaction and scored in mild to severely retarded range on the McCarthy Scales of Children's Abilities (McCarthy, 1972)	Single-case, multiple baseline design; pre–posttest	LAP (fine motor, gross motor, writing, matching, counting, comprehension, naming, object play); social interaction, on-task, language, and deviant behavior	Increase in LAP scores to normal level for their ages; increase in social interactions across settings to same level as nonhandicapped classmates
19 children in intensive treatment group: mean CA = 33 months, mean MA = 19 months at diagnosis; 19 children in less intensive treatment group: mean CA = 35 months, mean MA = 17.4 months at diagnosis; diagnosis of autism primarily based on NSAC (1978) definition and conducted independently	Pre–posttest comparison of intensive versus less intensive treatment groups; at onset of treatment, groups did not differ significantly on 17 measures (e.g., MA, speech, play); progress of children is being followed; some children have now been followed for as long as 10 years	School placement; IQ; social–emotional adjustment	50% of the intensive treatment group "recovered" as defined by successful completion of the first grade, normal IQ, and good social–emotional adjustment as rated by teachers; no child "recovered" in less intensive treatment group; substantial gains were also observed for other outcome categories for the intensive treatment group

teacher assume more of a role in treatment, the children have been found to behave more spontaneously and in the presence of natural cues.

Lovaas's (1980, 1982) experimental design included both an intensive treatment group that received 40 hours or more of treatment per week and a less intensive treatment group that received 10 hours of treatment per week. In other respects the nature of intervention was the same for all children. As summarized in Table 4, the intensive application of this approach resulted in substantial improvement for about half the autistic children. They attained IQs, school placements, and social–emotional ratings not different from normal peers. Children receiving a less intensive version of this approach did not, in any of 19 cases, achieve such gains.

Another intensive and comprehensive project reporting dramatic results is that of Phillip Strain at the University of Pittsburgh. Rather than beginning with 1-to-1 treatment, Strain and his colleagues (Hoyson, Jamieson, & Strain, 1984; Strain, Hoyson, & Jamieson, 1985; Strain, Jamieson, & Hoyson, 1985) offered a preschool classroom program serving both autistic and nonhandicapped children. The six participating autistic children entered the program at between 30 and 53 months of age and were diagnosed using the DSM-III criteria (APA, 1980). In addition to showing severe behavior and communication problems, their scores on the McCarthy Scales of Children's Abilities (McCarthy, 1972) indicated mild to severe mental retardation.

Like that of Lovaas, this program used behavioral strategies in a structured approach and actively involved parents. Some unique aspects were the use of group instruction and nonhandicapped peers whose interactions with the autistic children helped facilitate social skills. The instruction of children in groups was intended to make best use of the availability of nonhandicapped peers to teach social behavior and related skills associated with later school success. Each child's curriculum was highly individualized within the developmental sequences described in the Learning Accomplishment Profile (LeMay, Griffin, & Sanford, 1977).

Strain's results were remarkable. The six autistic children who completed 2 years of the program showed increases in eight developmental domains of the Learning Accomplishment Profile to normal levels for their ages. On observational measures, the autistic children engaged in positive social interactions as frequently as their nonhandicapped classmates. The rate of progress on the Learning Accomplishment Profile doubled for both the autistic and the nonhandicapped children. Although Strain and his colleagues (Strain, Hoyson, & Jamieson 1985) cautioned that their project is too recent to allow a comparison of the follow-up of the progress of the children with those in Lovaas's study, both projects have reported dramatic outcomes.

The third comprehensive program, based at the Princeton Child Development Institute (Fenske, Zalenski, Krantz, & McClannahan, in press), serves children ranging widely in age. The components of this program include a day school and treatment program, group homes, parent training, preparation for transition to other programs, and follow-up after discharge. This program also has a behavioral orientation. In a retrospective analysis, Fenske et al. (in press) found that early treatment (before 60 months) led to positive treatment outcomes in two thirds of their cases. Although the extent of the gains was not as dramatic as that of Lovaas or Strain, the Fenske et al. (in press) study is important because it compared children who began treatment before age 5 with those who began treatment later. Only one child of the nine in the later-treatment group achieved a positive outcome.

Although these three studies have dealt with a limited number of children, and in the case of Strain's program have had too little opportunity to follow the progress of the children, their results are highly encouraging and will surely influence future early intervention efforts. Other researchers should look to these studies to determine the critical factors for future research and service.

Critical Factors in Successful Programs

In concluding this review it may be useful to identify common features of these successful comprehensive programs.

1. *Structured, behavioral treatment.* All three took a behavioral approach, targeted specific skills, structured lessons clearly, and offered positive consequences for learning.

2. *Parent involvement.* Although the approaches and emphases differed, all three programs involved parents and taught them skills for teaching their own children and generalizing these skills to new settings.

3. *Treatment at an early age.* Fenske et al. (in press) found an advantage to early intervention over later treatment. Lovaas began his program for children under $3\frac{1}{2}$ years of age, but Strain's program included children aged 30–53 months.

Two of these programs reported outcomes more positive than any previously reported for children with autism or mental retardation. After a minimum of 2 years of treatment, Strain reported that all six children no longer showed the characteristics of autism, and Lovaas reported that about 50% of the children "recovered," some of whom have maintained this status for over 10 years. Two additional characteristics of these programs stand out:

4. *Intensive treatment.* Many details of treatment surely differ but the key factor in Lovaas's and Strain's approaches may be their intensive treatment. Children participated in structured treatment for several hours a day, 5 days a week, year-round, and the parents carried over these activities at home. Lovaas's

(1980, 1982) project included a comparison group that receved the same treatment on a less intensive basis. No child in the less intensive treatment group "recovered."

5. *Generalization.* A second aspect of Lovaas's and Strain's programs that may have been critical is the emphasis on generalization of skills. Virtually all programs for autistic children recognize the importance of generalization of skills to new settings and take steps, such as involving parents, to aid generalization. However, Lovaas placed particular emphasis on teaching autistic children in natural settings at home, at school, and in the community, involving parents and peers, and teaching the skills needed for success in preschool and kindergarten. Strain involved nonhandicapped classmates and families in active teaching roles aimed at facilitating generalization.

Although the literature on early intervention for autistic children that met the documentation criteria described earlier is small, the three studies in Table 4 provide great encouragement. The achievements of the children in the Lovaas and Strain programs constitute findings of a remarkable, if not radical, nature. They are even more striking in that initially the children not only showed the characteristics of autism but also of mental retardation. Continued follow-up of these children and replication are essential next steps.

IMPLICATIONS FOR RESEARCH AND PRACTICE

The research on early intervention clearly indicates that autism is a severe and complex handicap that is not affected by casual or infrequent attempts at treatment. Through education and treatment, adaptive behaviors can be taught to children with autism, and the factors noted earlier appear to be crucial elements in success. When considering early intervention for children classified as autistic, it is important to determine whether these elements are part of a particular program and to evaluate how effectively they are implemented. Future research and practice should build upon these findings and explore new variations on these themes as well.

Finally, a number of related issues should be considered by both researchers and practitioners. These are as follows:

1. New approaches to parent involvement should be a focus of further research in an effort to ease stress on parents and give them pratical skills in working with their children. Schopler and Mesibov's (1984) book points in this direction, and resources such as Harris's (1983) book can provide the clinician with detailed information on how to develop and implement parent training programs.

2. Additional preschool curricula for autistic children should be developed to

help teachers specify clear instructional objectives in practical areas, such as language, social skills, self-help skills, and independent behavior.

3. New means of promoting generalization of skills from the nursery school or clinic to natural settings are needed.

4. The use of nonhandicapped peers in teaching social skills was demonstrated by Strain, Hoyson, & Jamieson (1985), but more data on the usefulness and limitations of this approach are needed.

5. Current identification procedures are reliable and valid when properly applied to older children (Parks, 1983), but early identification of autism is still difficult, and many children are not identified until age 4 or 5 when much time for early intervention has been lost. Moreover, further research is needed on early identification, early intervention, and continuity of services as children move into the school years.

ACKNOWLEDGMENTS

Preparation of this manuscript was supported in part by the Office of Special Education and Rehabilitative Services, U.S. Department of Education, Contract Number 300-82-0366. The opinions expressed do not necessarily reflect the position or policy of the U.S. Department of Education, and no official endorsement by the U.S. Department of Education should be inferred.

REFERENCES

Alpern, G. D., & Boll, T. J. (1972). *Developmental Profile manual.* Indianapolis: Psychological Development Publications.

American Psychiatric Association. (1980). *Diagnostic and statistical manual of mental disorders* (3rd ed.). Washington, DC: American Psychiatric Association.

August, G. J., Raz, N., & Baird, T. D. (1985). Brief report: Effects of fenfluramine on behavioral, cognitive, and affective disturbances in autistic children. *Journal of Autism and Developmental Disorders, 15,* 97–107.

Ayers, A. J., & Tickle, L. S. (1980). Hyper-responsivity to touch and vestibular stimuli as a predictor of positive response to sensory integration procedures by autistic children. *The American Journal of Occupational Therapy, 34,* 375–381.

Bachrach, A. W., Mosley, A. R., Swindle, F. L., & Wood, M. M. (1978). *Developmental therapy for young children with autistic characteristics.* Baltimore: University Park Press.

Baker, A. F. (1983). Psychological assessment of autistic children. *Clinical Psychology Review, 3,* 41–59.

Beisler, J. M., & Tsai, L. Y. (1983). A pragmatic approach to increase expressive language skills in young children. *Journal of Autism and Developmental Disorders, 13,* 287–303.

Bettelheim, B. (1950). *Love is not enough: The treatment of emotionally disturbed children.* Glencoe, IL: Free Press.

Bettelheim, B. (1967). *The empty fortress: Infantile autism and the birth of self.* New York: Free Press.

Bloch, J., Gersten, E., & Kornblum, S. (1980). Evaluation of a language program for young autistic children. *Journal of Speech and Hearing Disorders, 45,* 76–89.

Bristol, M. M. (1984). Family resources and successful adaptation to autistic children. In E. Schopler & G. B. Mesibov (Eds.), *The effects of autism on the family* (pp. 289–310). New York: Plenum.

Bristol, M. M., & Schopler, E. (1983). Stress and coping in families of autistic adolescents. In E. Schopler & G. B. Mesibov (Eds.), *Autism in adolescents and adults* (pp. 251–278). New York: Plenum.

Brown, J. L. (1960). Prognosis from presenting symptoms of preschool children with atypical development. *American Journal of Orthopsychiatry, 30,* 383–390.

Campbell, M., Anderson, L. T., Deutsch, S. I., & Green, W. H. (1984). Psychopharmacological treatment of children with the syndrome of autism. *Pediatric Annals, 13,* 309–313, 316.

Campbell, M., Cohen, I. L., & Anderson, L. T. (1981). Pharmacotherapy for autistic children: A summary of research. *Canadian Journal of Psychiatry, 26,* 265–273.

Campbell, M., Geller, B., & Cohen, I. L. (1977). Current status of drug research and treatment with autistic children. *Journal of Pediatric Psychology, 2,* 153–161.

Cohen, M. (1981). Development of language behavior of an autistic child using total communication. *Exceptional Children, 47,* 379–381.

Coleman, M., & Gillberg, C. (1985). *The biology of the autistic syndromes.* New York: Praeger.

Dunlap, G., & Koegel, R. L. (1980). Motivating autistic children through stimulus variation. *Journal of Applied Behavior Analysis, 13,* 619–627.

Fenske, E. C., Zalenski, S., Krantz, P. J., & McClannahan, L. E. (in press). Age at intervention and treatment outcome for autistic children in a comprehensive intervention program. *Analysis and Intervention in Developmental Disabilities,*

Freeman, B. J., & Ritvo, E. R. (1984). The syndrome of autism: Establishing the diagnosis and principles of management. *Pediatric Annals, 13,* 284–288, 290, 294–296.

Geller, E., Ritvo, E. R., Freeman, B. J., & Yuwiler, A. (1982). Preliminary observations on the effect of fenfluramine on blood serotonin and symptoms in three autistic boys. *The New England Journal of Medicine, 307,* 165–168.

Groden, G., Domingue, D., Chesnick, M., Groden, J., & Baron, G. (1983). Early intervention with autistic children: A case presentation with pre-program, program and follow-up data. *Psychological Reports, 53,* 713–722.

Harris, S. L. (1983). *Families of the developmentally disabled: A guide to behavioral interaction.* New York: Pergamon.

Harris, S. L., & Wolchik, S. A. (1979). Suppression of self-stimulation: Three alternative strategies. *Journal of Applied Behavior Analysis, 12,* 185–198.

Harris, S. L., Wolchik, S. A., & Milch, R. E. (1982). Changing the speech of autistic children and their parents. *Child and Family Behavior Therapy, 4,* 151–173.

Harris, S. L., Wolchik, S. A., Weitz, S. (1981). The acquisition of language skills by autistic children: Can parents do the job? *Journal of Autism and Developmental Disorders, 11,* 373–384.

Hemsley, R., Howlin, P., Berger, M., Hersov, L., Holbrook, D., Rutter, M., & Yule, W. (1978). Treating autistic children in a family context. In M. Rutter & E. Schopler (Eds.), *Autism: A reappraisal of concepts and treatment* (pp. 379–411). New York: Plenum.

Hewett, F. M. (1964). Teaching reading to an autistic boy through operant conditioning. *American Journal of Orthopsychiatry, 17,* 613–618.

Hoyson, M., Jamieson, B., & Strain, P. S. (1984). Individualized group instruction of normally developing and autistic-like children: The LEAP curriculum model. *Journal of the Division for Early Childhood, 8,* 157–172.

Johnson, M. R., Whiteman, T. L., & Barloon-Noble, R. (1978). A home-based program for a preschool behaviorally disturbed child with parents as therapists. *Journal of Behavior Therapy and Experimental Psychiatry, 9,* 65–70.

Kanner, L. (1943). Autistic disturbances of affective contact. *The Nervous Child, 2,* 217–250.

Kaufman, B. N. (1976). *Son-rise.* New York: Warner Books.

Knobloch, P. (1982). *Teaching and mainstreaming autistic children.* Denver: Love.

Koegel, R. L., Rincover, A., & Egel, A. L. (1982). *Educating and understanding autistic children.* San Diego: College-Hill.

LeMay, D., Griffin, P., & Sanford, A. (1977). *Learning Accomplishment Profile—Diagnostic edition.* Chapel Hill, NC: Chapel Hill Training–Outreach Project.

Lovaas, O. I. (1980). Behavioral teaching with young autistic children. In B. Wilcox & A. Thompson (Eds.), *Critical issues in educating autistic children and youth* (pp. 220–233). Washington, DC: U.S. Department of Education, Office of Special Education.

Lovaas, O. I. (1981). *Teaching developmentally disabled children. The ME book.* Baltimore: University Park Press.

Lovaas, O. I. (1982, August). *An overview of the young autism project.* Paper presented at the meeting of the American Psychological Association, Washington, DC.

Marcus, L. M., & Baker, A. F. (1986). Psychological assessment of autistic children. In R. J. Simeonsson, *Psychological and developmental assessment of special children.* Newton, MA: Allyn & Bacon.

McCarthy, D. A. (1972). *Manual for the McCarthy Scales of Children's Abilities.* New York: Psychological Corporation.

Miller, S. B., & Toca, J. M. (1979). Adapted melodic intonation therapy: A case study of an experimental language program for an autistic child. *Journal of Clinical Psychiatry, 40,* 201–203.

National Society for Autistic Children. (1978). National Society for Autistic Children definition of the syndrome of autism. *Journal of Autism and Childhood Schizophrenia, 8,* 162–167.

Nordquist, V. M. & Wahler, R. G. (1973). Naturalistic treatment of an autistic child. *Journal of Applied Behavior Analysis, 6,* 79–87.

Olley, J. G., & Marcus, L. M. (1984). Considerations in the assessment of children with autism. In S. J. Weaver (Ed.), *Testing children: A reference guide for effective clinical and psychoeducational assessments* (pp. 71–84). Kansas City, MO: Test Corporation of America.

Parks, S. L. (1983). The assessment of autistic children: A selective review of available instruments. *Journal of Autism and Developmental Disorders, 13,* 255–267.

Prior, M. R., & Gajzago, C. (1974). Recognition of early signs of autism. *The Medical Journal of Australia, 2,* 183.

Reichler, R. J., & Schopler, E. (1976). Developmental therapy: A program model for providing individual services in the community. In E. Schopler & R. J. Reichler (Eds.), *Psychopathology and child development* (pp. 347–371). New York: Plenum.

Ritvo, E. R., & Freeman, B. J. (1984). A medical model of autism: Etiology, pathology and treatment. *Pediatric Annals, 13,* 298–302, 304–305.

Ritvo, E. R., Freeman, B. J., Geller, E., & Yuwiler, A. (1983). Effects of fenfluramine on 14 outpatients with the syndrome of autism. *Journal of the American Academy of Child Psychiatry, 22,* 549–558.

Ritvo, E. R., Freeman, B. J., Yuwiler, A., Geller, E., Yokota, A., Schroth, P., & Novak, P. (1984). Study of fenfluramine in outpatients with the syndrome of autism. *The Journal of Pediatrics, 105,* 823–828.

Rutter, M. (1978). Diagnosis and definition of childhood autism. *Journal of Autism and Childhood Schizophrenia, 8,* 139–161.

Rutter, M. (1983). Cognitive deficits in the pathogenesis of autism. *Journal of Child Psychology and Psychiatry, 24,* 513–531.

Rutter, M., Shaffer, D., & Sheperd, M. (1975). *A multi-axial classification of child psychiatric disorders.* Geneva, Switzerland: World Health Organization.

Salvin, A., Routh, D. K., Foster, R. E., & Lovejoy, K. M. (1977). Acquisition of modified American sign language by a mute autistic child. *Journal of Autism and Childhood Schizophrenia, 7,* 359–371.

Schopler, E., Andrews, C. E., & Strupp, K. (1979). Do autistic children come from upper-middle class parents? *Journal of Autism and Developmental Disorders, 9,* 139–151.

Schopler, E., & Mesibov, G. B. (Eds.). (1983). *Autism in adolescents and adults.* New York: Plenum.

Schopler, E., & Mesibov, G. B. (1984). *The effects of autism on the family.* New York: Plenum.

Schopler, E., Mesibov, G., & Baker, A. (1982). Evaluation of treatment for autistic children and their parents. *Journal of the American Academy of Child Psychiatry, 21,* 262–367.

Schopler, E., & Reichler, R. (1971). Parents as cotherapists in the treatment of psychotic children. *Journal of Autism and Childhood Schizophrenia, 1,* 87–102.

Schopler, E., Reichler, R., DeVellis, R. F., & Daly, K. (1980). Toward objective classification of childhood autism: Childhood Autism Rating Scale (CARS). *Journal of Autism and Developmental Disorders, 10,* 91–103.

Schopler, E., Reichler, R. J., & Renner, B. R. (1985). *The Childhood Autism Rating Scale—CARS.* New York: Irvington.

Short, A. B. (1984). Short-term treatment outcome using parents as co-therapists for their own autistic children. *Journal of Child Psychology and Psychiatry, 25,* 443–458.

Simeonsson, R. J., Cooper, D., & Scheiner, A. P. (1982). A review and analysis of the effectiveness of early intervention programs. *Pediatrics, 69,* 635–641.

Simeonsson, R. J., & Simeonsson, N. E. (1981). Medication effects in handicapped preschool children. *Topics in Early Childhood Special Education, 1(2),* 61–75.

Speers, R. W., & Lansing, C. (1965). *Group therapy and childhood psychosis.* Chapel Hill, NC: University of North Carolina Press.

Strain, P. S., Hoyson, M. H., & Jamieson, B. J. (1985). Normally developing preschoolers as intervention agents for autistic-like children: Effects on class deportment and social interactions. *Journal of the Division for Early Childhood, 9,* 105–115.

Strain, P. S., Jamieson, B. J., & Hoyson, M. H. (1985). Learning Experiences . . . An Alternative Program for Preschoolers and Parents: A comprehensive service system for the mainstreaming of autistic-like preschoolers. In C. J. Meisel (Ed.), *Mainstreamed handicapped children: Outcomes, controversies and new directions* (pp. 251–269). Hillsdale, NJ: Erlbaum.

Tinbergen, N., & Tinbergen, E. A. (1983). *Autistic children: New hope for a cure.* Winchester, MA: Allen & Unwin.

Wing, L. (1985). *Autistic children: A guide for parents and professionals* (2nd ed.). New York: Brunner/Mazel.

Wing, L., & Gould, J. (1979). Severe impairments of social interaction and associated abnormalities in children: Epidemiology and classification. *Journal of Autism and Developmental Disorders, 9,* 11–29.

Wolf, M. M., Risley, T., & Mees, H. (1964). Application of operant conditioning procedures to the behavior problems of an autistic child. *Behavior Research and Therapy, 1,* 305–312.

Chapter 8

Early Intervention for Children with Visual Impairments

MYRNA OLSON

Department of Special Education
The University of North Dakota
Grand Forks, North Dakota 58202

INTRODUCTION

Children born with severe visual impairments are found at the rate of approximately 1 per 3,000 live births. One survey reported 6,450 legally blind children (birth–5 years) in the United States (National Society for the Prevention of Blindness, 1980). It is difficult to describe this population of children because, despite the small numbers, they are a very heterogeneous group, varying widely in type, severity, and specific etiology (Barraga, 1976). The developmental course is equally diverse: Some children learn visually and become print readers; some function visually for mobility purposes but are primarily tactual or auditory learners; still others have no usable vision for mobility or educational purposes. On the other hand, even a few months of vision gives a child an advantage in the area of conceptual understanding of the visual world.

The specific time of onset and etiology of visual impairments are important factors with regard to the overall functioning of an individual child. For example, children who are blind from birth do not struggle with the social and psychological adjustment of loss that later blinded children experience. Moreover, some structural eye conditions require repeated surgery, interrupting children's education and spearating them from their home environments. A few have medical conditions that are progressive, and total blindness occurs during their school

297

THE EFFECTIVENESS OF EARLY INTERVENTION
FOR AT-RISK AND HANDICAPPED CHILDREN

years. Certain causes of visual impairment are secondary to conditions that affect
other senses and/or the child's psychological functioning. Finally, the presence
of certain congenital eye anomalies can leave the child cosmetically unattractive.
Without cosmetic surgery, a child may suffer from social stigma related to his or
her appearance.

The focus of this chapter will be upon children who are congenitally severely
visually impaired or who have lost their vision very early in life. It should be
noted that the relatively low incidence of visually impaired children coupled with
their heterogeneity adversely affects attempts to study them as a group. This is
especially the case when attempting to evaluate the effectiveness of early intervention. To place these and related issues in perspective, the following sections
will present background information on visual impairments in terms of their
functional significance, their etiology, their developmental course, and assessment strategies. Discussions of the forms early intervention has taken for this
group of children and an analysis of their effectiveness will follow.

FUNCTIONAL CLASSIFICATION BY SEVERITY

Barraga (1976) noted that as far back as the 1800s there has been a lack of
precision in the use of terms relating to those who have visual impairments or
who are totally without sight. Physicians, psychologists, and educators have
used numerous terms such as *medically blind, braille blind, educationally blind,
visually limited,* and having *low vision.* Most recently the terms *visually impaired* and *visually handicapped* have been used widely. Both denote the total
group of children who have impairments in the structure or function of the eye,
regardless of the nature and extent of the impairment. These terms imply that
even with the best possible correction, the impairment interferes with incidental
or normal learning through the sense of vision (Taylor, 1973).

As with all other disability areas, there has been a need for a medical and legal
definition of visual deficits. Currently, *legal blindness* is defined as visual acuity
for distant vision of 20/200 or less in the better eye, with best correction, or
visual acuity of more than 20/200 if the widest diameter of field of vision
subtends an angle no greater than 20° (National Society for the Prevention of
Blindness, 1966). Hathaway (1959) has provided the following classification for
children who are partially seeing: (1) Children having visual acuity of 20/70 or
less in the better eye after all necessary medical or surgical treatment has been
given and compensating lenses provided but having a functional, usable residue of
sight and (2) children with a visual deviation from the norm who, in the opinion
of the eye specialist, can benefit from the special educational facilities provided
for the partially seeing.

Professionals who have worked in education or rehabilitation settings do not
find legal definitions very useful in terms of assessing an individual's functional

vision. Two individuals with identical acuities (e.g., 20/200) may function in extremely different ways. One may be highly mobile, read print well, and function much like a sighted person. The second individual may have difficulty reading print, have total loss of vision at night, and may function more like a blind person (Kolk, 1981). Perhaps the most important consideration is the functional visual efficiency a child exhibits. The concept of visual efficiency includes visual acuity (distance and near), visual fields, ocular motility, binocular vision, adaptations to light and dark, color vision, and accommodation (Lowenfeld, 1973). For the educator, the child's functional vision is important in terms of where materials are placed, their size, the colors chosen, and the light selected (Langley & DuBose, 1976).

ETIOLOGICAL CONSIDERATIONS

Prenatal and perinatal causes of visual deficits include genetic factors, alterations of embryonic development, central nervous system damage (e.g., maternal infections during pregnancy), and complications at the time of birth. Hatfield (1975) found that prenatal factors were responsible for approximately one half of all blindness. Of these factors, 83% were presumed to be hereditary or genetic in origin. The remaining 17% in the prenatal category included such causes as intrauterine infections and exposure to certain drugs and medications.

Those losing vision postnatally are known as the adventitiously blind. There is some evidence that children who lose all functional vision before age 3 do not recall facts about their environment (e.g., colors, shapes, distance, size, and proportions). Most children blinded after this age do retain the concepts with some visual referent (Kolk, 1981). Common specific causes of adventitious blindness in young children include accident or traumatic injury (e.g., dart gun), secondary complications of other disorders (e.g., diabetes), specific biological changes (e.g., retinal detachment or tumor), secondary effects of surgery (e.g., lens removal), and inflammatory and progressive disorders. Table 1 summarizes the statistics reported in 1980 by the National Society for the Prevention of Blindness relating to causes of legal blindness in children from birth to the age of 5 years.

DEVELOPMENTAL PROFILE

Despite the many differences among children with severe visual impairment, there are some commonalities in their developmental profiles. The following subsections will examine these commonalities in the major areas of development as well as the impact these children have on their families.

TABLE 1

Leading causes of legal blindness in children from birth to five years[a]

Causes of legal blindness (1978)	Percent diagnosed
Congenital cataracts Opacity of the lens resulting from the physiochemical change in state of the lens protein. Often genetic; also associated with intrauterine infections.	16.3
Optic nerve atrophy Degeneration of the optic nerve in any part of its course. Multiple specific etiologies.	12.4
Retrolental fibroplasia (RLF) A scarring of the regina caused by the growth of blood vessels into the retina. Associated with RLF are corneal opacification, cataracts, and enophthalmos (i.e., apanophthalmopathy). Note: From the 1940s to the 1960s RLF was the most common cause of visual impairment because during that time oxygen was vigorously administered to premature infants. It was eventually found that excess oxygen concentrations causes the growth of blood vessels in the retina to go awry. Today, the incidence of RLF is less except among the smallest and sickest of survivors of neonatal intensive care; for these infants the level of oxygen often must remain high to make survival possible, and factors in addition to oxygen alone are felt to contribute to this new epidemic of RLF.	9.3
Anophthalmus/microphthalmus A congenital malformation in which one or both eyes are smaller than normal or totally absent. Associated ocular defects are high hyperopia, aniridia, cataracts and certain somatic abnormalities (e.g., clubfoot, cleft palate).	6.2
Congenital glaucoma A congenital condition in which increased intraocular pressure causes pathologic changes in the optic disc and defects in the visual field.	6.2
Retinoblastoma A tumor arising from the retina itself, fatal if untreated. Involvement is bilateral in about 30% of the cases and frequently hereditary (Kirk, 1981).	3.9

Motor Development

Children who are considered to have light perception only experience their world differently and thus may have selective lags in motor and locomotor development (DuBose, 1979). Fraiberg (1977) noted that the blind children she studied engaged in rolling, independent sitting, independent standing, and step-

TABLE 1 (*Continued*)

Causes of legal blindness (1978)	Percent diagnosed
All other cases	45.7

Examples:

Albinism

  A disease affecting the metabolism of melanin (dark pigment). It is
  inherited as a recessive trait and affects dark-skinned races more
  than light-skinned. Ocular signs present at birth include eyebrows
  and lashes that are white, conjunctivas that are hyperemic, irises
  that are gray or red, and pupils that appear red. The macula is
  poorly developed and the subject has severe photophobia.
  Incompletely developed maculae make the vision defective,
  resulting in a searching type of nystagmus.

Cortical blindness

  A lesion in the occipital lobe of the brain and/or its connections
  caused by injury, tumor, or degeneration. The condition is
  suspected if pupils respond to light normally and the fundi show no
  changes, yet other signs indicate that the child is blind for
  educational purposes.

Retinal detachment

  A condition wherein the neural layer of the retina detaches or
  separates from the pigment epithelium. Causes include breaks in the
  retina congenitally, from traumatic injury, or from the buildup of
  subretinal fluid due to inflammations of the retina or choroid. Most
  of the retina may become detached within a few hours or it may
  take years.

Retinitis pigmentosa

  A degeneration of the retinal rods accompanied by a secondary
  atrophy of the remainder of the retina including the pigment
  epithelium. The etiology is genetic with multiple modes of
  inheritance.

[a] *Note:* Based on *Vision Problems in the United States* by the National Society for the Prevention of Blindness, 1980, New York: Operation Research Department, Author.

ping movements (while the hands were held) at approximately the same time as most sighted infants. These motor tasks require a low and relatively stable center of gravity, which allows blind children to remain close to their immediate base of support. On the other hand, Fraiberg reported that considerable lags have been observed among blind infants on motor milestones that require projection of their bodies into space (elevating upper torso by own support, raising self to sitting, pulling to stand, crawling, or walking). Running, hopping, jumping, and skipping have also been found to be delayed among older blind preschoolers.

In normal development, the infant's hands unite him with the outside world as he reaches for something he sees. Reaching for objects (occurring for sighted infants at approximately 4–5 months) has been found to occur much later (8–9 months) for blind infants, even with intervention. At the time when most sighted infants begin intentionally reaching, the blind infant often maintains her hands at shoulder length in a neonatal posture. A rattle placed in the child's hand will be firmly grasped but dropped when another is introduced. When a favorite toy is dropped, the child's hands typically do not search for it. A blind infant's grasp appears to develop within the range for sighted infants; however, it is clumsy and unpracticed. More significantly, a blind infant's hands do not naturally unite at midline. Even when such an infant is capable of various grasps, he or she often chooses a more primitive grasp (e.g., raking grasp over a neat pincer grasp) to locate a small item efficiently. Finally, the holding of two objects simultaneously (one in each hand) and the transfer of objects has been found to be delayed in blind infants (DuBose, 1979).

Scott (1982) described the problems blind children have in developing good body image. She attributed this difficulty to the fact that blind children have not been able to observe their own bodies or those of other people—their sizes and shapes, how and where their arms and legs are attached, and the arrangement of facial features. This lack of body image becomes apparent when blind children are asked to draw, model, or describe their bodies. They often cannot estimate whether or not their bodies "fit" into a particular space. There is no opportunity to observe good posture and graceful body movements nor to visually monitor their own in a mirror.

Language Development

Visually impaired children with little or no vision do not display the same range of gestural language as children with normal sight (Scott, 1982). Although blind infants begin smiling at approximately the same time as sighted infants, this behavior often decreases over time (Freedman, 1964). Because they do not see what other people do with their faces or bodies when they are happy, sad, or angry, they cannot consciously assume those gestures. The result is often an inappropriate facial or bodily expression or even a total lack of such expression.

Warren (1977) concluded that blind children develop expected language, although not without intervening differences, before age 4 or 5. During the first year of life little difference is noted between blind and sighted infants in their early vocalizations and imitations; this is attributed to the fact that these early behaviors are dependent primarily on neurophysiological maturation and performance factors. Fraiberg (1977), in fact, found that blind babies imitated words above the mean for sighted babies.

By 14 months sighted babies say two words under test conditions, but blind babies do not achieve this until an average of approximately 18.5 months. Fraiberg has explained this difference by suggesting that representational behavior is involved. Without visual experiences, the blind child must rely solely on experiences gained from hearing or touch and thus has a deprived experiential base. The fact that a blind child's mobility is delayed may also hamper his or her language development in that experiences in locating and naming objects are fewer. A 6-month lag has also been noted in the ability of blind children to form two-word sentences. Again, the lack of exposure to attributes, actions, and qualities would be expected to affect the concept development needed to put sentences together (DuBose, 1979). However, Fraiberg (1977) did find that blind infants are able to use words to make their wants known at the same level as sighted infants. It is suggested that wants are established from internal or need states: blindness, therefore, does not impede verbal expression of those needs.

Sighted children of approximately $2\frac{1}{2}$ years of age begin representing themselves in their world of play. Blind children tend not to exhibit this behavior nor do they use the pronouns *I* or *me* until between 3 and $4\frac{1}{2}$ years of age (DuBose, 1979).

Cognitive Development

Table 2 illustrates the sighted infant's progress from reflexive response to representational behavior during the sensorimotor period and further outlines the effects blindness has at the various stages of cognitive development. As noted, some blind infants show no pupillary reflex or visual tracking, and there is also a definite delay in the acquisition of skills between 4 and 9 months. At this stage the blind infant fails to reach for objects. Because of the lack of sensory stimulation, the blind child's sensorimotor experiences are not easily integrated. By the end of the first year, the auditory sense begins to substitute for vision so the world can take on an organization.

Fraiberg (1968) found that the most obvious cognitive delay is in the development of object concept. Directly related to the delay in object concept is the blind child's difficulty in attaining a sense of object permanence and failure to engage in sustained search behavior. Spatial concepts and an understanding of causality are further inhibited by the delay in object concept. Moreover, when the blind child is unable to gain sufficient information from the environment, an understanding of the relatedness of objects to other objects, events, persons, and experiences is lessened. These deficiencies subsequently affect higher level cognitive skills such as classification and conservation (Piaget & Inhelder, 1969).

TABLE 2

Effects of blindness on sensorimotor development

Period	Expectations	Blindness
1. Reflexes (0–1 month)	Behavior is characterized primarily by reflexive responses to infant's own body and to some aspects of external world; some refinement of reflexive behavior occurs as infant discovers, for example, that some objects are suckable and some are not	1. No pupillary restrictions to light in some cases
2. Primary circular reactions (1–4 months)	Infant begins to repeat selectively those actions that produce interesting or satisfying effects; these actions are primarily directed to infant's own body rather than to external objects	1. No visual tracking 2. No examination of feet and hands 3. No intentional grasping of objects
3. Secondary circular reactions (4–9 months)	Behaviors that produce effects in external world that are satisfying or interesting to infant are reproduced; this marks the beginning of the infant's effective orientation to the external world	1. Body-centered sensations continued 2. Failure to follow rapid movements of persons and objects 3. Failures to understand the cause or source of object activation
4. Coordination of secondary circular reactions (9–12 months)	Beginnings of intentionality are seen in that infant begins to coordinate own behavior with respect to external world in more complex ways; use of specific ends demonstrates increasing organization of world; infant begins to anticipate effects of own actions and those of other people	1. Failure to attend visually to objects or persons or imitate movements 2. Failure to realize similarity in objects; thus, old schema not generalized to new objects 3. Failure to see a distant goal to attain it 4. Failure to perceive self in relation to environment 5. Initiation of interaction with adult to repeat an action less likely

TABLE 2 (*Continued*)

Period	Expectations	Blindness
5. Tertiary circular reactions (12–18 months)	Behavior clearly involves active trial-and-error experimentation with world; behavior becomes more flexible in that infant can systematically vary own actions to obtain a specific goal; infant seems to seek novelty to learn more about world	1. Failure to see relationships between action and solution that can be accomplished to produce activity 2. Less problem solving in environment 3. Failure to attack barriers to secure toys 4. Failure to see the usefulness of tools to assist in securing goals
6. Invention of new means through mental combination (18–24 months)	Internalized thought begins; child need no longer engage in overt trial-and-error behavior, but rather can think about possible behaviors and effects that they would have; according to Piaget, this stage frees child from own perceptions and behaviors and child begins to imagine behaviors and their consequences	1. Delayed internalization of action schema 2. Failure to categorize objects by salient dimensions 3. Previously observed adult behavior not imitated in pretending

Note: "Working With Sensorily Impaired Children" (Table 7-3) by R. R. Fewell, 1983, in *Educating Young Handicapped Children: A Developmental Approach* (2nd ed., pp. 248–249), S. G. Garwood (Ed.), Rockville, MD: Aspen Systems.

Social and Emotional Development

One of the first signs of social behavior is smiling. As previously indicated, blind babies begin smiling at approximately the same time as sighted babies; however, the smiling becomes less frequent over time. Lairy and Harrison-Covello (1973) commented that open displays of affection during the second year remain induced responses; blind children behave as if they are not the initiators of a relationship. Independence from the mother is delayed in that separation anxiety usually persists beyond the second year. A cognitive delay in object permanence would obviously have a bearing on this social behavior.

Fewell (1983) noted that a child's loss of vision may alter the acquisition of social targets largely because the context of the situation and/or the person interacting are difficult to read. Additional problems in establishing social relationships occur because most people neither appear to understand blindness nor know what to expect from blind individuals. Any behavior the blind child displays that is unfamiliar may be perceived as potentially threatening. Perhaps the most common atypical behaviors observed in blind children and blind adults are self-stimulating in nature and are referred to as *blindisms*. These blindisms include such mannerisms as body rocking or swaying, pendulum head movements, and eye poking. Some attribute these behaviors to the lack of visual stimulation; the body seeks more stimulation through moving (Knight, 1972). Others have suggested that because seeing requires a considerable expenditure of energy, the lack of vision necessitates energy being spent in another way (Hayes & Weinhouse, 1978). Interventions to prevent or reduce these mannerisms may be valuable in reducing some of the social interaction problems these children experience.

Self-Care Development

Reflecting on the means by which each of us learned to eat, toilet, dress, and groom ourselves, we find the role of visual imitation quite apparent. It follows, then, that totally blind children require more deliberate tactual/auditory intervention to learn these self-care skills. The sequence for learning them is similar to that for sighted children; the timelines are simply longer. When caregivers do too many things for blind children, the delay in independent performance becomes even greater (Fewell, 1983).

Impact on Families

In her longitudinal study of 10 blind infants, Fraiberg (1968) described the home situations of these children. She found that nearly all of the parents were immobilized by grief and felt they were without hope. Initial feelings of shock, disappointment, anger, and fear predominated. Usually the baby books had not been touched; no pictures of the baby had been taken. The gift toys were put away because parents felt the babies could not do anything with them anyway. Grandparents, relatives, and friends participated in a kind of conspiracy of silence; no one used the word *blind*. Visitors did not coo at the babies; no one said they were cute or adorable. Few parents were receiving any response from their children from holding or cuddling; most felt that their baby was happier in the crib. As will be discussed in a later section, Fraiberg found that through twicemonthly visits parents were helped in establishing nonvisual affectional bonds with their children and were assisted in overcoming some of the developmental effects of visual impairment. As the babies became more interactive and mobile, parents and other family members saw them as more competent and thus could accept the children more completely.

IDENTIFICATION AND DEVELOPMENTAL
ASSESSMENT OF BLIND CHILDREN

Identification and assessment of blind children are, of course, essential steps prior to providing intervention services and also serve to define the population of children included in studies of early intervention. There are several visual screening instruments that are useful in this regard and are described in the following.

Visual Screening

Severely visually impaired children are often identified at birth by medical personnel or in the first few months of life by their parents. Signals of visual difficulty may include such things as cosmetic appearance of the eyes, lack of visual tracking, lack of interest in lights and visual stimuli, or eyes that are not aligned. Occasionally, however, a severe visual deficit is not discovered until a child enters an educational program. There are five visual screening devices used most frequently throughout the United States with preschool children.

The New York Association for the Blind's Flash-Card Vision Test for Children (1966) is a test that is successfully used with children as young as 27 months of age. Three symbols (apple, house, umbrella) are presented in Snellen-acuity notation. Children verbally or manually label or match symbols at 10 ft or less to determine visual acuity.

The Home Eye Test (Boyce, 1973) is a test that can be used with children 3 years of age or older. It can be administered by parents at home and is reliable and inexpensive. The kit consists of an ''E'' chart with instructions for training and administration. Test distance is at 10 ft.

The Snellen Symbol Chart (National Society for the Prevention of Blindness, 1980) is a chart of symbols that is read at a distance of 20 ft. It is most effective with children who have good coordination and have no known perceptual difficulties. Symbols can be seen by the normal eye at 200 ft.

Stycar Vision Tests (Sheridan, 1976) are test batteries for children with limited verbal and coordination skills. Children are shown a set of familiar toys or objects and are asked to name them at a distance of 10 ft. If children are unable to name the toys, they can match them to a duplicate set.

Assessment of Functional Vision in Severely Handicapped Children (Langley, 1980) is a scale that can be administered in the first 2 years. It assesses presence and nature of the visual response, size and distance vision, visual reaction to impinging stimuli, and integration of vision with cognitive and motor processes.

Developmental Assessment

Historically, assessment devices used with blind children have been those that are standardized on sighted populations. However, unless norms based on blind children have been established, it is inappropriate to draw conclusions from the scores obtained on these tests. The astute diagnostician uses the appropriate items from a particular test without trying to draw global conclusions regarding the child's developmental status compared to sighted children. In this way, the assessment instruments become a tool for program planning and evaluation of early intervention strategies; the child's performance is referenced against his or her own performance over time.

In order to make more items from sighted tests appropriate for use with blind preschoolers, several adaptations can be made in terms of test administration and materials presented.

Test Administration

Procedurally, a well-defined assessment area aids the examiner in presenting items to the visually impaired child. Pieces of cloth or large trays placed upon a table surface provide necessary boundaries for such a child. When a child without sight enters a test setting he or she is often distracted by sounds and/or anxiety about the unknown. For this reason, it is important to choose a room that is as quiet as possible. The child should then be oriented to the room both tactually and auditorily.

Scott (1982) noted that a blind child's conceptual understanding may contain gaps and/or be based on faulty assumptions. Rather than assume that the child understands a test direction, the examiner must verify this by having the child demonstrate a conceptual understanding of it. An example is seen wherein a child is asked to find a tactual representation that is the "same" as the one presented. The examiner must have the child demonstrate his or her interpretation of the word *same* before the child's ability to tactually discriminate can be assessed. Along with verifying a child's conceptual understanding, it is important that the examiner model expected test responses (e.g., pointing to objects, grouping objects, giving body gesture or verbal responses). In addition, it is often necessary to extend the suggested time limits of a test that is normed on the sighted. Any deviation from standard procedure such as this should be noted by the examiner with interpretations of the child's performance written accordingly.

Materials Presentation

Preschool assessment instruments often include a wide array of objects, pictures, and printed symbols. When these instruments have been designed for sighted children, it may be necessary to substitute larger objects, pictures, or symbols. In addition, it is often helpful to use bright colors that are highly contrasted for children with residual vision and pictures; symbols may need to be represented tactually. Examiners may use such things as string, rubber bands, or yarn glued to paper to illustrate a form tactually. The Sewell Raised Line Drawing Kit (available through the American Printing House for the Blind, 1976) can also be utilized for illustrating fine lines tactually.

Developmental Assessment Tools

Three scales have been specifically developed for children with severe visual deficits: (1) Callier–Azusa Scale (Stillman, 1976) presents developmentally based descriptions of behavior in areas of motor development, perceptual development, daily living skills, and socialization. It is especially useful for children who might be deaf and blind or multihandicapped and it has no age limits. (2) Project Vision Up (Croft & Robinson, 1976) is a developmental scale for children birth to 8 years of age. It assesses developmental behaviors through card sorting and can also be used with mentally handicapped or multihandicapped children. (3) The Oregon Project (Jackson County Education Service District, 1978) is an observational checklist designed for children from birth to 6 years of age. It has subareas of cognition, language, gross motor, fine motor, self-help, and socialization.

Cognitive Tests

Two tests of cognition have been specifically designed for the preschool visually handicapped child. The Interim Hayes–Binet Scale of Intelligence (Howe Press, 1942) is commonly given to children 3 years and older and is based on the 1937 edition of the Stanford–Binet Intelligence Scale. Visual items have been eliminated so that it is highly verbal in nature. Special training is needed to administer and score this test. The Perkins Binet Intelligence Test (Davis, 1980) can be given to 5- and 6-year-olds. It provides verbal and performance scales and is highly predictive of academic achievement.

For children under the age of 3 the Bayley Scales of Infant Development (Bayley, 1969) are used. This test has a mental scale, a motor scale, and an infant behavior record. Because it is standardized on infants with sight, all visual items are inappropriate. Special training is required in administration and scoring.

Language Tests

The following language tests are of value: (1) The Receptive Expressive Language Assessment for the Visually Impaired (Raynor, 1971) is an adaptation of the Receptive Expressive Language Scale (Bzoch & League, 1970) for sighted children. It can be administered to children from birth to 72 months of age. (2) The Tactile Test of Basic Concepts (American Printing House for the Blind, 1976) is an adaptation of the Boehm Test of Basic Concepts for Sighted Children (Boehm, 1971). It can be given to 5- and 6-year-old children to assess their knowledge concepts needed for kindergarten readiness. (3) The Sequenced Inventory of Communication Development (Hedrich, Prather, & Tobin, 1984) includes receptive and expressive scales that allow assessment in an informal play atmosphere. The most effective age range for use is 4–48 months. This instrument is standardized on the sighted but used often with blind children.

Motor Tests

For the motor area, two tests should be considered. A screening test that assesses awareness of body planes, body parts, body movements, laterality, and directionality is Cratty and Sam's Body Image Screening Test for Blind Children (Cratty & Sams, 1968). The Peabody Developmental Motor Scales (Folio & Fewell, 1983) is an instrument used to assess gross motor development from birth to 7 years and fine motor development from birth to 6. Scoring allows the child credit for minimum success rather than a pass or failure.

Social Development Tests

The only test of social development specifically for the blind is the Maxfield Buchholz Scale of Social Maturity for Preschool Blind Children (Maxfield & Bucholy 1957). It evaluates children from birth to 6 years of age in the areas of motor development, dressing, eating, locomotion, socialization, communication, and occupation. The test requires the parent or primary caregiver to report the child's progress in these areas.

FORMS EARLY INTERVENTION HAS TAKEN

Beginning in 1968, with strong support at the federal level through the Handicapped Children's Early Education Program, services to young handicapped children in the United States have improved dramatically. Prior to this time, it was estimated that 75% of this population were unserved, and individual states still vary from having mandatory education for the handicapped from birth to having no legislation for early intervention. This state of affairs is further compounded in the area of services for the young visually handicapped child in that there is a severe shortage of professionally prepared teachers (Peabody, 1982).

Programs for visually handicapped preschoolers are found in public schools, community agencies, and early childhood centers as well as in the traditional state or private residential schools. The trend is increasingly toward mainstreaming those children who have no other major disabilities than the lack of vision.

Larger school districts might begin by providing a home-based program for blind infants. Vision specialists come into the house and talk with parents about the developmental progress of their child. Some assessment is usually conducted and a program of infant stimulation is established on the basis of that assessment. Typically, the vision specialist demonstrates teaching techniques for the parents and also sets up a follow-through program for the parents to carry out between visits.

Many districts provide some center-based programming for children younger than age 3 with severe visual impairments. If the child has no other handicaps, he or she may be served in a regular preschool setting with regular visits from a vision specialist. Some centers combine home-based programming with center-based time for children between 3 and 5 years of age. Blind children who have other significant handicaps are usually served in center-based programs for the severely/multiply handicapped. It is not unusual to see a classroom with five or six children (ages 3–5); this group of children may display combinations of handicaps such as cerebral palsy, spina bifida, deafness and blindness, and even Down's syndrome. Rarely does one see a center serving children with severe visual impairments only.

By the age of 5, most school districts provide preschool handicapped classrooms in public school buildings; again, partly because of the low incidence of blindness, one sees "normal" blind children in regular kindergarten rooms served by itinerant vision specialists. Multihandicapped blind children are found in classrooms with children having a variety of handicapping conditions.

Because early intervention for blind preschoolers often takes place in mainstreamed settings or in settings with multihandicapped youngsters, it is more difficult to identify teaching strategies that are specific for blind children. Nonetheless, certain themes emerge whether the program is developmentally based or takes a behavioral approach. In the section that follows several intervention strategies and themes are described.

General Intervention Strategies Commonly Employed

Sensory Stimulation

With a deficit in vision, it is crucial that any remaining vision is utilized to the greatest extent possible. Providing infants and young children with high-contrast items (e.g., yellow on black) and an interesting visual environment that they can learn to scrutinize visually through practiced "looking" is essential. Through their fingertips blind children explore, label, classify, compare, and will eventually read.

The refinement of the tactual sense is essential and usually begins with encouraging tactual exploration of various surfaces. It is important that blind children learn to recognize and label real objects before they are given miniature replicas of those objects.

The auditory modality is the major channel for the blind child's learning. It is necessary to help young blind children identify the nature of sounds as well as their relative locations. They need practice lengthening their auditory attention spans and strengthening their auditory memory skills and their comprehension.

The sense of smell will alert the blind child to danger or pleasure. These smells need to be deliberately introduced and associated with their origin and meaning (e.g., poisons for danger; food, clothing, and shoes for location within stores).

The sense of taste will also serve the blind child as a receptive channel and should therefore be stimulated as broadly as possible. Parents need to introduce foods with varying textures, temperature, and tastes as soon as the child is on solid food. Children should also be encouraged to handle the food and self-feed as soon as they are capable of doing so.

Affective Expression

The earliest concern in the area of affective development is that a substitution for visual bonding with the parent takes place. Sighted infants respond to the human face and will subsequently smile in response to their parents' faces. This helps establish a bond between parent and child. When vision is absent, tactual and auditory bonds must be substituted. Parents are generally encouraged to persist in holding and cuddling their newborn blind infants, even though the children often initially resist the tactual contact. As children grow, they need to be given feedback about their own body language and facial expressions. Further, an understanding of how the voices of others are paired with facial or body gestures to convey fine nuances of meaning needs to be gained.

As discussed earlier, blind children often develop stereotypic mannerisms referred to as *blindisms*. Most teachers try to help blind children become aware of their blindisms by touching the children, giving them verbal reminders, or reinforcing children for not engaging in the behavior. When it appears that the blindism is more frequent at times when the child is idle, the teacher may try to engage the child in meaningful independent activities. Oftentimes, these activities involve the hands or the entire body (e.g., block play, sand play, water play, obstacle courses). It has been helpful to give children acceptable outlets for pent-up energy. Examples might be to teach children to clasp their hands, to rotate their feet, or simply to hold a small object to squeeze or rub very subtly. The point to be made here is that sighted people engage in mannerisms; the difference is that these mannerisms are viewed as acceptable and less noticeable than those often engaged in by blind children.

Orientation and Mobility

The child who must learn to negotiate his or her environment with little or no vision requires added incentives to move about. Sighted infants see things that evoke their curiosity; blind infants must be enticed to pursue objects out of their immediate reach. Adelson and Fraiberg (1977) noted that children are not able to utilize their auditory sense for purposeful reaching until the age of 9 or 10 months. It thus becomes important to introduce objects to blind children and to subsequently help them follow through with coactive movement to relocate objects. As children move out in their environments, it is important to make those environments safe for exploration and also to fill them with interesting perceptual cues for orientation. Sharp table edges can be padded, breakable items removed, and protective movements or search patterns taught. The child can be shown how to hold one hand (palm outward) over the forehead area while walking in an unfamiliar area and/or stooping to retrieve a dropped object. Homes and preschool classrooms can provide tactual clues on the walls or floors to assist children in orienting themselves. Children can be taught to listen for environmental sounds and smells.

Independence in the accomplishment of daily living skills is essential. Blind children do not learn to bathe, groom, dress, feed, or toilet themselves without direct teaching because they cannot learn by casual observation as sighted children do. This can be frustrating for parents in that the child will necessarily take longer to accomplish these tasks independently. Parents can greatly reduce the child's anxiety by being patient and by being relaxed when they move through an activity the first time.

Another important area that requires direct intervention to develop involves midline skills. Blind children need to learn to operate with their hands together on an object with each hand performing a different task. Toys that are activated by turning knobs or handles with one hand while being held in the other are especially helpful. Containers (e.g., pots, bowls) that can be held and filled with small objects (e.g., measuring spoons, jar lids) are also particularly useful.

Cognitive Development

Toys can be utilized for teaching the child causality. When toys vibrate or continue to move after the child pushes or hits them, children can begin to understand the effects of their actions. By modeling and physically prompting a blind child to search for a toy that is out of reach, one can help the child to develop a sense of object permanence and ideas for solving simple problems.

Blind children learn that objects in the environment have multiple uses by being shown how to use objects in a variety of ways. In teaching skills of classification, it is important to help the child focus on particular characteristics objects have that make them alike or different. The child should have the opportunity to feel the objects while verbally repeating these characteristics. Furniture and objects in the environment should be maintained in their same and appropriate place to assist young children to order their environment.

When teaching skills related to reasoning, blind children should ideally be given actual concrete experiences to help them arrive at the appropriate conclusions. Blind children often have distorted ideas about real objects because they are given tactual experiences with small replications of real-world objects. Initially, real objects should be used along with frequent checks of their conceptual understanding. When teaching new concepts, it is often helpful to relate things to the child's own body, clothes, or toys. It is not uncommon for blind children to center on one object or behavior. Adults should help broaden the child's interest in people, events, and objects if or when this does begin to happen. Finally, to help blind children develop an understanding of conservation they should be provided with opportunities to handle the same materials in different conditions. By rolling the same mass of clay into various shapes, filling different-shaped containers with the same cup of rice, or filling different-sized containers with the same glass of water, the child experiences the principle of conservation.

Communication Readiness

In preparation for reading, preschool children should be exposed to the medium in which they will communicate (i.e., braille or large print). Sighted youngsters start kindergarten with an awareness of print letters, words, and books that provides motivation and a readiness for reading instruction. Likewise, it is important that visually handicapped children are exposed to braille or large print through books that are read to them as well as through seeing objects in their environment labeled.

Written expression for most youngsters is braille writing or typing. Preschool children are generally allowed to manipulate the moving parts of a braille writer as they develop the hand–finger strength to depress certain keys simultaneously. This experimentation can be likened to the scribbling a sighted child might do with paper and pencil.

Common Aids/Appliances

Many of the aids and appliances used with the preschool population are directed toward children having usable vision (e.g., devices that enlarge print, pictures). Because the focus of this chapter is on the severely visually impaired child, these low-vision devices will be omitted from the following descriptions.

Concept Teaching

A number of tactual objects and two-dimensional tactual diagrams are available for purchase from the American Printing House for the Blind. These objects and diagrams represent concepts often illustrated for sighted children through pictures. Teachers commonly glue such materials as yarn, string, rubber bands, cloth materials, or electricians' tape to heavy paper to make their own tactual diagrams for children. A thermoform machine can be utilized to make plastic replicas of tactual diagrams or of braille material. The thermoform machine is basically an electric oven that softens the plastic and, by suction, molds the plastic over the master sheet.

Reading/Writing

Before preschool blind children read, they may be given recorded materials on records or on cassette tapes. The controls on record players and tape recorders have been made with tactual symbols so that the children can locate the appropriate control and operate the machines independently.

When a child has developed sufficient reading readiness skills a set of materials often used is the Mangold Program of Developmental Perception and Braille Letter Recognition (Mangold, 1976). This is a series of lessons that teaches the child the mechanical skills necessary for reading braille. The American Printing House (APH) for the blind has developed a number of tactual discrimination materials that assist a child in developing readiness for reading braille. Also available from APH is a new reading series entitled *Patterns* (Caton & Pester, 1981) developed specifically for blind preschool and primary age children. Braille symbols are introduced in order of their ease of recognition. Stories are written so that blind children can relate to them sensorily (e.g., tactual, auditory descriptions rather than visual descriptions of experiences).

The braille writer is often introduced to blind preschoolers so that they may become familiar with its operation. Some may formulate braille symbols by depressing combinations of the six keys by kindergarten; most children are still developing finger strength and coordination at this time.

Blind kindergarteners are taught to write their names with pen or pencil so they can sign their names and write a printed emergency message. Letters of the alphabet are presented to the child in raised format (for finger tracing) and/or in grooved templates (for tracing with a pen or pencil). Often the teacher forms the child's name with yarn glued to paper so that the child may gain an understanding of letter sequence and spacing.

Mathematics

The blind preschool child is often given an abacus for the purpose of learning to count. Measuring devices such as rulers come with braille embossing so that a blind child can learn about the relative size of things in the environment.

Orientation and Mobility

Preschool blind children, on rare occasion, are taught to use a long white cane for mobility. A majority of schools and agencies believe, however, that few children have developed sufficient hand–foot coordination to use this device properly. However, the Mowat Sensor, (Sensory Aids Corporation, 1977) a hand held ultrasound travel aid that vibrates at different rates to warn the child of obstacles, can be used.

Recently, some orientation and mobility instructors have used the Binaural Sensory Aid (Telesensory Systems Incorporated, 1970) with blind preschool children. This aid consists of a pair of glasses that sends out high frequency sounds from the nosepiece and provides the child with echoes that vary in pitch, depending upon the distance one is from an obstacle. Some instructors have attained a high degree of success with this device in teaching the child spatial concepts and relative distances.

Art

Teachers of preschool blind children are called upon to use the tactual medium in the art projects they present. Perhaps one of the most useful devices for helping a blind child benefit from art activities is a screenboard. This is a teacher-made item that consists of a piece of metal screen mounted on a lap-size flannel board. Regular paper is placed over the screenboard and crayon is used to scribble, color within boundary lines, draw shapes, or make letters. Because of the roughness of the screen below, the crayon particles leave a tactual trail that is detectable by the child's fingers.

SUMMARY OF THE RESEARCH ON THE EFFECTIVENESS OF EARLY INTERVENTION

Early intervention research on populations of visually handicapped children is very limited in both scope and quality. Ferrell (personal communication, August, 1983) of the American Foundation for the Blind commented that those working with children with visual impairments have not yet found ways to determine adequately the effectiveness of early intervention. In spite of our long history serving young children and their families, we must contend with small numbers of children (with great variance in their visual conditions, intellectual capabilities, and educational experiences) and limited resources that make data collection difficult. The consequence of this situation is that studies are often descriptive in nature and involve only a small number of subjects. Careful controls are not established and generalization to a larger population of visually impaired children has not been possible. Nevertheless, since 1969 seven studies have been conducted with visually impaired young children that have attempted to provide a minimal level of objective information on the effectiveness of early intervention. These seven studies are summarized in Table 3. Studies were excluded that did not describe intervention parameters, identify the severity of visual handicaps, or include experimental designs that attempted to yield reasonable efficacy data or provide appropriate outcome measures.

As a review of Table 3 will reveal, five of the studies were fairly extensive, with the time span for intervention ranging from 6 weeks to 3 years. This allows for teacher–student and teacher–parent rapport to be established and for skills to be stabilized over time (Adelson & Fraiberg, 1974; Allegheny County Schools, 1969; Bregani et al., 1981; Fraiberg, 1977; O'Brien, 1976). As noted, it was reported that early intervention made a substantial difference in helping blind children perform on a par with sighted children in three studies (Adelson & Fraiberg, 1974; Fraiberg, 1977; Olson, 1983). However, a weakness in research design is reflected in all of those studies that compared visually impaired children to their nonhandicapped peers. Most tests used to determine developmental level were normed on sighted youngsters; where researchers chose appropriate test items it would be difficult to conclude on par performance if one were to look at the whole child. Further, documented increases due to intervention were often vague and subjective in nature (Adelson & Fraiberg, 1974; Allegheny County Schools, 1969; Fraiberg, 1977; O'Brien, 1976).

A continuing trend from the earliest to the current studies seemed to be the involvement of parents in the education of their children. Five of the seven studies reported professionals guiding parents in their interactions with visually impaired preschoolers in the home setting. An additional study reported parent education meetings as part of the intervention. Nevertheless, it was not always clear from the description of the intervention what the impact on the total family had been. More specificity in terms of parent training techniques would also increase the value of these studies to those hoping to replicate the techniques (Adelson & Fraiberg, 1974; Allegheny County Schools, 1969; Bregani et al., 1981; Fraiberg, 1977; O'Brien, 1976; Rogow, 1982).

Particular intervention strategies emerged across several of the studies. Children were given sensory experiences in every modality; they were helped to develop body awareness through movement exercises; early independence was heavily encouraged, as was guided exploration of the child's environmental surroundings; and concrete experiences were routinely paired with verbalizations of those experiences (Adelson & Fraiberg, 1974; Allegheny County Schools, 1969; O'Brien, 1976; Rogow, 1982).

Three studies suggested that planned interactions with other professionals (medical personnel, social workers, and psychologists) contributed to their success. However, without additional controls regarding possibly confounding variables, these findings can only be considered suggestions at this time (Allegheny County Schools, 1969; Bregani et al., 1981; O'Brien, 1976).

CONCLUSIONS AND RECOMMENDATIONS

As has been emphasized, early intervention research in the area of visual impairment is meager, although historically teachers and parents have reported observational rather than statistical support for the effectiveness of programs and particular strategies within those programs. The small number of children present a problem in the establishment of a sound research design. Variability in the population of children with visual problems is extremely high. Not only do they differ in terms of their home and educational backgrounds and their intellectual, language, and social developmental levels, but they also vary tremendously in terms of the etiologies of their impairments and functional use of residual vision. It is nearly impossible to generalize from the findings of particular intervention

TABLE 3

Summary of early intervention studies for visually impaired children

Reference	Nature of intervention	Intervention parameters	Setting	Role of parents
Adelson & Fraiberg (1974)	Helped child unite sound with touch during parent–child interactions and during play	Professional visited home bimonthly and filmed monthly until child was past 2 years of age	Professional worked with parents in the home	Initial observation followed by guided interaction with child
Allegheny County Schools (1969)	Children received training in the following areas: Movement in space, self-help skills, use of residual vision, socialization and body image; a major principle was to assure no physical restrictions; independence and exploration were highly encouraged	Six weeks of training, full days; daily staffings to provide frequent program changes	Center	Parent education meetings were held; caseworkers provided counseling
Bregani, Ceppelini, Cerabalini, Contini, Damascelli, Livingstone, Premoli, & Rocca (1981)	A team of professionals from clinical psychology, medicine, and clinical social work: Individual team members visited the child's home weekly to help parents provide age-appropriate play and learning experiences that are supportive of the psychomotor and emotional development of a blind child; a major purpose of the intervention was to prevent and treat severe psychological disturbances	One-hour weekly home visits to the home over 1 year's time; entire team discussed diagnostic findings of each session and maintained input about progress and future strategy	Home	Parents were worked with directly, although the focus was not to give parents psychological interpretations of their own attitudes; rather, the emphasis was on getting the child to be an active participant in his or her own growth and development
Fraiberg (1977)	Visits to home by educational person to guide parents in their interactions with their blind children	Twice monthly; 9 visits from birth to the end of the third year	Home	Parents received guidance in dealing with their children

Child characteristics	Experimental design	Outcome measures	Results
Ten children who were totally blind (light perception only) and had no other handicapping conditions; ages ranged from 1 month to 8 months; all children were followed past second birthday	Post-only comparisons with sighted norms and with a group of blind infants in a previous study by Norris, Spaulding, & Brodie (1957)	Selected items from Gesell & Amatruda (1962) and Bayley Scales of Infant Development (1969)	The two blind groups showed similar patterns of development that differed from sighted norms; however, the treatment group exceeded the blind comparison group (from a previous study) especially over time (suggesting a cumulative effect)
Seven children ages 3–5 who were designated legally blind and at varying developmental levels; all were ambulatory and had not received any prior treatment	Pre–post tests	1. A scale of Orientation and Mobility of Young and Blind Children (Lord, 1967) 2. Body Image of Blind Children Screening Test 3. Videotapes over time	An increase in several items were reported; visitors who observed noted improvement from pre to post
Eight prematurely born children with retrolental fibroplasia, ranging in age from 8 months to 2 years	Pre–post tests	Scale of Psychomotor Development of Brunet-Lezine plus tests from Fraiberg's research (1977); neurological and ocular examinations were also given	All eight cases had documented decreases in behavioral stereotypes, a definite catching up in psychomotor development, and objective improvement in verbal communications and in the relationship between child and parent
Ten congenitally blind infants with no more than light perception and who had no other sensory or motor deficits or signs of central nervous system damage	Ongoing observation of single-subject pre–post tests in areas of: (1) attachment behavior, (2) behavior toward inanimate objects, (3) gross and fine motor development, (4) language, and (5) self- and object concepts	Motion picture samples of behaviors were scored, tabulated, and cross-checked before comparisons to sighted norms	In those areas of development where comparable data were available, the infants receiving the intervention came closer to sighted-child ranges than blind-child ranges

(*continued*)

TABLE 3 (*Continued*)

Reference	Nature of intervention	Intervention parameters	Setting	Role of parents
O'Brien (1975)	Body awareness, braille readiness, perceptual motor development, physical education, preschool development plan, social education, auditory language and visual training; Itinerant and classroom services were provided; Parents, social workers, and teachers received special training in the fostering of perceptual independence	Intervention activities (for purposes of pilot study) occurred over 8 months from pretests to posttests	Home and Learning Center	Demonstration teaching in the home plus parent meetings and counseling sessions
Olson (1983)	Introduction of a novel and a commercial toy providing various levels of structured verbal and tactual assists to accomplish exploration and ultimate solution of the toys	The experimental group was legally blind and had more years of early education (mean = 2.7 years) than did the comparison group of normally sighted children (mean = 1.6 years)	Home or classroom	Present in some cases but not directly involved
Rogow (1982)	Structured social routines (in the form of nursery rhymes) were presented verbally while paired with physical assists to accomplish action sequences	Three children were worked with for 30 minutes per day in the home over 10 months; 7 children were worked with for 90 minutes per week at their schools over 10 months	Home/school	Unclear

studies. Many of the studies that have been carried out with blind children have focused on describing their development and behavior as compared to sighted children. Yet there has been a lack of attention to developmental processes. It is most difficult to plan intervention strategies to avoid developmental lags when we really do not totally understand the many variables causing these lags.

Despite all of these recognized problems and deficiencies, available studies suggest several trends. First, early intervention efforts appear to have the potential to make a difference in helping blind children perform closer to the developmental expectations of sighted children. Second, the setting of the intervention does not seem to be a crucial factor in the success of a particular intervention. It did not seem to matter whether home-based, center-based, and combination programs were provided. Rather, an important variable may have been carryover

Reference	Nature of intervention	Intervention parameters	Setting	Role of parents
Children birth–8 years with vision sufficiently impaired that with best correction interferes with successful functioning in school or in their environment; Learning Center Program served 23 children; Home Program served 10 children	Pre–post tests and checklists	Visual Efficiency Scale; school health forms; developmental checklists; Bolea Pictorial Self-Concept Scale; Boehm Test of Basic Concepts (1971) case studies and anecdotal records Instruments developed through project:pupil status report, developmental checklist of behaviors and skills, social and developmental history, and psychological evaluation		Overall level obtained in 9 of 12 areas was above expectation; program highly effective in that 87% of objectives attempted were accomplished
Thirty children ages 2 years 1 month to 6 years 3 months; 15 legally blind children formed the experimental group; the comparison group was comprised of 15 children with normal sight	Each visually impaired child was matched with a normally sighted child for age, sex, and socioeconomic status; performance ratings were given on the exploration and success at solving the two toys; Post-only comparisons were then made based on the initial difference between the two groups (early intervention as opposed to later intervention)	Performance in exploration and toy solutions was rated by teachers of the visually handicapped who independently viewed and scored behavior in 10 different categories		No significant difference found between the two groups in the interactions with either toy; Possibility that additional years of early education for blind group were responsible for fact that no deficits on toy task were found
Eight female and two male children ranging in age from 15 months to 7 years; subjects had a broad range of visual impairments, secondary handicaps, and ambulatory abilities	Baseline data gathered from parents, teachers, videotapes provided a comparison with data gathered every 2 months	Piagetian stages of language development were used for determining child's functional level of communication		All subjects demonstrated an increased awareness of their role in social interaction; intentionality was seen in the use of social signals to show willingness, readiness, and comprehension of the social nature of the structured routine; Seven nonverbal subjects acquired a variety of social signals to indicate initiation and participation

between the home and the center. Finally, parents and educators might increase the chance for the child's success through planned interactions with other related child health and development professionals.

The available data suggest also that our research efforts in the field of visual impairment cannot afford the luxury of studying group norms or group averages. Even with more extensive resources, children with severe visual impairments are simply too few in number and too heterogeneous in functioning for traditional experimental designs to be emphasized in a systematic fashion. More single-subject longitudinal studies need to be initiated. These studies should be both highly qualitative (richly documenting every detail of a blind child's early experience) and quantitative in nature. Because the number of blind children being studied is small, it is imperative that researchers do not work in isolation. It would be best if some common data collection mechanism could be agreed upon and findings shared across investigations. Such efforts may allow us to be in a better position in subsequent years to evaluate more adequately the effectiveness of early intervention for visually impaired children.

REFERENCES

Adelson, E., & Fraiberg, S. (1974). Child development project. *Child Development, 45,* 114–126.

Allegheny County Schools. (1969). *A demonstration project on developing independence in preschool handicapped children.* Pittsburgh, PA: Author. (ERIC Document Reproduction Service No. ED 032 699)

American Printing House for the Blind. (1976) *Tactile test of basic concepts.* Louisville, KY: Author.

Barraga, N. (1976). *Visual handicaps and learning.* Belmont, CA: Wadsworth.

Bayley, N. (1959). *Bayley scales of infant development.* New York: Psychological Corporation.

Boehm, A. (1971). *Boehm test of basic concepts for sighted children.* New York: Psychological Corporation.

Boyce, V. S. (1973). The home eye test program. *Sight-Saving Review, 43,* 43–48.

Bregani, P., Cepellini, C., Cerebalini, R., Contini, G., Damascelli, A., Livingstone, J. B., Premoli, M., & Rocca, A. (1981). Blind children: Prevention of emotional disturbances by early intervention with parents and child. *Courier, 31,* 256–262.

Bzoch, K., & League, R. (1970). *Receptive expressive emergent language assessment scale.* Tallahassee, FL: Anhinga Press.

Caton, H., & Pester, E. (1981). *Patterns.* Louisville, KY: American Printing House for the Blind.

Cratty, B., & Sams, T. (1968). *Cratty and Sam's body image screening test for blind children.* New York: American Foundation for the Blind.

Croft, N., & Robinson, L. (1976). *Project vision up.* Boise, ID: Boise Education Production and Training Foundation.

Davis, C. (1980). *Perkins-Binet tests of intelligence for the blind.* Watertown, MA: Howe Press of the Perkins School for the Blind.

DuBose, R. (1979). Working with sensorily impaired children. Part 1: Visual impairments. In S. G. Garwood (Ed.), *Educating young handicapped children* (pp. 323–359). Germantown, MD: Aspen Systems.

Fewell, R. (1983). Working with sensorily impaired children. In S. G. Garwood (Ed.), *Educating young handicapped children: A developmental approach* (2nd ed., pp. 248–249). Rockville, MD: Aspen Systems.

Folio, M. R., & Fewell, R. (1983). *Peabody developmental motor scales.* Allen, TX: DLM Teaching Resources.

Fraiberg, S. (1968). Parallel and divergent patterns in blind and sighted infants. *Psychoanalytic Study of the Child, 23,* 264–300.

Fraiberg, S. (1977). *Insights from the blind.* New York: Basic Books.

Freedman, D. G. (1964). Smiling in blind infants and the issue of innate vs. acquired. *Journal of Child Psychology and Psychiatry, 5,* 171–184.

Gesell, A., & Amatruda, C. (1962). *Developmental diagnosis.* New York: Hoeber.

Hatfield, E. (1975). Why are they blind? *Sight-Saving Review, 45,* 3–22.

Hathaway, W. (1959). *Education and health of the partially sighted child* (4th ed.). New York: Columbia University Press.

Hayes, C., & Weinhouse, E. (1978). Applications of behavior modification to blind children. *Journal of Visual Impairment and Blindness, 74,* 139

Hedrich, D., Prather, E., & Tobin, A. (1984). *Sequenced inventory of communication development.* Seattle, WA: University of Washington Press.

Howe Press of the Perkins School for the Blind. (1942). *Interim Hayes Binet scale of intelligence.* Watertown, MA: Author.

Jackson County Education Service District. (1978). *Oregon project* Medford, OR: Author.

Kirk, E. (1981). *Vision pathology in education.* Springfield, IL: Thomas.

Knight, J. (1972). Mannerisms in the congenitally blind child. *New Outlook, 9,* 297–302.

Kolk, C. (1981). *Assessment and planning with the visually impaired.* Baltimore: University Park Press.

Lairy, G. C., & Harrison-Covello, A. (1973). The blind child and his parents: Congenital visual defect and the repercussion of family attitudes on the early development of the blind. *Research Bulletin, American Foundation for the Blind, 25,* 1–24.

Langley, M. B. (1980). *Assessment of functional vision in severely handicapped children.* Chicago, IL: Stoelting.

Langley, M. B., & DuBose, R. (1976). Functional vision screening for severely handicapped children. *The New Outlook for the Blind, 70,* 346–350.

Lord, F. (1967). *Preliminary standardization of a scale of orientation and mobility skills of young children.* Washington, DC: U.S. Department of Health, Education and Welfare, Office of Education.

Lowenfeld, B. (1973). *The visually handicapped child in school.* New York: Day.

Mangold, S. (1976). *Mangold program of developmental perception and braille letter recognition.* Castro Valley, CA: Exceptional Teaching Aids.

Maxfield, K., & Bucholz, S. (1957). *Maxfield and Bucholz scale of social maturity for preschool blind children.* New York: American Foundation for the Blind.

National Society for the Prevention of Blindness. (1966). *N.S.P.B. fact book: Estimated statistics on blindness and visual problems.* New York: Author.

National Society for the Prevention of Blindness. (1980). Vision problems in the United States. New York: Operation Research Department, Author.

New York Association for the Blind. (1966). *Flashcard vision test for children.* New York: Author.

Norris, M., Spaulding, P. J., & Brodie, F. H. (1957). *Blindness in children.* Chicago, IL: University of Chicago Press.

O'Brien, R. (1976). *Alive. . . Aware. . A person: A developmental model for early childhood services.* Rockville, MD: Montgomery County Public Schools.

Olson, M. (1983). A study of the exploratory behavior or legally blind and sighted preschoolers. *Exceptional Children, 50,* 130–138.

Peabody, R. (1982). Intervention strategies and the state of education for the visually handicapped. In M. Lewis & L. T. Taft (Eds.), *Developmental disabilities: Theory, assessment, and intervention* (pp. 55–61). New York: SP Medical and Scientific Books.

Piaget, J., & Inhelder, B. (1969). *The psychology of the child.* New York: Basic Books.

Raynor, S. (1971). *Receptive expressive language assessment for the visually impaired.* Mason, MI: Infant Program for Visually Impaired.

Rogow, S. (1982). Rhythms and rhymes: Developing communication in very young blind and multi-handicapped children. *Child: Care, Health and Development, 8,* 249–260.

Scott, E. (1982). *Your visually impaired student.* Baltimore, MD: University Park Press.

Sensory Aids Corporation. (1977). *Mowat sensor.* Bensenville, IL: Author.

Sewell, E. P. Corporation. (1981). *Sewell raised line drawing kit.* Woodside, NY: Author.

Sheridan, M. (Ed.). (1976). *Stycar vision test.* Nashville, TN: NFER Nelson Publishing Company.

Stillman, R. (Ed.). (1976). *Callier-Azusa scale.* Reston, VA: Council for Exceptional Children.

Taylor, J. L. (1973). Educational programs. In B. Lowenfeld (Ed.), *The visually handicapped child in school* (pp. 155–184). New York: Day.

Telesensory Systems Incorporated. (1970). *Binural sensory aid*. Palo Alto, CA: Author.

Warren, D. H. (1977). *Blindness and early childhood development*. New York: American Foundation for the Blind.

Chapter 9

An Analysis of the Effectiveness of Early Intervention Programs for Hearing-Impaired Children

KATHRYN P. MEADOW-ORLANS

Center for Studies in Education and Human Development
The Gallaudet Research Institute
Gallaudet University
Washington, DC 20002

INTRODUCTION

Hearing impairments may be classified by type (sensorineural, conductive, or mixed), time of onset (at birth or after birth), by severity (on a continuum from mild to profound), and by etiology. All of these classifications are interactive, and each is important for the early diagnosis of hearing impairment and for the nature and effectiveness of the intervention employed. The relationship between type and severity of hearing loss is especially important. Conductive hearing loss involves the middle ear and is likely to be less severe than a sensorineural loss that is related to a wide range of injuries or abnormalities of the auditory nerve, the cochlea, the organ of Corti, or the central nervous system (Davis, 1978a). When the time of onset is at or before birth (congenital hearing loss), the most prevalent causes include genetic factors, complications of pregnancy such as intrauterine infection or Rh incompatibility, and prematurity or birth complications such as asphyxia and/or mechanical injury. Onset after birth (acquired hearing loss) is usually divided into the periods before and after the acquisition of

325

THE EFFECTIVENESS OF EARLY INTERVENTION
FOR AT-RISK AND HANDICAPPED CHILDREN

language, the former having more severe consequences. Formerly, the important cut-off point was accepted to be the third year of life; more recently, the critical age was reduced to 18 months, and some developmental psychologists and child linguists believe that important linguistic information is acquired from the age of 6 months. Important specific causes of acquired hearing loss include central nervous system infections and head trauma.

Severity of impairment is expressed in terms of decibel (dB) loss or hearing threshold level. To about 25 dB, the hearing loss is probably insignificant. A mild hearing loss (25–40 dB) means the individual has difficulty hearing whispers and faint speech; a moderate loss (41–55 dB) causes difficulties with normal speech. A moderately severe loss (56–70 dB) is serious enough for a child to have difficulties acquiring language. A severe hearing loss (71–90 dB) creates difficulties in the understanding even of strongly amplified speech, and a profound loss (greater than 90 dB) means that even maximally amplified speech is not understood (Dubose, 1979, p. 366). Although 350,000 of 5% of school-age children have hearing thresholds outside the normal range in at least one ear, fewer than 55,000 of these require special education because of their hearing impairments (Hobbs, 1975).

This smaller group—those who may well benefit most from early intervention—will be the focus of this chapter. These children are likely to be severely or profoundly hearing-impaired and to have become deaf before the age of 3 years.

PREVALENCE AND ETIOLOGY OF HEARING IMPAIRMENT

Each year the Center for Assessment and Demographic Studies at Gallaudet College conducts a survey of all educational programs serving hearing-impaired children and youth in the United States. For the 1983–1984 school year, data were collected on 53,184 children from every state and from Puerto Rico, Guam, and the Virgin Islands. As in most handicapping conditions, boys were overrepresented, accounting for almost 54% of the children. Only 4% of the children in the 1983–1984 survey were younger than 3 years old; 10% were older than 3 but younger than 6 years of age. The underrepresentation of children at the youngest ages reflects both a paucity of educational programs for children below the age of 3 and the difficulties of achieving early diagnosis. According to Simmons (1978), the average age for detection of deafness approaches 8 months only in a few medical centers; the national average is still between $2\frac{1}{2}$ and 3 years of age. Two thirds of the students were classified as white, 18% black, 11% Hispanic, and 4% "other." Three fourths of the children were deaf from birth and 93% were deaf before the age of 3; 44% were classified as profoundly impaired, and an additional 21% as severely impaired (see Figure 1).

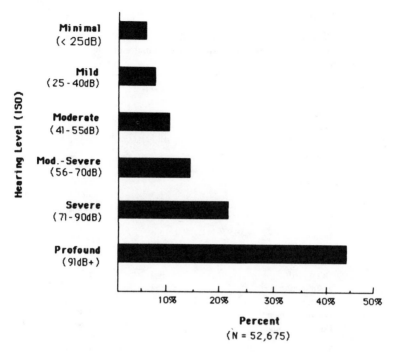

Fig. 1. Percent distribution of students enrolled in special educational programs for the hearing-impaired according to degree of hearing loss: United States, 1983–1984. From Center for Assessment and Demographic Studies, Gallaudet University, Washington, DC, courtesy of Dr. Michael Karchmer, Director, and Arthur Schildroth, Research Associate. ISO = International Standards Organization.

Table 1 shows the relative importance of various causes of deafness for this population. Maternal rubella with resulting congenital rubella syndrome accounted for almost 15% of the impairments, but this figure has decreased significantly from previous years when victims of the 1963–1965 rubella epidemic were still enrolled in school programs. In fact, cytomegalovirus infection is currently the intrauterine infection with greatest prevalence in terms of potential hearing impairment (Hanshaw, 1982). Also important as a reported cause is heredity, with 12% of the children known or presumed to be deaf for this reason. It is believed that this figure greatly understates the proportion of children with a genetic cause, because many (perhaps over half) of those with an ''unknown'' etiology or ''unavailable data'' are presumed to be genetic in origin. Prematurity (with its associated complications) is an ever-increasing cause of hearing loss in the present era of improved low birthweight survival with neonatal intensive care.

TABLE 1

Cause of deafness for children enrolled in special
educational programs for the hearing impaired in the
United States, 1983–1984[a]

Cause	Percent (%)	N
Maternal rubella	14.7	7,555
Trauma at birth	2.4	1,233
Complications of pregnancy	3.3	1,704
Heredity	12.1	6,257
Prematurity	4.3	2,203
Rh incompatibility	1.3	668
Meningitis	7.8	4,032
High fever	3.2	1,644
Mumps	.2	98
Infections	2.7	1,382
Measles	.7	354
Otitis media	3.4	1,757
Trauma after birth	.8	398
Other	8.0	4,106
Not determined	20.5	10,579
Data not available	19.2	9,873
Total		51,503[b]

[a]*Note:* from Center for Assessment and Demographic Studies, Gallaudet College, Washington, DC.

[b]Multiple causes reported for 6.6% of children.

EARLY IDENTIFICATION OF CHILDHOOD DEAFNESS

Studies conducted between 1970 and 1975 resulted in the identification of seven factors that place about 7% of newborn babies at risk for hearing impairment (Davis, 1978b): "(1) Familial deafness (congenital sensorineural hearing loss in first cousin or closer); (2) Bilirubin level: 20 mg/100 ml of serum or over; (3) Rubella (or other nonbacterial intrauterine infection such as cytomegalovirus) during pregnancy; (4) Congenital malformations of ear, nose, or throat (any first-arch syndrome); (5) Birth weight 1500 grams or less; (6) apnea and cyanosis (apgar score 1–4); and (7) Severe infection (neonatal)'' (p. 259). There is widespread agreement among specialists that children who are at risk from one or more of these seven factors should be tested for hearing loss soon after birth. Methods for this assessment are, however, highly controversial. Davis (1978b) stated that an arousal test has the most support, and that "such arousal is regularly elicited in normal infants by a narrow-band noise (3000 Hz) or white noise presented at 90 or 100 db SPL (Sound Pressure Level) for a duration of 2 seconds'' (p. 260). Gerber's (1977) text includes seven chapters related to methods of audiometric testing of infants: behavioral, impedance, respiratory, cardiovascular, electroencephalic, evoked cochlear potentials, and evoked brainstem potentials. Some of these methods have yet to be used extensively. Simmons (1978, pp. 22–23) has reported his experience with newborn screening in the Stanford University nurseries. Of 10,981 babies screened in a 7-year period, 28 were confirmed to have moderate to severe hearing losses; only 1 baby with a significant loss at birth was not identified through use of an automated (computerized) "crib-o-gram," which records movements of babies in their cribs in response to an hourly test stimulus. The ratio of babies with hearing impairments was 1 in 800 in the well-baby group, but the ratio was 1 in 61 for the intensive care nursery. Simmons (1978) stated that it is possible to estimate the presence or absence of even a mild hearing loss with at least 95% accuracy in 90% of the babies who have reached 7 months of age. The crib-o-gram procedure is not, however, widely utilized at the present time.

MEDICAL, SURGICAL, AND PROSTHETIC INTERVENTIONS

Once hearing loss has been confirmed, the question of treatment and intervention arises immediately (Boothroyd, (1982). Medical interventions, such as prescription drugs to control ear infections, are usually less important for children with sensorineural hearing losses, although the addition of a conductive loss stemming from middle-ear effusion can decrease the hearing threshold even further and interfere with use of hearing aids. Surgical interventions can include the correction of congenital abnormalities of the outer and middle ear and the insertion of tympanostomy tubes for the treatment of chronic middle-ear effusion. There have been some experiments with the surgical implantation of electrodes in the auditory nerve, but most specialists do not recommend this procedure for young hearing-impaired children (Boothroyd, 1982). There is increasing interest in experiments with cochlear implants (House & Urban, 1973); approximately 1,000 procedures have been completed with adults in several countries around the world (Schein, 1984). Because of potential problems with the surgical procedure and with the device itself, many medical and audiological experts are reluctant to expose children to the risks, especially when results with adults are less than completely satisfactory. Some believe that, even with improvements, only postlingually deafened people may benefit from implants (Freeman, Carbin, & Boese, 1981, p. 73).

Hearing aids are fitted for children at increasingly younger ages; today many preschool and infant programs routinely provide young students with individual hearing aids (Moores, 1982). Technical advances have enabled smaller devices to be more powerful (M. C. Pollack, 1975; Rubin, 1976) and many educators place great emphasis on the importance of supplying amplification very early in the belief that habituation leads to better utilization of residual hearing. In fact, children have been fitted with hearing aids at as early as 21 days of age (Griffiths, 1975). One program reported that children who received hearing aids before the age of 2 improved their level of awareness for speech using amplification by more than 10 dB in a 28-month training period (Horton, 1974, p. 482). However, there is considerable variability in speech reception capabilities among children, even among those with very similar audiograms (Stark, 1979, p. 231). As in so many areas of intervention with hearing-impaired children, there is broad disagreement about types of hearing aids that are most beneficial, depending on the type and severity of the hearing loss. One of the major problems in fitting an infant with a hearing aid is that neither the type nor severity of the loss may have been clearly determined. The inability of a very young child to express discomfort with specificity heightens the danger of overamplification as well.

There are numerous types of hearing aids, including portable, desk. and group amplification systems. Young children use personal hearing aids that can be worn. These are ordinarily air-conduction (rather than bone-conduction) systems, of which there are four types: body, behind-the-ear, eyeglass, and in-the-ear. The body-type aid is considered optimal for young children by some audiologists. It is the largest of the four and is worn in a pocket or placed in a harness, with a cord leading from the aid to a receiver attached to an individually fitted ear mold. Another likely choice for the young child is a behind-the-ear aid, which fits behind the auricle against the mastoid and contains a hard plastic ear loop that hooks over the ear. Attached to the ear hook is a tube connecting the mold to the hearing aid (Bess & McConnell, 1981, p. 157). These smaller aids have become more widely used with recent developments that enable greater power. The particular aid prescribed will depend on the type and severity of the hearing loss, although it is generally believed that children whose hearing threshold is greater than 40 dB (moderate or greater hearing loss) can benefit from a hearing aid. Considerations for an individual choice of aid include the amount of amplification it provides (*gain*), the relationship between the amount of gain and the *frequency response,* the maximum power output (*saturation sound pressure level*), and the fidelity of the signal provided (*harmonic distortion*) (Bess & McConnell, 1981, p. 155). Regardless of the type of hearing aid prescribed for a child, consistent monitoring is necessary. For example, rapid growth requires that ear molds be replaced every 2 to 3 months. Cooperation among several kinds of specialists is necessary for optimal intervention.

THE HISTORY AND NATURE OF EDUCATIONAL
INTERVENTIONS

The specialist who is likely to have most frequent contacts with the young hearing-impaired child is the teacher trained in deaf education. Most states require that special education programs be provided for hearing-impaired children by the age of 3; many provide programs from birth onwards. These programs emphasize in varying degrees efforts to teach hearing-impaired children to speak and to lipread, to acquire language, to facilitate social and interactional skills, to promote emotional and cognitive development, to improve parent–child communication, and to reduce family stress around the diagnosis of a hearing impairment.

The nature of educational programming is influenced by the fact that congenital sensorineural deafness is a low-incidence handicap. Thus, affected children are scattered over a wide geographic area, which makes the provision of services more difficult. This was one reason for the establishment (in Los Angeles) of the John Tracy Clinic correspondence course for parents of young deaf children, which has served many thousands of families since 1943. Lessons were mailed to families, and individual responses to questions from parents were written as parents and children progressed through the course. This has evolved into home-based programs that emphasize visits to parents in their own homes by teachers, although these visits are often combined with periodic group meetings of parents at the school or clinic site. It is important to note that these earlier home-based as well as center-based programs have traditionally relied upon oral methods of instruction (see subsequent discussion).

A number of early intervention programs gained new or additional impetus from funding by the Federal Bureau for the Education of the Handicapped through the Handicapped Children's Early Education Program in the early 1970s. Model programs supported by this agency included some of the traditional ones, and others such as the Ski-Hi program in Utah (Clark & Watkins, 1978) developed specifically for families scattered in less-populated areas, and one at the University of California in San Francisco where the emphasis was on parent counseling and the early introduction of "total communication" (Schlesinger & Meadow, 1972; 1976).

In describing the nature of exemplary early intervention programs for young deaf children, an important dimension is the kind of communication used by teachers and encouraged in parents. As noted, some programs utilize only oral communication: speech for adults to children, speech plus speechreading (lipreading) for children. Others use a method called total communication: simultaneous use of spoken and signed English. A few programs use a system of "cued speech" consisting of hand shapes of phonetic representations of English

TABLE 2

Outline of educational program types by preferred communication mode

Program type	Distinctive features	Examples (references)
Aural-only (also called acoustic method, unisensory method, auditory method, acoupedics)	Emphasis on training of residual hearing; no visual stimuli, including speechreading, allowed to compete	Beebe, Pearson, & Koch, 1984; D. Pollack, 1984
Aural-plus-oral (also called oral-only)	Hearing aids emphasized, child allowed to observe speaker's face if auditory message not received	Cole & Paterson, 1984; McConnell, 1974
Aural-plus-oral-plus-visual	Hearing aids plus speech and speechreading plus some system of expressing language manually	
Cued speech	Uses a limited number of hand shapes to express phonetic sounds simultaneously with spoken words	Cornett, 1967; Nicholls, 1979
Rochester Method	Fingerspelling (using the hand to form individual letters comprising the spoken words of the message)	Quigley, 1969; Scouten, 1967
Simultaneous or combined method	Use of signs adapted from American Sign Language (ASL) (Pidgin Sign English or Manual English) together with spoken language	Brasel & Quigley, 1977; Stuckless & Birch, 1966
Total communication	1. Use of one of several artificial sign language systems designed to reproduce spoken English precisely	Atchley, 1984; Bornstein, 1974; Somers, 1984
	2. Uses ASL without speech in informal, social situations; uses oral-only or signed English plus oral in educational settings	Freeman, Carbin, & Boese, 1981; Quigley & Paul, 1984

combined with spoken English. Regardless of communication mode, *all* early intervention programs fit children with hearing aids. The training of residual hearing is an important aspect of any early education approach. Some programs, referred to as "aural-only," rely only on the training of residual hearing.

A survey conducted in 1978 showed that 38% of all educational programs for deaf children utilized the combined oral/aural approach, with the remaining 62% using the total communication approach (Jordan, Gustason, & Rosen, 1979). A 1982 survey of 107 parent–infant programs found that 56% of the center-based programs and 44% of the home-based programs used the total communication approach; 34% of the center-based and 39% of the home-based programs utilized the oral/aural approach; 6% and 13%, respectively, used the aural-only approach; and 2% of each type of program used a fingerspelling/oral and a cued-speech approach (H. B. Craig, 1983, p. 91). (Fingerspelling refers to the use of hand shapes to form each letter in order to spell the complete spoken message. This is also called the Rochester Method.) Although programs are fairly evenly divided today in their use of oral-only and total communication approaches, before about 1970 sign language of any kind was strictly excluded from all educational programs serving young children. Today, communication mode continues to be a subject of bitter controversy among many parents and educators. A summary of the various combinations of communicative interventions is found in Table 2.

THE DEVELOPMENTAL COURSE IN DEAF CHILDREN

Some understanding of the expected course of development in children with hearing impairments is important background for the assessment of early intervention strategies. As in many childhood disabilities, the precise nature of the child's differential response to the environment may be difficult to detect. Because most parents of deaf children have no previous experience with congenital deafness (approximately 90% are hearing parents and fewer than 10% are deaf), they may never consider that their child has a hearing loss. In several studies, parents of hearing-impaired children have reported difficulties with the diagnostic process. In Florida, for example, 24% of surveyed parents of preschool deaf children claimed to have suspected their child's hearing loss before the child was 6 months old, but only 12% of the children's impairments were confirmed by that time. In 45% of these cases, the pediatrician was the first contact person. Although 26% of the initial hearing tests were reported to have been administed by pediatricians, they identified only 11% of the cases (Haas & Crowley, 1982). A Canadian study reported that 80% of the families interviewed felt that family physicians had a tendency to disagree with or to dismiss parents' suspicions about their infants' deafness (Williams & Darbyshire, 1982, p. 27). A survey of parents of children in five Ontario schools for the deaf revealed that the hearing loss was first suspected by parents in 77% of the cases (Shah, Chandler, & Dale, 1978). These authors concluded that physicians too rarely used parental suspicions as indicators for referral and testing.

The difficulties and frustrations of securing a firm diagnosis add to the trauma of learning about a child's handicap (Meadow, 1968a). Feelings about the child's hearing loss and worries about future development are certain to influence the developmental course. Accordingly, in describing this developmental course for deaf children it is helpful to compare differences that appear in deaf children with hearing parents with those of deaf children with deaf parents. The family environments of the two groups are quite different. Whereas the diagnosis of deafness is a shock for hearing parents, this is usually not the case for deaf parents. Although communication is an immediate problem for hearing parents, deaf parents most often communicate with each other in sign language (either Manual English or American Sign Language) and thus are quite prepared to communicate with their hearing-impaired child in the visual mode. Because early intervention programs that utilize total communication are, to some extent, attempting to replicate the family environment established by deaf parents some information on the developmental course for children using total communication will also be presented. Detailed comparisons, however, of early intervention programs using different communication modes will be presented in a later section of this chapter.

Language Acquisition and Development

The acquisition of language through oral-only means is an extremely slow and difficult process for a child who is severely or profoundly deaf from birth. One excellent oral program reports that the child who performed best in a 12-month training period, in terms of spoken words produced, had 10 words by the age of 27 months; another produced 3 words by the age of 30 months after 3 months of training. All seven children in this program had produced at least 1 word after 12 months of training, at which time they ranged in age from 23 to 44 months (Lach, Ling, Ling, & Ship, 1970). Another oral-only program reported testing 27 children between the ages of 2 and $3\frac{1}{2}$ years of age. Initially their receptive language age scores were at the 5-month-old level; at the end of the $1\frac{1}{2}$-year time period these scores were at the 11-month-old level (Geers, 1979). A third oral-only program reported a mean expressive language age of 14.6 months and a mean verbal comprehension age of 18.6 months after a 1-year training period. At that time 24 children had a mean age of 52.4 months (Chambers et al., 1981).

In contrast, several studies of the sign language acquisition of deaf children with deaf parents have concluded that the linguistic development of these children is much like that of spoken language development of hearing children with hearing parents. In some instances, sign approximations have been observed at ages earlier than first words have been reported. One investigator followed a deaf child of deaf parents between the ages of 10 and 21 months. This child produced 20 signs at age 10 months, two-sign utterances at 10 months, and three-sign utterances at 18 months (McIntire, 1977). Another deaf child of deaf parents produced sign approximations at 10 months and two signs at 12 months. She had

9 two-sign combinations at 17 months of age and 117 signs by the age of 19 months (Schlesinger & Meadow, 1972).

Maestas y Moores (1980) reported modifications some deaf parents make in linguistic interactions with their infants that may accelerate acquisition of language. For example, these parents were observed to use touch in a variety of ways to reinforce interaction, to sensitize their infants to basic aspects of space and time in signing and fingerspelling, and to help the infants to attend visually. Parents often signed on the body of the infant (also reported in Schlesinger & Meadow, 1972) and molded or physically guided the infant's hands. Many different styles and ways of combining modes and language forms were observed, including code switching in Spanish–English–sign–voice by one pair of parents. Erting's (1985) research with deaf children with deaf parents and with hearing parents illustrates vividly the important influence played by linguistic attitudes in the language experiences of deaf preschoolers.

Finally, some studies can be cited of deaf children of hearing parents exposed both to oral (spoken) and manual (signed English) communication through total communication educational programs. Language acquisition, development of inflections and of fingerspelling are impressive. One child had a vocabulary of 348 signs at the age of 3 years; at 40 months she had produced 604 signs. At 35 months, 10% of her utterances were produced in speech only, 22% in signs only, and 68% were produced simultaneously in speech and sign (Schlesinger & Meadow, 1972). Another child was reported to sign 65 words and speak 10 words at the age of 18 months; at 22 months, he signed 136 words and spoke 10 words (Stoloff & Dennis, 1978). At the age of 13 months, another child (who received intervention before she was 8 months old) produced 226 signs by the time she was 21 months old (Schlesinger, 1983). A teacher's record of another child's signed utterances between the ages of 4 and 5 years included "The crocodile will eat the fish," "The people are come movie here?," "You will hurry," "I will drive later when I grow like Debbie." This child did not receive a hearing aid until she was 28 months old; her parents began signing to her at age 30 months, and she started in a preschool program at the age of 34 months (Champie, 1981).

These accounts of individual children illustrate some of the possible optimal linguistic achievements of deaf children exposed early to bimodal communication. Based on her research with three-year-old deaf preschoolers with hearing parents, Day (1986) suggests that while the acquisition and use of language by signing deaf children follows expected patterns, there are nevertheless subtle differences. She saw a delay in questioning and responding in the children and believes that hearing parents may use reduced amounts of explanatory or heuristic language with their deaf children. Schlesinger (1985) proposes that parental feelings of powerlessness in communicating with their deaf children contribute to differences in language style; MacKay-Soroka (1985) reports that the quality of the signed messages of bimodal (hearing) mothers to their deaf children were less adequate than were the spoken messages of mothers of orally-trained deaf children.

Interactions of Young Deaf Children with Their Mothers

Most educational programs for young deaf children emphasize the importance of parents', especially mothers', participation. Mothers are expected to spend a great deal of time with their children to become knowledgeable about the use of hearing aids and speech training and, in total communication programs, to become fluent in sign language. These expectations may have some unintended consequences for interactions between deaf children and their mothers. Seven interactional studies of deaf children and mothers were published between 1970 and 1983 (Goss, 1970; Greenberg, 1980; Henggeler & Cooper, 1983; Hyde, Power, & Elias, 1980; Meadow, Greenberg, Erting, & Carmichael, 1981; Schlesinger & Meadow, 1972; Wedell-Monnig & Lumley, 1980). Investigators utilized a variety of procedures for recording and analyzing data, and they compared deaf child–hearing mother dyads to a variety of comparison groups. Nevertheless, a cohesive and noncontradictory set of findings emerged: Hearing mothers of deaf children were clearly found to be more dominating of and intrusive with their children. They tended to spend more time teaching their children and to be rated as tense and antagonistic. The deaf children, on the other hand, were described as less compliant, less attentive, and less responsive than were the hearing children with whom they were compared. Perhaps the conflict between teachers' imperatives to communicate more and the deaf child's inability to communicate orally created pressure on mothers to try harder and harder to elicit responses. Thus, deaf children may have been bombarded increasingly with messages they did not understand, have attended less frequently, and have become more recalcitrant. The very behaviors that were sought appeared less frequently than they might have otherwise (Meadow, 1980).

Moreover, both hearing mothers and their deaf children seemed to enjoy their interactions together to a lesser extent (Schlesinger & Meadow, 1972). Although hearing mothers of deaf children were the *most* interactive, their deaf children were *least* interactive compared to dyads of hearing mothers and hearing children (Wedell-Monnig & Lumley, 1980). Interactions were seen as less reciprocal, with some indications that this characteristic becomes exaggerated as the children become older (Hyde et al., 1980). In contrast, communication between members of the hearing mother–hearing child dyads occurred in longer episodes and was more elaborated; more turns were taken around a specific topic before interaction was interrupted or a new topic introduced.

Greenberg's (1980) study is of particular interest in view of the preceding discussion of language acquisition in deaf children exposed to oral and to total (simultaneous) communication. In his study, no differences were found between the simultaneous and orally communicating children for 11 categories of communicative behavior. However, the simultaneous children had a significantly higher percentage of spontaneous communications (37%) than did oral children (20%). Simultaneous children also showed more sociable and cooperative behavior and more compliance with mothers' requests. They touched their mothers more frequently and averted their gaze less frequently than did the dyads communicating orally only. The simultaneous dyads showed longer and more complex interactions and spent more total time interacting with each other. Later, Meadow et al. (1981) compared the 28 children studied by Greenberg with a group of 7 deaf children with deaf parents and a group of 14 hearing children with hearing parents. In that comparison, the deaf child–deaf mother and hearing child–hearing mother dyads were shown to have the most frequent and most complex interactions. The oral-only deaf child–hearing mother dyads had the least frequent and least complex interactions, and the simultaneous deaf child–hearing mother dyads were intermediate in the ranking.

Academic Achievement

The educational achievement level of deaf students has been called a "shameful indictment of our educational programs" (Moores, 1982, p. 297). An analysis of Stanford Achievement Test (SAT) scores of about 17,000 hearing-impaired children in 288 programs showed that the highest scores (achieved by 19-year-olds) were grade 4.4 for paragraph meaning and grade 6.7 for arithmetic computation (DiFrancesca, 1972; Gentile & DiFrancesca, 1969). The problems encountered by most deaf children in language development help to explain these academic deficiencies.

A series of studies has been conducted comparing deaf students with deaf parents (using sign language) to deaf students with hearing parents (who used oral-only communication). One dimension for comparison in these studies of school-age children was academic achievement, usually based on SAT scores. Meadow (1968b) compared 32 matched pairs of deaf-parent and hearing-parent students and found the deaf-parent group with significantly higher scores. They exceeded their hearing-parent partners by an average of 2.1 years for arithmetic scores and 1.25 years for reading scores. Stuckless and Birch (1966) compared 38 pairs of students on Metropolitan Achievement Test scores. Those with deaf parents were in the 76th percentile for reading compared to those with hearing parents who scored in the 57th percentile for reading. Balow and Brill (1975) compared 421 deaf students with hearing parents to 34 deaf students with (two) deaf parents. The deaf student–hearing parent group had average SAT scores (total battery) at grade level 7, but the deaf student–deaf parent group had average scores at grade level 8.4. Vernon and Koh (1970) were able to utilize a somewhat more sophisticated design for their group comparisons. They matched genetically deafened children with hearing, oral-only parents with 32 deaf children with deaf signing parents. This helped to insure that none of the hearing-parent children had central nervous system involvements related to the cause of deafness. All comparisons of SAT scores favored the deaf-parent (manual) group over the hearing-parent (oral) group. Differences in reading-related scores ranged from 1.4 to 2.4 grades.

Finally, Brasel and Quigley (1977) reported a study comparing deaf children with deaf parents to deaf children with hearing parents, which introduced two additional variables believed to contribute to more and less successful educational outcomes for each of the two groups. As in the other studies described in this section, all the hearing parents used oral-only methods of communication and all the deaf parents used sign language for communication. However, the hearing-parent group was subdivided into those children who received intensive oral training before the age of 2 years and those who received less intensive oral training, which began after they were 2 years old (but before age 4). The deaf-parent group was also subdivided into those whose parents used Manual English routinely in the home and those whose parents used American Sign Language routinely. There were 18 children in each of the four groups. At the time of testing, their mean age was 14.8 years, with hearing loss greater than 90 dB, performance IQ 90 or higher, and no significant handicaps in addition to deafness. On the four language-related subtests of the SAT, the group whose deaf parents used Manual English performed at a level significantly above that of the three other groups; the group with hearing parents and later intervention consistently ranked lowest. The authors concluded that the grammatically correct Manual English input provides deaf children with a heightened opportunity to generate a language base that can be applied to the printed page and that also enabled them to generate grammatically correct written English.

It seems clear from this review of the developmental course for deaf children that deaf children with hearing parents in particular have numerous problems that affect virtually all aspects of development. However, the developmental course of deaf children of deaf parents and the involvement in total communication programs for deaf children of hearing parents suggests the potential for achieving a more positive outcome. Accordingly, the oral-only tradition (which always includes hearing aids) can be considered a contemporary baseline from which it is possible to evaluate new efforts at early intervention. This is the approach that will be taken in the following section. Nevertheless, the field has been and continues to be fraught with bitter controversies. These issues have to do primarily with communication mode but also surround questions of the type and timing of the application of hearing aids, the variety of sign language to be selected, and whether segregated or integrated (mainstreamed) education should be selected. Some, but not all, of these questions have been addressed in program evaluations for young hearing-impaired children and are discussed in the following sections.

EVALUATION OF EARLY INTERVENTION WITH HEARING-IMPAIRED CHILDREN

Despite a strong interest in the area, little systematic research has been published that enables us to evaluate, in any definitive way, the outcomes of early interventions with young deaf or hard-of-hearing children. Boothroyd (1982) suggested a number of reasons for this lack: the absence of norms for evaluating performance or achievement levels of this group, the difficulty of controlling relevant variables, and the tendency of educators to describe only their star pupils while giving the impression that they are "typical." Moores (1982) pointed to the general problems of evaluating early intervention, but emphasized that the low incidence of deafness multiplies these problems and that difficulties of child–evaluator communication compound the research design complexities. He believes that the most important reason for the lack of research, however, is "the highly emotional nature of the question of methodology with . . . young deaf children" (p. 240).

Greenberg and Calderon (1984) pointed to the many difficulties of using measures developed for normal children with young deaf children, particularly around items related to sound and speech. Questions of developmental and linguistic achievements of hearing-impaired children are very complex. Moreover, there are issues related to the timing of the intervention, which, in turn, is related to the timing of the diagnosis of hearing loss—a difficult and complex problem in itself. The severity of a child's hearing loss and the nature of that loss influences the type of hearing aid that will be prescribed, the child's ability to benefit from the aid in varying environments, and the effectiveness of language-related activities. Family variables will also play a role in the success of intervention. For example, in homes where parents are less available to participate in the intervention process, children receive less intensive training. Similarly, availability of programs in a particular area is certainly a factor, and the quality of programs and teachers varies greatly. Children who have handicapping conditions in addition to their hearing loss present different problems (as many as 30% of hearing-impaired children do have additional conditions that have a negative impact on their ability to benefit from intervention). All of these variables interact separately and in combination with decisions for educational placement and methodology. The result is that it becomes exceedingly difficult to design evaluation research that takes account of the many conditions influencing children's developmental and educational progress, especially language development, in relation to a specific program of intervention.

TABLE 3

Studies of deaf children: early versus late intervention[a]

Reference	Nature of intervention	Intervention parameters	Setting	Role of parents
Balow & Brill (1975)	Oral-only preschool training	Parent-child involvement in John Tracy Clinic: 1. Summer session: $N = 36$ 2. Regular preschool classes, 1 or 2 years: $N = 15$ 3. Regular preschool classes, 3 or 4 years: $N = 21$ 4. Correspondence course: $N = 240$	Clinic or correspondence with clinic	Intensive for on-site participants; variable for correspondence course participants
Brasel & Quigley (1977)	Traditional oral-only preschool programs (many different programs)	Children with hearing parents: 1. Intensive oral training, initiated before age 2 years 2. Less intensive oral training, begun after age 2, before age 4 Children with deaf parents: 1. Home language = Manual English 2. Home language = ASL	Various programs from across the United States	Hearing parents: Group 1: intensive involvement Group 2: minimal involvement Deaf parents: Educational involvement not described
W. N. Craig (1964)	Oral-only preschool training	Children began program between ages of 2 years 10 months and 4 years 6 months; both day and residential pupils served; daily schedule involved individual tutoring and group activities	Preschool units in 2 state residential schools for deaf children	Not reported; minimal at best

Nevertheless, 13 reports of the results of interventions with hearing-impaired children are presented in Table 3. (This includes all that could be located.) Despite the many difficulties in conducting scientifically valid early intervention studies for this population of children, the existing studies do address certain key issues noted earlier and allow some important recommendations to be made regarding the effectiveness of early intervention. These studies fall into two groupings, each addressing a specific issue. The first set consists of eight reports comparing outcome measures for hearing-impaired children based on ''earlier'' versus

Child characteristics	Experimental design	Outcome measures	Results
Graduates of 16 classes of the California School for the Deaf, Riverside (1956–1971)	Retrospective analysis of student records; statistical control	SAT (Geutile & DiFrancesca, 1969) administered at high-school graduation	Tracy Clinic outcomes with IQ controlled for SAT total battery were as follows: regular classes for 3 or 4 years (8.2) > regular classes for 1 or 2 years (6.8) (summer session only not significant, 7.2)
			Children with *some* clinic experience (7.2) scored higher than those with no clinic experience (6.8)
4 groups, 18 each; mean CA 14.8, hearing loss 90+ dB; performance IQ 90+; no significant additional handicaps; deafness confirmed before 1.3 years; parents' socioeconomic status rating higher for group with early intensive oral training	Retrospective; histories of preschool education extracted from records, families contacted through present schools for posttesting	Test of Syntactic Ability (Quigley & Power, 1971); SAT (Geutile & DiFrancesca, 1969)	Children whose *deaf* parents used *Manual English* scored highest on all 10 measures; children with *hearing* parents and late, *less* intensive oral training scored lowest on all 10 measures; children whose *deaf* parents used ASL scored higher than children with hearing parents and early intensive training
Experimental group: 151 children who entered preschool between ages 2 years 10 months and 4 years 6 months Control group: 92 children who entered 2 schools between ages 5 and 7 Testing completed when students were between ages 6 years 8 months and 16 years 6 months; hearing loss: 60+ dB; performance IQ Nebraska (Hiskey, 1941); Leiter (1940): +64	Retrospective comparisons of early versus late placement	Lipreading Test for Words and Sentences (author); Gates Reading Tests for word recognition and paragraph reading (primary and advanced forms) (Gates & McGinitie, 1965)	No significant differences in scores of students with preschool training in comparison to those without preschool

(continued)

"later" intervention. The second set consists of five reports that provide cross-program comparisons of intervention methods.

Early Versus Later Intervention with Hearing-Impaired Children

In Table 3, eight studies are summarized in which investigators attempted to assess the influence of early intervention on education and/or language development

TABLE 3 (*Continued*)

Reference	Nature of intervention	Intervention parameters	Setting	Role of parents
Greenstein, Greenstein, McConville, & Stellini (1975)	Parent–Infant Program at Lexington School for the Deaf: strong oral program; emphasis on parent support, mental health team available	Weekly 90-min sessions with teacher for auditory training program; weekly parent-group workshops; program involved children until 40 months of age	Center-based parent-child program	Strong emphasis on parent involvement; parent education in cognitive, language, affective development
Levitt (1986); Levitt, McGarr, & Geffner (1986)	Curriculum in state-supported special education programs; probably consisted of traditional oral-only programs	Early special education defined as prior to age 3.	Schools for the deaf (state-supported) in New York State	Variable
Horton (1975); Liff (1973); McConnell (1974)	Bill Wilkerson Hearing and Speech Center program for infants and children: parent-oriented program to develop child's ability to understand and develop spoken language in oral-only tradition	Visits to demonstration home, work with teacher, weekly sessions with audiologist to check hearing aids	Practice at home to encourage use of language in everyday, familiar settings	Central to program

Child characteristics	Experimental design	Outcome measures	Results
Early enrollment group ($N = 9$) had mean CA of 12.67 months (all admitted before 16 months); late enrollment ($N = 10$) group had mean CA of 20.9 months (all admitted after 16 months); hearing loss +70 dB; means for groups were comparable: 96–105 dB unaided, 42–54 dB aided; groups 1 and 2 had hearing parents; A third group consisted of 11 hearing-impaired children with deaf parents enrolled at 7 months ($N = 11$)	Comparisons of repeated measures, nonrandom assignment; groups determined by age at admission to program	REEL language scale (Bzoch & League, 1971); POLA language assessment; assessment of mother–child videotape; teacher ratings of communication (authors' measures included in report)	Early admission children of both hearing and deaf parents scored significantly higher than late admission children on all language measures; differences significant for: REEL 24 months receptive and total; 36 months expressive POLA: 40 months expressive, elicited, imitative, and total Mother–infant communication: For early admission groups, *more:* child looking at mother, simultaneous looking, child vocalizing to mother, and movement to mother; teacher ratings: early admission mothers received significantly higher ratings
All children born in 1962 attending state-supported schools for the deaf in New York State in 1972	Longitudinal (testing done in 4 successive years, ages 10–14), retrospective data gathered on early education and hearing aid history	Test of Syntactic Ability (Quigley, Wilbur, Power, Montanelli, & Steinkamp, 1976); written language sample; Phoneme Reception Test (Smith, 1972, 1975); Children's Nonsense Syllable Test (authors); speech intelligibility: (adopted from NTID Rating Scale (Johnson, 1975).	Age when hearing aid fitted correlated with age special education began; age of special education (earlier the better) correlated with high reading scores and with superior speech and language skills (age 3 or younger)
Group 1 began hearing aid use before age 3, $N = 6$ (at median age of 27 months) Group 2 began hearing aid use after age 3, $N = 5$, (at median age of 48 months) Group 3, normal-hearing children judged by teachers to be "average achievers" Median hearing level: Group 1, 87 dB; Group 2, 84 dB	Posttesting only (nonrandom groups) at time children were in 2nd grade	Lee (1966) Developmental Sentence Types	Group 1 (early intervention) and Group 3 (normal hearing) not significantly different in any comparison of type or level of utterance; Group 1 produced 75% of utterances at sentence level compared to 32% of Group 2; Group 1 had 8% noun-type utterances compared to 19% for Group 2; verbal-type utterances occurred 79% of time in Group 1 compared to 49% for Group 2; in addition, Group 1 integrated in class with Group 3; Group 2 in self-contained class for hearing impaired because language judged inadequate for integration

(*continued*)

TABLE 3 (*Continued*)

Reference	Nature of intervention	Intervention parameters	Setting	Role of parents
Watkins (1984)	Home intervention designed to monitor hearing aid usage, provide language training, check mother's teaching/intervention techniques	Weekly visits by home trainer; parents given option of either oral-only or total communication approach to education	Experimental Group 1: home intervention before age 2½; Group 2: home intervention after age 2½; Group 3: center-based instruction (not Ski-Hi program); Group 4: no intervention before age 5	Primary intervention agents for intervention groups
White & White (1986)	Traditional oral-only preschool; primary focus the development of spoken languae	Weekly 90-min sessions with teacher for auditory training program; parent workshops	Infant Center, Lexington School for the Deaf	Strong parent emphasis

^aAbbreviations: ASL, American Sign Language; dB, decibels; NTID, National Technical Institute for the Deaf; POLA, Preschool Oral Language Emergent Language (revised by White & White for this study).

of hearing-impaired children. W. N. Craig's (1964) early study reflects some of the historical development of education for deaf children. It drew on students from two residential schools, both of whom accepted residential students as young as 3 years of age at that time. Comparisons of students with early intervention (before age 5) with those who began their training after the age of 5 showed no significant differences in scores on a lipreading test or on reading tests. Another (unpublished) study from the same period, with similar schools, reported the same absence of differences in later performances (Phillips, 1963). Even though retrospective studies are extremely difficult to interpret, the two studies were used for a period of time in debates about the value of early intervention for hearing-impaired children. Today there would be wide agreement that residential placement is not appropriate for children so young. Services of itinerant teachers and more widespread preschool programs in local schools have made this option unnecessary.

The Brasel and Quigley (1977) study, included in Table 3, was also discussed

Child characteristics	Experimental design	Outcome measures	Results
N = 23 per group; 4 groups matched for hearing loss $\bar{X}$ > 84 dB); additional handicaps (3 subjects in each group with some additional handicap); age at testing 105.5–132.6 months; social position of Group 4 parents significantly lower than parents in Groups 1, 2, and 3	Posttesting only, no random assignment: testing completed when children were 7 years or older	Elicited Language Inventory (Carrow, 1974); Peabody Picture Vocabulary Test (Dunn, 1965); Developmental Sentences (Lee, 1966); Arizona Articulation Proficiency Scale (Fudala, 1974); Woodcock–Johnson (reading, math, writing, language) (Woodcock & Johnson, 1977); social-emotional adjustment (Meadow, 1983); Parent attitudes, Ski-Hi (Clark & Watkins, 1978); communication evaluation and hearing aid management, parent communication (authors)	Early versus late home intervention (Group 1 versus Group 2): few significant differences; late preschool versus no preschool (Group 3 versus Group 4): also few significant differences; comparisons between combined Groups 1 and 2 versus Groups 3 and/or 4: Groups 1 and 2 favored on 22 of 24 comparisons
N = 46, prelingually deaf infants, enrolled at 8–30 months of age; 80+ dB hearing loss Group 1: Deaf parents, entered before 18 months old, N = 5 Group 2: Deaf parents, entered after 18 months old, N = 4 Group 3: Hearing parents, entry before age 18 months, N = 9 Group 4: Hearing parents, entry after age 18 months, N = 28	Posttest only	WREEL (adaptation of REEL: Bzoch & League, 1971)	No differences on 7 of 10 measures for children with deaf versus hearing parents; children with hearing parents scored higher than those with deaf parents for babble and jargon; children with deaf parents higher for expression on parts of speech, combinations of words and sounds; early entry students scored higher than late entry students on 9 of 10 comparisons, no difference for 1 comparison

Assessment; REEL, Receptive and Expressive Emergent Language; SAT Stanford Achievement Test; WREEL, Revised Receptive Expressive

in a previous section because of their comparisons of achievement of deaf children with deaf and with hearing parents. An additional factor in their comparison of deaf children with hearing parents was the age at which intervention began. They reported that those children who received intensive training that began at age 2 or earlier performed at higher achievement levels than did children who received less intensive training that began between the ages of 2 and 4 years.

The six remaining studies included in Table 3 represent differing approaches to intervention. Liff's (1973) study and the Greenstein, Greenstein, McConville, and Stellini (1975) study were designed to evaluate progress of children who entered center-based preschool programs at younger or older ages. These two programs are well known and strong in the oral-only tradition: the former is the Bill Wilkerson Hearing and Speech Center program in Nashville, Tennessee, and the latter is the Lexington School for the Deaf in New York City. Both programs emphasize early amplification and intensive work with audiologists attached to the program. The Nashville report evaluated children who began to use a hearing aid before 3 years of age compared with children whose hearing aid usage began after they were 3 years old. (This means that deafness was *diagnosed* and *intervention* began earlier for group one, because all intervention in the Nashville center automatically would include fitting a hearing aid.) By the time these two groups of children had reached the second grade, those with earlier intervention were integrated in a class of hearing children with whom their language scores were comparable. In contrast, children with later intervention were in a special self-contained class and demonstrated lower language levels.

The Greenstein et al. (1975) study was conducted with younger children who began their educational programs at a younger age: Mean age at first enrollment for two groups of children with hearing parents was 13 months and 21 months, respectively. Mean age of enrollment for another group with deaf parents was 7 months, reflecting the lesser difficulties deaf families have in achieving an early diagnosis for their hearing-impaired children. In two different language measures, the early admission group of children with hearing parents scored significantly above the later admission group of children with hearing parents. Differences between children with deaf parents and those with hearing parents in the early admission group were not significant.

Likewise, White and White (1986) combined the variables of parental hearing status and early (prior to 18 months) versus later intervention (between 18 and 30 months of age) in their evaluations of language development in a preschool age sample. The pattern of their results is similar to that of the Brasel and Quigley study in that they report that deaf children with deaf parents achieved more rapid expressive language development, compared to deaf children with hearing parents (although the latter group was observed to babble and use spoken or vocalized jargon more frequently). Children with hearing parents receiving earlier intervention out-performed those whose intervention began at a later age. However, in the very small groups of children with deaf parents (one group contained four subjects; the other, five) those who entered late scored higher than those who entered early.

The study reported by Balow and Brill (1975) reflects quite a different kind of intervention from those just discussed. These investigators conducted a retrospective analysis of school achievement for all graduates of the California School for the Deaf at Riverside, a state residential facility. Included in the school files were records of each student's preschool experience. Many graduates had had some level of early training through the John Tracy Clinic in Los Angeles. Group 1 had attended a 6-week summer preschool session with their parents, Group 2 had participated in preschool center-based programs at the clinic for either 1 or 2 years, Group 3 had attended these preschool classes for 3 or 4 years, and Group 4 had contact with the Clinic program through the Correspondence Course for Parents. The results indicated that Group 3, with 3 or 4 years of preschool experience, had highest scores on the SAT battery at the time of their high school graduation; students with *some* contact with the Clinic (Groups 1–4) had higher SAT scores than did other students who had no contact of any kind.

There are several problems with this study, although it is a useful effort to utilize existing data to answer an important question. Because all the students were attending residential school at the time of their graduation from high school, we can assume that they are a select group, not representative of all hearing-impaired students. Similarly, the equivalence of the groups is a concern, as it is in all studies that are either retrospective or employ nonrandom assignment. In this study we have no information on the socioeconomic status of parents, although we might believe that those whose parents had contacted the Tracy Clinic were more privileged than those whose parents did not.

The extensive study by Levitt, McGarr, and Geffner (1986) enabled them to avoid some of the pitfalls of the other retrospective studies summarized in this section. Over a 15-year period, these investigators identified all hearing-impaired children born in the year 1962 who were attending state-supported special education schools or programs in 1972. Testing of students was completed in four successive years when the students were ages 10 to 14. Information on many background variables was also collected. All these complex data were subjected to highly sophisticated statistical techniques based on a complex understanding of the importance of hearing level, IQ, socioeconomic status, and so forth. From this wide-ranging analysis, the authors concluded that their most important observation was the strong positive correlation between early intervention and later speech and language development. This correlation was particularly high in the oldest group of students, which the authors believe to be evidence that early gains are maintained throughout the child's life.

The final study evaluating early versus late interventions with hearing-impaired children is an evaluation of a very different program model from those discussed previously (Watkins, 1984). This is the Ski-Hi program, based in Utah and designed for children who live in areas where no center-based educational program is available. Ski-Hi trains teachers who go to the children's homes weekly to work with them and their parents (Clark & Watkins, 1978). The teachers usually do not have full-time jobs with a school district but are paid on the basis of time spent with students. Parents are given the option of selecting oral-only training or total communication training for their children. Those who opt for total communication learn sign language through watching videotapes on equipment provided by the program. This evaluation study compared four groups of children matched for hearing level. Group 1 received home-based intervention (Ski-Hi) before the age of $2\frac{1}{2}$, Group 2 received home-based intervention (Ski-Hi) after age $2\frac{1}{2}$, Group 3 received a different (center-based) intervention after age $2\frac{1}{2}$, and Group 4 received no training before entering kindergarten. A wide-ranging battery of tests was administered to the 92 children when they reached the age of 7 (see Table 3). Few differences emerged between Groups 1 and 2 or

TABLE 4

Studies documenting deaf children's progress: program comparisons

Reference	Nature of intervention	Intervention parameters	Setting	Role of parents
Greenberg (1983); Greenberg, Calderon, & Kusché (1984)	Intensive counseling and total communication (TC) (American Sign Language) program participants compared with participants in "minimal treatment" traditional programs, oral and/or total communication	Initial counseling and guidance (following diagnosis); weekly home visits by teacher for educational activities, auditory/speech training, sign training; weekly home visits by deaf adult for sign language instruction; group sign classes weekly; occasional parent group activities; psychiatric consultation available	Home-based program with some activities available in center	Intensive involvement with entire family
Moores (1985); Moores, Weiss, & Goodwin (1978)	7-program evaluation; programs varied from structured academic/cognitive to unstructured socialization emphasis; instructional communication systems included oral-only (2 programs); TC (2 programs); Rochester/finger-spelling (1 program); oral or TC option (1 program); plus transition from oral to TC (1 program)	Intervention began at age 2 years, provided until age 5; half-day sessions, 5 days per week	3 of 7 programs conducted in state residential schools for deaf children, 3 in public day school settings, 1 in split setting; all under auspices of public school systems	Not reported; can assume variable efforts and success with parent involvement

between Groups 3 and 4. However, when Groups 1 plus 2 were compared with Groups 3 plus 4, the Ski-Hi groups performed at a superior level in 22 of the 24 comparisons made.

Despite the difficulties and problems with some of the studies reported in this section, the balance of evidence, particularly strongly reflected in the Levitt study, points to the importance of very early intervention for improving later achievement levels of hearing-impaired children. Given conflicting reports, however, we must await future studies for more definitive answers.

Child characteristics	Experimental design	Outcome measures	Results
12 children in experimental (E) program; 16 in control (C): mean age: 43.8 months (E), 47.1 months (C); age at first intervention: 20.4 (E), 23.9 (C); hearing loss (unaided): 97.1 dB (E), 94.2 (C); hearing loss (aided): 72.5 dB (E), 70.8 dB (C)	2-group posttest design with experimental (E) and comparison (C) groups matched as closely as possible	Family Questionnaire on Resources and Stress (Holroyd, 1973); Developmental Profile (Alpern & Boll, 1972); videotaped assessments of parent-child communication/interaction (author); Leiter Performance IQ (Leiter, 1969)	For developmental level: Leiter IQ, E = 125.4, C = 117.3, no significant differences; on Alpern–Boll, E children scored significantly higher in social, communication, and academic areas and on abstract concept of time (both comprehension and expression) than C group; maternal and child communicative skills favored E groups; mothers in E group experienced less perceived stress
No significant developmental delays; no significant differences in demographic variables *except* for age at introduction of manual communication: 20.8 months (E), 33.2 months (C)			
N = 60; age range 2.6–4.6 at year 1; Age at onset of hearing loss: 2 or younger; no severe additional handicaps; hearing loss: 70+ dB (mean = 98.5 dB)	Longitudinal; data collected in each of 4 successive years; comparisons of children in each of 7 programs	Metropolitan Achievement Test— Primer Battery (Durost, Bixler, Wrightstone, Prescott, & Balow, 1971); Receptive, Expressive, and Word intelligibility scales (author)	Metropolitan Achievement Test Reading: Rank 1 = Rochester Rank 7 = Oral-only Arithmetic: Rank 1 = TC Rank 7 = Oral-only Combined scores: Rank 1 = Rochester Rank 7 = Oral-only Receptive Language Scale Rank 1 = individualized Rank 7 = oral/TC transition Expressive Language Scale Rank 1 = TC Rank 7 = Rochester Work Intelligibility Scale Rank 1 = Oral plus individualized (tie) Rank 2 = All others (tie)

(continued)

Effects of Intervention Procedures: Program Comparisons

In response to the growing pressure for visual supplements, several systems of manually coded English were developed, all based on signs from American Sign Language, but using English word order and adding prefixes and/or inflections for the representation of English grammar and syntax. Programs developed in the

TABLE 4 (*Continued*)

Reference	Nature of intervention	Intervention parameters	Setting	Role of parents
Musselman, Lindsay, & Wilson (1985)	Many different programs included; all options: auditory only, oral-only and total communication (TC), both home-based and center-based; total communication used primarily as a remedial option	Home-visiting teachers and hospital programs provided about 60 hr of instruction per year; senior kindergarten, half-day, 5 days per week (100 hr per year)	Participating programs serve 80% of preschoolers in Ontario; 20 programs school-based, 20 programs provide itinerant services to only a few children	Varied
Quigley (1969)	Study 1: experimental groups exposed to fingerspelling in classrooms; control groups experienced combined manual and oral communication in classroom	Data collected over a 5-year period	6 matched residential schools for deaf students	No data collected
	Study 2: experimental groups exposed to fingerspelling in controlled way in both classroom and dormitory, beginning at preschool level; control group in oral-only program	Intervention continued for 4 years	2 residential schools with similar programs	Little or no involvement

Child characteristics	Experimental design	Outcome measures	Results
N = 153; age at first testing, 3–5 years; Leiter IQ mean = 115 (Leiter, 1969); WISC-R mean = 109 (Wechsler, 1974); age at first intervention, 6–54 months, mean = 18 months; hearing loss: 70+ dB; 95% began training before the age of 3½	Longitudinal, time-lag design with 4 cohorts; each child tested 3 different times in 4-year period	Language Assessment Battery (LAB) (Reich, Keeton, & Lindsay, 1978); Assessment of Children's Language Comprehension Test (Foster, Giddan, & Stark, 1973); Phonological Level Speech Evaluation (Ling, 1976); Mother–Child Communication (authors); Gates–MacGinitie Test of Reading Ability (Primary, Form A) (1965); Metropolitan Achievement Tests for math (Durost et al., 1971); Social development (Alpern & Boll, 1972)	Age, unaided hearing loss and IQ consistently predicted the level of linguistic development Effects of communication mode: Speech measures: auditory > oral > TC LAB (receptive) TC > auditory and oral LAB (proposition comprehension) TC > auditory and oral Speech: Auditory > oral > TC Mother–child: TC > auditory and oral Social development TC > auditory and oral (round 1 only) Educational achievement: no significant difference Effects of early versus late entry: LAB: auditory and oral modes, late > early; TC, early > late (±18 months old)
Experimental schools, N = 112; control schools, N = 110; no significant differences for CA (13+ years old), IQ (mean = 106), time in school (8.4 years), hearing loss (89 dB), or age at onset (3.5 years)	Yearly testing for 5 years; experimental (E) = fingerspelling; control (C) = simultaneous group	Speechreading (W. N. Craig, 1964; Utley, 1946); SAT (Kelley et al., 1969); written language (stories), (author); Cloze procedures (Moores, 1967), speech (Hudgins, 1949)	Year 5 data Speechreading: Words: E = 70.7, C = 74.3[a] Sentences: E = 67.9, C = 69.3[a] Speech intelligibility: E = 25.5, C = 22.2[a] Stanford Achievement Test Par. meaning E = 5.1, C = 4.4[a] Combined reading E = 4.9, C = 4.3[a] Combined arithmetic E = 6.4, C = 5.6[a] Battery median E = 5.9, C = 5.0[a] Written language and Cloze procedures E > C 7 of 8 comparisons[b]
Experimental subjects, N = 16; control subjects, N = 16; no significant differences for CA (mean = 7.8), hearing loss (about 98 dB), IQ (Leiter, 1940), or WISC IQ (Wechsler, 1949); CA at onset: experimental group, 12.6 months, control group, 11.8 months	Controlled introduction of fingerspelling, yearly testing for 4 years, beginning with preschool; posttesting only	Speechreading (Utley, 1946); SAT (Kelley et al., 1966); Metropolitan Reading Tests (Wrightstone, Aronow & Moskowitz, 1963); Gates Vocabulary and Comprehension (Gates & MacGinitie, 1965); written language samples (author)	Speechreading: Words: E = 44.9, C = 39.8[a] Sentences: E = 37.7, C = 23.2[a] Reading: SAT paragraph meaning: E = 2.3, C = 2.1[a] SAT word meaning: E = 2.3, C = 2.0[a] Other reading tests: E > C, 5 of 5[b] Written Language measures: E > C 4 of 5[b] C > E 1 of 5[b]

1970s incorporating one of these systems into their oral and auditory methods were called total communication programs.

Five studies can be cited that have investigated outcomes of early intervention with varying language modes, utilizing more than one educational program for comparative purposes. These studies are summarized in Table 4. The two earliest, completed by Quigley (1969) focused on the effects of the use of fingerspelling (Rochester Method) with deaf children.[1] Quigley's first study evaluated about 220 students in six residential schools for the deaf: three schools where the Rochester Method was used routinely in the classroom, three where the "simultaneous" or "combined" method of manual English plus speech was used. (This method was the precursor of the total communication method, which uses a more precise English format.) In the fifth year of the comparison, test results showed no significant differences between the fingerspelling groups (referred to as the experimental group) and the simultaneous method groups (referred to as control) for lipreading or speech. However, significant differences favoring the fingerspelling group were found on SAT scores and written language evaluations.

Quigley's second study compared two groups of children entering two different residential schools for the deaf (mean age 7.8 years). One school routinely used the Rochester Method (experimental group), the other school routinely used an oral-only method (control group). At the end of a 5-year period of schooling, tests showed no significant differences between the two groups on a measure of speech reading for single words. The measure of speech reading for groups of words (sentences) significantly favored the group exposed to fingerspelling in conjunction with spoken language. The SAT scores for word meaning favored the experimental group, but the SAT scores for paragraph meaning did not differ significantly. Four of five other reading test scores favored the experimental group; the pattern of written language evaluations was less clear.

A third study summarized in Table 4 was conducted by Moores and his colleagues (Moores, 1985; Moores, Weiss, & Goodwin, 1978) at the University of Minnesota. This was an ambitious longitudinal project, designed to evaluate the progress and achievement of hearing-impaired children in a number of different preschool programs utilizing a variety of methods in a variety of settings. Data collection began in 1970, just when many changes were taking place in the field of deaf education. This is reflected in the history of methodologies used in the seven programs throughout the 4 years when data were being collected. Initially, four programs used an oral-only or aural-only approach; one used total communication, one used the Rochester Method, and one was in transition from oral-only to the Rochester Method. In the second year, one aural-only program

---

[1]Quigley's (1969) study number 1 utilized students beyond preschool age. Because of the paucity of evaluations of communication mode, it is included here.

dropped out of the research and a second total communication program was added; one oral-only program entered a transitional period while shifting to total communication; the Rochester program shifted to the provision of either oral-only or total communication on an individualized basis.

At the end of the third year of the research program, 57 hearing-impaired students were tested on the Metropolitan Reading Test (Hildreth, Griffiths, & McGauvran, 1969). They scored above the norms for hearing children for matching, alphabet, and copying subtests. They scored below the norms on the numbers subtest. "The relatively poor performance on the numbers test may be due in part to the fact that all questions on this test were presented vocally" (Moores, 1985, p. 171). Similarly, the scores of the deaf children on the Illinois Test of Psycholinguistic Abilities (Kirk, McCarthy, & Kirk, 1969) were almost identical to the mean of the standardization sample of hearing children. In comparisons across programs, the single consistently oral-only program received the lowest mean scores of any program for reading, arithmetic, and combined scores; the second oral-only program (in process of transition to total communication in the fourth year of data collection) ranked next to lowest. The Rochester program and the consistently total communication program ranked either first or second on the reading, arithmetic, and combined scores; the total communication program ranked first and the Rochester program ranked last on ratings for expressive communication.

Moores concluded that there is a complex interaction among and between many program variables that determines outcomes for individual children and groups of children. These variables include program emphasis, structure, orientation, and methodology. He believes that the programs enrolling children who consistently out-performed others had two special common features. One of these was an emphasis on cognitive/academic progress as well as on socialization skills from the beginning of a child's training. Children who were enrolled in programs emphasizing only communication or only socialization showed progressively retarded educational achievement as they entered the primary grades. The second common feature of the two more successful programs was a coordinated use of intensive training in audition, speech, and manual communication (i.e., total communication) from the very earliest educational efforts onward.

The fourth study summarized in Table 4 reports an evaluation of an experimental program conducted through Children's Hospital Diagnostic Center in Vancouver, British Columbia. Twelve children and families who had participated in this program for at least 12 months, beginning prior to the child's second birthday, were compared with 12 matched children and families who participated in a variety of more traditional programs (Greenberg, 1983; Greenberg, Calderon, & Kusché, 1984). The nontraditional aspects of the experimental program included the early and intensive use of sign language, which was taught through family visits by a deaf adult. This early contact with deaf adults is a significant departure from other programs. The second broad difference between the experimental programs and those from which the control group families were recruited was the emphasis on family counseling. This was provided by the program director (himself deaf) and by a consulting psychiatrist. Children in the comparison group received auditory and speech training (as did the children in the experimental group). They received some training in manual communication also, but this was initiated when the children had a mean age of 33.2 months, compared to sign language initiation in the experimental group at a mean age of 20.8 months. When the evaluation measures were administered, children in the experimental group were about 44 months old, children in the comparison group were about 47 months old (approximately 2 years after interventions were begun).

Developmental measures showed no significant differences between the two groups' performances on physical or self-help skills. However, there were significant differences, favoring the experimental group, on measures of social, academic (i.e., cognitive), and communication development. Comparative analyses of mother–child interactions were completed demonstrating that mothers in the experimental group gave fewer commands and more frequent reinforcements to their children, were more likely to communicate at times when the child was attending visually, demonstrated more enjoyment in the interaction, and held more elaborate conversations. Analysis of language during these interactions showed longer word–sign combinations for children in the experimental group.

This evaluation study is the only one in the literature that attempts to measure comparative stress levels in participating families. Because parent counseling was an important part of the experimental intervention strategy, this outcome measure is of great interest. The Family Questionnaire on Resources and Stress (Holroyd, 1973) was utilized as the measure for this variable. On the total scale score, experimental families exhibited significantly lower stress levels compared to the other group of families. Experimental families also showed lower stress levels for eight of the nine subscales, although differences were significant in only two instances.

The final study summarized in Table 4 (Musselman, Lindsay, & Wilson, 1985) was a complex longitudinal project conducted in Ontario, Canada, which included 80% of the children enrolled in public preschool programs for the hearing-impaired ($N = 153$). An enormous pool of data was collected, with three complete rounds done during the 4-year period of research. As reported by other investigators, children exposed consistently to auditory training programs tended to have more residual hearing, to have higher IQ scores, and to come from families with higher socioeconomic status. Children in total communication programs were at the opposite end of the continuum on these three measures, and those in auditory/oral (oral-only) programs were intermediate on measures of the three characteristics. Because children in the total communication programs were relatively disadvantaged, we might expect them to perform less well on most measures. This was not the case, however. On the language measures, the total communication children scored highest, followed by children in auditory programs, with children in oral programs scoring lowest. The same pattern was found in evaluations of mother–child interaction. In the area of speech production, however, the auditory program children ranked first, only slightly better than the performance of children in oral programs, but much higher than children in total communication programs. On measures of social development, total communication children scored significantly higher at the time of the first round of data collection, although these differences disappeared later.

Of the children in the Ontario study, 95% began their education before they were $3\frac{1}{2}$ years old. Data were analyzed to compare those whose training began before the age of 18 months and those who began later. It appeared that children in total communication programs performed better if they had earlier intervention, whereas those in auditory and oral programs performed better if they began their training later. This finding was unexpected by the investigators, and they offered three provocative hypotheses as possible explanations: First, they suggested that the late starters in auditory and oral programs have less profound hearing handicaps, which was the reason for later discovery and diagnosis of the impairment; second, they suggested that the intense formal training offered by auditory and oral programs creates burn-out in children by the time they are 5 or 6 years old; third, they suggested that language is better learned through informal interaction than through formal structured training.

All five studies summarized in Table 4 showed enhanced achievement of hearing-impaired children exposed to some method of oral-plus-visual communication when groups with that form of intervention were compared with children exposed to oral-only communication. The addition of a measure of family stress was a special contribution of Greenberg's study. It is, of course, difficult to separate the many variables that contribute to optimal achievement of deaf children and to positive adjustment of the children and their families. However, these four studies have laid a strong foundation for future work.

IMPLICATIONS AND RECOMMENDATIONS

Recommendations for intervention can be fairly straightforward on one level: Referral to a medical specialist *and* to an experienced pediatric audiologist should be automatic for any child whose parents suspect that a hearing loss exists and for any child who does not ''pass'' a hearing screening. When parents do not voice a suspicion of hearing loss, the physician should consider such a referral for young children with frequent ear infections or with language delays and difficulties. Knowledge that hearing aids can be usefully applied at a very early age and that early educational intervention if properly designed can reduce the impact of hearing loss can help parents deal effectively with an unfamiliar and ambiguous situation.

One of the difficult ambiguities of hearing impairment is determination of the degree of loss in young infants. Repeated testing may be necessary before amplification is recommended. Audiologists are often associated with a clinic or educational program offering services for parents and hearing-impaired infants or young children. A physician who is knowledgeable about the kinds of programs available in the immediate service area is better equipped to make helpful referrals. Merely passing on to parents a comprehensive list of available programs can be a real service. Many parents complain that they had incomplete information about educational issues and services before they became involved in a single program.

We are only now beginning to develop systematic intervention programs and to understand the factors responsible for improving the outcomes for young hearing-impaired children and their families. Nevertheless, based both on clinical experiences and the outcomes of early intervention studies, it seems reasonable to suggest that the hallmarks of excellence in early intervention programs for young hearing-impaired children include the following:

1. A strong emphasis on parent counseling, probably in the form of both parent groups and individual sessions. This means that staff people should have some training in counseling and/or should have regular access to an experienced mental health professional. Groups both for mothers and for fathers, singly or together, seem optimal.

2. Staff people with training in audiology who check hearing aids daily to make sure they are working properly. On-site capabilities, either in the home or at the center, to test hearing aids and to provide new ear molds when necessary are essential.

3. Staff training in and strong commitment to encouraging speech and developing oral skills. A natural interactional approach to the development of these skills seems optimal, and the inclusion and encouragement of parental involvement is of prime importance.

4. Inclusion of sign language as a "normal" program component for all parents and children. The view that sign language is a helpful communicative adjunct for all hearing-impaired children and a necessary tool for language acquisition in severely and profoundly deaf children helps parents avoid the painful choice of oral *or* sign language training and encourages a more rapid adjustment to the child's hearing handicap. A moderate rather than a militant approach to teaching and learning a different communicative mode is a positive indicator.

5. A flexible approach to matching family language needs and program capacities. This means that staff would have, or attempt to include, varieties of sign

language that are used by deaf parents enrolled in the program and that the sign language system taught to hearing parents is one they can learn most readily—probably a sign language system based on English grammar and syntax with fewer rather than more complex inflectional forms. Sign language training should include help for communicating in a visual mode as well as mere vocabulary and structure. Encouragement of body language, facial expression, and attention-getting strategies is helpful to parents who are accustomed to rely more exclusively on auditory communication.

6. The presence of deaf persons in the program as staff or as resources, either full-time or part-time, is indicative of a positive attitude about the condition of deafness that can be very helpful to parents' envisioning their children as productive, competent, contented hearing-impaired adults. Interaction with deaf adults can help hearing-impaired children begin to develop a positive identity.

REFERENCES

Alpern, G. D., & Boll, T. J. (1972). *The developmental profile.* Indianapolis, IN: Psychological Development Corporation.

Atchley, T. (1984). Taft hearing impaired school. In D. Ling (Ed.), *Early intervention for hearing-impaired children: Total communication options* (pp. 15–52). San Diego: College-Hill.

Balow, I. H., & Brill, R. G. (1975). An evaluation of reading and academic achievement levels of 16 graduating classes of the California School for the Deaf, Riverside. *The Volta Review, 77,* 266–276.

Beebe, H. H., Pearson, H. R., & Koch, M. E. (1984). The Helen Beebe Speech and Hearing Center. In D. Ling (Ed.), *Early intervention for hearing-impaired children: Oral options* (pp. 15–64). San Diego: College-Hill.

Bess, F. H., & McConnell, F. E. (1981). *Audiology, education, and the hearing impaired child.* St. Louis: Mosby.

Boothroyd, A. (1982). *Hearing impairments in young children.* Englewood Cliffs, NJ: Prentice-Hall.

Bornstein, H. (1974). Signed English: A manual approach to English language development. *Journal of Speech and Hearing Disorders, 3,* 330–343.

Brasel, K. E., & Quigley, S. P. (1977). Influence of certain language and communication environments in early childhood on the development of language in deaf individuals. *Journal of Speech and Hearing Research, 20,* 96–107.

Bzoch, K. R., & League, R. (1971). *Assessing language skills in infancy: A handbook for the multidimensional analysis of emergent language.* Gainesville, FL: Tree of Life Press.

Carrow, E. (1974). *The Carrow Elicited Language Inventory.* Boston: Teaching Resources Corporation.

Chambers, L. W., Neville-Smith, C., House, A. M., Roberts, J., Canning, E., O'Reilly, B., Cox, M., & O'Neill, M. (1981). Serving the needs of hearing impaired preschool children in rural areas. *Canadian Journal of Public Health, 72,* 173–180.

Champie, J. (1981). Language development in one preschool deaf child. *American Annals of the Deaf, 126,* 43–48.

Clark, T. C., & Watkins, S. (1978). *The Ski-Hi Model, A comprehensive model for identification, language facilitation, and family support for hearing handicapped children through home management, ages birth to six.* Logan, UT: Project Ski-Hi.

Cole, E. B., & Paterson, M. M. (1984). The McGill University project. In D. Ling (Ed.), *Early intervention for hearing-impaired children: Oral options* (pp. 119–180). San Diego: College-Hill.

Cornett, R. O. (1967). Cued speech. *American Annals of the Deaf, 112,* 3–13.

Craig, H. B. (1983). Parent–infant education in schools for deaf children: Results of CEASD survey. *American Annals of the Deaf, 128,* 82–98.

Craig, W. N. (1964). Effects of preschool training on the development of reading and lipreading skills of deaf children. *American Annals of the Deaf, 109,* 280–296.

Davis, H. (1978a). Abnormal hearing and deafness. In H. Davis & S. R. Silverman (Eds.), *Hearing and deafness* (pp. 87–146). New York: Holt, Rinehart & Winston.

Davis, H. (1978b). Audiometry: Other auditory tests. In H. Davis & S. R. Silverman (Eds.), *Hearing and deafness* (pp. 222–265). New York: Holt, Rinehart & Winston.

Day, P. S. (1986). Deaf children's expression of communicative intentions. *Journal of Communication Disorders* (in press).

DiFrancesca, S. (1972). *Academic achievement test results of a national testing program for hearing impaired students, United States: Spring 1971* (Series D, No. 9). Washington, DC: Office of Demographic Studies, Gallaudet College.

Dubose, R. F. (1979). Working with sensorily impaired children, Part II: Hearing impairments. In S. G. Garwood (Ed.), *Educating young handicapped children, A developmental approach* (pp. 361–398). Germantown, MD: Aspen Systems Corporation.

Dunn, L. M. (1965). *Peabody Picture Vocabulary Test.* Circle Pines, MN: American Guidance Service.

Durost, W. N., Bixler, H. H., Wrightstone, J. W., Prescott, G. A., & Balow, I. H. (1971). *Metropolitan achievement tests.* New York: Harcourt Brace Jovanovich.

Erting, C. J. (1985). Cultural conflict in a school for deaf children. *Anthropology and Education Quarterly, 16,* 225–243.

Foster, R., Giddan, J. J., & Stark, J. (1973). *Assessment of children's language comprehension.* Palo Alto: Consulting Psychologists Press.

Freeman, R. D., Carbin, C. F., & Boese, R. J. (1981). *Can't your child hear?* Baltimore: University Park Press.

Fudala, J. B. (1974). *Arizona articulation proficiency scale.* Palo Alto: Western Psychological Services.

Gates, A. I., & MacGinitie, W. H. (1965). *Gates-MacGinitie Reading Test.* New York: Teachers College Press.

Geers, A. E. (1979). Evaluating educational effectiveness at the pre-school level—Is it possible? In A. Simmons-Martin & D. R. Calvert (Eds.), *Parent–infant intervention* (pp. 269–279). New York: Grune & Stratton.

Gentile, A., & DiFrancesca, S. (1969). *Academic achievement test performance of hearing impaired students, United States: Spring, 1969* (Series D, No. 1). Washington, DC: Office of Demographic Studies, Gallaudet College.

Gerber, S. E. (1977). *Audiometry in infancy.* New York: Grune & Stratton.

Goss, R. N. (1970). Language used by mothers of deaf children and mothers of hearing children. *American Annals of the Deaf, 115,* 93–96.

Greenberg, M. T. (1980). Social interaction between deaf preschoolers and their mothers: The effects of communication method and communicative competence. *Developmental Psychology, 16,* 465–474.

Greenberg, M. T. (1983). Family stress and child competence: The effects of early intervention for families with deaf infants. *American Annals of the Deaf, 128,* 407–417.

Greenberg, M. T., & Calderon, R. (1984). Early intervention: Outcomes and issues. *Topics in Early Childhood Special Education, 3*, 1–9.

Greenberg, M. T., Calderon, R., & Kusché, C. (1984). Early intervention using simultaneous communication with deaf infants. *Child Development, 55*, 607–616.

Greenstein, J. M., Greenstein, B. B., McConville, K., & Stellini, L. (1975). *Mother–infant communication and language acquisition in deaf infants*. New York: Lexington School for the Deaf.

Griffiths, C. (1975). The auditory approach: Its rationale, techniques and results. *Audiology and Hearing Education, 1*, 35–39.

Haas, W. H., & Crowley, D. J. (1982). Professional information dissemination to parents of preschool hearing-impaired children. *The Volta Review, 84*, 17–23.

Hanshaw, J. B. (1982). On deafness, cytomegalovirus, and neonatal screening. *American Journal of Diseases of Children, 136*, 886–887.

Henggeler, S. W., & Cooper, P. F. (1983). Deaf child-hearing mother interaction: Extensiveness and reciprocity. *Journal of Pediatric Psychology, 8*, 83–95.

Hildreth, G., Griffiths, N. L., & McGauvran, M. E. (1969). *Manual of directions Metropolitan Readiness Tests*. New York: Harcourt, Brace & World.

Hiskey, M. S. (1941). *Nebraska Test of Learning Aptitude for Young Deaf Children*. Lincoln: University of Nebraska.

Hobbs, N. (1975). *The futures of children*. San Francisco: Jossey-Bass.

Holroyd, J. (1973). *Manual for the questionnaire on resources and stress*. Los Angeles: UCLA Neuropsychiatric Institute.

Horton, K. B. (1974). Infant intervention and language learning. In R. L. Schiefelbusch & L. L. Lloyd (Eds.), *Language perspectives—Acquisition, retardation, and intervention* (pp. 469–491). Baltimore: University Park Press.

Horton, K. B. (1975). Early intervention through parent training. In M. E. Glasscock, III (Ed.), *The otolaryngologic clinics of North America: Vol. 8, No. 1. Symposium on sensorineural hearing loss in children: Early detection and intervention* (pp. 143–157). Philadelphia: Saunders.

House, W. F., & Urban, J. (1973). Long term results of electrode implantation and electronic stimulation of the cochlea in man. *Annals of Otolaryngology, 82*, 504–517.

Hudgins, C. V. (1949). A method of appraising the speech of the deaf. *The Volta Review, 51*, 597–601, 638.

Hyde, M. B., Power, D. J., & Elias, G. C. (1980). *The use of the verbal and nonverbal control techniques by mothers of hearing-impaired infants* (Research Report No. 5). Australia: Brisbane College of Advanced Education, Centre for Human Development Studies. Mt. Gravatt, Queensland.

Johnson, D. (1975). Communication characteristics of NTID students. *Journal of the Academy of Rehabilitative Audiology, 8*, 17–32.

Jordan, I. K., Gustason, G., & Rosen, R. (1979). An update on communication trends at programs for the deaf. *American Annals of the Deaf, 124*, 350–357.

Kelley, T. L., Madden, R., Gardner, E. F., & Rudman, H. C. (1966). *Stanford Achievement Test Technical Supplement*. New York: Harcourt, Brace & World, Inc.

Kirk, S. A., McCarthy, J. J., & Kirk, W. D. (1969). *Examiner's manual: Illinois test of psycholinguistic abilities* (rev. ed.). Urbana, IL: Board of Trustees of the University of Illinois.

Lach, R. D., Ling, D., Ling, A. H., & Ship, N. (1970). Early speech development in deaf infants. *American Annals of the Deaf, 115*, 522–526.

Lee, L. (1966). Developmental sentence types: A method for comparing normal and deviant syntactic development. *Journal of Speech and Hearing Disorders, 31*, 311–330.

Leiter, R. G. (1940). *The Leiter International Performance Scale*. Vol. I: *Directions for the Application and Scoring of Individual Tests*. Santa Barbara State College Press.

Leiter, R. G. (1969). *The Leiter International Performance Scale*. Chicago: Stoelting.

Levitt, H. (1986). Interrelationships among the speech and language measures. In H. Levitt, N. S. McGarr, & D. Geffner (Eds.), *Development of language and communication skills in hearing-impaired children* (ASHA Monograph), Washington, DC: American Speech, Hearing and Language Association, (in press).

Levitt, H., McGarr, N. S., & Geffner, D. (1986). Introduction. In H. Levitt, N. S. McGarr, & D. Geffner (Eds.), *Development of language and communication skills in hearing-impaired children* (ASHA Monograph), Washington, DC: American Speech, Hearing and Language Association (in press).

Liff, S. (1973). *Early intervention and language development in hearing impaired children.* Unpublished master's thesis, Vanderbilt University, Nashville, TN.

Ling, D. (1976). *Speech and the hearing-impaired child: Theory and practice.* Washington, DC: A. G. Bell.

MacKay-Soroka, S. (1985). *Referential communication between mothers and their deaf children.* Unpublished doctoral dissertation, University of Toronto.

Maestas y Moores, J. (1980). Early linguistic environment: Interactions of deaf parents with their infants. *Sign Language Studies, 26,* 1–13.

McConnell, F. (1974). The parent teaching home: An early intervention program for hearing-impaired children. *Peabody Journal of Education, 51,* 162–170.

McIntire, M. (1977). The acquisition of American Sign Language configurations. *Sign Language Studies, 16,* 247–266.

Meadow, K. P. (1968a). Parental responses to the medical ambiguities of deafness. *Journal of Health and Social Behavior, 9,* 299–309.

Meadow, K. P. (1968b). Early manual communication in relation to the deaf child's intellectual, social, and communicative functioning. *American Annals of the Deaf, 113,* 29–41.

Meadow, K. P. (1980). *Deafness and child development.* Berkeley: University of California Press.

Meadow, K. P. (1983). *Meadow/Kendall social emotional assessment inventory for deaf and hearing-impaired children* (rev. ed.). Washington, DC: Gallaudet College.

Meadow, K. P., Greenberg, M. T., Erting, C., & Carmichael, H. (1981). Interactions of deaf mothers and deaf preschool children: Comparisons with three other groups of deaf and hearing dyads. *American Annals of the Deaf, 126,* 454–468.

Moores, D. F. (1967). *Application of "Cloze" procedures to the assessment of psycholinguistic abilities of the deaf.* Unpublished doctoral dissertation, University of Illinois.

Moores, D. F. (1982). *Educating the deaf: Psychology, principles, and practices* (2nd ed.). Boston: Houghton Mifflin.

Moores, D. F. (1985). Early intervention programs for hearing impaired children: A longitudinal assessment. In K. E. Nelson (Ed.), *Children's language* (Vol. 5) (pp. 159–195). Hillsdale, NJ: Erlbaum.

Moores, D. F., Weiss, K. L., & Goodwin, M. W. (1978). Early education programs for hearing-impaired children: Major findings. *American Annals of the Deaf, 123,* 925–936.

Musselman, C. L., Lindsay, P. H., & Wilson, A. (1985). *Linguistic and social development in preschool deaf children.* Toronto, Ontario: Ministry of Colleges and Universities.

Nicholls, G. H. (1979). *Cued speech and the reception of spoken language.* Master's thesis, McGill University, Montreal.

Phillips, W. D. (1963). *Influence of preschool training on achievement in language arts, arithmetic concepts, and socialization of young deaf children.* Unpublished doctoral dissertation, Columbia Teachers College.

Pollack, D. (1984). An acoupedic program. In D. Ling (Ed.), *Early intervention for hearing-impaired children: Oral options* (pp. 181–254). San Diego: College-Hill.

Pollack, M. C. (Ed.). (1975). *Amplification for the hearing-impaired.* New York: Grune & Stratton.

Quigley, S. P. (1969). *The influence of fingerspelling on the development of language, communication, and educational achievement in deaf children.* Urbana: University of Illinois.

Quigley, S. P., & Paul, P. V. (1984). ASL and ESL? *Topics in Early Childhood Special Education, 3,* 17–26.

Quigley, S. P., & Power, D. J. (1971). *Test of Syntactic Ability, rationale, test logistics, and instructions.* Urbana, IL: Institute for Research on Exceptional Children.

Quigley, S. P., Wilbur, R. B., Power, D. J., Montanelli, D. S., & Steinkamp, M. W. (1976). *Syntactic structures in the language of deaf children* (Final Report, Project No. 232175). Urbana–Champaign: Institute for Child Behavior and Development, University of Illinois.

Reich, C., Keeton, A., & Lindsay, P. (1978). *A language assessment battery for hearing-impaired children.* Interim report to the Ministry of Education on Contract No. 253-U. Toronto: Ontario Institute for Studies in Education.

Rubin, M. (1976). Hearing aids for infants and toddlers. In M. Rubin (Ed.), *Hearing aids, current developments and concepts,* (pp. 95–101). Baltimore: University Park Press.

Schein, J. D. (1984). Cochlear implants and the education of deaf children. *American Annals of the Deaf, 129,* 324–332.

Schlesinger, H. S. (1983). *Interventions with children who have early deficits.* Paper presented at the Annual Meetings of the American Psychoanalytical Association, Philadelphia.

Schlesinger, H. S. (1985). Deafness, mental health, and language. In F. Powell, T. Finitzo-Hieber, S. Friel-Patti, & D. Henderson (Eds.), *Education of the hearing impaired child* (pp. 103–116). San Diego: College-Hill.

Schlesinger, H. S., & Meadow, K. P. (1972). *Sound and sign, childhood deafness and mental health.* Berkeley: University of California Press.

Schlesinger, H. S., & Meadow, K. P. (1976). Emotional support for parents. In D. L. Lillie, P. L. Trohanis & K. W. Goin (Eds.), *Teaching parents to teach.* New York: Walker & Co. for Technical Assistance Development System, The University of North Carolina at Chapel Hill.

Scouten, E. L. (1967). The Rochester Method, an oral multisensory approach for instructing prelingual deaf children. *American Annals of the Deaf, 112,* 50–55.

Shah, C. P., Chandler, D., & Dale, R. (1978). Delay in referral of children with impaired hearing. *The Volta Review, 80,* 206–215.

Simmons, F. B. (1978). Identification of hearing loss in infants and young children. In M. E. Glasscock, III (Ed.), *The otolaryngologic clinics of North America: Vol. 11, No. 1. Symposium on sensorineural deafness* (pp. 19–28). Philadelphia: Saunders.

Smith, C. R. (1972). *Residual hearing and speech production in deaf children.* Unpublished doctoral dissertation, City University of New York.

Smith, C. R. (1975). Residual hearing and speech production in deaf children. *Journal of Speech and Hearing Research, 18,* 795–811.

Somers, M. N. (1984). The parent–infant program at Kendall Demonstration Elementary School. In D. Ling (Ed.), *Early intervention for hearing-impaired children: Total communication options* (pp. 183–230). San Diego: College-Hill.

Stark, R. E. (1979). Speech of the hearing-impaired child. In L. J. Bradford & W. G. Hardy (Eds.), *Hearing and hearing impairment* (pp. 229–248). New York: Grune & Stratton.

Stoloff, L., & Dennis, Z. G. (1978). Matthew. *American Annals of the Deaf, 123,* 442–447.

Stuckless, E. R., & Birch, J. W. (1966). The influence of early manual communication on the linguistic development of deaf children. *American Annals of the Deaf, 111,* 452–460, 499–504.

Utley, J. (1946). A test of lipreading ability. *Journal of Speech Disorders, 2,* 109–116.

Vernon, M., & Koh, S. D. (1970). Early manual communication and deaf children's achievement. *American Annals of the Deaf, 115,* 527–536.

Watkins, S. (1984). *Long-term effects of home intervention on hearing impaired children.* Unpublished doctoral dissertation, Utah State University.

Wechsler, D. (1949). *Wechsler Intelligence Scale for Children: Manual.* New York: The Psychological Corporation.

Wechsler, D. (1974). *Wechsler Intelligence Scale for Children* (revised). New York: The Psychological Corporation.

Wedell-Monnig, J., & Lumley, J. M. (1980). Child deafness and mother–child interaction. *Child Development, 51,* 766–774.

White, S., & White, R. (1986). The effects of hearing status of the family and age of intervention on reception and expressive oral language skills in hearing-impaired infants. In H. Levitt, N. S. McGarr, & D. Geffner (Eds.), *Development of language and communication skills in hearing-impaired children* (ASHA Monograph), Washington, DC: American Speech, Hearing and Language Association (in press).

Williams, D. M. L., & Darbyshire, J. O. (1982). Diagnosis and deafness: A study of family responses and needs. *The Volta Review, 84,* 24–30.

Woodcock, R. W., & Johnson, M. B. (1977). *Woodcock-Johnson Psycho-Educational Battery.* Hingham, Massachusetts: Teaching Resources Corporation.

Wrightstone, J. W., Aronow, M. S., & Moskowitz, S. (1963). *Developing reading test norms for deaf children.* American Annals of the Deaf, *108,* 311–316.

Part IV

Current and Future Perspectives

Chapter 10

Early Intervention for At-Risk and Handicapped Children: Current and Future Perspectives

MICHAEL J. GURALNICK
FORREST C. BENNETT

Child Development and Mental Retardation Center
University of Washington
Seattle, Washington 98195

INTRODUCTION

Since the late 1960s, we have witnessed the emergence of a complex array of intervention programs designed for young children at risk for developmental problems and for those with documented handicaps. This period has truly been a remarkable one, marked by an enormous creative output, a willingness to experiment, and a resourcefulness that has altered permanently our concepts and expectations regarding the nature of the development of young at-risk and handicapped children. Equally impressive changes have occurred with regard to the provision of services to meet the special needs of these children and their families.

Although the field has struggled with relatively limited information base and some restrictive developmental models, especially during the early phases, the experience of a generation of involvement with early intervention has yielded a strong commitment that these efforts should be pursued from many directions and across many dimensions. Encouragement at the federal level, state mandates, local support for services in many communities, the growth of specialized multidiscipline personnel preparation programs, the rapid expansion of research

THE EFFECTIVENESS OF EARLY INTERVENTION
FOR AT-RISK AND HANDICAPPED CHILDREN

interests in all aspects of early childhood, and advocacy by parent and professional groups are only partial reflections of the vigorous efforts on behalf of these children.

At this same time critics have emerged asking for justification of these programs and questioning the extent of the accomplishments that actually occur as a direct result of involvement in the various forms of early intervention. The questions that have been raised seem both fair and appropriate and, of course, comprehensive programmatic efforts such as early intervention must be responsive to issues concerning their effectiveness. In fact, the necessity for and interest in evaluating programs of this nature should not require prompting from critics. Evaluation, especially efficacy evaluation, is a process that should occur as part of the normal course of events, utilizing many different approaches and being carried out at many different levels. Accordingly, an analysis such as the one presented in this volume should only be considered as part of a continuous process of evaluation, re-direction, and re-evaluation.

We would contend that at this point in time a meaningful appraisal of the effectiveness of early intervention for at-risk and handicapped children must occur in a broad context—one that has as its goals the presentation and analysis of viable hypotheses and recommendations based on existing evidence, the refinement of significant questions that need to be addressed, the identification of patterns and trends, and the establishment of future directions for research and program development. Global or absolute declarations of success or failure do not fit within this framework and, frankly, cannot adequately reflect an understanding of both the restrictions imposed on research in this area and the complex interactions occurring among the types and characteristics of the intervention programs themselves, the children involved, family factors, and numerous other variables. Those seeking global answers are certain to be disappointed; those drawing global conclusions are certain to be easily challenged.

How one interprets the information contained in this volume will depend to some extent upon who is doing the interpreting. As has been stressed in the previous chapters, we must be wary of simplistic approaches and interpretations and recognize at the outset that we are all subject to biases that work to filter selectively some information and amplify other information. Our chapter authors themselves are not free of this bias and we have encouraged them to present their views and to make their recommendations. Although keeping track of outcomes with a scorecard is of minimal value, we hope that the tabular format in each of the chapters has at least helped to establish a clearer perspective for the reader of the available data base.

No attempt will be made here to arrive at statements regarding the effectiveness of early intervention that extend across its many domains based on the information contained in the preceding chapters. That, of course, would run counter to a major theme of this book. However, it is possible to extract issues, principles, and directions that are applicable across the various early intervention efforts. Accordingly, in this final chapter, general topics and issues that may be particularly valuable in interpreting current findings and pointing toward future directions will be discussed. Specifically, topics focusing on the following will be considered: (1) the role of parents, (2) expectations of outcomes, (3) best practice models, (4) motivational, social, and emotional factors, (5) training issues, and (6) the significance of developmental continuity and the evaluation of long-term effects. Finally, a brief section on biomedical and specific nonstandard approaches to early intervention will be included, even though the focus of this volume has been on experiential approaches. However, given the visibility of many biomedical interventions in the media, the potential for radical and dramatic change, and the existence of enthusiastic and vigorous supporters for one or another treatment, we felt our volume would be incomplete if these approaches were omitted.

THE ROLE OF PARENTS

Parent involvement in most early intervention research reviewed in this volume focused primarily on their role as adjuncts to developmental and educational instruction. In some instances parents carried major instructional responsibilities, first receiving training themselves and then providing intervention to their child along with maintaining progress records. In other cases, parents extended center-based activities into their home, reinforcing learning activities that were part of the intervention curriculum. Parents were also the recipients of counseling in some form in existing programs, but this appeared to be a much less well developed component. Advice on community services and information on the development of at-risk or handicapped children were provided as well, usually in a group format.

Partly in response to concerns over the limited impact on child development that early intervention programs have been able to demonstrate as a result of parent involvement (Casto & Lewis, 1984; Halpern, 1984), this relatively narrow role of parents in early intervention programs is now being carefully reconsidered. Contemporary models are far more comprehensive, focusing on family systems that emphasize the mutually interacting network of forces that influence all involved (e.g., Bronfenbrenner, 1977; Friedrich, Greenberg, & Crnic, in press). Moreover, such models have helped prompt research seeking to identify variables that can mitigate the effects of the additional stresses created by children with handicaps or those at risk. The promotion of coping strategies and the role of family resources including social support networks add important dimensions to early intervention programs (Bailey & Simeonsson, 1984; Gallagher, Beckman, & Cross, 1983).

Within this framework the family truly becomes a more prominent and direct focus of the early intervention program. In the simplest sense it is recognized that sound family functioning is essential for providing a supportive and developmentally appropriate environment for the child with special needs. Accordingly, effective intervention with families is likely to yield developmental benefits to children. Crucial questions in the future will be concerned with how to translate and integrate family interaction models into early intervention programs, how to develop useful instruments to assess the factors of interest, and how to establish the network of services and identify professionals capable of assisting families to develop effective coping and adaptive strategies.

A second contemporary direction suggests that a rigid emphasis on the teaching roles of parents found in many early intervention programs may well be a questionable practice. It has been argued that the approach to training parents to carry out curriculum-based intervention activities can run counter to the establishment of adaptive parent–child relationships (Affleck, McGrade, McQueeney, & Allen, 1982). In contrast, a relationship-focused model is put forth as an alternative in which the promotion of warm, reciprocal, and supportive parent–child relationships are the primary goals. Within this approach, parents do receive technical information and skills training from professionals such as that regarding the special characteristics of their children (e.g., expected delays in smiling, the need to wait for a response, strategies to enhance communication with visually impaired children). However, the information and assistance is provided to parents in a framework designed to ensure that they remain the key solvers of problems and are encouraged to build relationships with their children in as natural a manner as possible.

Recent theoretical developments and research in the area of the long-term implications of adaptive parent–child interactions support the importance of this approach (Sroufe, 1983). As noted in the first chapter in this volume, one basis for children's socially competent functioning can be found in these early parent–child relationships. Accordingly, strategies that promote secure attachments are likely to yield important developmental benefits. Once again, however, early intervention programs are challenged to develop models and techniques to bring this relationship-focused approach into the mainstream of early intervention services.

All of these perspectives lead to the inevitable conclusion that a much more sensitive and clearly *individualized* approach to parents and families will be required of early intervention programs in the future (Turnbull & Winton, 1984). Many parents are willing to serve as therapists and can do so in a very effective manner (e.g., A. M. Gross, Eudy, & Drabman, 1982). For many parents, adopting an instructional role places them in an activist position of promoting development—a role in which they feel comfortable. It does not necessarily follow that the parent–child relationship will be damaged as a consequence. The critical point here is the need to consider these and related perspectives within a broader context. This individualization can only be accomplished by a thorough understanding of contemporary approaches to family functioning.

EXPECTATIONS OF OUTCOMES

Evaluations of the effectiveness of early intervention programs have considered a wide array of developmental domains. However, the malleability of cognitive development has been the principal interest of researchers for many of the disability and at-risk populations addressed in this volume. When these studies are aggregated to allow statistical analyses using the technique referred to as meta-analysis (Glass, 1976), overall gains of about one-half to one standard deviation for environmentally at-risk (Casto & White, 1985) and handicapped children (Casto & Mastropieri, 1986) are obtained. In fact, even where more specific disability information is available as seen in the previous chapters, including the prevention of the decline in cognitive development for children with Down syndrome and those at risk due to environmental factors, it appears that on the average a gain of one-half to one standard deviation on standard intelligence tests during the life of the intervention is the best we can expect on the basis of existing data. Of course, speculation such as this contains numerous pitfalls and flaws. Meta-analysis is certainly not free from statistical and conceptual problems (Jackson, 1980), nor are any of the analytic approaches to this issue. Moreover, we have argued at various points in this volume that such global efforts provide only very limited information that is useful in determining the efficacy of early intervention. The primary value of this actuarial or aggregate approach may reside in its ability to provide a framework within which to interpret reports which vary markedly from this range (e.g., Lovaas, 1982) and alert us as to whether or not our programs are having an impact that is consistent with this pattern.

There is, of course, a range of effectiveness across children that this actuarial approach does not address. Some children are extremely responsive; for others a particular program will have minor effects. In turn, these effects will vary for different developmental domains. Unfortunately, as the reviews of the preceding chapters have indicated, the field has only a limited ability to predict responsiveness for cognitive or any other measure at the individual child level, thereby hindering empirically based clinical and programmatic decision making. Sufficient evidence is available to suggest that factors such as the type and severity of a child's handicap, family factors, available social supports, the presence of behavior problems, child temperament, and related variables all interact with early intervention program dimensions (e.g., type, quality, duration, or intensity) to govern the eventual outcomes. A sign of progress in the field will be our increasing ability to predict variations in effectiveness. Once that occurs strategies can be developed to help guide the design of specific early intervention programs to maximize their effectiveness for individual children.

How then can future research studies move closer to this goal? One approach is to define and describe our research samples more systematically and carefully. This has been one of the weakest areas in efficacy research, limiting our ability to relate child characteristics and associated factors to outcomes, as well as providing an additional threat to the validity of the studies themselves. Progress, however, does require that researchers attempt to provide more conscientiously relevant information about the sample or samples under investigation (see Kopp & Krakow, 1982). Developmental and chronological age, family characteristics and educational levels, health factors, and particularly accompanying disabilities and related marker variables (e.g., cognitive dysfunctions, language delays or disorders, sensory impairments, motor difficulties, prematurity, and birth weight) are among the important types of information that should be provided. Unfortunately, the information available from existing intervention studies is often inadequate.

A second and parallel approach is to provide a more detailed description of the interventions themselves. The tables in each of the preceding chapters reflect the fact that critical information is often omitted, and readers are frequently left with only meager descriptions of the actual events that occurred as part of the early intervention program. Clearly, more adequate descriptions and even objective data regarding actual compliance with a program's objectives are needed. One major task for the future will be the development of categories and coding systems that reflect the richness and complexity of the interventions but yield useful qualitative and quantitative descriptive data.

BEST PRACTICE MODELS

Ideally, of course, experimental designs that allow random assignment of subjects on a prospective basis to contrast or control groups and to intervention groups would provide the most appropriate and valid information. Experiments in this form are a real possibility for certain at-risk groups and can provide the needed information. For children with documented handicaps, however, only relatively rare occasions will exist to allow truly comprehensive experiments of this type to be carried out, although limited questions typically focusing on the timing of early intervention or comparisons between treatment and no-treatment options prior to age 3 years can be effectively and ethically conducted (e.g., use of wait list controls, comparisons to children being closely monitored but not receiving interventions, or taking advantage of the absence of services for very young children in certain localities).

Even in the absence of controlled investigations, however, as more studies are conducted, more detailed information from samples and from programs can be gathered to determine if any patterns or trends exist. Such patterns, of course, can only suggest possible combinations of variables that produce the best outcomes. Because there are so many variables involved, even numerous studies may not allow isolation of sample-by-program factors that may be having the most influence on the outcome measures. As noted, variability of subject samples is usually quite extensive, even when focusing on children with well-defined disabilities. In fact, even where important distinctions among subgroups within a disability category exist (see chapter on communication disorders, Chapter 6 in this volume) intervention programs have not adjusted to these variations.

How then is it possible to eventually identify early intervention practices that are likely to consistently produce superior results, that is, outcomes that fall above the average gain for effective programs for that disability? Despite numerous difficulties, a process that seeks to detect patterns of change based on diverse sources of information may be the best available strategy. By integrating existing information, by generating hypotheses regarding the most probable best practices, and by systematically developing a series of smaller scale experiments, a best practice models approach can be established, which may ultimately provide the most meaningful and useful tests of the effectiveness of early intervention.

When establishing such a best practice model, one source of information is the intervention strategies that appear to correspond to the best outcomes based on previous studies. Within data sets numerous correlations with outcomes exist that can be used to generate hypotheses about those approaches to be included in a best-practice model. A second source of information is the large number of studies using single-subject designs that intensively apply intervention techniques. Although the sample is a limited one, in this context intervention strategies can be tested and replicated quite carefully and, in many instances, experimental control over those strategies can be maintained. Of equal importance is the fact that this approach can be readily carried out within the context of a service program. This type of research–service model has been available for some time (Guralnick, 1973) and can be used as one framework for a best practice approach.

Small-scale group studies focusing on certain issues, approaches, models, instructional strategies, and so on within certain disability or at-risk groups provide a third important source of information for a best practice model. Direct comparisons of one or another approach avoid ethical concerns regarding the need for control samples not receiving any systematic intervention. Significant issues that have appeared throughout this volume that are amenable to this strategy include the intensity of intervention debate, comparisons between highly structured and less structured programs, and the effects of different forms of parental involvement. Consistent and educationally or clinically useful outcomes generated by these smaller scale interventions can make invaluable contributions to best practice models.

The importance of conducting small-scale studies of components of early intervention is underscored by the fact that the vast majority of the early intervention programs reviewed in the various chapters of this volume were highly experimental in nature. That is, they were often speculating as to what the best practices might be—relying on existing models of development and family functioning, devising and revising curricula while delivering services, training a relatively inexperienced staff, and trying to figure out how best to work with and utilize the information provided by professionals from multiple disciplines. The reader need only consider the oral-only versus total communication approaches to serving hearing-impaired children, the problems now detected in the area of peer relationships, recent results on information-processing strategies employed by young developmentally delayed children, and current views of the influence of social ecologies and family systems models to appreciate the rapid changes that best practice models will need to incorporate.

The next 10 years will, it is hoped, provide a more accurate assessment of the magnitude of effects that can be expected from participation in early intervention programs through such a best practice approach. The intent of this approach is to maximize the value of early intervention practices through progressive refinements of programs. For this to be feasible, not only is careful documentation of samples and descriptions of actual interventions needed as discussed earlier, but it is also essential to establish criteria for documenting change related to comprehensive models that have made a concerted effort to incorporate the various sources of information described earlier. Clearly, consistent positive changes compatible with program goals and objectives as well as changes that are at the upper ranges of those expected on the basis of previous efforts are important. Moreover, we suggest that improved *predictability* of outcomes for children and families should be a critical criterion for this best practice approach. Once a sufficient level of sophistication has been achieved to allow reasonable predictability of outcome, special procedures and corresponding small-scale experiments can be designed to focus specifically on one or another of the least responsive subgroups. Successful efforts here will, in turn, be incorporated into a best practice model.

In a real sense, the best practice approach is consistent with the natural course of events. Researchers and program developers typically build upon prior work and refine their efforts in a long, difficult, but needed process. Unfortunately, the field has developed in many, often unrelated, directions with rationales for specific approaches difficult to justify. What is called for here, however, is a much more systematic and planful approach to this process—one that requires the thoughtful development of programs and a careful allocation of resources.

MOTIVATIONAL, SOCIAL, AND EMOTIONAL FACTORS

The call to consider assessments of motivational, social, and emotional factors as significant indices of the impact of early intervention programs has been compelling in its logic (Taft, 1983; Zigler & Trickett, 1978), but has not as yet found a clear role in efficacy studies. In part, these delays reflect the relatively short history of these constructs, especially those related to aspects of social competence (Anderson & Messick, 1974) and to difficulties in devising appropriate assessments. Moreover, even when defined and measured, only limited intervention strategies have been available to address these factors. Best practice models will certainly need to consider these important domains.

Fortunately, there are signs that this field is undergoing rapid change. Not only are advances occurring in clarifying concepts in this area, but recent interest has stimulated the development of instrumentation that is now capable of providing valuable assessments of important aspects of motivational, social, and emotional development. For example, advances have occurred in assessing overall emotional development of infants and young children (Greenspan & Porges, 1984; Sroufe, 1979; Sroufe, Schork, Motti, Lawroski, & LaFreniere, 1984), temperament (Carey, 1981), mastery motivation (Yarrow & Messer, 1983), relationships with peers (Rubin & Ross, 1982), broad aspects of social competence (Kohn, Parnes, & Rosman, 1979), and the identification of behavior problems in young children (Behar & Stringfield, 1974).

When at-risk and handicapped populations are evaluated with these and related instruments, it becomes readily apparent that special attention must be given to these developmental domains. For example, overall, young handicapped children exhibit major deficits in their relationships with peers (Guralnick, 1986) and various groups of children exhibit substantial behavior problems even during the early years (Escalona, 1982; Thompson, 1984). In addition, certain groups of children have unusual difficulties in displaying affect (Emde, Katz, & Thorpe, 1982) and in gaining self-control (Kopp, Krakow, & Vaughn, 1983).

Clearly, major advances have occurred in our understanding of these variables and their importance to development as a whole. However, resolutions of many ambiguities regarding the constructs involved need to occur, and assessment instruments, at least for experimental purposes, must be developed. Considering the now well established unique and unusual problems at-risk and handicapped children experience in motivational, social, and emotional domains, the challenges for the next generation of early intervention programs to provide effective services in these areas are considerable. Primary among the problems that must be addressed is the development of assessment instruments that can be easily utilized by educators, pediatricians, psychologists, and child development specialists in general that provide a framework and direction for intervention. For the most part, existing instruments are too cumbersome for use in this manner and provide only limited information as to the intervention strategies that might be most effective.

In fact, there are very few systematic intervention programs that can be called upon in the motivational, social, and emotional areas. Those that are developed in the future will, ideally, recognize that to be effective they must be truly comprehensive in nature. A meaningful understanding of parent–child relationships, interactions with other family members, and an ability to integrate motivational, social, and emotional issues into virtually all activities of the intervention program will be essential.

TRAINING

Properly preparing personnel to work in the array of early intervention programs remains an essential issue for the future. At one level, the need for professionals from virtually every discipline thoroughly grounded in developmental principles, having the knowledge and clinical skills of their own discipline, expressing a willingness and ability to work within the multidisciplinary or interdisciplinary process, and exhibiting a special knowledge of children at risk and those with documented handicaps, continues to increase with the growing number and diversity of service programs. Preparing personnel for the provision of services to infants is particularly perplexing, however. Do we need to train a new cadre of infant specialists? Will professionals emerge from downward extensions of training programs for teachers in early childhood and special education? Are certain health disciplines (such as nursing) more appropriate, given the special needs of this population? As our service models evolve for these very young children, we will be in a better position to establish the credentials and training programs for professionals in this field.

As noted in the first chapter of this volume, physicians, especially pediatricians, have played a very important but complicated role in early intervention. Some physicians have been highly critical of the evidence supporting the effectiveness of early intervention and have raised concerns about the potential harm of such interventions (Ferry, 1981). At the same time, however, primary care pediatricians in particular have historically been criticized by parents and professionals for failing to detect problems at the earliest reasonable time and making appropriate referrals, lacking general technical knowledge of the medical and developmental issues facing at-risk and handicapped children, and being insensitive to the plight of families and children with special needs (see Guralnick & Richardson, 1980, for review).

Not surprisingly, existing research, although very limited, suggests considerable ambivalence and wide variations with regard to physicians' referral practices and attitudes toward early intervention (Adams, 1982; Esposito, 1978). It may well be that, for pediatricians in particular, these varying views can be traced in part to insufficient or inadequate training in relation to at-risk and handicapped children. In fact, existing surveys have clearly shown that practicing pediatricians perceive their training during residency to be inadequate in these and related biosocial areas (Dworkin, Shonkoff, Leviton, & Levine, 1979; The Task Force on Pediatric Education, 1978). Other surveys of residency training programs themselves prior to 1980 support these views, indicating that pediatric residents rarely received systematic clinical training experiences with at-risk or handicapped children (Becker, 1978; Guralnick & Richardson, 1980).

In a recent national-in-scope effort to alter this state of affairs, a carefully defined and tested curriculum for residents in the field of developmental pediatrics has been developed (Bennett, Heiser, Richardson, & Guralnick, in press) and thoroughly evaluated (Bennett, Guralnick, Richardson, & Heiser, 1984; Guralnick, Bennett, Richardson, Heiser, & Shibley, in preparation). Designed for at least a 1-month rotation, over 40 pediatric residency programs across the country are currently utilizing the curriculum. Ten interrelated units constitute the core of this rotation in developmental pediatrics: (1) basic principles of child development and screening, (2) knowledge of developmental disorders, (3) aspects of prevention, (4) developmental diagnosis and assessment, (5) interdisciplinary process and team functioning, (6) families, (7) management of handicapping conditions, (8) attitudes, (9) community services and resources, and (10) controversial research issues. Topics related both directly and indirectly to early intervention are prominent features of many of these curricular units. It is hoped that as pediatric residents move into practice, improvements in their knowledge, clinical skills, and attitudes towards at-risk and handicapped children gained as part of their experience in this developmental pediatrics rotation will be reflected in the decisions that are made with regard to early intervention.

CONTINUITY AND LONG-TERM EFFECTS

The absence of systematic attempts to evaluate the long-term effects of early intervention is a major source of concern in the field. In fact, any form of follow-up beyond the intervention period to determine how children progressed was a rare occurrence in the early intervention literature. The significance of evaluating the long-term impact of early intervention is self-evident, and if research with disadvantaged children is any indication for other at-risk and handicapped children (Lazar & Darlington, 1982; Bryant & Ramey, Chapter 2 in this volume), its public policy implications can be far reaching.

Despite the apparent appeal of judging the effectiveness of early intervention in terms of its longer-term outcomes, the relationship between early and later effects is quite complex (see Emde & Harmon, 1984). In part, the expectations of long-term impact are tied to individual researchers' conceptualizations as to whether developmental continuity or developmental discontinuity best characterizes the course of human development. For example, if one subscribes to a strong continuity position, believing that intervention during the early years will govern subsequent developmental progress to a substantial degree, then the absence of long-term effects would be devastating. Those who contend that children are highly vulnerable to inadequate developmental support at various points in the life cycle would not be surprised if short-term effects gradually eroded over time unless equally specialized programs were available. In essence, this latter position requires that continuity of programming must occur in order to assure continuity of outcomes. Moreover, how long-term effects may manifest themselves—in what form, over what time period, and under what conditions— are only a few of the questions that must be considered.

The understanding of continuity and change is certainly a core issue in human development. Our developmental models are only now beginning to yield a framework that allows us to understand the processes and transactions that occur across time. Through such approaches (e.g., Sroufe & Rutter, 1984) it may be possible to understand ultimately the numerous direct and indirect effects of early experiences in general, and perhaps even to predict the forms, patterns, and timing of later outcomes (Clarke & Clarke, 1984; Horowitz, 1980; Rutter, 1980). A crucial task in the future for those involved in early intervention programs for at-risk and handicapped children will be to monitor these developments and incorporate those concepts that seem useful in promoting our understanding of the long-term impact of early intervention.

BIOMEDICAL ISSUES AND NONSTANDARD INTERVENTIONS

Although this volume has intentionally focused on the effectiveness of experiential developmental interventions, it is worth noting in this concluding chapter that an ever-increasing array of controversial therapies, dietary hypotheses, and biomedical approaches continue to be advocated and advertised for at-risk or handicapped infants and young children (Golden, 1980). These unproved, and frequently unusual, interventions often attract widespread media interest and acclaim despite their total lack of investigative support or even research effort. Thus, vulnerable parents of vulnerable children are bombarded with personal testimonials and promises of great developmental gains (even cures) and must attempt the difficult process of distinguishing sound, worthy early interventions from questionable, possibly dangerous, recommendations. Certainly, more than ever, today the primary health care provider and child development specialist must function as a scientific consumer–critic for families with at-risk or handicapped children.

Examples of popular, controversial therapies include "patterning" as advocated by Doman and Delacato (see chapter on children with motor handicaps, Chapter 5 in this volume), sensory integration according to Ayres, and developmental optometry consisting mainly of visual tracking exercises (see Silver, 1975, for discussion of these therapies). Each of these approaches attempts to reorganize and retrain the central nervous system by means of primitive, repetitive, intensive movements and postures. Unfortunately, this type of neurophysiological retraining has not been found to fulfill proponents' extensive claims and, particularly in the case of patterning, incorporates questionable biomedical practices such as rebreathing (breathing under a bag to increase the ambient carbon dioxide content) into the overall treatment program.

The attractive hypothesis that dietary eliminations or supplementations can rapidly and dramatically improve childhood development and behavior is quite widespread in contemporary society. Avoidance of artificial food colors and additives (Feingold diet), refined sugar, and a variety of potentially allergenic foods (e.g., cow's milk, eggs, nuts, chocolate, wheat, corn, or strawberries) by at-risk or handicapped children continues to be strongly recommended by many despite the extreme paucity of documentation of significant benefit (M. D. Gross, 1984; Stare, Whelan, & Sheridan, 1980). Of even greater concern is the popular use of very large, potentially toxic, amounts of vitamins and minerals (the orthomolecular hypothesis) for infants and young children with many different types of developmental disabilities. This approach has been rejected for children with Down syndrome by several investigations (Bennett, McClelland, Kriegsmann, Andrus, & Sells, 1983; Smith, Spiker, Peterson, Cicchetti, & Justine, 1984). Additionally, supplementation of individual metabolites such as 5-hydroxytryptophan or pyridoxine to children with Down syndrome has been found to be ineffective (Pueschel, Reed, & Cronk, 1984).

Medical management and interventions for at-risk or handicapped young children include both respected and proved as well as controversial and unproved strategies. These children, of course, require quality, competent primary health care supervision including regular, periodic developmental assessment to facilitate the recognition and early identification of developmental and behavioral abnormalities. This population of children has an increased incidence of both acute and chronic health problems (e.g., infectious diseases, nutritional inadequacies, impaired growth, seizure disorders, congenital malformations) and, thus, generally requires more frequent and intense medical assessment and intervention in such forms as physical and neurological examinations, laboratory tests, radiological procedures, and a wide variety of appropriate medications (e.g., antibiotics, anticonvulsants, bronchodilators, and decongestants). Similarly, handicapped children in particular have an increased likelihood of requiring a variety of surgical interventions such as palliation and/or repair of major birth defects, orthopedic correction of deformities and contractures associated with physical impairments, shunting of excessive cerebrospinal fluid, correction of strabismus, and placement of tympanostomy tubes in the management of chronic otitis media with conductive hearing loss.

An increasing number of psychotropic medications have proved to be selectively and cautiously indicated and effective for some of the commonly encountered dysfunctional behaviors of young children with aberrant development. It is beyond the scope or intent of this volume to explore this expanding treatment modality in detail, but the reader should recognize the potential utility of such agents as major tranquilizers for severely disturbed and disruptive handicapped children, stimulant medications for severe attentional deficits and impulsivity, antidepressants for a variety of indications, and, of current research interest, fenfluramine for some of the cardinal behaviors associated with autism (Ritvo et al., 1984). It should be emphasized that these medications are most appropriately and effectively used in conjunction with available experiential interventions— not in isolation as the sole management approach, but rather as one piece of a comprehensive, individualized intervention plan.

Finally, unusual and unconventional biomedical interventions abound for developmentally disabled infants and children, just as they do for any chronic disorder. Two such approaches, in particular, merit mention because they are currently receiving increased attention and publicity, principally as applied to children with Down syndrome. Cell therapy, which involves the intramuscular injection of fresh fetal lamb brain tissue into the infant or young child, has been offered in parts of Europe and now the United States. Its proponents claim to alter dramatically many of the morphologic and developmental characteristics of Down syndrome. However, these claims have been completely undocumented by clinical investigations, and this treatment places the child at potential risk for serious anaphylactic allergic reactions (Pruess & Fewell, 1985). Reconstructive facial surgery has recently been advocated by several European and North American centers for cosmetic and self-esteem purposes; to improve lip, tongue, and oral function and thereby aid speech; to diminish nasal obstruction and reduce the frequency of upper respiratory infection; and to increase the child's general developmental level by normalizing appearances and minimizing any negative environmental expectations (Rozner, 1983). Unfortunately, none of these worthwhile goals has, as yet, been convincingly demonstrated. Clearly, a cautious, conservative, informed posture regarding nonstandard interventions that offer simple, rapid solutions to complex, chronic problems seems most appropriate.

CONCLUDING COMMENTS

In this final chapter, we have highlighted six major issues likely to alter the future impact of early intervention for children and families as well as affect our ability to adequately document outcomes. Although other topics are certain to emerge, such as biobehavioral approaches (Gibson & Fields, 1984), these six issues may well provide important directions for future program development. In fact, the comprehensive assessment of the state of the effectiveness of early intervention presented in this volume has clearly suggested that future research efforts must become more systematic. It is hoped that a consideration of the concepts, issues, and outcome patterns described in the preceding chapters will provide a useful framework in this regard. To be successful, however, this effort will require a new level of collaborative relationships among service providers, community support systems, researchers, and practitioners from numerous disciplines. How well early intervention can improve the outcomes for different groups of at-risk and handicapped children and how well we can document its effectiveness is in the hands of the next generation of early intervention programs.

REFERENCES

Adams, G. L. (1982). Referral advice given by physicians. *Mental Retardation, 20,* 16–20.

Affleck, G., McGrade, B. J., McQueeney, M., & Allen, D. (1982). Promise of relationship-focused early intervention in developmental disabilities. *Journal of Special Education, 16,* 413–430.

Anderson, S., & Messick, S. (1974). Social competency in young chitdren. *Developmental Psychology, 10,* 282–293.

Bailey, D. B., Jr., & Simeonsson, R. J. (1984). Critical issues underlying research and intervention with families of young handicapped children. *Journal of the Division for Early Childhood, 9,* 38–48.

Becker, L. D. (1978). Training pediatricians to serve learning-disabled children and their families. *Clinical Pediatrics, 17,* 355–358.

Behar, L., & Stringfield, S. (1974). A behavior rating scale for the preschool child. *Developmental Psychology, 10,* 601–610.

Bennett, F. C., Guralnick, M. J., Richardson, H. B., Jr., & Heiser, K. E. (1984). Teaching developmental pediatrics to pediatric residents: The effectiveness of a structured curriculum. *Pediatrics, 74,* 514–522.

Bennett, F. C., Heiser, K. E., Richardson, H. B., Jr., & Guralnick, M. J. (in press). *A curriculum in developmental pediatrics.* Chicago: Eterna International.

Bennett, F. C., McClelland, S., Kriegsmann, E. A., Andrus, L. D., & Sells, C. J. (1983). Vitamin and mineral supplementation in Down's syndrome. *Pediatrics, 72,* 707–713.

Bronfenbrenner, U. (1977). Toward an experimental ecology of human development. *American Psychologist, 32,* 513–531.

Carey, W. B. (1981). The importance of temperament–environment interaction for child health and development. In M. Lewis & L. A. Rosenblum (Eds.), *Genesis of behavior: Vol. 3. The uncommon child* (pp. 31–55). New York: Plenum Press.

Casto, G., & Lewis, A. C. (1984). Parent involvement in infant and preschool programs. *Journal of the Division for Early Childhood, 9,* 49–56.

Casto, G., & Mastropieri, M. A. (1986). The efficacy of early intervention programs: A meat-analysis. *Exceptional Children, 52,* 417–424.

Casto, G., & White, K. (1985). The efficacy of early intervention programs with environmentally at-risk infants. In M. Frank (Ed.), *Infant intervention programs: Truths and untruths* (pp. 37–50). New York: Haworth Press.

Clarke, A. D. B., & Clarke, A. M. (1984). Constancy and change in the growth of human charac-
    teristics. *Journal of Child Psychology and Psychiatry, 25,* 191–210.
Dworkin, P. H., Shonkoff, J. P., Leviton, A., & Levine, M. D. (1979). Training in developmental
    pediatrics. *American Journal of Diseases of Children, 133,* 709–712.
Emde, R. N., & Harmon, R. J. (Eds.). (1984). *Continuities and discontinuities in development.* New
    York: Plenum Press.
Emde, R. N., Katz, E. L., & Thorpe, J. K. (1978). Emotional expression in infancy: II. Early
    deviations in Down's syndrome. In M. Lewis & L. A. Rosenblum (Eds.), *The development of
    affect* (pp. 351–360). New York: Plenum Press.
Escalona, S. K. (1982). Babies at double hazard: Early development of infants at biologic and social
    risk. *Pediatrics, 70,* 670–676.
Esposito, R. R. (1978). Physician's attitudes toward early intervention. *Physical Therapy, 58,* 160–
    167.
Ferry, P. C. (1981). On growing new neurons: Are early intervention programs effective? *Pediatrics,
    67,* 38–41.
Friedrich, W. N., Greenberg, M. T., & Crnic, K. A. (in press). Empirical studies of handicapped
    children and their families: Measurement issues in conceptual framework. In S. Landesman-
    Dwyer & P. Vietze (Eds.), *Research on the impact of residential settings on mentally retarded
    persons.* Baltimore: University Park Press.
Gallagher, J. J., Beckman, P., & Cross, A. H. (1983). Families of handicapped children: Sources of
    stress and its amelioration. *Exceptional Children, 50,* 10–19.
Gibson, D., & Fields, D. L. (1984). Early infant stimulation programs for children with Down
    syndrome: A review of effectiveness. In M. Wolraich & D. K. Routh (Eds.), *Advances in
    developmental and behavioral pediatrics* (Vol. 5, pp. 331–371). Greenwich, CT: JAI Press.
Glass, G. V. (1976). Primary, secondary, and meta-analysis of research. *Educational Researcher, 5,*
    3–8.
Golden, G. S. (1980). Nonstandard therapies in the developmental disabilities. *American Journal of
    Diseases of Children, 134,* 487–491.
Greenspan, S. I., & Porges, S. W. (1984). Psychopathology in infancy and early childhood: Clinical
    perspectives on the organization of sensory and affective-thematic experience. *Child Develop-
    ment, 55,* 49–70.
Gross, A. M., Eudy, C., & Drabman, R. S. (1982). Training parents to be physical therapists with
    their physically handicapped child. *Journal of Behavioral Medicine, 5,* 321–327.
Gross, M. D. (1984). Effect of sucrose on hyperkinetic children. *Pediatrics, 74,* 876–878.
Guralnick, M. J. (1973). A research-service model for support of handicapped children. *Exceptional
    Children, 39,* 277–282.
Guralnick, M. J. (1986). The peer relations of young handicapped and nonhandicapped children. In
    P. S. Strain, M. J. Guralnick, & H. M. Walker (Eds.), *Children's social behavior: Develop-
    ment, assessment, and modification* (pp. 93–140). New York: Academic Press.
Guralnick, M. J., Bennett, F. C., Richardson, H. B., Jr., Heiser, K. E., & Shibley, R. E. (in
    preparation). *An experimental evaluation of outreach training in developmental pediatrics.*
Guralnick, M. J., & Richardson, H. B., Jr. (Eds.). (1980). *Pediatric education and the needs of
    exceptional children.* Baltimore: University Park Press.
Halpern, R. (1984). Lack of effects for home-based early intervention? Some possible explanations.
    American Journal of Orthopsychiatry, 54, 33–42.
Horowitz, F. D. (1980). Intervention and its effects on early development: What model of develop-
    ment is appropriate? In R. R. Turner & H. W. Reese (Eds.), *Life-span developmental psychol-
    ogy: Intervention* (pp. 235–248). New York: Academic Press.
Jackson, G. B. (1980). Methods for integrative reviews. *Review of Educational Research, 50,* 438–
    460.
Kohn, M., Parnes, B., & Rosman, B. L. (1979). *A rating and scoring manual for the Kohn Problem

Checklist and Kohn Social Competence Scale. New York: The William Alanson White Institute of Psychiatry, Psychoanalysis, & Psychology.

Kopp, C. B., & Krakow, J. B. (1982). The issue of sample characteristics: Biologically at risk or developmentally delayed infants. *Journal of Pediatric Psychology, 7,* 361–374.

Kopp, C. B., Krakow, J. B., & Vaughn, B. (1983). Patterns of self-control in young handicapped children. In M. Perlmutter (Ed.), *The Minnesota symposia on child psychology: 16. Development and policy concerning children with special needs* (pp. 93–128). Hillsdale, NJ: Erlbaum.

Lazar, I., & Darlington, R. (1982). Lasting effects of early education: A report from the consortium for longitudinal studies. *Monographs of the Society for Research in Child Development, 47* (2–3, Serial No. 195).

Lincoln, A.J., Courchesne, E., Kilman, B. A., & Galambos, R. (1985). Neuropsychological correlates of information-processing by children with Down syndrome. *American Journal of Mental Deficiency, 89,* 403–414.

Lovaas, O. I. (1982, August). *An overview of the young autism project.* Paper presented at the meeting of the American Psychological Association, Washington, DC.

Pruess, J. B., & Fewell, R. R. (1985). Cell therapy and the treatment of Down syndrome: A review of research. *Trisomy 21, 1*(1), 3–8.

Pueschel, S. M., Reed, R. B., & Cronk, C. E. (1984). Evaluation of the effect of 5-hydroxytryptophan and/or pyrodoxine administration in young children with Down syndrome. In S. M. Pueschel (Ed.), *The young child with Down syndrome* (pp. 59–83). New York: Human Sciences Press.

Ritvo, E. R., Freeman, B. J., Yuwiler, A., Geller, E., Yokota, A., Schroth, P., & Novak, P. (1984). Study of fenfluramine in outpatients with the syndrome of autism. *Journal of Pediatrics, 105,* 823–828.

Rozner, L. (1983). Facial plastic surgery for Down's syndrome. *Lancet, 1,* 1320–1323.

Rubin, K. H., & Ross, H. S. (Eds.). (1982). *Peer relationships and social skills in childhood.* New York: Springer-Verlag.

Rutter, M. (1980). The long-term effects of early experience. *Developmental Medicine and Child Neurology, 22,* 800–815.

Silver, L. B. (1975). Acceptable and controversial approaches to treating the child with learning disabilities. *Pediatrics, 55,* 406–415.

Smith, G. F., Spiker, D., Peterson, C. P., Cicchetti, D., & Justine, P. (1984). Use of megadoses of vitamins with minerals in Down syndrome. *Journal of Pediatrics, 105,* 228–234.

Sroufe, L. A. (1979). The coherence of individual development: Early care, attachment, and subsequent developmental issues. *American Psychologist, 34,* 834–841.

Sroufe, L.A. (1983). Infant–caregiver attachment and patterns of adaptation in preschool: The roots of maladaptation and competence. In M. Perlmutter (Ed.), *The Minnesota symposia on child psychology: 16. Development and policy concerning children with special needs* (pp. 41–83). Hillsdale, NJ: Erlbaum.

Sroufe, L. A., & Rutter, M. (1984). The domain of developmental psychopathology. *Child Development, 55,* 17–29.

Sroufe, L. A., Schork, E., Motti, F., Lawroski, N., & LaFreniere, P. (1984). The role of affect in social competence. In C. Izard, J. Kagan, & R. Zajonc (Eds.), *Emotions, cognition and behavior* (pp. 289–319). New York: Cambridge University Press.

Stare, F. J., Whelan, E. M., & Sheridan, M. (1980). Diet and hyperactivity: Is there a relationship? *Pediatrics, 66,* 521–525.

Taft, L. A. (1983). Critique of early intervention for cerebral palsy. In T. B. Brazelton & B. M. Lester (Eds.), *New approaches to developmental screening of infants* (pp. 219–228). New York: Elsevier.

The Task Force on Pediatric Education. (1978). *The future of pediatric education.* Evanston, IL: American Academy of Pediatrics.

Thompson, R. J., Jr. (1984). Behavior problems in developmentally disabled children. In M. Wolraich & D. K. Routh (Eds.), *Advances in developmental and behavioral pediatrics* (Vol. 5, pp. 265–330). Greenwich, CT: JAI Press.

Turnbull, A. P.,& Winton, P. J. (1984). Parent involvement policy and practice: Current research and implications for families of young, severely handicapped children. In J. Blacher (Ed.), *Severely handicapped young children and their families: Research in review* (pp. 377–397). Orlando, FL: Academic Press.

Yarrow, L. J., & Messer, D. J. (1983). Motivation and cognition in infancy. In M. Lewis (Ed.), *Origins of intelligence: Infancy and early childhood* (2nd ed.) (pp. 451–477). New York: Plenum Press.

Zigler, E., & Trickett, P. K. (1978). IQ, social competence, and evaluation of early childhood intervention programs. *American Psychologist, 33,* 789–798.

Index

A

Adaptive behavior, mental retardation and, 116
Adjustment problems, 17
Affective development, correspondence with cognitive development, in Down syndrome children, 121–122
Affective expression, strategies for developing in visually impaired children, 312
Art, aids and appliances used in teaching with visually impaired children, 318
Articulation disorders, 214, 215–216
  early intervention procedures for, 229–232
  effectiveness of intervention for, 242–243
Assessment
  developmental, *see* Developmental assessment
  for intervention for developmentally delayed children, 134–135
  of intervention for motor handicapped children, 188–189
    behavioral observation measures in, 189
    nonstandardized tools for, 189
    standardized tools for, 188
  of language development, 234–237
  of motivational, social, and emotional factors, 372–374
  of severity of developmental delay, 116–117
Ataxia, 177
Athetoid cerebral palsy, 176
Auditory stimulation, of neonate, 90
Autism, 275–293
  classification of, 277–278
  course of development in, 278–281
  early intervention for
    approaches to, 282–283
    criteria for studies to review and, 283–284

future research and practice directions for, 292–293
  review of effectiveness of, 285–292
family stress associated with, 281–282
incidence, etiology, and definition of, 276–277
Autonomic nervous system instability, of premature/low birthweight infants, 107

B

Bayley Mental Development Index (MDI), 48, 62
Bayley Scales of Infant Development, 48, 188
Behaviorally based approaches, for developmentally delayed children, 131–132
Behavioral observation, in assessment of intervention for motor handicapped children, 189
Best practice models, 370–372
Biologic risk, 5, 79–109
  environment of premature/low birthweight infant and, 85–87
  intervention parameters and setting for, 92–93
  nature of population at, 80–85
  neonatal intervention rationale and, 87–90
  outcome measures and, 93–94
  recommendations regarding, 106–109
  results of neonatal developmental intervention and, 94–106
  subject selection for intervention and, 93
  types of intervention with, 90–92
Birthweight, low and very low
  defined, 80
  incidence of, 80–81
Blindness, defined, 298

383